KW-757-554

INTELLIGENCE AND IMPERIAL DEFENCE

British Intelligence and the Defence of the Indian Empire 1904–1924

Richard J. Popplewell

FRANK CASS
LONDON

First published 1995 in Great Britain by
FRANK CASS & CO. LTD.
Newbury House, 900 Eastern Avenue, London IG2 7HH

and in the United States of America by
FRANK CASS
ISBS, 5804 N.E. Hassalo Street, Portland, Oregon 97213-3644

Copyright © 1995 Richard J. Popplewell

British Library Cataloguing in Publication Data

Popplewell, Richard James
    Intelligence and Imperial Defence:
    British Intelligence and the Defence of
    the Indian Empire, 1904–24. – (Cass
    Series: Studies in Intelligence)
    I. Title   II. Series
    327.1241054

    ISBN 0-7146-4580-X (cloth)
    ISBN 0-7146-4227-4 (paper)

Library of Congress Cataloging-in-Publication Data

Popplewell, Richard James.
    Intelligence and imperial defence : British intelligence and the
defence of the Indian Empire, 1904–1924 / Richard James Popplewell.
        p.   cm. — (Cass series—studies in intelligence)
    Includes bibliographical references and index.
    ISBN 0-7146-4580-X (cloth); 0-7146-4227-4 (paper)
    1. India—Politics and government—1857–1919 2. India—Politics
and government—1919–1947. I. Title. II. Series.
DS480.3.P66 1995
327.1241'054'09041—dc20   95-16884
                                                                   CIP

*All rights reserved. No part of this publication may be reproduced in any
form or by any means, electronic, mechanical, photocopying, recording
or otherwise, without the prior permission of Frank Cass and
Company Limited.*

Typeset by Vitaset, Paddock Wood, Kent
Printed in Great Britain by
Bookcraft Ltd, Midsomer Norton, Avon

CASS SERIES: STUDIES IN INTELLIGENCE

(Series Editors: Christopher Andrew and Michael I. Handel)

University of Plymouth Library

Subject to status this item may be renewed
via your Voyager account

http://voyager.plymouth.ac.uk

Exeter tel: (01392) 475049
Exmouth tel: (01395) 255331
Plymouth tel: (01752) 232323

90 0281458 2

Also in this series

To my parents and to the
memory of my grandfather

UNIVERSITY OF PLYMOUTH
LIBRARY SERVICES

Item No.	281458 2
Class No.	327.12 POP
Contl No.	0 7146 4580 X

Contents

Kayasth – One of the four basic castes of Hindu society; the writer caste.

Lakh – One hundred thousand.

Local Government – Correct term for the provincial administrations of British India.

Mufassil – Hinterland; particularly the country as opposed to Calcutta.

Pandit – A learned man, especially in languages.

Pathan – Tribal group from the North-West Frontier.

Political and Secret Department – Department of the India Office, London, which dealt with the Government of India's Foreign and Political Department. As such it was primarily concerned with the princely states of India and the Persian Gulf. In no sense did it constitute a 'secret service'.

Raj – Rule; especially the British administration and rule in India.

Sadhu – Hindu ascetic, holy man.

Samaj – A society.

Samiti – A society.

Sepoy – Native infantryman of the Indian Army.

Swadeshi – Literally 'of, or pertaining to, one's own country'; in political terms, use of Indian goods.

Theosophist – Member of religious movement drawing on Hinduism and Buddhism.

Thug – Professional robber and assassin, whose motives were at least in part religiously-inspired.

Thuggee – Act of robbery and murder committed by a *Thug* in honour of the Hindu goddess Kali.

Zamindar – Large landowner.

Introduction

This is the first book to appear on the British intelligence operations based both in India and London, which defended the Indian Empire against subversion during the first two decades of the twentieth century. If nothing else, it will help to fill a gap in the existing literature on British intelligence by showing which organizations served India, who controlled them, and the scale on which they operated.

Specifically, this book is about the operations of British intelligence against the revolutionary movement which emerged in India after 1907. The assumptions of the book are the following: in the period 1907–17 the Raj faced a serious threat from Indian revolutionaries; this threat was a major stimulus to the growth of British intelligence operations on a global level; and imperial intelligence played an important role in defending the British Empire during the First World War. It follows that the subject matter here concerns two grey areas: first, the intelligence system of the British Empire, which has scarcely been studied; second, the Indian revolutionary movement, whose significance has been underplayed. To begin with, something needs to be said about the Indian revolutionary movement.

In the period 1914–16 it appeared to the British that the main threat to the continuance of their rule in India came from terrorists whose activities were centred on bases both within the sub-continent and in many other parts of the world. It needs to be asked why historians have all but ignored this subject. The conventional picture is that though not all was well with the Raj at this time, nationalist opposition to it was kept well within bounds. Indeed, it is assumed that the British were rather fortunate to face, as their main local adversaries, the Indian National Congress and the home rule leagues led by Annie Besant and Tilak. These groups played according to gentlemanly, non-violent rules of political opposition. It is true that there were a few hotheads

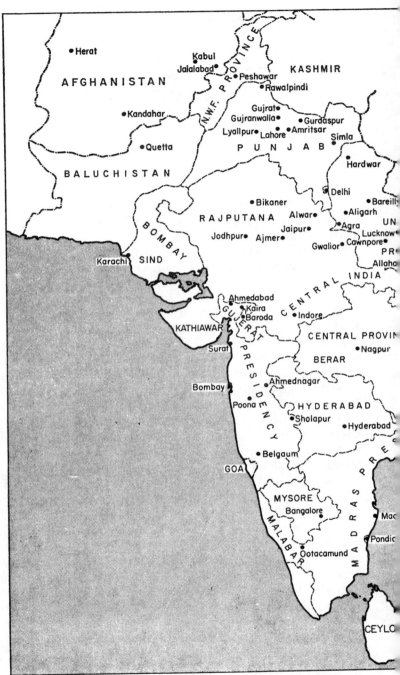

Indian Empire in 1914 (from *Watershed in India 1914–1922*
by Sir Algernon Rumbold, Athlone Press, 1979)

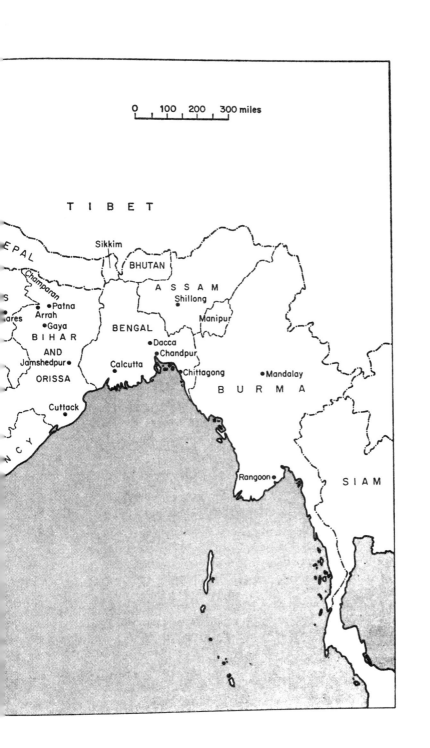

0   100   200   300 miles

T I B E T

NEPAL

Champaran

Sikkim

BHUTAN

A S S A M

Shillong

Patna
Arrah
Gaya

Manipur

ares

B I H A R

BENGAL

Dacca
Chandpur

AND

Jamshedpur

Calcutta

Chittagong

Mandalay

ORISSA

B U R M A

Cuttack

NCY

Rangoon

S I A M

inside India willing to shed blood; but they were only a handful and made no impression whatsoever on the ordered ranks of the Raj.[1]

Standard works on the First World War do not refer to the Indian revolutionaries at all.[2] Moreover, they remain unknown to the overwhelming majority of contemporary Indians. Here there is a marked difference between them and the 'freedom fighters' of the Second World War; Subhas Chandra Bose and the soldiers of the Indian National Army who fought with Japan against Britain are now regarded with admiration by many Indians. Existing works on the Indian revolutionaries of the First World War have done little to restore their memory from oblivion, even where this has been the main aim of the author. Indian studies of the armed struggle against the Raj in this period contain many examples of revolutionaries finding 'martyrdom', but scarcely any of them achieving anything.[3] Indeed, though they never say so explicitly, Indian historians have shown that the revolutionaries of the early twentieth century had little immediate impact in their own day, and failed to a considerable extent because of their own breathtaking incompetence. To modern nationalists they are not an edifying example, while at the time their endeavours proved to the overwhelming majority of Indians that violence would do nothing to weaken the power of the Raj. In this sense, the revolutionaries' abysmal failure only served a purpose which they had never intended or wanted; it increased the popularity of M.K. Gandhi and his message of non-violent resistance to British rule in India.

Complete failure is the primary reason why the Indian revolutionary movement of the early twentieth century has been overlooked. A second reason is the vastly greater success of the non-violent opposition to the Raj centred on Gandhi after 1919. But both these explanations are centred on the Indian nationalist movement itself. Studies of the Indian revolutionary movement need also to take into account the attitude of the British towards it. The British had no interest in publicizing the problems they had faced as a result of the Indian terrorism during the First World War. Thereafter, they deliberately underplayed its seriousness. For example, a look at the public statements of Lord Hardinge, who was Viceroy in the critical years 1910–16, would lead one to suppose that the Government of India was not at all bothered by Indian terrorists at home, let alone in other parts of the world. But Hardinge's numerous memoranda contained in the secret proceedings of the Indian Home Department paint a very different picture.

4

That the British were successful in keeping the revolutionary threat quiet is shown by the lack of attention paid to the Indian revolutionary movement today. However, they were able to do so only because of the completeness of the success which their counter-subversive measures achieved during the First World War. This does not mean that the victory was lightly won or that the threat seemed a slight one at the time. In fact, the British were able to defeat the Indian revolutionaries only by developing a complex intelligence network on a global scale. This network was centred on both Delhi and London and embraced North America, the Far East, many of the countries of Europe, as well as India itself. The covert means which the British used in the fight against terrorism was another reason why they were unwilling to publicize their achievement.

So this book is principally concerned with how the British were able to suppress the Indian revolutionary movement at very little obvious cost to themselves. Besides being primarily concerned with British intelligence, it differs from previous works on the Indian revolutionary movement in two main respects. First, it is concerned with events both within India and abroad. The scale of the threat posed by the revolutionaries can only be fully understood when it is appreciated that the British in India felt at the time that they were facing a terrorist threat which was fuelled from centres abroad.[4] Second, previous works on the Indian revolutionary movement have only looked at the concrete achievements of the revolutionaries. These were minimal, amounting in human terms to no more than a score or so casualties on the side of the British. Much more important, however, were the less tangible fears which the revolutionary movement engendered in the minds of the rulers.

Even at the concrete level, however, it would be a mistake to underestimate the seriousness of the revolutionary threat to the Raj. To repeat, it is misleading to regard the Indian revolutionary movement as powerless simply because it failed so completely in the end. In terms of military strength, the revolutionaries were not weak in comparison with the British presence in India, which was tiny even before the First World War led to a heavy drain on the manpower of the Raj. One key occurrence should be referred to. In the years 1915–16 the province of Bengal, which constituted roughly one third of the territory of British India, with a population of about 80 million, threatened to became ungovernable as a result of a local terrorist campaign. This was at a time when the British war effort was faring badly both against the

Germans on the Western Front, and more immediately against the Turks in the Near East. The fears created by the Indian terrorists directly affected British strategy in the Near East. Undoubtedly they were one of the factors which encouraged an apparently reckless British campaign against the Turks in Mesopotamia, which ended in the surrender of a British army at Kut at the beginning of 1916. The British had overextended themselves in this campaign to a considerable degree because they wished to impress Indian public opinion with their military strength.

In the years 1914–16, internally generated terrorism seemed a potentially serious threat to the British regime in India. But this is reckoning without the activities of Indian revolutionaries abroad. During the First World War, these extended at one time or another to Canada, the United States, Japan, China, Siam, Germany, Italy, France, Switzerland, Britain, Sweden, Russia and even some parts of Africa. Furthermore, Indian revolutionary activities were just one element in a complex of German colonial subversion whose main targets involved not just India, but also Persia and East Africa.

Something now needs to be said about what this book does not cover. There is little here about mainstream Indian nationalism. The Indian National Congress receives hardly more attention in these pages than the obscure Indian revolutionary leader, Har Dayal. But does British intelligence against the Indian revolutionaries equate with Indian imperial intelligence? What about the mainstream nationalists, who were much more important in the long term? The simple fact is that the intelligence agencies of the British Empire were not concerned with spying on non-violent nationalists.

Finally, this leads to another broad issue with which this book is concerned: what does the history of British intelligence reveal about the nature of British rule in India? Is it true that the Empire was dependent on a spy service which existed on a scale unthinkable, for ideological reasons, in Britain itself? The answer is that even at the height of the First World War, British Indian intelligence was always run on a very small scale, despite its expansion in geographical terms. It will be shown that British sensitivities about the use of spies and covert action in this period were as strong in the Indian empire as they were in London. Above all, the Government of India felt that intelligence should be a means of imperial defence, and not an arm of oppression bound to create new enemies for the Raj.

*　　*　　*

6

I would like to express my gratitude, first of all, to my PhD supervisors, Dr Christopher Andrew of Corpus Christi College, Cambridge, and Dr Chris Bayley of St. Catherine's College, Cambridge. I owe no less thanks to Dr John Ferris of Calgary University, Alberta, Canada, for his valuable advice and encouragement. In particular, I would like to thank him for the very helpful and detailed source references which he gave me, particularly for Chapters 1 and 2. His generous help with source references saved me months of work.

I am grateful also to Dr Nicholas Hiley of New Hall College, Cambridge, for help with the source material for Chapter 7, and to Mr J.A.D. Wallinger, who provided me with the information he had about his uncle Arnold Wallinger's career. I have benefited also from the advice and encouragement of Professor Michael Handel, of the US Naval War College, Portsmouth, Rhode Island. Last, but not least, I would like to thank Mrs Norma Marson of Frank Cass & Co. who has kindly given me time, advice and assistance.

NOTES

1. The best recent book dealing with British Indian politics, Judith Brown's *Modern India*, states quite correctly that during the Great War 'only a tiny minority of political activists were involved in or countenanced violence, and it was never generalized on a continental scale'. J.M. Brown, *Modern India* (Oxford: Oxford University Press, 1985), Chapter 6, 'War and the Search for a New Order', Part i, 'The Catalyst of War and the Official Design', p. 196.
2. The exception is Keith Robbins's *The First World War* (Oxford: Oxford University Press, 1984). But even here there is no more than a brief reference to events inside India during the First World War.
3. For example, Arun Coomer Bose, *Indian Revolutionaries Abroad, 1905–1922* (Allahabad: Indian Press Private, 1971).
4. The most satisfactory account of the Indian revolutionary movement is T.G. Fraser's unpublished PhD thesis, 'The Intrigues of German Government and the Ghadr Party Against British Rule in India, 1914–1918'. Fraser, however, underestimated the seriousness of the Indian revolutionary movement within India, because he did not study events within Bengal.

1

British Intelligence in Nineteenth-century India

Espionage in India has a very ancient history. There are extensive references to spies in the most ancient Hindu religious texts. In the *Rigveda* and other epics, watchers, or *śpasas* keep mankind under surveillance on behalf of the thousand-eyed god, Varuna. These religious works contain unambiguous prescriptions for the conduct of earthly affairs:

> As the wind moves everywhere and penetrates all created beings, so also should the king penetrate everywhere by the means of his unidentified agents.[1]

The recorded history of espionage in India begins with Kautilya's classic treatise on statecraft, the *Arthashastra*, which was probably written around 300 BC.[2] It is the earliest extant book dealing systematically with espionage, though it explicitly draws on several earlier Indian works.[3] According to tradition, and possibly historical fact, Kautilya was the chief adviser to the Chandragupta Maurya, who founded the first great Indian empire in 321 BC. In the extent of their conquests, the Mauryas far exceeded any previous Indian rulers. By the death of Chandragupta's successor, Bindusara, in 272 BC, the Mauryan Empire controlled virtually all the Indian sub-continent. This success was the result not only of the Mauryas' prowess on the battlefield, but more importantly stemmed from the centralized administration which they imposed. Espionage played a key role in this system, and helped to maintain the Mauryan Empire for almost one and a half centuries before its end around 180 BC.

According to the *Arthashastra*, both domestic and foreign espionage was essential to the security of the state and the maintenance of large networks of spies was one of the ruler's most important duties. The *Arthashastra* describes no less than 28 distinct categories of agents, with over 50 sub-types. Their tasks included the prevention of treason among high officials and the monitoring of public opinion, as well as fighting crime.[4] Spies were generally indispensable to the preservation of a vast, heterogeneous empire with poor communications. Though a prescription for ideal government, the *Arthashastra* undoubtedly describes a state of affairs approximating to reality. The greatest Mauryan emperor, Ashoka, who ruled 268–31 BC, referred in inscriptions to agents who brought him news and generally kept him informed on public opinion.

Over a millennium later, spying was just as important to the Mogul Empire of the sixteenth and seventeenth centuries, which was the next to equal the Mauryan in geographical expanse. The Mogul central government maintained a network of news-writers or intelligence-gatherers who reported on its noble officials or *mansabdars* and on the local notables or *zamindars* who formed the base of the administration. The *zamindars* were themselves obliged to supply regular reports on local conditions.[5]

What of the third empire to control the Indian sub-continent? The period between 1761, when the French presence was virtually destroyed, and the suppression of the Indian Mutiny in 1858 saw the establishment of British rule in India. At the beginning of the eighteenth century, the British presence in India was still essentially that of a trading colony, whereas by 1858, they had direct control of two-thirds of the sub-continent. Almost all the rest of India was in the hands of native princes, who were in no position to oppose Britain's wishes. The only really independent territories left were the tiny French enclaves at Chandernagore and Pondicherry, and the Portuguese presence at Goa.

British government in India retained many elements of continuity with the Mogul administration.[6] In particular the British, like the Moguls, depended upon a relatively small, elite and largely foreign civil service to run their empire, namely the famous Indian Civil Service (ICS). At the beginning of the twentieth century the ICS numbered only 1,300. Like the Moguls, the British were obliged, because of India's poverty, to leave the lower administration poorly paid, badly motivated and native-staffed. But one of the most notable differences between the two empires was the unwillingness of the British to continue the Mogul practice of controlling both civil service and population through the extensive and systematized use of espionage. A strong aversion to the use of spies was one of the alien traditions of government which the British brought to India.[7]

There are many reasons why one might expect the British to have used espionage in India. To begin with, there is Kipling's depiction of the Raj in his novel *Kim*, which is just as dependent upon its secret agents as those of the Mauryas and the Moguls.[8] It is surprising that the British did not revert to native traditions of intelligence-gathering at an early date. Apart from the continuing inadequacy of the Indian bureaucracy, there are other reasons why any government in India might feel the need for domestic espionage. First and foremost is the volatile nature of Indian society, which has always been deeply divided by race and religion. This problem was exacerbated by the vast size of the sub-continent. The difficulties of procuring information about outlying areas, and about movements of public opinion, were enormous. In many ways, therefore, the British Indian Empire of the nineteenth and early twentieth centuries AD might have seemed to have been in as much need of spies as the Mauryan Empire of the third and fourth centuries BC.

The period in which the Indian Empire was founded was characterized by a great ignorance on the part of the British of the vast territories which they were taking over. This may be seen even as the result of their military success, for in expanding so rapidly their resources became overstretched. Even when British rule was firmly established, in the second half of the nineteenth century, members of the ICS were often very poorly informed of local conditions. In 1863, the Chief Justice of Bombay, where the British had been long established, complained:

> the Chief administrators of our vast Indian Empire . . . are often, if not habitually, in complete ignorance of the most patent facts . . . around them.[9]

There was, however, one key difference between the Mogul and British administrations. Since the senior officers of the British Army and of the administration were all white and thousands of miles from home there was no danger of their turning against the central authority, unlike the Mogul officials whom they supplanted. In this respect at least, the nineteenth-century British had less need of an espionage service than the Moguls.

The Government of India was slow to place intelligence in any

10

form on a regular footing. It finally did so not for political reasons, but in order to deal with organized crime. The gradual collapse of the Mogul Empire from the end of the seventeenth century onwards had resulted in a massive breakdown of law and order in large areas of central and northern India. Just one aspect of this general problem was the growth of *thuggee*, a religiously inspired form of banditry. The *Thugs* were a fraternity of murderers whose activities stretched throughout India, though they were particularly prevalent in the northern provinces and in the central Deccan. The *Thugs* murdered and then robbed their victims in honour of the Hindu goddess Kali. Typically they would strangle their victims with a cloth which had a coin dedicated to Kali knotted into one of its corners. Thus they were able simultaneously to profit themselves and to perform acts of religious devotion – though which aspect of their craft most motivated them is open to question.[10] Significantly, the *Thugs* included many otherwise monotheistic Muslims in their ranks. The British involved in the suppression of *Thuggee*, however, believed that the *Thugs* considered 'the persons murdered precisely in the light of victims offered up to the goddess'.

For a long time the British government knew almost nothing of the *Thugs'* existence. Captain (later Colonel Sir) William Sleeman, magistrate in the district of Nursingpur in central India from 1822–24, and who was later to be in charge of the destruction of the *Thugs* throughout India, recorded that

> if any man had then told me that a gang of assassins by profession resided in the village of Kundélee, not four hundred yards from my court, and that the extensive groves of the village of Mundésur, only one stage from me . . . was one of the greatest *bhils*, or places of murder, in all India . . . I should have thought him a fool or a madman; and yet nothing could have been more true: the bodies of *a hundred travellers* lie buried in and among the groves of Mundésur . . .

The British first became aware that the *Thugs* were a problem in 1810 when some of their Indian soldiers failed to return from leave. It turned out that in each case these sepoys had joined groups of other travellers on their way home, and after two or three days were never seen again. Over the next few years the British acquired more evidence of the seriousness of the problem in central India. Yet they took no more than local measures to deal with it.

11

The British decision to destroy the *Thugs* root and branch came as part of a general drive towards more efficient government which started under Lord Bentinck, who was Governor-General in the years 1828–33.[11] In 1830 Bentinck established the famous Thagi and Dakaiti Department with William Sleeman as its first General Superintendent. The highest total strength of officers in the Department during the campaign against the *Thugs* was just 18, though their duties covered not only British India, but the princely states as well. None the less, the establishment of the Thagi and Dakaiti Department marked the beginning of a concerted British campaign against the *Thugs*.

British tactics were straightforward and effective. Their immediate aim was to obtain information which they did by offering captured *Thugs* the choice of hanging or turning approver. Philip Meadows Taylor, an officer of the Thagi and Dakaiti Department, recalled that

> when they found that their only chance of life lay in giving correct information, they unequivocally denounced their associates.

By 1837, 483 *Thugs* had become informers. The British had to build a special jail at Jabalpur in the Central Provinces to keep them safe from their former associates who were still at large. After they had secured informers, the British verified their evidence by exhuming the corpses of the *Thugs'* victims. This led them to the discovery that *Thuggee* existed on a large scale throughout the whole of India. It later proved that between 40 and 50 gangs of *Thugs* had been at work, murdering possibly 20–30,000 people a year. One *Thug* admitted to have been 'directly concerned in the murder of seven hundred and nineteen persons', and boasted to his captors that if he 'had not been in prison twelve years, the number would have been a thousand!'[12] In its first five years, the Thagi and Dakaiti Department's operations led to the conviction of over 3,000 *Thugs*. Meadows Taylor stressed the thoroughness of the operations which the Department conducted in collaboration with the provincial police forces. He claimed that

> no body of men could traverse the country in any direction without being subject to the strictest scrutiny by the police, and by informers who were stationed with them upon all the great thoroughfares and in the principal towns.

By 1863 the Thagi and Dakaiti Department had extirpated the *Thugs* from British India but it continued to work against them in the princely states.[13]

The discovery of the scale of the *Thugs'* operations over the 20 years between 1810 and 1830 revealed the great inadequacy of the British government's information about the land it ruled. The revelations about the *Thugs* had great impact not just on India, but also in Britain itself, where any literature on the subject sold very well to a horrified but inquisitive public. None the less, this failure of criminal intelligence did not lead the Government of India to question whether the information at its disposal about other aspects of Indian society or politics might be deficient.

The British most seriously lacked information about one key element in Indian society: the native army. On 10 May 1857 they were caught completely by surprise when the Army of Bengal mutinied. The immediate cause was the issue of cartridges for the new Enfield rifles with which the sepoys had recently been equipped. Before use, soldiers had to bite the cartridges. The problem for Indian soldiers was that they were greased either with beef fat, which made them contaminating to Hindus, or with pork fat, which Muslims could not eat. The threat of religious defilement proved the spark that lit a powder-keg of grievances which had built up in recent years within the ranks of the Army of Bengal. By the end of May 1857 the revolt had spread over large areas of north-central India.

This is not the place to discuss the causes of the Indian Mutiny. Suffice it to say that they were extremely complex and that the British had anticipated none of them. The surprise of the British government at the outbreak of the Mutiny, like its unawareness of the scale of the *Thugs'* operations up to the 1830s, shows its failure both to understand Indian conditions fully or to obtain information about them. This was not, however, a failure of a British intelligence organization, because there was no organization systematically gathering political intelligence in British India.

By the middle of 1858, the British had suppressed the Indian Mutiny but at considerable financial cost to the Home Government, which in return took over formal control of India from the East India Company. An immediate precaution was the reorganization of the Indian Army, within which the proportion of native to British troops was reduced. The Mutiny may also have prompted the Government of India to improve its knowledge about the sub-continent. As one writer has noted:

Towards the end of the century the British, concerned to know what was happening in the country lest tension should erupt as unpredictably and savagely as in 1857, and anxious to make the best use of limited resources, began to make a wide range of inquiries into such matters as educational standards, access to administrative posts, or the transfer of land between social groups.[14]

The less tangible consequences of the rebellion may have been just as important. It is often said that the British were left with a 'mutiny complex', which amounted to a sometimes irrational fear of their Indian subjects arising in times of disturbance. Yet there was one precaution against Indian unrest which the nineteenth-century British never took – the institutionalization and systematic use of political intelligence.

It was not until five years after the Mutiny that the Government of India made any move to improve the sources of political intelligence at its disposal. In 1863, it officially endowed the Thagi and Dakaiti Department with the task of collecting 'secret and political' information. Even so, the Department did not receive any additional facilities for carrying out these new duties, while it continued to combat *Thuggee* in the princely states.

The Government of India's reluctance to set up a regular political intelligence service is a clear indication of the security which the British now felt in face of their Indian subjects and very strongly suggests that references to a 'mutiny complex' on the part of the British are greatly exaggerated. Indeed, it will be seen that in the period up to 1914, when serious unrest broke out in Bengal, British attitudes towards the population of India were marked by a high degree of complacency.

The British reaction to the Mutiny was in fact very restrained. They learned one thing from the experience. This was that, provided the gross mistakes of 1857 were not repeated, no challenge to British rule could be generated from within India. Even from the viewpoint of 1858, it was clear that the Mutiny had had no real chance of over-throwing the British government. Geographically, it had been restricted to some areas of north-central India while Bombay, Bengal, Madras and the Punjab were completely untouched by the unrest. Even where rebellion did break out, it never amounted to a general revolt against the British. In particular, the rebels failed to secure the support of the peasants. If the British took only limited precautions

14

against the recurrence of Indian unrest, this was because in the conditions of the second half of the nineteenth century they did not feel any such measures to be necessary.

To practically all nineteenth-century Indians, the Mutiny showed that armed resistance to the British was useless. In the half-century that followed, only one politico-religious movement attempted to offer an armed threat to the Raj. This was a Muslim fundamentalist sect, the Wahabis. The Wahabi movement had been founded in Arabia in 1691 by Muhammad, son of Abdul Wahab. The Wahabis wanted both to purify the Muslim faith and to rid Muslim lands of the 'infidel'. Though there were very few inside India, the Wahabis concerned the British on two counts. First, any Muslim revivalist movement posed a nebulous threat as something potentially able to unite Muslims throughout India. In the 1840s the British feared, but did not find, a Wahabi conspiracy extending as far south as Madras.[15] Understandably, British suspicions of Muslims were heightened after 1857, when some believed that the Mutiny was a Muslim conspiracy to restore the Mogul empire. The mutinous troops had, after all, made the last Mogul Emperor, the 82-year-old Bahadur Shah, their nominal leader. But, in fact there was no basis for a Muslim conspiracy against the British.

The second reason why the Wahabis concerned the British was that they had links with the fierce Muslim tribes to the north-west of India and in Afghanistan. A small Wahabi colony existed across the North-West Frontier. These 'Hindustani fanatics', as the British styled them, were the descendants of Wahabis who had emigrated from the Punjab in 1824 in order to wage holy war against the 'infidel' Sikh regime which had taken control there as Mogul power declined. During the Mutiny of 1857 they attempted to cause trouble on the frontier and were closely associated with the Wahabis inside India. In following years, the Wahabi movement in India created serious disturbances, which extended over Bengal, Bihar, the Punjab and the North-West Frontier. The British only finally suppressed them in 1871.[16] Thereafter the Hindustani fanatics remained a constant source of trouble on the Frontier. Their numbers were maintained by a trickle of recruits from India, some of whom were common criminals escaping justice. Their fighting strength amounted to about 400 in 1916.[17]

The British undoubtedly felt acute concern about connections between religious revivalism and political unrest. Nevertheless, even at its strongest, in the 1860s, the Wahabi movement did not lead to a major development of British intelligence in India. At this time Bengal, as the province most seriously affected by the Wahabis, had a relatively large detective police force, composed of a Deputy Inspector-General, four Assistants and 32 Head Constables. However, even this force was disbanded in 1870, so that in 1901 Bengal had, according to the government, 'no efficient detective staff'.[18]

One explanation of the very restrained reaction of the British to Wahabis may be the lack of interest shown in India by the Muslim powers beyond its western borders. The Wahabis had connections with the warlike tribes of Arabia, but this hardly amounted to a threat to Britain's imperial interests. Most importantly, during most of the nineteenth century neither Persia nor the Ottoman Empire showed any interest in India's Muslims. The Persian kingdom was not only chronically weak, but also predominantly Shiite Muslim in composition. India's Muslims on the other hand were overwhelmingly Sunnis. The Ottoman Empire, though ruled by Sunnis, was too absorbed in defending itself against Russia and against rebellion in its Balkan provinces to risk offending Britain. It was only from the 1890s to the outbreak of the First World War that the Ottomans began to think of subverting the British Indian Empire by presenting themselves as protectors of Muslims.

After their suppression, the Wahabis remained a nuisance though not a serious threat. The British still viewed them in this light after 1872, when a Wahabi convict assassinated the Viceroy, Lord Mayo, while he was visiting a penal colony. This was an isolated act but it led the Government of India finally to consider the establishment of a political intelligence service. Mayo's successor, Lord Northbrook (1872–76), wrote that the murder made obvious the need for 'a detective police for political purposes' at the disposal of the central government. He gradually organized such a force under Major Edward Bradford, the Superintendent of the Thagi and Dakaiti Department. Northbrook claimed that by 1876, when he left India, Bradford 'had the means, through his agents in all parts of India, of knowing anything of consequence that might be going on among disaffected classes'.[19] In 1878 the next Viceroy, Lord Lytton, wrote that the Thagi and Dakaiti Department 'is virtually our Secret Police Department'.[20]

None the less, by 1881, Northbrook's scheme to set up a political intelligence agency under the Government of India had fallen through.[21] There is no indication that Northbrook's initiative amounted to more than encouraging the Thagi and Dakaiti Department and endowing it with funds with which to procure local informers. The regular staff of the Department did not increase, and now amounted to just a handful of clerks. One thing is certain; at this time the quality and amount of political intelligence at the disposal of the central government depended on the interest which the Viceroy personally showed in acquiring it. It is noticeable that the sudden interest in political intelligence shown by Northbrook and Lytton in the 1870s coincided with increased fears of the Russian threat on the North-West Frontier.

Though Northbrook was eager to improve intelligence, political conditions in British India did not greatly perturb him. On the one hand, he advised Lord Ripon, who was Viceroy in 1880–84:

> People are apt to forget that there is no substantial assurance in the condition of the masses in India, or of substantial change in their feelings.[22]

But on the other hand, both Northbrook and Bradford were confident that Indian opinion need not be feared provided that taxes were not raised. They thought that this assessment was borne out when the Indian public reacted with complete indifference to British set-backs in the Second Afghan War of 1878–80.[23]

The events of 1857 made it clear that no group of Indians could successfully oppose the British on their own. Before Gandhi developed techniques of non-violent resistance to the Raj after the First World War, there was only one way that the British regime in India could conceivably be undermined: by the combination of some form of internal unrest with foreign aggression. In the nineteenth century there was only one power which might have been able to put British rule in India in jeopardy: Russia. British fears of a Russian threat dated from 1807, when Napoleon proposed a Franco-Russian attack on India. This danger was short-lived, disappearing altogether when he launched his disastrous invasion of Russia in 1812. But the threat to India re-emerged at the end of the 1820s when the Russian empire began to expand eastward. After inflicting crushing defeats on Persia and the Ottoman Empire in 1828, Russia began to expand into the Caucasus and to explore Central Asia, where the independent khanates of Bokhara, Khokand and Khiva were one step removed from routes into British India through Afghanistan. From this time onwards, the British became seriously concerned about a direct threat to India. This took some time to unfold, largely because the Russians became bogged down in a major war against the Muslim tribes of the Caucasus, but by the mid-1860s the Russians had crushed the Caucasian tribes and their advance on the Central Asian khanates began. Bokhara and Khokand fell in 1868, followed by Khiva in 1875. The danger to India now seemed acute to many British statesmen, including Northbrook and Lytton. At the beginning of the nineteenth century, the British and Russian empires were more than 2,000 miles apart; by its end, the Tsar's lands were, in places, only 20 miles from India.

There was some debate within the British government about what form a potential Russian threat might take. Disagreement existed over whether the Russians really could invade India through Afghanistan, given the nature of the terrain there and the warlike nature of the Afghans, but it was agreed that the Russians would not even have to invade India in order to make British rule there untenable. Some British statesmen argued that all that the Russians needed to do to bring down the Raj was to mount sustained pressure on the North-West Frontier. The Indian Army at its current strength could certainly not repulse a serious Russian threat. Indeed, it had on occasion enough difficulties in fighting the tribes of the region. Yet there seemed no possibility that the Indian Army could be either substantially increased in size or modernized. The finances of India were too poor to allow this, and any major increase in taxation would undermine Indian support for the Raj. Thus, the British argued, a Russian threat could make British rule in India unsustainable for financial reasons alone. The most dangerous form that Russian aggression could take would be pressure on the frontier in combination with subversion among the Indian princes, who still controlled one third of the sub-continent.

In response to the Russian threat, the Government of India made limited attempts to improve both its political intelligence within India, and the sources of military information at its disposal about the lands to the north from where the Russians might attack. Throughout this period, British information-gathering in the lands beyond India's frontiers had two basic goals. The first was to find out all possible invasion routes to India, and the feasibility of the Russians sending a large army through them. The second was to discover whether the Russians had been in the desolate regions to the north of India, and if so, what influence they had had. At the beginning of the nineteenth century, the whole of Central Asia was uncharted territory. The last non-Asiatic ruler to invade India by land was Alexander the Great, and neither the Russians nor the British knew very much about the invasion routes from the north. Much of the territory to the north and north-west of the Indian sub-continent was so inaccessible that, even at the beginning of the twentieth century, European geographical knowledge of the region was far from complete.

The exploration, espionage and intrigue which the British and Russians conducted in Afghanistan and Central Asia by the British and Russian empires in the period 1810–1907, is commonly referred to as the 'Great Game'. The term was coined in the early nineteenth century by one of the British participants in this struggle, but it only became famous after the publication of Kipling's novel *Kim* in 1901.

The British players of the Great Game can be divided into three general categories. The first were the officers of the Indian Army and the Government of India's Political Department, which roughly equated to its Foreign Office. The second category were British travellers of independent means, some of whom were even more eager than the Government of India to discover a Russian threat. The most notable, William Moorcroft, was a veterinary surgeon who started his adventures across the border in search of horses. He became convinced of a mounting Russian threat to India, and in 1819 started exploring on his own initiative. He was the first Englishman to reach the river Oxus, and provided the Government of India, and the Royal Geographical Society, with a mass of information about Central Asia.[24]

The third category of intelligence-gathering were Indian hillmen, whom the British recruited to go into areas too dangerous for Europeans, even in disguise. The British chose these men for their exceptional intelligence, and trained them in the arts of clandestine surveying before sending them across the frontier, often in the disguise of Muslim holy men or Buddhist pilgrims. There is very little information about this group. It remains unclear how many there were, and how important their reporting was because they left no written records of their work. But, given the very poor quality of British information about the lands beyond India's northern borders, their work is very unlikely to have been on a serious scale.

The most important British players in the Great Game were the officers of either the Indian Army or the Political Department. It was their opinions which carried weight. It should be noted that neither the Army nor the Political Department had intelligence sections at this date. The British officers – a mere handful – who carried out secret operations beyond India's frontiers in no way saw themselves as spies. They had many features in common. Most of them started their careers as explorers and intelligence-gatherers at a very early age. All were highly proficient linguists, often capable of passing for Asians. They were also bound together by a lack of regard for danger, which in several cases crossed the bounds of irresponsibility. The phrase, the Great Game aptly evokes the attitude of these men and their dashing, almost playful, attitude to exploration.

On one occasion, above all, this outlook contributed to disaster. Alexander 'Bokhara' Burnes was the most celebrated of all British adventurers in Central Asia. As an Indian Army officer in his twenties he had befriended not only Ranjit Singh, the ruler of the Punjab, but also his mortal enemy, Dost Mohammed, the Emir of Afghanistan. Burnes's greatest achievement had been to get through to the Central Asian city of Bokhara, where hardly any Europeans had ever set foot. As one of the Raj's greatest experts on Central Asia, he accompanied the British force which occupied Kabul in 1838 in the capacity of Political Officer. In 1841 the mission ended in disaster when the Kabul population revolted. Burnes and many British were killed in the city itself. The rest were wiped out by Afghan tribes on the notorious 'retreat from Kabul'. Burnes undoubtedly contributed to the disaster. Up to the end he refused to believe that Kabul was about to revolt against British occupation. This led to his own death, and also helped lull the British commanders into a false sense of security.

Burnes was equalled in his failure to understand his Asian adversaries by his fellow player of the Great Game (and the inventor of the phrase), Captain Arthur Conolly. While the Indian Army was in Kabul, Conolly set out on a diplomatic mission to the Emir of Bokhara. Ignoring local warnings, he introduced himself to the Emir as a British officer. He soon found himself at the bottom of a vermin-infested pit, accompanied by a few local criminals. But he did not have to wait long for European company. At the end of 1838, Colonel Charles Stoddart arrived to the rescue, presenting himself to the Emir in full regimentals. The Bokharans executed both Conolly and Stoddart in 1841, shortly after the Afghans had massacred the British on their retreat from Kabul.

The fate of Conolly and Stoddart illustrates an interesting aspect of the Great Game: it was rarely secret. Several of the participants published accounts of their adventures. Explorers and intelligence-gatherers had considerable influence upon the British and Indian governments' fears of Russian expansionism. Generally the published works of practitioners of the Great Game were Russophobe, arguing that the best way to halt the Russian advance was by 'forward policies': either the British should invade potential targets them- selves; or they should support satellite states blocking the Russian advance. These works were influential in overcoming the opposite school which argued for a policy of 'masterly inactivity', on the grounds that Russia could never pose a serious threat to India. 'Forward policies' led to two needless Afghan wars, and culminated in Francis Younghusband's invasion of Tibet in 1903–4 in search of non-existent Russian agents.

The geographical contribution of these explorers is debatable. It is impossible to assess how useful their work was in detecting possible Russian invasion routes, for the invasion never came. Their efforts hardly amounted to an extensive and sustained intelligence operation, nor did they lead to full knowledge of the geography to the north of India. Tibet, in particular, was uncharted territory before the British invaded it in 1904.

Lytton was clear about the inadequacies of British intelligence work on India's northern borders. He was very critical of Sir Henry Norman, who had been Commander-in-Chief of the Indian Army under Northbrook. Norman had discouraged the creation of a Military Intelligence Department. As a result, Lytton found that the Govern- ment of India was in 'an extraordinary state of ignorance' about the states on its borders. He noted the example of the Jowakis, a small independent tribe whose lands were enclosed on three sides by the Punjab. In 1878 Lytton claimed that 'we were more completely ignorant of its interior than we are now of the centre of Africa . . .'.[25] To rectify this situation, Lytton's government set up a tiny Military Intelligence Department which cost about £3,000 a year.[26]

In conclusion, the British appear never to have launched a sustained intelligence effort in Afghanistan and Central Asia. Their information-gathering in this region was a very makeshift affair, which depended on the initiatives of individual members of the British and Indian governments, and of the explorers themselves.

More important than the Great Game was what was going on inside India. The British were aware that there was some Russian intelligence activity in India but they were surprisingly unconcerned about it. On the eve of the Second Afghan War, in 1878, Lytton wrote casually that there is, undoubtedly, at this moment, in India, a certain number of emissaries – foreigners, ostensibly Persians and Afghans – supposed to be acting in the interests of the Russian Government, and whose movements have been more or less traced in Northern India.[27]

India never experienced a spy-scare like that in Great Britain in the years immediately preceding the First World War, when irrational fears of German espionage gripped both public and government.[28] The Government of India's restraint is further indicative of its lack of concern about the possibility of any armed threat from its Indian subjects.

The failure of Northbrook's scheme to improve the Government of India's central intelligence in response to the Wahabi movement has already been described. The Russian threat led to some concern about intelligence-gathering at the provincial level. By 1878 the central government had become concerned about the inadequate sources of intelligence at the disposal of the Local Governments of British India. It noted that in some provinces no official had the duty of receiving and distributing 'confidential or secret communications on subjects of political or military importance'. Communication of such information between provinces was inadequate. There was 'no recognized channel through which suspected persons can be watched, or suspicious phenomena traced, from one province to another'. The Government of India was so ignorant of what was happening in the provinces that it was uncertain whether intelligence officers already existed in provinces other than the Punjab.[29]

The Punjab government had set up a Special Branch in 1876 whose duty was to receive and distribute confidential and secret information – of both a political and general character – from different parts of the province.[30] Apparently this arrangement worked well, providing a useful link between the Local Government and the police. The staff of the Special Branch was very small; consisting of one police officer, two clerks and one native inspector, and costing Rs.4,800 a year.[31]

Inspired by the example of the Punjab, in 1878, Lytton requested that Local Governments 'pay great attention to all sources of information regarding foreign emissaries, intrigues, or unusual political or social phenomena'. He emphasized, however, that he did not want 'to create an extensive system of secret police' or to interfere with the jurisdiction of the Local Governments. He suggested that the provincial governments should appoint an officer as their confidential agent to handle secret information in the same way that the General Superintendent of Thagi and Dakaiti served the central government. These officers were to communicate with the central government through the Thagi and Dakaiti Department.[32] But the officers appointed were not employed full-time on intelligence work. For example, in Bombay these duties were carried out by the Under-Secretary of the Judicial Department; in Bengal by the Private Secretary to the Lieutenant-Governor; in Madras by the Chief Secretary to Government.[33] Because the organization for collecting information remained weak both at the centre and in the provinces and because Lytton did not give a precise indication of the subjects on which the information should be collected, the reforms amounted to very little.[34]

Even the extent to which princely intrigues concerned the British should not be exaggerated. Their real concern was definitely not princely intrigue in its own right, but that some of the princes might ally with the Russians. The British saw this only as a potential threat, never as a likely one. Malhar Rao, the Gaekwar of the Western Indian State of Baroda, was the only internal political threat perceived by Northbrook's administration. In 1875 the British deposed him and exiled him to Madras for the brutal administration of his state and for the attempted poisoning of the British Resident. Lytton subsequently ordered the Government of Madras to watch all communications between him and men of Northern India and to open his mail, which he regarded as an extreme step.[35]

The British, like the Moguls, maintained news-writers within the domains of the Indian princes, but they did so erratically and on a small scale. The Foreign Department of the Government of India, which handled relations with the princes, never intended to organize 'a staff of regularly paid news-writers or spies in the Native States'. In the 1880s Sir Mortimer Durand, the Indian Foreign Secretary, dismissed such agents as generally worthless, and felt that even their successful use would lead to suspicion on the part of the Native governments.[36]

Within the Native States the Foreign Department was officially represented by the Political Service, which was largely staffed by British ex-army officers. They were sent as 'Residents' to princely courts, where one of their duties was to acquire intelligence 'by familiar intercourse with natives of all classes'. On occasion they were

23

expected to pay for information with 'secret service funds'. However, they no more constituted an espionage service than any other European diplomatic corps. The acquisition of intelligence was not their primary function and performance varied greatly according to the willingness of individual Political Officers.[37]

The Thagi and Dakaiti Department continued to operate in the princely states right up to the beginning of the twentieth century but it never had extensive facilities for criminal investigation, such as might, if need arose, be put to political purposes. Only five senior officers conducted criminal investigation for the whole of the Indian Empire and the Native States. Besides the General Superintendent and his Assistant in the Central Special Branch, one officer was stationed in Central India, one in Rajputana, and another in Hyderabad, the largest of the Native States. The Central India and Rajputana Agencies were tiny. Even the Hyderabad officer controlled an office establishment of only six clerks, 'an executive branch' consisting of nine Inspectors and Deputy-Inspectors, and a 21-man 'menial establishment'.[38] This meant that more members of the Hyderabad section were concerned with sweeping floors than with detecting criminals.[39]

The Government of India's anxiety that Russia might exploit the grievances of Indian Princes reached its height during the Viceroyalty of Lord Dufferin (1884–88). For a brief time, it seemed possible that opportunities might be open for Russian subversion in the key strategic province of the Punjab.

By 1820 the Sikhs of the Punjab had formed a strong independent state under their great one-eyed leader Ranjit Singh. In 1839 Ranjit died and this led to a period of instability which lasted until 1849, by which time the British had annexed all the Punjab. British rule in the Punjab was widely accepted by the local population and when the Mutiny came in 1857, the Punjabis provided substantial support for the British. This confirmed their importance to the Raj. In particular, the Indian Army drew heavily on Sikhs, whom the British regarded not only as loyal, but also as the foremost 'martial race' in British India.

When Ranjit Singh died, his son, Dhulip, was a minor and was never more than a tool in the hands of various Sikh factions who fought one another for dominance in the Punjab in the years 1839–49. After their annexation of the Punjab, the British formally deposed him and took him to England, paying him a large pension in return for the renunciation of his rights to Ranjit Singh's kingdom. But by 1885 Dhulip had run into financial difficulties, and threatened that unless the India Office increased his pension, he would return to the Punjab. In March that year he issued an address to the Sikhs, complaining of his 'ill-treatment' at the hands of the English, and set out for India. When detained by the British at Aden, he fled to Russia, where he proclaimed himself 'a rebel now in earnest'.[40] At the beginning of 1887 he left Russia for India, where he found asylum in the French enclave of Pondicherry.[41]

At this time the local Special Branch was watching popular feeling in the Punjab, sending in weekly reports to the central government. On 8 February 1887 the Government of India ordered the Lieutenant-Governor of the Punjab to increase his intelligence activities and 'to ascertain by means of special and private enquiries the feelings with which the native army and native states in the Punjab regard His Highness's aspirations'.[42] The Thagi and Dakaiti Department sent a single native detective to the Punjab. He reported that certain groups among the Sikhs showed great interest in Dhulip Singh, but that only one clan would rise on his behalf.[43] Colonel Henderson, the General Superintendent of the Thagi and Dakaiti Department, believed, however, that the agent, who was a Muslim, was biased against the Sikhs on religious grounds. His reports were not supported by the reports of the local Special Branch.[44] In fact, the main intelligence operation in the Dhulip Singh case was carried out by Henderson himself, who simply interviewed local notables in the Punjab/North-West Frontier region. They convinced him that there was no significant popular sympathy for Dhulip Singh and that there were no Russian or other agents active on his behalf.[45]

Even before Colonel Henderson had carried out his investigations, Dufferin informed the Secretary of State that

> if the Russians were to come with Dhulip Singh in their right hand, the rumour of such a circumstance would undoubtedly have an inconvenient effect.[46]

But he added

> I should be sorry to think that the foundations of our Empire were so unsubstantial as to be really endangered by the intrigues of such a personage.[47]

Yet apart from the Wahabi unrest of the 1860s, the Dhulip Singh conspiracy was the most serious danger the British perceived within India in the later nineteenth century. Even the small regular intelligence

25

agency at the Government of India's disposal had proved adequate in assessing this threat.

The Dhulip Singh conspiracy imposed no urgency for the reform of Indian intelligence. None the less, in 1887, Lord Dufferin's government attempted to improve its sources of intelligence independently of the Dhulip Singh affair. The Central Office of the Thagi and Dakaiti Department was reorganized for the last time before its abolition in 1903. It was renamed the Central Special Branch of the Thagi and Dakaiti Department and was strengthened by the addition of an Assistant General Superintendent and a three-man office staff.[48] Thus the General Superintendent, who already acted informally as the Viceroy's senior intelligence officer, was placed in charge of the Government of India's official intelligence office. The functions of the Central Office remained those defined in 1878 – to collate and distribute the information received from the provinces in weekly reports to the Government of India. It was expected to conduct enquiries for the government on only a limited scale.

In its reforms of 1887, Lord Dufferin's government recognized that the fundamental problem of intelligence-gathering in India lay in the absence at the local level of regular organizations with the task of securing information, be it criminal, military or political in character. The Government of India had placed little authority behind its recommendations of 1878, and ten years later it still did not know whether Local Governments other than the Punjab disposed of any sort of intelligence office. Now the government wanted to 'be fully informed of everything affecting the public peace and order, which can be made the subject of observation'. The central government proposed that each Local Government should set up a Special Branch on the Punjab model. An officer entitled 'Assistant to the Inspector General of Police, Special Branch' was to be in charge, assisted by a staff whose maximum strength was set at three men. The staff in the quiet Central Provinces and Madras were to be even smaller. The total cost of the local and the Central Special Branches was expected to be Rs.93,600 (£6,240), half paid by the central government and half by the provinces. The Special Branches were to submit weekly reports to the Local Governments in two forms. The *Secret Police Abstract* was to contain information about 'foreign and resident suspects, religious leaders and sects', in order to enable the local police to carry out surveillance. It was also to contain information on the native press and native societies.

How were the central and the provincial Special Branches to operate within such small dimensions? The answer was that they would rely for information mainly on the local police 'whose agents are everywhere found'. The Special Branches might make enquiries through 'either policemen who have shown aptitude for secret service or informers whose intelligence and fidelity have been tested'. Henderson, the head of the Thagi and Dakaiti Department, who was responsible for carrying out the reforms, believed that their 'training and experience . . . qualify them to observe all movements and indications of popular feeling'. He divided the areas in which information was concerned into nine categories, placing the greatest emphasis on those relating to political threats to the Raj.[49]

There was a large element of wishful thinking in the scheme. Henderson himself realized that the local police had been of little use in reporting on popular feeling in the Dhulip Singh affair. Indeed, they seemed to have been oblivious of it. This is hardly surprising, since no one had ever been in any doubt about the quality of the Indian police which suffered from two basic problems: first, there were too few of them to control the whole sub-continent; and second, the lower ranks were poorly paid, poorly motivated and as a rule not well educated. Even in preventing ordinary crime they left very much to be desired. In 1856, on the eve of the Mutiny, senior members of the East India Company concluded that the police were 'all but useless for the prevention and sadly inefficient for the detection of crime'. William Edwards, a British official, wrote even more candidly about the brutality and corruption of the police in 1859, describing them as a 'scourge to the people' and as one of the chief grounds of popular dissatisfaction with the British government.[50] In 1902, a Police Commission set up to reform the police found that the lower ranks were just as useless as they had been half a century earlier.[51]

In respect of intelligence work, the performance of the police was at best variable from province to province. The Home Department, which was the Government of India's Ministry of the Interior, remarked that in some provinces the observation of popular feeling formed 'a regular and well-understood part of police duties' while in other provinces the police never reported on such matters or did so 'in a perfunctory way'.[52] Inevitably, police intelligence was very much dependent upon the efficiency of underpaid inspectors and sub-inspectors who did not receive special training for intelligence work and who had simultaneously to carry out their ordinary duties.

The reforms of 1887 amounted simply to an attempt to make the local police forces aware of the need to provide intelligence and to establish a basic flow of information from the provinces to the centre, and between the provinces. Such arrangements had been greatly deficient hitherto. The scheme was not so much an attempt to anticipate any outbreak of popular unrest as a recognition that intelligence, political or otherwise, scarcely existed in British India.

On one issue, Dufferin's administration was emphatic; it intended neither 'to organize an extensive system of Secret Police to act independently of Local Governments and Administrations', nor to set up a system of espionage 'through which the people would be harassed by spies and informers'.[53] The government clearly felt the constraint of public opinion by this date. In 1881, Dufferin's predecessor, Lord Ripon had written as follows on the subject of repressive measures in general:

> I hold as strongly as any man that we must be careful to maintain our military strength; but, whatever may have been the case in the past, we cannot now rely upon military force alone; and policy as well as justice, ought to prompt us to endeavour to govern more and more by means of, and in accordance with, that growing public opinion, which is beginning to show itself throughout the country.[54]

In the final decades of the nineteenth century, Indian society started to change relatively rapidly and relations between rulers and ruled were altered as a result. From the point of view of the British, one of the most obvious changes was the growth of public opinion, one manifestation of which was the mushrooming of the vernacular press throughout India. By the time Dufferin wrote, the Indian press was ready and able to comment on government policies. This had not been the situation three decades earlier at the time of the Mutiny.

All the British rulers from the 1880s onwards, and probably earlier still, shared Ripon's concern that British rule in India had to be made palatable to the Indians. In fact, in a fundamental way British rule in India was always vulnerable. Compared with the native population, the British were a tiny minority. It was one thing to crush an armed threat to the Raj; the British were able to do this in 1857, and again during the First World War, when they were faced by a serious outbreak of terrorism. What they could not afford was to alienate the

Indian public on a substantial scale. The maintenance of British rule in India depended upon the acquiescence and participation of the ruled.

At the end of the nineteenth century the British were still thinking of Indian opinion as something which was essentially passive; in other words, Indians might respond for better or worse to British political measures but they did not have the strength or the experience to take initiatives of their own. Public opinion at this time might encourage the British to take certain policies such as avoiding the use of espionage, but could not force them to do so.

One group which was conspicuous by its complete absence from the discussions leading up to the reform of intelligence in 1887 was the Indian National Congress, which had been founded in 1885. It was intended to be a forum which would express the opinions of all India. From this time onwards Indian nationalism was to be a slowly increasing factor in the politics of British India. However, the Congress at this time wanted to work alongside the government, introducing minor reforms. Moreover, it was restricted to a very narrow clique of wealthy and educated Indians. At his farewell speech at the end of 1888, Dufferin dismissed the Congress as representing only 'a microscopic minority' of Indians. Furthermore, the Congress found it difficult to secure unity on any but the least controversial issues, such as entry into the Indian Civil Service (ICS), increased Indian participation in the legislative process and economic questions. At this time the British did not perceive a constitutional organization as anything like a threat.

According to an old but untrue story, British intelligence had an indirect role in the birth of the Indian National Congress. It is worth recounting this, in order to dispel some of the myths surrounding the secret service of the Raj. It used to be claimed that Lord Dufferin had encouraged the foundation of the Congress, so as to channel Indian discontent into manageable, constitutional channels. The Congress thus served as a 'safety-valve' on behalf of the British rulers. By the end of the First World War some Indian nationalists were already using this interpretation in order to condemn the Congress, whose policies they regarded as too moderate.

What is the origin of this story? Undoubtedly, a retired ICS officer, Allan Octavian Hume, played an important role in setting up the Congress. By the 1880s, Hume had come to see himself as an unofficial adviser to the government, regularly presenting it with what he saw as prophetic warnings about the discontented state of Indian public opinion.[55] Hume later claimed that his involvement with the Congress was partly the result of having read seven volumes of secret reports on the situation in India in 1878. These convinced him that India was threatened by a serious outbreak of violent unrest. However, Hume never said exactly what these reports were, which naturally led historians to the conclusion that they were the products of the Raj's extensive secret police. As one Indian writer notes:

> So deeply rooted had become the belief in Hume's volumes as official documents that in the 1950s a large number of historians and would-be historians, including the present writer, devoted a great deal of time and energy searching for them in the National Archives. And when their search proved futile, they consoled themselves with the thought that the British had destroyed them before their departure in 1947.[56]

In reality, the reports which Hume saw came from a dubious collection of Indian mystics on whom he, as a believer in the occult, placed great reliance. William Wedderburn, who was also involved in the foundation of the Indian National Congress stated this explicitly in his biography of Hume.

There are several other reasons which disprove the traditional story about British involvement in the foundation of the Congress. First, as has been shown throughout this chapter, the intelligence facilities of the Raj at this time were barely existent, either for domestic or foreign information-gathering. Second, whatever information they provided, it did not lead the Government of India to fear revolution. The story is, however, of interest in that it is one of the old myths about the strength of the British secret service in India. This myth is similar to that concocted by Rudyard Kipling in his novel *Kim* of an all-seeing, far-sighted Raj. This leads to the conclusion that both nationalist writers and the staunchest imperialists were badly ill-informed about an important facet of British rule in India. British intelligence was not concerned in any way with the creation of the Congress, nor was it to become concerned with this constitutional organization in the period covered by this book.

What then, were the targets of the Raj's tiny intelligence operations at the end of the nineteenth century? At this time the British were, as usual, very much concerned about potential religiously inspired unrest.[57] At the time there were important developments within

Hinduism: on the positive side there was the growth of Hindu reform movements, but the other side of the coin of greater Hindu self-definition was an increase in communal violence between Hindus and Muslims. This, of course, was very worrying to the government. Even worse, was outright opposition to the Raj on religious grounds, though this as yet motivated only a minute section of the Hindu community.

In the 1890s popular unrest broke out in the Maharashtra region of the Bombay Presidency. Conscious political protest was limited to a small group – the Chitpavan Brahmins, who dominated the town of Poona. One of their main grievances was economic; they were concerned that their privileged access to government employment was being curtailed.[58] But the unrest also had a basis in anti-British Hindu religious feeling.

The trouble in Poona was to no small degree thanks to the activities of one man, Bal Gangadhar Tilak, who was to be one of the greatest Indian nationalist leaders of the twentieth century. Tilak was the first Indian nationalist leader to attempt to create a mass following. The methods which he used in the Poona District in the 1890s were innovative. The key to his strength at this time was the combination of political demands against the British with orthodox Hinduism. He put over his message to a wide audience through his newspapers, the *Mahratta* and the *Kesari*, and by organizing festivals. In 1894 he organized a public celebration in Poona in honour of the elephant-headed god, Ganesh, whose cult he had revived. Another favourite for devotion was the Maharashtrian hero, Shivaji, who had successfully fought the Moguls in the seventeenth century. Both god and hero were powerful rallying symbols, allowing Tilak to spread his nationalist message in a language which ordinary people could understand. The final element in Tilak's armoury of propaganda was the use of devoted Hindu youths. Tilak's young disciples spread anti-government and anti-Muslim tracts which called on Hindus to prepare for the expulsion of an alien power.[59] Through these youths, Tilak tried to reach into the villages, where they served as 'famine agents' and as political preachers.

Tilak's campaign at first caused the British annoyance, but little concern. Through compromise the Local Government was able to take the sting out of Tilak. He had proved weak for several reasons. First, because the Hindus to whom he appealed were divided among themselves by caste. For all his ingenuity, Tilak was still basically speaking for the elite Brahmin caste, and specifically the Chitpavan

31

sub-caste. His movement was further weakened because its appeal was strictly regional. For example, Shivaji had little appeal to men further north, whose territory the Maharastrian hero had extensively devastated. Finally, Tilak was repulsive to Muslims, to whom he was as hostile as he was to the British.

Although the political movement in Poona was later seen by the British as one of the first significant nationalist challenges to the Raj, at the time it only caused serious concern because of one of its side-effects. In 1897 Poona was the scene of the first assassination of a government official since Lord Mayo's murder in 1872. This act was of much greater concern to the British than Tilak's agitation.

In May 1897 there was an outbreak of plague in Poona. The plague commissioner, Mr Rand, ordered the compulsory evacuation of infected houses, but in such a way as to offend orthodox Hindus. Tilak, in his paper *Kesari*, described Rand, as a tyrant. On 22 June two brothers named Chapekar murdered Rand and a Lieutenant Ayerst who happened to be travelling with him. The Rand murder led the British to suspect a deep-rooted conspiracy at Poona. It is true that the Chitpavan Brahmins were a disaffected group, but their discontent did not extend to violence. The Chapekars were thus untypical. They were members of a terrorist society, but one which had no more than a handful of members. None the less, in February 1899 the Secretary of State for India, Lord Hamilton, wrote to the Viceroy, Lord Curzon:

> The methods which the agitators have there pursued are singularly like those adopted in Ireland – an ostensible constitutional party, a virulent and seditious press writing on the border land of legality, and an inner circle of desperadoes.[60]

This was the situation which the British most feared in India at the end of the nineteenth century. It should be noted, however, that such comparisons between India and Ireland by British statesmen are extremely few and far between.

In fact, the situation in Poona was already under control by the time Hamilton wrote. A small Bombay Special Branch and the local police were able cope with a new and unexpected threat to the Raj. The agitation which Tilak encouraged centred on the anti-plague measures and died away when the plague abated. Likewise the Chapekars were caught and executed. Tilak was jailed 18 months later.

Like previous challenges to the Raj in the nineteenth century, the unrest in Poona in the 1890s did not lead to any major intelligence operation, even after terrorism erupted. Why were the British reluctant to set up a secret service in India? Two practical reasons for failing to systematize domestic espionage have already been mentioned. First, India was too poor to allow the British to employ powerful forces of control. The army was incapable of resisting a major invasion; the police force was unable to stop crime; and the bureaucracy amounted to no more than the bare minimum for holding the country together and for collecting taxes. If, therefore, Indian intelligence had minimal dimensions, it was no different from other elements of the government. There is no doubt that the British did feel constrained by financial considerations when discussing their intelligence arrangements.

The second reason why the British did not want to use domestic intelligence on anything more than a minimal scale was Indian public opinion. From the 1880s onwards, successive viceroys were well aware that expansion of intelligence could be counter-productive. Terrorists like the Chapekars could not shake the Raj; but British rule would be weakened if popular support, or at least acquiescence, was undermined.

But these practical reasons are an insufficient explanation for the British reluctance to expand Indian intelligence in the nineteenth century. The British had a genuine distaste for spies. This was part of the ideological baggage which they brought with them to India, and which was surprisingly resistant to local conditions.

It is important to look briefly at attitudes to domestic intelligence in Britain. From the later seventeenth century on, British governments used spies only intermittently at home for fear of alienating popular opinion. In the eighteenth and nineteenth centuries, England, Scotland and Wales were relatively free from spies. The British held this to be one of the marks which made their society superior to those of the European continent. It seems that after 1848, domestic political espionage stopped altogether in Britain. There is no doubt that British public opinion was very hostile to the idea of domestic espionage and spying abroad was not held to be any less distasteful. Britain had neither a regular foreign intelligence service nor a counter-intelligence service until 1909.

But it would be an exaggeration to say that Victorian statesmen held espionage in absolute abhorrence. When good intelligence was clearly necessary, the Victorians were ready to have recourse to espionage. In the period 1790 to 1830, spies were used to counter the dangers of Jacobin subversion within Britain resulting from the French Revolution; and thereafter, to guard against the dangers of unrest in the troubled decades following the Napoleonic Wars.

The second half of the nineteenth century saw the birth of the Special Branch of the Metropolitan Police. This was the nearest that the later Victorians came to having a domestic intelligence service in Britain. Initially, the Special Branch came into being as a result of the government's desire to avoid having to set up anything resembling a secret police force. Britain had begun to offer asylum to political refugees from the continent, as a result of which the government received heavy criticism from European powers which believed that nothing was being done to control the activities of their exiled subversives. With the minimum level of surveillance of foreign refugees which the Special Branch provided, the British government felt able to dismiss such foreign criticisms. Another stimulus to the continued existence of the Special Branch was the Irish bombing campaign in England between 1881 and 1884. In default of any regular intelligence apparatus, it was left to the Special Branch to fight the terrorists.

One area where the British had regularly used spies was Ireland, where unrest was always on the cards. Undoubtedly espionage played an effective and continuous role there in maintaining British domination. Most importantly, in the 1790s, the use of spies had crippled whatever chances nationalist rebels had had. The British used spies to counter the threat posed by Irish Americans. One famous British agent, Henri le Caron, infiltrated the top levels of Irish nationalist circles in the United States in the 1870s and 1880s.[61]

When needs required, the Victorians did have recourse to spies.[62] Although they held spies to be undesirable, whether for domestic or foreign intelligence, they did not hesitate to use them when threatened by subversion, and certainly in the face of armed threat. They were not unaware of the benefits to be gained from espionage for defending their Empire. What the Victorians lacked was the notion of intelligence as first, a permanent component of government or of foreign policy; and second, something which was the preserve of professionals.

If the Victorians did not use spies extensively, this was also because of a careful calculation of the damage that might be caused to the image of government in the eyes of the public which usually meant that the use of spies was counter-productive. The same attitude applied to considerations of foreign espionage. The benefits to be gained had to be offset against the damage which might result to Britain's foreign relations.

Throughout most of the nineteenth century, the British had the option of using espionage or not. The period between the end of the Napoleonic Wars in 1815 and the outbreak of the Boer War in 1899 was one of peace for the Empire. The only war fought against a European power after 1815 was against Russia in the Crimea, from 1854 to 1855. In this period there were no major threats to Britain itself, and the only thing to disturb the general peace was expansion of the Russian empire. This raised intermittent fears about the security of India, but to some British statesmen it was not clear that there was a Russian threat at all. What is more, the Russians made no attempts to spread subversion in India. Thus if the Victorians had only limited use for espionage, this was because it was not that necessary.

This is true of the British Empire at global level. It does not fully answer the question of why the British in India did not 'go native' and continue existing traditions of intelligence-gathering. As already noted, there were several reasons why conditions in India might naturally have led governments to use domestic espionage on a considerable scale. Britain's freedom from spies in the later nineteenth century had been made possible by the development of an effective police force. This was something that India did not have.

The first point to note is that India was controlled by men who shared the common Victorian aversion to the use of spies. From the 1790s onwards, the conduct of the British authorities in India was closely scrutinized by the home government on all issues of importance. In this sense, attitudes towards espionage at home had a direct relevance to what went on in India. But there was more to it than this. The British rulers of India shared the views about espionage of their colleagues in the India Office in London. Their distaste for spies amounted to more than just practical concern about Indian public opinion. There was a feeling that India should have 'enlightened' government. This feeling was particularly strong after Lord Bentinck became Viceroy in 1828. He was heavily influenced by the Utilitarians, a prominent group of English reformist social and political theorists, whose main representatives were Jeremy Bentham and James and John Stuart Mill. The Utilitarians looked to the government and legal system of the state to play a leading role in improving society. Bentinck attempted to apply some of their ideas for what he saw as the progress of India, but his hopes for such an 'improvement' were not

35

fulfilled. None the less, from this time onwards the British administration was guided by what it saw as its mission in India. Whether the British belief in themselves was justified or not is not relevant here; what matters is that the British had such a self-image.

A particular concern which exercised the minds of some of the British rulers was that they should not seem to be using the methods of the Russian empire, which many of them held to be a model of despotism. Educated British understanding of the Tsarist state was frequently defective in the nineteenth and early twentieth centuries but attitudes towards Russia are significant because they show what the British did not want their empire, or indeed their own country, ever to resemble. Specifically, in the context of intelligence, the British despised the supposedly ubiquitous Tsarist secret police. Dufferin informed Lord Cross, the Secretary of State for India, that when reforming Indian police intelligence,

> we had to go to work very cautiously, for unfortunately everything that is conducted through the ordinary official channels seems ultimately to leak out, and of course it would not do for the native press to get it into their heads that we were about to establish a Third Section after the Russian pattern.[63]

Thus there were powerful impediments to the development of political intelligence in British India, namely the combination of poverty, the force of public opinion both in India and in Britain and the ideology of the Government of India itself, as well as practical doubts about the effectiveness of large-scale and regular intelligence operations. These factors ensured that British intelligence operations in nineteenth-century India remained on a tiny scale.

APPENDIX

British Intelligence Requirements within India in the late nineteenth century[64]

Henderson wrote in 1887: the main points on which it is the duty of the 'Special Branch' to keep government fully informed are the following:

(a) All political movements, sects, leaders and publications, and the like;
(b) Information regarding religious sects, changes in doctrine and

practice having a political significance; propagandism;

(c) The arrival, sojourn, departure and proceedings generally of suspicious characters and foreigners, special attention being paid to foreign emissaries; and to the movements of wandering gangs of criminals, the presence in any place of noted criminals and any circumstances regarding their habits that may come to notice;

(d) Rumours or published opinions disturbing the public peace; popular feelings and rumours;

(e) Religious excitement, such as caused by kine-killing contrary to rule, etc; comments on laws and government measures;

(f) Illicit trade in arms and ammunition, special reports being made of all Arms Act cases;

(g) Recruiting for the Indian Army or for Native States;

(h) Affairs in trans-frontier and Native States and rumours regarding them;

(i) Constitution, objects, and proceedings of native societies, whether established for political, or ostensibly for other, objects.

NOTES

1. Manu, IX, 306, quoted in S.D. Trivedi, *Secret Services in Ancient India: Techniques and Operation* (New Delhi: Allied Publishers Private, second edn, 1988).
2. Kautilya's *Arthashastra* was first translated by R. Shamasastry (Mysore, 1951). The main scholarly version of the text is the three-volume edition by R.P. Kangle (Bombay, 1963–72). A more recent and more accessible version is the edited version by L.N. Rangarajan (New Delhi, 1992). The date of composition of the *Arthashastra* has not been conclusively established. In *The Structure and Composition of the Kautilya Arthashastra* (PhD thesis, University of Iowa, 1968), T.R. Trautmann attacked the traditional view that the treatise was written around 300 BC and was the work of a single author. According to Trautmann, the *Arthashastra* was composed around 150 AD and was not written by one person. According to Rangarajan (op. cit.), Trautmann's thesis is based on 'the flimsy theoretical ground that authorship can be proved by analysing the frequency of "mundane high frequency words"', such as 'and', 'then', 'also', etc. As regards single authorship, Kautilya several times refers to himself by name. He is surely at least partly responsible for the work, even if it was expanded and revised by later writers. Stronger criticisms of the traditional view are that 'the rules of government laid down by the *Arthashastra*, pertain to a small state and not a vast empire as that of Candragupta' (R.C. Majumdar *et al.* (eds), *The History and Culture of the Indian People*, Vol. II). Moreover, it is said that the author does not refer to Chandragupta. But in and before 300 BC the Mauryan Empire was essentially an expanding single kingdom. If Chandragupta is not mentioned in the text, nor is any other ruler. Undoubtedly the sections in the *Arthashastra* relating to espionage do correspond to Mauryan practice. This is shown by comparison with the Emperor

Ashoka's references to agents who used to bring him news and keep him informed on public opinion.

3. According to Trivedi op. cit., 'The genius of Kautilya lies in his systematic codification of the wide variety of scattered information available on this subject'.

4. Trivedi, ibid., makes the unsubstantiated claim that the techniques of the Mauryan Empire were in many ways more advanced than those of modern secret services.

5. S.P. Blake, 'The Patrimonial-Bureaucratic Empire of the Mughals', *Journal of Asian Studies*, Vol. XXXIX, No. 1 (Nov. 1979). J.F. Richards, *Mughal Administration in Golconda* (Oxford: Oxford University Press, 1975).

6. Blake notes that 'like the Mughals, the British divided governmental authority into two main branches, military and revenue; they kept the basic Mughal administrative subdivisions and centralized civil power at each level in the hands of one person; and they adopted, especially after the Mutiny of 1857, the Mughal position that the state's role should be limited to collecting taxes and maintaining law and order'. 'The Patrimonial-Bureaucratic Empire of the Mughals', op.cit.

7. For details about British aversion to spying at home and in Europe, see C.M. Andrew, *Secret Service* (London: Heinemann, 1985), Ch. 1, 'Victorian Prologue'.

8. Gerald Morgan in 'Myth and Reality in the Great Game', *Asian Affairs*, Vol. LX [new series, Vol. IV, part I (February 1973)], lists the various agencies in the Indian Empire who might have carried out espionage, but did not. Remarkably he neglects to discuss the activities of the Thagi and Dakaiti Department and the provincial Special Branches which really had the task of collecting political intelligence.

9. Quoted in J.M. Brown, *Modern India. The Origins of an Asian Democracy* (Oxford: Oxford University Press, 1985), p. 56.

10. It is a great exaggeration to argue that the *Thugs* were not motivated by religion. This was the case put forward by Hiralal Gupta in the *Journal of Indian History* (August 1959). He argued that the *Thugs* were not a religious sect in any meaningful sense. They were generally people whose wealth and power had been diminished as the British took power. Gupta's main thesis is that the presentation of the *Thuggee* as a religious group was 'a convenient way of disowning responsibility for its actual origin in the British period'. There are numerous problems with this argument. Captured *Thugs* had a habit of boasting about their exploits in the service of the goddess Kali. If they were not seriously motivated by religion, why did they not simply refer to themselves as dacoits, or ordinary robbers? The penalties, if anything, would have been less. Gupta's case rests on the fact that evidence for the existence of *Thuggee* comes almost entirely from the British period. This is not surprising since it was only the British who attempted systematically to destroy the *Thugs* and to compile evidence about them.

11. The head of the British Government of India was known as the Governor-General in the period up 1857. After 1858, when the British Crown formally took over control of the Indian government from the East India Company, the Governor-General was known also, and more commonly, as the Viceroy.

12. 'Author's Introduction', Philip Meadows Taylor, *Confessions of a Thug* (first published, 1838; reprinted Oxford: Oxford University Press, 1986).

13. The Government of India hoped that the regular police, who had been recently reorganized, would be able to deal with other forms of organized crime. Letter from Northbrook to Ripon, 24 Nov. 1881, Northbrook Papers, IOLR MSS.EUR.C.141. Letter from the Viceroy in Council to the Secretary of State, dated Fort William, 11 February 1904 in J&P 493/04 in IOLR L/PJ/6/670.

14. Brown, *Modern India*, op. cit., p. 152.

15. A. Butterworth, 'District Administration in Madras, 1818–1857', p. 38, in *The Cambridge History of India*, Vol. VI, 'The Indian Empire, 1858–1919' (Cambridge 1932).

16. W.W. Hunter, *The Life of the Earl of Mayo*, Vol. II (London, 1876), pp. 306–7.

A. Seal, *The Emergence of Indian Nationalism*, p. 13, quoting Selections from the Records of the Government of Bengal, XLII, 'Papers connected with the trial of Moulvie Ahmedoollah' (Calcutta, 1866).

17. J.C. Ker, *Political Trouble in India* (Calcutta: Editions Indian, reprint 1973), pp. 306–7.

18. Extract from letter from the Government in Bengal, dated 12 December 1901, in *Proposed Organization of a Detective Police in Each Province*. IOLR HD/Pol: Feb. 1904, nos. 158–9 in P/6818.

19. Letter from Northbrook to Mr William Taylor (a journalist?), 10 Jan. 1878, Northbrook Papers, IOLR MSS.EUR.C.144/7.

20. Letter from Lytton to the Duke of Buckingham, Governor of Madras, 19 June 1878, Lytton Papers, IOLR MSS.EUR.E.218/25B.

21. Letter from Northbrook to Ripon, 24 Nov. 1881, Northbrook Papers, IOLR MSS. EUR.C.141/1.

22. Letter from Northbrook to Ripon, 6 May 1881, Northbrook Papers, IOLR MSS. EUR.C.141/1.

23. Letter from Northbrook to Ripon, 27 May 1881, Northbrook Papers, IOLR MSS. EUR.C.141/1.

24. Peter Hopkirk, *The Great Game. On Secret Service in High Asia* (London: John Murray, 1990), pp. 89–108.

25. Letter from Lytton to Viscount Cranbrook, 15 July 1878, Lytton Papers, IOLR MSS. EUR.E.218/25B.

26. Ibid.

27. Letter from Lytton to the Duke of Buckingham, op. cit.

28. For a discussion of the British spy scare, see D. French, 'Spy Fever in Britain', *Historical Journal*, Vol. XXI (1978) and Andrew, *Secret Service*, op. cit.

29. Enclosures of a letter to the Secretary of State for India, no. 179, 15 Nov. 1887. Extract from the proceedings of the Government of India, Home Department, Simla, 29 Oct. 1878. Cross Papers, IOLR MSS.EUR.E.243/23.

30. Ibid.

31. Enclosures of a letter to the Secretary of State for India, no. 179, 15 Nov. 1887. Enclosure no. 1. 'Memorandum on the Formation of an Intelligence Department under the Government of India'. Cross Papers, ibid.

32. Enclosures of a letter to the Secretary of State for India, no. 179, 15 Nov. 1887. Extract from the proceedings of the Government of India, Home Department, Simla, 29 Oct. 1878, op. cit.

33. Ibid.

34. Enclosures of a letter to the Secretary of State for India, no. 179, 15 Nov. 1887. Enclosure no. 2, dated Simla, 1 Oct. 1887. From A.P. MacDonnell, Secretary to the Government of India, Home Department, to the Chief Secretaries to the Governments of Madras, Bombay, and Bengal; the Secretaries to the Government of North-Western Provinces and Oudh and the Punjab; the Chief Commissioner of Central Provinces; and the Resident at Hyderabad for Berar. Cross Papers, IOLR MSS.EUR.E.243/23.

35. Letter from Lytton to the Duke of Buckingham, 19 June 1879, op. cit.

36. Enclosures of a letter to the Secretary of State for India, no. 179, 15 Nov. 1887. Enclosure no. 3, dated 29 Oct. 1887, from H.M. Durand, Secretary to the Government of India, Foreign Department, to the Resident at Hyderabad, the Agents to the Governor-General in Rajputana, Central India, and Baluchistan; the Residents in Mysore, Cashmere, Baroda, and Nepal; and Political Residents in the Persian Gulf and Turkish Arabia. Cross Papers, IOLR MSS.EUR.E.243/23.

37. Ibid.

38. In 1903 the Thagi and Dakaiti Department's secret service fund amounted to only Rs.300 (£20) per annum. Its total annual cost in that year was Rs.37,268 (£2,485).

Letter from the Viceroy in Council to the Secretary of State, dated 11 Feb. 1904.
39. That the British felt a need to spy on the Native States is another myth created by Kipling. See especially Ch. 11 of *Kim*. In the early twentieth century the Government of India suspected only one of the Indian Princes, the Gaekwar of Baroda. Lord Minto, however, assured Lord Morley that the Bombay CID had nothing to do with Baroda. Minto to Morley, Morley Papers, MSS.EUR.D.573/21.
40. Dhulip Singh's activities in Europe were not watched by Indian agents. Henderson noted that the information on Dhulip Singh's activities in Paris was 'very meagre'. The Government of India had no information about his doings in Russia. Summary of correspondence in the case of Maharajah Dalip Singh, prepared by Colonel P.D. Henderson, 13 June 1887. Part 4, 'Disloyal Proceedings of Maharaja Dalip Singh' and Part 5, 'Proceedings of Maharaja Dalip Singh after his Departure from Aden', Cross Papers, IOLR MSS.EUR.E.243/23.
41. Ibid. Part 3, 'Proceedings in connection with the residence in Pondicherry of Sardar Thakur Singh Sindhanwalia'.
42. 'Summary of correspondence in the case of Maharajah Dalip Singh' prepared by Colonel P.D. Henderson, 13 June 1887. Cross Papers, IOLR MSS.EUR.E.243/22.
43. Letter from Dufferin to Cross and enclosure, 7 July 1887, Cross Papers, IOLR MSS. EUR.E.243/23.
44. Summary of correspondence in the case of Maharajah Dalip Singh, prepared by Colonel P.D. Henderson, 13 June 1887. Part 1, 'Popular feeling about Dalip Singh's expected arrival in India'. Cross Papers, IOLR MSS.EUR.E.243/22.
45. Extract of a letter from Colonel Henderson, Superintendent of Thuggee and Dacoity, to Secretary, Foreign Department, on the supposed interest taken by the Sikhs in Dulip Singh's movements, June 1887. Cross Papers, IOLR MSS.EUR.E.24/22.
46. Letter from Dufferin to Cross, 22 Feb. 1887, Cross Papers, IOLR MSS.EUR.E.243/22.
47. Letter from Dufferin to Cross, 17 April 1887, Cross Papers, ibid.
48. Notes of a conference held at Government House, Rangoon, between Sir Frederic Fryer and four of his officers, and President, two members, and the Secretary of the Police Commission, 31 Jan. 1903. The office staff comprised of one Native Attaché, one Inspector and one Head Clerk. The officer appointed Assistant General Superintendent as Mr D.E. McCracken, who had formerly been Assistant to the Inspector-General of the Punjab. The Central Special Branch cost Rs.15,600 (£1,040) annually. J&P.493/04 in IOLR L/PJ/6/670.
49. See Appendix to this chapter.
50. Quoted in Bipan Chandra, *India's Struggle for Independence* (New Delhi: Penguin, 1989), p. 42.
51. J&P 493/04 in IOLR L/PJ/6/670.
52. *Memorandum on the Formation of an Intelligence Department*, Cross Papers, IOLR MSS.EUR.E.243/23.
53. Enclosures of a letter to the Secretary of State for India, no. 179, 15 Nov. 1887. Enclosure no. 1, *Memorandum on the Formation of an Intelligence Department under the Government of India*, Cross Papers, IOLR MSS.EUR.E.234/23.
54. Quoted in Brown, *Modern India*, p. 100.
55. See for example, the account of Hume's political career in Anil Seal, *The Emergence of Indian Nationalism* (Cambridge: Cambridge University Press, 1971).
56. Bipan Chandra, *India's Struggle for Independence*, op. cit., pp. 63–6. I have relied on this work for this interpretation of Hume's role in the foundation of the Indian National Congress.
57. See Appendix to this chapter.
58. See Valentine Chirol, *Indian Unrest* (London: Macmillan, 1910).
59. *Sedition (Rowlatt) Committee Report* (Calcutta, Bengal Secretariat Press), 1918. Ch. 1, 'Revolutionary Conspiracies in Bombay'. Chelmsford Papers, IOLR MSS.

EUR.E.264/43.
60. Hamilton Papers, IOLR Hamilton to Curzon, Vol. I, 10 Feb. 1899. Quoted in M.N. Das, *India Under Morley and Minto* (London: George Allen & Unwin, 1964), Ch. IV, 'Politics in India', p. 105. Hamilton was particularly concerned that the Mahratta Brahmins, who were the main force behind the unrest, were dominant in the Deccan police and in the administration generally. Hamilton Papers, 8 June 1899.
61. J.A. Cole, *Prince of Spies. Henri Le Caron* (London: Faber & Faber, 1984).
62. See Bernard Porter, *The Origins of the Vigilant State. The London Metropolitan Police Special Branch before the First World War* (London: Weidenfeld & Nicolson, 1987) and *Plots and Paranoia. A History of Political Espionage in Britain 1790–1988* (London: Unwin Hyman, 1989). Porter overemphasizes Victorians' aversion to espionage. This makes the difference between them and twentieth-century British starker.
63. Letter from Dufferin to Cross, 17 April 1887, Cross Papers, IOLR MSS.EUR.E.243/22. The Third Section had, incidentally, been abolished in 1880. Dufferin ought to have referred to the *Okhrana*, as the Tsarist secret police was popularly known from the time he wrote until the Russian Revolution.
64. *Memorandum on the Formation of an Intelligence Department*, Cross Papers, IOLR L/PJ/7/670.

2

The Reform of Indian Intelligence under Lord Curzon

In 1899 Lord Curzon became Viceroy. He brought with him a determination to reform and improve British rule in India, not seen since the crusading spirit of Bentinck's administration in the 1830s. One of the least efficient parts of the Indian administration was obviously the police. In 1902, Curzon appointed a Police Commission which had the task of conducting a general enquiry into the pay, strength and efficiency of the police throughout British India. It completed its work in 1903.[1]

Like his predecessors, Curzon had only limited success in improving the ordinary ranks of the police. He, too, was unable to solve the root cause of their inefficiency, namely India's poverty, which prevented the development of a relatively efficient bureaucracy, such as the British knew at home. In one area of his police work, however, Curzon enjoyed more success – the reform of police intelligence. This was an aspect of the Police Commission's work which he personally thought to be of great importance. Under Curzon, Indian domestic intelligence assumed the basic structure which it was to retain until the Raj came to an end in 1947. Furthermore, the governmental guidelines under which it operated were to remain generally in place in the decades up to the Second World War. Curzon's reform of police intelligence can be divided into two areas. First, a Department of Criminal Intelligence (DCI) was attached to the Government of India at the centre. Though Curzon never intended it to play such a role, it was soon to become both the central domestic and foreign intelligence agency of the Raj. Second, Criminal Investigation Departments (CIDs) were set up in all the provinces of British India. These reforms will now be examined in turn.

In October 1903 the Police Commission abolished the Thagi and Dakaiti Department.[2] It believed that the original reason for its existence – the suppression of special forms of organized crime such as *Thuggee* – no longer existed even in the Princely States, where the Department was still performing investigations. The Commission was dissatisfied with the performance of the Department's Central Special Branch as a criminal intelligence agency, since it had failed to keep abreast of recent developments in crime.[3] The development of India's railway, postal and telegraphic networks had rendered it obsolete by giving greater mobility to criminals. Part of the problem lay with inadequate police intelligence organization in the provinces. The Commission felt that the local police were unable to cope

> with a political or other movement, the ramifications of which extend[ed] beyond the limits of a single province, and particularly when the problem to be solved [was] the unravelling of organized crime committed by agents moving over wide areas of country.[4]

The provincial Special Branches were weak and did not supply information to the Central Special Branch.[5] But the Police Commission still attributed some of the blame for the deficiencies of the provincial police to the Central Special Branch, claiming that it lacked the authority, staff, administrative experience and specialized knowledge necessary for co-ordinating enquiries into organized crime.[6] The Government of Bengal was more critical, describing it as 'a farce', because the information which it provided was meagre and arrived too late to be of any use at the local level. These opinions of the Indian intelligence system were shared by other Local Governments.[7] The only thing in favour of the Central Special Branch's recent performance was that it had served as a rudimentary political intelligence agency.[8]

In a series of discussions with the governments of eight provinces, the Police Commission prepared the guidelines which were to regulate the operation of the new Department of Criminal Intelligence, which was to replace the Thagi and Dakaiti Department.[9] Its basic function was to collect information obtained from the Criminal Investigation Departments, which absorbed the Special Branches in the provinces, and to communicate it to the central and local governments. Such information fell into two categories. The first was information dealing with special forms of crime, particularly those which had been rendered more difficult by the development of communications. The groups with whom it would principally deal were the criminal tribes, *dakaits* (armed robbers) working large areas, forgers, counterfeiters and poisoners. The second category of information was 'intelligence upon political matters, including social, religious, and political movements not necessarily of a criminal character'.[10] However, nowhere in their discussions did the Police Commission encounter any suggestion that India needed a central intelligence department because of developments in the political climate.

Curzon's administration set about improving its police intelligence at a time when the external dangers which had faced India in the nineteenth century were decreasing. The threat perceived from Russia declined quickly after the outbreak of the Russo-Japanese War of 1904–5, which dramatically exposed Tsarist weakness, and disappeared completely when Great Britain, France and Russia formed the Triple Entente in 1907. Inside India the political situation appeared to have taken a turn for the better by the beginning of the twentieth century. Any fears which the British ever had of intrigues on the part of the Indian Princes subsided completely after the threat from Dhulip Singh proved fanciful. The mass movement organized by Tilak around Poona appears with hindsight to have been a portent of future troubles with Indian nationalists; but it did not seem so at the time. There was no longer any serious unrest in western India when the DCI and the CIDs were set up, and in the discussions leading to their formation no one even mentioned the name of Tilak. More surprisingly, the Police Commission did not once refer to the need for better supervision of the nationalist press, though this was a duty with which the DCI and the CIDs were in a short while to be very much concerned.[11]

Curzon was the first Viceroy to identify the Indian National Congress squarely with anti-British forces and realize that it served as an embryonic focus of all-Indian nationalism which might be able to undermine British power. In the last two decades of the nineteenth century, Congress politicians had started to make limited demands for a greater share in political power and for greater control over the way in which India's finances were spent. Yet Curzon saw the Congress as an easy target for destruction rather than a serious threat. In 1900 he made the famous statement that

> The Congress is tottering to its fall, and one of my greatest ambitions while in India is to assist it to a peaceful demise.

He certainly did not have the Congress in mind when he reformed Indian intelligence, and it does not receive a single mention in the deliberations of the Police Commission of 1902–3. There are other reasons why this was so. To the British, the Congress was not an obvious intelligence target. It was a completely public and not a secret organization, and remained so throughout the first two decades of the twentieth century.[12] Above all, from the British point of view, it was not involved in fomenting violent opposition to the Raj; indeed, most of the early nationalists associated with the Congress professed loyalty to British rule.

Thus the reform of police intelligence under Curzon was in no way stimulated by the existence of Indian nationalism of either the moderate variety represented by the majority of Congress politicians, or of the more extreme type represented by Tilak and his followers. The political climate in India changed rapidly after 1905 for reasons which will be discussed in the next chapter. But it should be noted here that Curzon's administration was not anticipating future developments in Indian politics when it set up the DCI and the CIDs. Lack of concern about the future of the Raj was as notable as confidence in the present in the proceedings of the Police Commission.

A final and conclusive reason why constitutional nationalists were not the preserve of British intelligence were the old British scruples about the use of spies. Worries that the Raj should not be thought to be introducing 'Russian methods' reappeared in the discussions of 1902–3. For example, the Lieutenant-Governor of the United Provinces wrote to the Police Commission, echoing Lord Lytton's observations of 1878:

> It would be objectionable and inconvenient to have a staff of secret Police in a province reporting direct to the Government of India matters regarding which the Local Government and the local authorities had not information. The staff would feel it necessary to justify their existence by reporting, and there would be a tendency for the new Department to develop into a centralized secret Police Bureau such as exists in the Russian Empire.[13]

Furthermore, as in the nineteenth century, the Government of India had no intention of alienating Indian public opinion by harassing moderate politicians. However, British inhibitions about the use of anything resembling domestic espionage went beyond concerns to avoid any inconvenience to moderate nationalists. They were a major reason why the Department of Criminal Intelligence was originally intended to have no regular investigative functions at all.

At first the Police Commission had wanted to attach to the Department of Criminal Intelligence a small detective establishment to deal with crimes which were beyond the detective resources of an individual Local Government, or which crossed the jurisdictions of several Local Governments. However, the India Office and almost all the Local Governments were as opposed to this as was the Government of the Punjab.[14] Partly this was a reflection of bureaucratic rivalries within the British government. At this time the different provincial administrations of British India had very strong individual characters and regional loyalties. This meant that Local Governments had a strong tendency to dislike interference from the central government of India, let alone from other Local Governments.[15]

The great regional diversity of India was another factor which discouraged the setting up of a detective branch of the central government. The Home Department, which was the Government of India's 'Home Office', wrote to the head of the Police Commission in January 1903:

> Experience shows that, if a member of a provincial police force is detached for duty outside the sphere of his ordinary employment, he is comparatively helpless amidst surroundings with which he is not familiar.[16]

Perhaps the most important precedent militating against the establishment of a detective police under the control of the Indian central intelligence derived not from the history of imperial intelligence, such as it was, but from the experience of the Special Branch of the Metropolitan Police during the so-called 'Dynamite War' against Irish Republican terrorists who had bombed mainland Britain in the 1880s.[17] Operations against the terrorists had initially suffered as a result of conflict between different police organizations. The Special Branch of the Metropolitan Police was the local agency concerned with combating terrorism, and it saw London, the terrorists' main target, as very much its patch. In 1885, however, the Home Office brought Edward Jenkinson, the Royal Irish Constabulary's 'spymaster general', over from Dublin along with a team of detectives, in order to help the Special Branch co-ordinate its work with that of the British provincial police forces. From the outset there was friction between Jenkinson's organization and the Metropolitan Police.[18] This prompted a detailed discussion of the respective roles of Jenkinson and the Met by the Home Secretary, Sir Richard (later Lord) Cross.[19] These discussions are of relevance to Indian police intelligence, because they provided the guidelines under which it was to operate. But before looking at these rules, one important point should be noted. The Government of India was drawing on the British experience. It was by no means trying to establish its own methods of working in the politically and ideologically sensitive area of criminal intelligence.

Cross developed a set of basic rules governing the operation of the central intelligence department under Jenkinson and the local investigating agencies, namely the Special Branch of the Metropolitan Police and the British provincial police forces.[20] The Police Commission translated these into Indian terms, and the Government of India took them over as the ground-rules of the DCI. The principal objective of the central department was the collection, collation and communication of information regarding certain specific types of crimes and criminals all over British India. However, while the central agency was to give all the help which local officers required in their investigations, local officers were responsible for the collection of information and for investigation. The final arbiter of any disputes between the DCI and the provincial organizations was the Home Department of the Government of India, which controlled the DCI.[21] The DCI did not have the independent authority to force the local CIDs to do anything they did not want to do. The Government of India alone had the power of giving orders to the Local Governments. The Police Commission noted that:

> If the central agency has formally granted to it the power of issuing orders to Local Governments, there will undoubtedly be jealousy, friction and consequent failure.

These rules amounted to a considerable restraint on the freedom of action and possibilities for development of the new Department of Criminal Intelligence. Essentially, therefore, the DCI was restricted to the work of a secretariat.

This was not, however, quite the whole picture. From the beginning the DCI, though debarred from operating as a regular intelligence-gathering agency, did have some facilities for using agents. The Police Commission laid down that

> though debarred from anything of the nature of investigation, the Central officer should be authorized to employ informants of his own and should be allowed secret service money for this purpose

on a liberal scale; the information so obtained should be used to supplement the information received from the [CIDs] of the various provinces.[22]

The Police Commission did not specify when the DCI was permitted to employ such agents. It should also be noted that the informants were not the same as political spies. They were clearly intended as auxiliaries to criminal investigation in the provinces. Furthermore, the DCI was not equipped with the funds to employ large numbers of agents.

Secret Service funds were included in the category of 'Miscellaneous annual expenditure'. In 1902 they comprised Rs.5,700 (£380) out of a total miscellaneous costs of Rs.7,400 (£493). The other major expense in this category was 'travelling allowances'. The exact figure of the Secret Service allowance granted to the DCI in 1904 is not known. The grant for 'travelling allowances' was Rs.5,000 (£333). It is likely, therefore, that the Secret Service allowance was about Rs.11,000 (£733) a year. This was a very small sum, particularly since the term 'Secret Service' covered a great number of headings. However, the new CIDs also had their own funds for such purposes.

The Department of Criminal Intelligence did not differ from the Central Special Branch in its main brief; nor initially was it different in composition, as the following Table shows.

At first the Government of India actually saved money by the reform of the central intelligence agency. The DCI cost Rs.25,400 (£1,693) more than the Central Special Branch every year, which was an insignificant sum. However, when this sum is deducted from the savings made when the Hyderabad branch of the Thagi and Dakaiti Department was transferred to the Princely Government, the reform left the Government of India over Rs.10,645 (£710) better off.[24]

Despite the restrictions placed upon it, the Department of Criminal Intelligence differed in certain important respects from the Central Special Branch of the Thagi and Dakaiti Department. Though it began with a very small staff, Curzon's administration expected that it would grow.[25] But the most important feature of the reform of the central agency lay in the office of the Director of Criminal Intelligence.[26] The Police Commission thought that the Director ought usually to be drawn from the Indian Civil Service, since he needed less the detective skills of a policeman than administrative ability 'to unite in concerted action, in some sections of their work, all the police

TABLE 1

COMPARISON BETWEEN ESTABLISHMENTS OF CENTRAL SPECIAL BRANCH
AND DCI[23]

CENTRAL SPECIAL BRANCH		DCI	
1. *Officers*		1. *Officers*	
General Superintendent		Director	
Assistant		Deputy Director	
Inspector			
Total cost	Rs.43,800	Total cost	Rs.57,996
per year	(£2,920)	per year	(£3,866)
2. *Clerical Staff*		2. *Clerical Staff*	
4 clerks	Rs.5,844	4 clerks	Rs.5,844
	(£390)		(£390)
3. *Menial Establishment*		3. *Menial Establishment*	
3 Indian servants	Rs.384	15 Indian servants	Rs.1,560
	(£26)		(£104)
Total Cost of Staff:	Rs.50,028	*Total Cost of Staff:*	Rs.65,400
	(£3,336)		(£4,360)
Miscellaneous Costs:	Rs.7,400	*Miscellaneous Costs:*	Rs.17,000
	(£493)		(£1,133)
TOTAL COST:	Rs.57,428	*TOTAL COST:*	Rs.82,400
	(£3,829)		(£5,493)
Differences in Costs:	Rs.24,972 a year		
	(£1,664) a year		

forces of India'. The type of official required for the post was 'a civilian used to dealing with Local Governments and conversant with the feelings that have to be conciliated and the local conditions that require to be conciliated in particular cases . . .'.[27] The Director had to have the diplomatic accomplishments of 'tact, address and ability, so as to obviate jealousy and friction, meet opposition courteously but firmly, and command respect'. Sir Andrew Fraser, the Chief Commissioner of the Central Provinces and Officer-in-Charge of the Police Commission placed great emphasis on the need for an able Director of Criminal Intelligence; he wrote:

> I have not the slightest doubt that in a very short time the central agency, provided that a good man is placed in charge of it, will be working in the smoothest way with the local departments.

The success of the operations of the DCI at this time were thus more dependent on the officer in command of the DCI than upon the bureaucratic structure at his disposal. Broadly speaking, this situation was to continue.

The first appointment to the post of Director of Criminal Intelligence was Harold (later Sir Harold) Stuart, the 43-year old Secretary to the Police Commission. On leaving Oxford he had joined ICS in 1881. He had spent most of his career in the Madras Presidency. The selection of Stuart as DCI is the clearest indication of the high status which the Department of Criminal Intelligence was intended to occupy inside the Government of India and in relation to the Local Governments. His permanent post in 1903 was Inspector-General of Police. He had already been earmarked for even higher things when the previous year he was appointed Officiating Deputy Secretary to the Government of India. He served as Director of Criminal Intelligence from 1904 until 1908 when he became Home Secretary to the Government of India.

Continuity with the old Central Special Branch was provided by the government's choice for the position of Deputy Director of Criminal Intelligence. This officer was henceforth to be a member of the Police Department, usually one of the Deputy Inspectors-General in charge of provincial CIDs.[28] Donald McCracken, who had been the Assistant General Superintendent of the Thagi and Dakaiti Department since 1878 was selected 'by reason of his extensive acquaintance with the working of both the Provincial and Central Special Branches'.[29]

On 19 April 1904 the Department of Criminal Intelligence started work. Its office was located permanently at Simla, the hill station in the foothills of the Himalayas where the Government of India used to spend the hot summer months. Unlike the rest of the government, it did not migrate to the capital, Calcutta, in the 'cold weather'.[30]

The police reforms of Curzon's administration differed fundamentally from those of Lytton and Dufferin in that they placed provincial intelligence on a much firmer footing. The CIDs were tiny relative to the population of the provinces, but their creation meant that for the first time the Local Governments had investigating intelligence agencies established on a permanent basis. Whatever the future problems between the centre and the provinces, the new CIDs were to provide the Department of Criminal Intelligence with far more extensive information than had been at the disposal of the old Central Special Branch.[31]

The DCI was set up in advance of the CIDs,[32] the latter being set up between 1903 and 1906. As in the case of the DCI, the Police Commission intended them primarily to counter ordinary crime, and political factors were not important in their formation.[33] This is further indicated by the fact that the CIDs were set up in all the provinces of British India, including those, like Madras, which had never experienced serious political unrest. Indeed, the Madras CID outnumbered that of the Punjab.

Despite the intermittent attempts of nineteenth century Viceroys to improve police intelligence, the Government of India had very few detective resources at its disposal at the beginning of the twentieth century. Thanks to Dufferin's reforms, the provinces of British India had their own Special Branches, but these were no more than small secretariats concerned with processing information rather than investigation. Only a few provinces had anything approaching a detective force. The Bombay Presidency, which had recently been affected by the unrest fomented by Tilak, was in advance of the other parts of British India in creating a detective police force. This amounted to a force of 13 men, along with a four-man intelligence branch operating at Poona.[34] In the entire Madras Presidency, which covered about a third of the territory of British India, the only detective force was the Intelligence Department of the Madras City Police, which had been formed in 1887. It consisted of only seven men.[35] In the strategically important and turbulent province of the Punjab there were, according to the Local Government, 'many excellent detectives in the Police . . . but the organization [was] purely local'.[36] On the other hand, in Bengal, the United Provinces and the Central Provinces there was no special detective agency at all.[37] Even in the provinces where detective branches did exist, the officers were uniformly of low rank, never higher than Inspector.

The new CIDs were large only in comparison with the almost non-existent detective agencies which they replaced; relative to the size of India they were still tiny. An important difference, however, was not so much in their size as in their status. In all cases they were headed by a senior police officer, at least a Superintendent, but usually a Deputy Inspector-General. Some of the CIDs expanded slightly after their creation so the figures for their initial full intended strength are given here. Two CIDs existed in the Bombay Presidency – one for Bombay City and one for the Province as a whole. In 1906 the provincial CID was 50-strong, while that attached to Bombay City numbered 51.[38] In the Madras Presidency in 1910, 55 CID officers covered the whole province.[39] In the United Provinces the CID had reached a total of 87 men by 1907.[40] Next door, in the Central Provinces the detective force came to only 41.[41] In the Punjab there were surprisingly only 34 officers in the CID.[42] In 1906 Bengal after Partition had a CID which was 70-strong, while that of the newly created Eastern Bengal and Assam was 18-strong.[43] In each province the Special Branches were incorporated into the CIDs, and continued at the same strength, as agencies for processing and distributing information produced by the CIDs.

No Viceroy in the nineteenth century managed to establish police intelligence as a recognized and essential part of government. By creating the CIDs and by conferring a high status upon the Director of Criminal Intelligence, Curzon's administration acknowledged the gathering of intelligence as a vital function of good government, and the agencies dedicated to its procurement as legitimate. But his accomplishment ought not to be exaggerated. Though they did not question the need for the CIDs in the provinces, Curzon's successors were less keen on the Government of India's central intelligence agency. The most important question about the DCI after Curzon was not whether it should be allowed to expand at home and abroad, but whether it should exist at all. By creating the DCI and the CIDs in 1904, Curzon tried to make the Government of India more efficient. Yet his achievement and intention were impressive only when compared with the ramshackle system which his government replaced and when the degree of prejudice within the administration against the idea of a secret police is taken into account.

The British in India retained the same attitudes towards spies as the ruling classes in England, even though they did not in India feel the security of being in an 'island fortress'. These attitudes towards espionage were characteristically British. If anything, the governments of the early twentieth century were even more reluctant to use espionage than those of the nineteenth century. This distinction ought not, however, to be laboured. In the nineteenth century the threats to the Raj from inside and outside India seemed greater than they were under Curzon. Moreover, Curzon set up a police intelligence network which was geared mainly to criminal intelligence and not to political espionage. His intentions in this respect differed from those of Lytton and Dufferin in the previous century.

NOTES

1. It was made up of seven members, five British and two Indian, with a secretary. Its president was Sir Andrew Fraser, the Chief Commissioner of the Central Provinces.
2. At the request of the Nizam's government, the entire Thagi and Dakaiti establishment in Hyderabad was incorporated into the Native Police. The Thagi and Dakaiti Department survived after a fashion with the continuance of the minuscule Rajputana and Central India Agencies, which were placed under the local Agents of the Foreign and Political Department. All intelligence relating to social or political movements in the Native States continued to come from the Political Officers. Letter from the Viceroy in Council to the Secretary of State, 11 Feb. 1904. J&P 493/04 in IOLR PJ/6/670.
3. Finance and Commerce Department, no. 51 of 1904. J&P 493/04 in IOLR L/PJ/6/670.
4. Demi-official from H.H. Risley, Officiating Secretary to the Government of India, Home Department, to Sir Andrew Fraser, KCSI, President of the Police Commission. In J&P 493/04.
5. Notes of a meeting held at Belvedere on Saturday, 24 January 1903, to discuss with Sir Andrew Fraser, the question of organizing a Central Criminal Investigation Department for India, in J&P 493/04.
6. Finance and Commerce Department, no. 51 of 1904, op. cit.
7. Notes of a conference held in the Council Chamber, Fort St. George, on 18 Feb. 1903 and notes of a conference held at Government House, Rangoon, between Sir Frederic Fryer and four of his officers, and President, two members, and Secretary of the Police Commission, 31 Jan. 1903, in J&P 493/04.
8. An India Office Minute of 1904 reviewed the performance of the Thagi and Dakaiti Department since its creation under Sleeman. It stated that: 'Its value and efficiency . . . varied with the energy and competence of the successive officers who . . . held the post of Superintendent but . . . it afforded a valuable means of making the Government acquainted with the movements of opinion in India'. Unsigned India Office Minute Paper, dated 11 February 1904, entitled 'A Central Criminal Intelligence Department for India', in J&P 826/04 in IOLR L/PJ/6/670. The writer of the Minute had served for five years as Home Secretary in India.
9. The provinces involved in the discussions were Burma, Madras, the United Provinces, Assam, Bombay, the Central Provinces and the Punjab. The British representative in the Princely State of Hyderabad in southern India was also consulted.
10. Finance and Commerce Department, no. 51 of 1904, op. cit.
11. See, generally, N.G. Barrier, *Banned: Controversial Literature and Political Control in British India, 1907–1917* (University of Missouri Press, 1974).
12. It was not difficult for the government to find out about the inner meetings of the Congress leaders. When Congress met in Calcutta at the end of December 1906, the Maharaja of Darbhanga informed the government of what Congress leaders said in private.
13. Semi-official letter from Sir J.D. LaTouche, Lieutenant-Governor of the United Provinces, to Sir Andrew Fraser, 7 March 1904, in J&P 493/04.
14. Finance and Commerce Department, no. 51 of 1904, op. cit. The exceptions were Assam and the Central Province. Notes of a conference held at Government House, Rangoon, on 31 Jan. 1903, op. cit.
15. Ibid. These characteristics of the Raj also come out strongly from the writings of former British Indian officials. See, for example, Sir Algernon Rumbold, *Watershed in India 1914–1922* (London: The Athlone Press, 1979).
16. Undated semi-official letter from H.H. Risley, op. cit.
17. This was furnished to the Police Commission by James Monro, who had been both Inspector-General of the Bengal Police and Assistant Commissioner of the London Met, in which capacity he had served for a short time as the first head of the Special Branch.

18. He brought over Irish detectives to work in London, but did not inform the Special Branch of their arrival. Some of the Irish detectives were arrested as a result.
19. *Note on the Proposed Establishment of a Central Criminal Investigation Department*, by Sir Andrew Fraser, 25 April 1903, in J&P 493/04, op. cit.
20. Ibid.
21. The Thagi and Dakaiti Department had been under the Political Department, since most of its work against crime was done outside British India.
22. Notes of a meeting held at Belvedere on 24 Jan. 1903, op. cit. Communication to the Director, Central Criminal Intelligence Department, Authorizing him to Incur the Secret Service Expenditure and to Exercise the Power Conferred under the Civil Service Regulations on the General Superintendent, Thagi and Dakaiti Department. HD/Pol: Aug. 1904, no. 152 in IOLR P/6819.
23. Note on the Proposed Establishment of a Central Criminal Investigation Department, op. cit.
24. India Office Minute Paper, 11 Feb. 1904, entitled *A Central Criminal Intelligence Department for India*, in J&P 826/04.
25. The India Office noted that a stronger staff was not required in 1904, since the 'local "Special Branches" had still to be reorganized, and it was upon material to be furnished by them that the Central Intelligence Department would depend for its occupation'. India Office Minute Paper, 11 Feb. 1904, op. cit. The Police Commission foresaw that the office of the Central Intelligence Department would eventually be 'a very large one'. Notes of a meeting held at Belvedere on 24 Jan. 1903, op. cit.
26. The Director of Criminal Intelligence was initially styled 'Director, Central Intelligence Department'. In April 1905 this title was officially altered to 'Director, Criminal Intelligence'. Letter from J.C. Fergusson, Under-Secretary to the Government of India, to the Local Governments, 14 April 1905, HD/Pol: April 1905, nos. 55–6, IOLR P/7060.
27. Finance and Commerce Department, no. 51 of 1904, op. cit.
28. Note on the Proposed Establishment of a Central Criminal Investigation Department, op. cit.
29. Letter from Finance and Commerce Department to the Secretary of State, 17 March 1904. Letter from the Secretary of State to the Viceroy, 20 April 1904. Letter from Stuart to the Secretary of the Home Department, 22 June 1904 and letter from W.S. Marris, Under-Secretary of the Home Department, to the Director, Central Criminal Intelligence Department, 16 July 1904, HD/Pol: July 1904, nos. 62–5, IOLR P/6819.
30. Letter from Stuart to the Secretary to the Government of India, Home Department, 1 July 1904, HD/Pol: Aug. 1904, nos. 98–9, IOLR P/6819.
31. Fraser wrote: 'There is no revolutionary change of system, it is true. The main principles that underlay the establishment of the Central Special Branch are the same as those which I advocate in regard to the information part of the new Department, which is proposed to take its place. But the new department goes much further, and will undoubtedly be far more efficient, because it is based on provincial departments far superior to any local agency hitherto existing because it provides for concerted action as well as communication of intelligence among the different provinces, and because it will have a much superior staff to carry on the work.' Note on the Proposed Establishment of a Central Criminal Investigation Department, op. cit.
32. The Department of Criminal Intelligence was set up in advance of the general reorganization of the police partly because the Police Commission hoped that the Director of Criminal Intelligence would act as an adviser during the general reform of the police, and partly because some important enquiries were then underway, which the Government of India felt that the Thagi and Dakaiti Department was not capable of dealing with. Specifically these were enquiries into forgery, counterfeiting and the arms traffic between the Native States and the frontier.
33. For example, Charles Cleveland, the Inspector-General of the Central Provinces, set

forward three reasons why the CPs needed a CID:

(a) Some difficult and important cases of local crime are, in my opinion, prematurely abandoned by the police for want of supplementary detective work.

(b) Crimes of considerable importance which, while constituting a serious danger to the Government and to the public, are not specially the business of any local police officer, eg: trading in arms and ammunition by 'Kabulis', trading in false coin . . . the operations of professional cheats and impostors, and corrupt practices of Government officers.

(c) The sounding of local opinion in critical times, eg, when there is much agitation between Hindus and Muhammedans, when people's minds are excited owing to a sudden rise in prices or to an outburst or revival of religious or race enthusiasm. At such times I think valuable information might be collected through special detectives. The local police officers are known, and even if they can be trusted to be loyal and honest may be hoodwinked by local agitators.

Letter from C.R. Cleveland, to the Assistant Secretary to the Chief Commissioner, Central Provinces, 28 Sept. 1901, in *Proposed Organization of a Detective Police Force in Each Province*. HD/Pol: Feb. 1904, nos. 158–67, IOLR P/6818.

34. Letter from J.L. Jenkins, Acting Secretary to the Government of Bombay, Judicial Department, to the Secretary of the Home Department, 31 Aug. 1901, in *Proposed Organization of a Detective Police Force in Each Province*, op. cit.

35. Its duties were: The investigation of special cases of crime; gathering information for the Special Branch and attending all public meetings or gatherings; enquiring into all cases of loss of currency notes and postal articles; watching the movements of suspected foreigners and criminal gangs; making confidential enquiries regarding the character and antecedents of persons about whom information is required by Government or other authority or into other matters which require to be dealt with as private and confidential. Letter from H.G. Stokes, Chief Secretary to the Government of Madras, to the Secretary to the Government of India, Home Department, 30 July 1901. In *Proposed Organization of a Detective Police Force in Each Province*, op. cit.

36. The Government felt that a regular, standing agency was needed 'for dealing with criminal organizations extending over several districts'. Letter from H.A. Casson, Judicial and General Secretary to the Government of the Punjab and its dependencies, to the Secretary to the Government of India, Home Department, 18 Sept. 1901.

37. Letter from L.M. Thornton, Secretary to the Government of the North-Western Provinces and Oudh, to the Secretary to the Government of India, Home Department, 30 Oct. 1901, in *Proposed Organization of a Detective Police Force in Each Province*.

38. 'Statement showing the number and costs of officers and men presently employed in the Criminal Investigation Department, Bombay Presidency, since its creation in 1905', in *Question in Council by the Hon'ble Mr. Gokhale Regarding the Strength and Cost of the Provincial Criminal Investigation Departments*. HD/Pol: Oct. 1911, nos. 69–99, in IOLR P/8712. 'Statement of strength and cost submitted by the Commissioner of Police, Bombay', in *Strength and Cost of the Executive Staff of the Criminal Investigation Department Employed on Political Work in the Various Provinces of India During the Period of 10 Years from 1903 to 1912*, HD/Pol: May 1914, no. 51, IOLR P/9458.

39. The CID was created in September 1906. Letter from A.G. Cardew, Acting Chief Secretary to the Government of Madras, Judicial Department, to the Secretary to the Government of India, Home Department, and 'Statement showing the number and cost of officers and men of the Criminal Investigation Department, Madras', in *Question in Council by the Hon'ble Mr. Gokhale Regarding the Strength and Cost of the Provincial Criminal Investigation Departments*, op. cit.

40. 'Statement showing the number and cost of officers and men of the Criminal Investigation Department, United Provinces (including fingerprint bureau)', in *Question in Council by the Hon'ble Mr. Gokhale Regarding the Strength and Cost of the Provincial*

Criminal Investigation Departments, op. cit.

41. 'Statement showing the number and cost of officers and men of the Criminal Investigation Department, Central Provinces, from 1 January 1908, the date of its constitution', in *Question in Council by the Hon'ble Mr. Gokhale Regarding the Strength and Cost of the Provincial Criminal Investigation Departments*, op. cit.

42. 'Statement showing the number and cost of officers and men of the Criminal Investigation Department, Punjab, for the years 1905–1910', in *Question in Council by the Hon'ble Mr. Gokhale Regarding the Strength and Cost of the Provincial Criminal Investigation Departments*, op. cit.

43. They are discussed in Ch. 4, below.

3

The Development of Indian Domestic Intelligence, 1904–14

A single assassin can achieve, with weapons, fire or poison, more than a fully mobilized army.

Kautilya, *Arthasastra*, ref. 9.6.54,55

The year 1905 saw the outbreak of serious unrest in India, caused by the decision of Curzon's administration to partition the province of Bengal. For the next 14 years, political trouble remained centred on Bengal, but soon also spread to other parts of India. It was at its worst in the years 1905–7. In the long term, the significance of this period lies in the emergence of more radical forms of Indian nationalism. At the time, the British were also concerned by the appearance of terrorism in several provinces of northern India. Before looking at the developments in British intelligence which were a response to unrest in India, it is necessary to recall the political events of the years leading up to the First World War.

Curzon's government did not foresee the scale of the unrest which followed the partition of Bengal in October 1905. The primary aim was to improve the administrative efficiency of the Raj.[1] At the time, Bengal was a massive province, whose population of 78.5 million amounted to just over a quarter of the total of British India,[2] and its administration was notoriously inadequate. In its place two new provinces were created: Bengal itself, and East Bengal and Assam. At the same time, part of the old province was attached to its western neighbour, Bihar and Orissa.

A subsidiary aim of the partition was political: Curzon hoped to reduce the power of the Indian nationalists. In the Government of India's view, the Congress drew much of its support from the educated

57

Bengali Hindu classes who dominated the old province. They were the so-called *bhadralok* or, as the British were fond of disparaging them, the '*Babu* agitators'. As Curzon put it, the government's aim was to 'dethrone' Calcutta which would then cease to be the 'centre from which the Congress Party is manipulated throughout Bengal, and indeed the whole of India . . . The centre of successful intrigue'.[3] A further aim was to benefit Bengali Muslims, leaving them indebted to the Raj. In Eastern Bengal and Assam, Muslims were overwhelmingly in the majority; the new province of Bengal was predominantly Hindu, though even here, Bengali-speakers were in a minority.

The *bhadralok* responded to the partition of Bengal with fury. Not only were their political power and prestige undermined, but they also saw the partition as a material threat to their job opportunities. They were able to put up opposition on a scale which the British had not thought possible. The *bhadralok* led an organized protest movement, for which they initially succeeded in attracting the support of the Hindu lower castes. The anti-partition campaign saw the rapid development of new forms of political protest. In the *swadeshi* and boycott movement, the educated Hindu classes found a way of spreading their own narrowly based discontent to a wider audience. *Swadeshi* means literally 'of, or from, one's own country'. As a political slogan after 1905, it stood for the use of only Indian produce only, with British imports boycotted. However, it was not only British goods which were shunned. The boycott movement was also intended to lead to the rejection of government service, government education and government law courts. In effect, the movement had two aims: to injure the British economy; and to paralyse the administration. The *bhadralok* were also quick to seize on the populist methods which Tilak had developed with some success for political agitation in the Poona district in the mid-1890s. The anti-partition campaign was made intelligible to the uneducated when clothed in religious language. The message of protest was carried out of the *bhadralok* stronghold of Calcutta into the countryside by groups of dedicated landlords, lawyers, students and even schoolboys.

From the British point of view, the *swadeshi* campaign was all the more serious because it soon spread from Bengal to other parts of India. Though it was only in Bengal that the movement achieved anything approaching a mass character, it none the less had a significant impact on Poona and Bombay, while finding resonances in the Punjab, the United Provinces and even the peaceful Madras Presidency in the south. Moreover in 1906 Congress took up the *swadeshi* cause, and at the same time put forward more radical demands of its own, calling for self-government in India.

The climax of this wave of political unrest was reached in 1907, the fiftieth anniversary of the Mutiny. There were widespread disturbances throughout northern India, which were particularly severe in Bengal and the Punjab. That year also marked the real outbreak of terrorism, from which India has never since been free. An unexpected event of 1907 was the appearance of Indian revolutionary parties in London, Paris and Vancouver.

The broadly based unrest in the Punjab seemed at first to be the most dangerous new development in British India. The Punjab was the key strategic province of India; first, because it formed a barrier to the well-armed tribes of the North-West Frontier and Afghanistan beyond; and second, because the local Sikh community was the primary recruiting ground for the Indian army. The troubles owed something to the inspiration of Bengal, but had more immediate local roots. As in Bengal, the immediate cause was the ill-thought out action of the government, which once again paid inadequate attention to popular opinion. At the end of the nineteenth century, the Punjab had been enriched by an extensive irrigation programme, which led to the creation of the so-called 'canal colonies' of Sikh farmers. The popularity of the Raj plummeted when in 1906 the Local Government introduced draft legislation which stressed that some new settlers' rights were limited, since they were tenants on government land. At the same time, the Local Government intended to raise taxes at time when the Punjab was undergoing temporary economic hardship.[4] At the beginning of 1907 the Punjab saw a spate of agitation and rural discontent. This made a marked impression on the British. As a leading contemporary expert on Indian affairs noted, it was the unrest in the Punjab which 'aroused public opinion at home to the reality of Indian unrest'.[5] British official response showed that the Raj had been shaken. In 1907, the Government of India vetoed the unpopular legislation. Lord Minto, who was Viceroy in the years 1905–10, acknowledged that this amounted to 'the appearance of surrender to agitation'. But he stressed that this was 'far less dangerous than to insist upon enforcing the unfortunate legislation proposed upon a warlike and loyal section of the Indian community'.[6]

Minto's action had immediate effect in the Punjab and the province was not to be troubled by popular discontent until 1919. By the end of

1907, unrest in the rest of India was subsiding. In December, divisions between the moderate and extremist factions in the Congress blew up amid scenes of violence. The main issue involved was the conduct of the *swadeshi* campaign, which the extremists under Tilak wanted to develop in the rest of India, at the same time as intensifying the rejection of all forms of co-operation with the Raj. The moderates, under the great liberal politician, Gokhale, insisted on restricting *swadeshi* to Bengal, and regarded non-co-operation as self-defeating. The Congress was unable to heal its divisions until 1916.

Just as the Congress had failed to maintain a united front, so too the *swadeshi* campaign in Bengal was beginning to fall apart. The real issues had only really concerned the *bhadralok*, particularly Calcutta professionals and the large land-owners. For all their ingenuity in developing new forms of political protest, they had only been able to create a mass movement up to a point and temporarily at that. Even many of the *bhadralok* had become concerned when the protest against the partition led to communal violence between Hindus and Muslims. By the middle of 1908, the *swadeshi* campaign was all but over.

The collapse of organized protest also owed a great deal to the actions of the government. Minto and Lord Morley, who was Secretary of State for India, 1905–10, countered the unrest in India with a judicious combination of repression and conciliation.

Gokhale had warned the extremists in the Congress not to under-estimate the power of the Raj. As he told them in 1907:

> You do not realize the enormous reserve of power behind the Government. If the Congress were to do anything such as you suggest, the government would have no difficulty in throttling it in five minutes.[7]

As Congress and the *swadeshi* movement broke down, the Government of India struck. Extremist newspapers were banned, while 16 Congress and *swadeshi* leaders were either arrested or deported. These included Tilak, who spent the next six years in Mandalay jail. In Bengal, strict measures were introduced with bans on mass meetings and restrictions on the press.

The British did not regard repression as an end in itself. Gokhale rightly calculated the power of the Raj from a nationalist perspective. The Government of India and the India Office, on the other hand, were made acutely aware in this period of the limitations on British power in India. First and foremost, British appreciation of threats to the Raj had now changed. Their fears of the Russians, and of plotting by the Princes, were replaced by a concern about a potential nationalist unrest which was far more dangerous in that it might both have a popular base and be geographically widespread. The *swadeshi* movement had shown the possibility of this development although still in only an embryonic form. Moreover, these years had seen not just an attempt to oppose a specific government measure, namely the partition of Bengal. The *swadeshi* campaign had also led to the strengthening of more radical nationalist demands. From the British point of view, Tilak and the extremist party in the Congress had put forward a programme which seemed to be aimed at doing away with British rule in India altogether. For a time it seemed possible that their programme might be adopted by the Congress as a whole, while their message had been widely taken up in many sections of the press.

After 1907 the Congress and the forces of Indian nationalism of both moderate and extremist complexion were greatly weakened. But for all this the Congress was now an established part of the political life of the Raj. Despite its temporary weakness, the government did now pay attention to the voice of the moderates, above all that of Gokhale, whom Morley regarded with great respect. Thus the attitude of the British rulers towards India had changed since the height of the Victorian age, when the view prevailed that good government was enough.[8] Already by the end of the nineteenth century, the government's attitude was marked by an awareness that Indian public opinion had to be taken into account. This was clearly shown in the discussions concerning the reform of Indian intelligence which took place under Lytton and Dufferin. After 1905, this concern for public opinion was more pronounced than ever. The British had become aware that the essential foundation of the Raj had become much less secure than it had seemed even at the turn of the century.

The policies followed by the government after 1905 might be summed up by the slogan: 'the rally of the moderates'. The British sought to win the support of most sections of Indian society and to make their rule palatable to them. Specifically they targeted the conservative classes in order to weaken the Congress, and above all to isolate the more militant nationalists.

As part of this programme, in 1906 Morley and Minto proposed a set of constitutional reforms. These were introduced in 1909, and are commonly known as the Morley–Minto Reforms, more correctly as the Indian Councils Act. They allowed Indians a share in the work of the provincial legislative councils, and made Indians eligible for appointment to the Viceroy's executive council as well as to the Secretary of State for India's advisory council in London. These reforms fell far short of allowing responsible government. None the less, they appeared a major development at the time. In Britain, Morley had the sensitive task of steering the necessary legislation through Parliament. In India, Minto had to win acceptance for the reforms from Indian moderate opinion. Both the Secretary of State and the Viceroy depended for their success on political quiet in India. Morley could not afford to be seen to be giving in to Indian nationalism; Minto had to avoid alienating Indian public opinion through severe measures against the extremists.

Policies of conciliation continued under Morley and Minto's successors, Crewe and Hardinge, who were respectively Secretary of State for India, 1910–15, and Viceroy, 1910–16. In 1912 they took two major steps. First, they reversed the partition of Bengal; and second, they transferred the capital from Calcutta to its old Mogul seat at Delhi. This was, among other things, an important symbolic gesture in moving the government back to its traditional Indian centre, and away from a seaport which had originally served Britain's economic needs.

The British approach undoubtedly worked, for a time, to create calm in India. The majority of Indian politicians accepted the Morley–Minto reforms favourably, even if some were disappointed that they did not lead to greater Indian participation in government. None the less, the British had one problem in implementing their policies of conciliation. This was the outbreak of terrorism after 1907, which meant that repressive measures were needed at a time when the Government of India had to be particularly sensitive to public opinion. This balancing act between the need to suppress terrorism and to court the moderates became particularly difficult after the First World War, when Britain's weakness gave the terrorists a great shot in the arm. In the period up to 1914, however, both the Government of India and the India Office felt strongly that any advantage to be gained from 'repression' would be greatly offset by the damage to the reputation of the Raj in the eyes of the great majority of Indians who had no connection with political violence. One of the measures which the British generally were least inclined to introduce in this period was the extension of domestic intelligence inside India. Before discussing the development of Indian intelligence in the years before the First World War, it is necessary to give a brief outline of the Indian revolutionary movement in this period.

The first stirrings of revolutionary violence in the twentieth century were in Western India. In 1904, V.D. Savarkar organized a secret revolutionary society, the *Abhinav Bharat*, in Poona. The first sign that revolutionary sentiment was spreading from this old trouble spot came after 1905 when several newspapers, mainly in Bengal, openly advocated violence. In 1907, there was an outbreak of terrorism in Bengal. This expansion of revolutionary activity is largely to be explained by the failure of the *swadeshi* movement and the temporary collapse of the extremist faction in Congress. A number of Hindu youths, primarily in Bengal, were frustrated by the weakness of non-violent nationalism.

The opening shot in the terrorist campaign came in 1907 with an unsuccessful attempt to assassinate Sir Andrew Fraser, the Lieutenant-Governor of Bengal and former head of Curzon's Police Commission. In April the following year two young Bengalis, Prafulla Chaki and Khudiram Bose threw a bomb at a carriage in which they thought Judge Kingsford, who had been responsible for jailing some of their fellow revolutionaries, was travelling. Instead they killed two English-women, Mrs and Miss Kennedy. This act provoked outrage throughout British India. The Government of India was already concerned by the activities of revolutionary agitators who had joined the *swadeshi* movement in various parts of northern India, and who went far beyond the *swadeshi* preachers in their calls for an end to British rule. Minto had already expressed his grave concern in November 1907 when he told the Viceroy's legislative council that the seeds of 'sedition' had been scattered even among the 'hills of the frontier tribes'.[9] The worst of his fears at this time was that not only would revolutionary agitation spread, but also that the terrorists would win extensive support among hitherto non-violent nationalists.

Despite Minto's fears, the British did not appreciate the full extent of the terrorist movement. As yet, acts of violence were limited, but revolutionary organizations were developing both in Bengal and in other parts of northern India. Developments in Bengal were much the most serious. There, by 1907, the revolutionaries had started a campaign whose aims were twofold; first, they intended to assassinate unpopular officials such as Kingsford, and to kill or intimidate informers and all potential witnesses to their acts; and second, they started to acquire funds in preparation for an extended campaign of political violence. This they aimed to do through carrying out armed robberies. More details of events in Bengal are contained in the next chapter.

By 1909 it seemed that both the mainstream nationalists and the terrorists had been defeated. Police enquiries had led to the uncovering of some terrorist groups. As a result, police surveillance was relaxed, partly as an economy measure, but mainly in order to appease public opinion. The wisdom of this action was called into question by some, though not all, members of the government when a group of terrorists carried out a sensational act, which shook the British both in India and in Whitehall: in December 1912 the Viceroy, Lord Hardinge, was very nearly killed by a terrorist bomb. More details of the renewed terrorist campaign will be given in this and subsequent chapters. Some idea of the scale of terrorism can be gained from the fact that 186 terrorists were either killed or convicted in the period 1908–18. This excludes many others put under house arrest for implication in terrorist activity during the First World War, and most importantly, the figure excludes revolutionaries abroad.

From the British point of view, one of the most troubling features of the Indian revolutionary movement was the speed of its growth. In 1907, Bengali terrorists had had to import basic knowledge of bomb-making.[10] In 1914, terrorism was still primarily a Bengali problem within the sub-continent, but this was not saying much, considering that Bengal accounted for about a quarter of the population of British India. But the most disturbing feature of the spread of political violence was the emergence of revolutionary centres abroad. In 1907 Indian revolutionary groups were to be found in London and Paris. Even worse, by the eve of the First World War, Indian immigrants to the United States and Canada had formed a revolutionary party, the *Ghadr* (revolt) movement, which could draw on the support of other members of the Indian diaspora in China and elsewhere in the Far East.

Before the First World War, the number of Indian terrorist acts remained small in comparison with the wave of anarchist terror in Europe in the 1890s or with the activities of Russian terrorists in the last two decades of the nineteenth century and first decade of the twentieth. In the 1890s, a wave of anarchist assassinations had carried off President Carnot of France, the Spanish Prime Minister, Canovas de Castillo, Empress Elisabeth of Austria, King Humbert of Italy, President McKinley of the United States, as well as a considerable number of police and state officials. In Russia, the vogue for terrorism reached the greatest proportions. A wave of assassinations started in the late 1870s and reached a climax with the killing of Tsar Alexander II in 1881. A second wave started at the turn of the century. In 1906–7 alone it led to the murder or attempted murder of 4,000 people. In each case the government was forced to introduce harshly repressive measures, which only increased the unpopularity of the already unpopular Tsarist regime.

The lessons to be learned from Russia were not encouraging to the British in India. The potential similarities in the situation were considerable. In Russia, the number of terrorists was small relative to the population, yet the damage they inflicted was great both in terms of lives lost and in terms of the regime's morale. Also, in Russia the terrorists were able to prosper because they had some sympathy from liberal opinion which, though not naturally disposed to violence, regarded the Tsarist autocracy as more inhuman than the often young and idealistic terrorists. In particular, middle-class sympathy for the revolutionaries was reflected in an embarrassingly high rate of acquittals for political crime in Russian law courts. Already in 1907 a similar situation was occurring in Bengal. The British were under few illusions that the nature of their government, though they held it to be on an incomparably higher moral plane than that of the Russian empire, made the soil of their colonies infertile to political violence. They had only to look at Ireland, where the revolutionary Fenian Brotherhood had launched an unsuccessful rising in 1867 and a bombing campaign in mainland Britain in the 1880s, and where peasant unrest, often directed against landlords, was endemic from the mid-1880s.

The British in India always faced a potential danger from political violence if only because of their numerical weakness. In 1911 the population of British India was 303 million, with the number of British troops in the sub-continent numbering only 73,500. Indian revolutionaries had to carry out only relatively few acts of terrorism in order seriously to shake British confidence. They almost succeeded in this at the end of 1912 when they attempted to assassinate the Viceroy.

Thanks to Curzon's reform of police intelligence, the Government of India found at its disposal a central agency already used to processing intelligence when serious political trouble broke out. Though small in scale, the Raj's intelligence arrangements were at least better than they had been in the nineteenth century. After the beginning of 1907 the Department of Criminal Intelligence ensured a regular, clear flow of information about the extreme nationalist movement and the native press from the provinces in the *Weekly Reports* of the Director of Criminal Intelligence, which it sent to both the central government and the Local Governments. These printed reports, divided under province and country, were concerned only with nationalist elements likely to incite or commit acts of violence: in other words, revolutionary agitators and terrorists.

The regular issue of the *Weekly Reports* shows that the DCI and the new provincial Criminal Investigation Departments were working together effectively. The raw material was provided by the CIDs in the Weekly Secret Abstracts sent in to the DCI. Following instructions laid down by the DCI, the information which they supplied was grouped under specific headings. These were: Afghanistan and trans-border; Native States and Foreign possessions in India; persons of note; foreigners; politico-religious and racial movements; religious and social excitement and propagandism; the native press; and miscellaneous subjects.[11]

The DCI's *Weekly Reports* were distinguished by a high degree of objectivity. It is true that the Indian police frequently depicted Indian 'extremists', particularly those abroad, as moral degenerates of one kind or another. But beyond pouring scorn upon the revolutionaries and deploring the conduct of their personal lives, particularly where women were involved, the DCI made no attempt to interpret the information they transmitted. Notably it did not try to inculcate a fear of revolutionaries in the minds of the Viceroy and his Council, in an attempt to justify its own existence or to encourage its expansion. This chapter will show that the DCI would have had no success even if it had taken to scaremongering, so great were the ideological barriers to the development of a political police force in India.

The efficient working of the Indian intelligence system was dependent on good personal relations between the DCI at the centre and the CIDs in the provinces. Sir Harold Stuart, the first Director of Criminal Intelligence, paid many visits to the officers of the Local Governments. The duties of the Director of Criminal Intelligence proved rigorous. After travelling 17,660 miles by rail during the 'cold' season of 1905–1906, Stuart complained:

> The food on many of the railways is execrable and on none is it good . . . I can assure the Government that my health has suffered and indigestion become chronic since I assumed charge of my present appointment . . . My unfortunate clerk suffers even more than I do . . .[12]

In June 1907 Charles (after 1912 Sir Charles) Stevenson-Moore succeeded Stuart as Director of Criminal Intelligence, holding this post until 1910.[13] Like Stuart, Stevenson-Moore was a Cambridge graduate. From 1885 to 1898 he had filled various routine posts in the ICS before being appointed Inspector-General of Police in Bengal. Also like Stuart, he was appointed DCI because he had combined experience of the civil service and of the police.

During Stevenson-Moore's term as Director, the strength of the DCI grew. In 1906 it set up a four-man fingerprint bureau, whose staff had increased to ten by 1910, in which year it also acquired a small photographic section and a graphologist.[14] The majority of the personnel of the DCI belonged to the clerical staff and 'menial establishment'. As in the old Central Special Branch, the DCI's clerks had to be either Europeans or Eurasians.[15] These sections grew steadily in the period before the First World War. The DCI started in 1904 with 19 clerks and servants; in 1911 there were 68, including the fingerprint and photographic departments.[16] However, the DCI was not given special treatment because it was in some ways responsible for the security of British rule. The Government of India treated it like any other department, and in 1910, for example, the Director was denied some additional members of staff because he would thereby acquire more *jemadars* and personal *peons* than the Inspector-General of Forests, the Director-General of Education and the Sanitary Commissioner.[17]

Though the clerical facilities of the DCI improved, the number of officers on the permanent staff remained small. The DCI started in 1904 with just the Director and Deputy Director of Criminal Intelligence, but by 1908 three other officers had joined them: the Assistant Director, the Personal Assistant to Director and the 'Government expert in handwriting'. In 1906 A.B. Barnard had replaced McCracken as Deputy Director and in December of that year a famous Muslim detective, Munshi Aziz-ud-Din, was appointed Assistant Deputy Director of Criminal Intelligence, after service as Assistant Commissioner in the Central Provinces.[18] This appointment proved a diplomatic asset for the DCI, since Aziz-ud-Din came to be a very popular figure with the officials at the India Office.[19] He left the DCI in January 1910 to become Deputy Commissioner in the Central Provinces. In this capacity, however, he continued to serve on secondment to the DCI in connection with the 'seditious movement'.[20]

The next officer post created on the staff of the DCI was that of

'Personal Assistant to the Director'. James Campbell Ker, a Scot, occupied this position from 15 August 1907 until December 1913. Like the Director, he did not come from the Indian Police Service but had started his career as an academic. Having left Glasgow University with a first-class honours degree in mathematics, he became a Fellow of Caius College, Cambridge. In 1901, at the age of 23, he gave up this position to enter the Indian Civil Service. Before joining the DCI he had served in the Bombay Presidency and in Sind. His duties as Personal Assistant to the Director were political. He prepared the *Weekly Reports* of the Director of Criminal Intelligence and drew up history sheets of the leading political agitators both in India and abroad.[21] Like many officers in the DCI, he came from a religious – in this case Scots Calvinist – family.

In 1906 the DCI acquired a detective capacity with the addition of four Inspectors. This reform was necessary because of a 'steady increase in the work of the office', which, for several reasons, was expected to continue. The CIDs had unearthed much organized crime which, before their creation, had gone undetected; and had brought about a general increase in the flow of information to the central government. The DCI itself was doing a lot of work connected with the criminal tribes. By this time it had not only to face an unexpectedly large amount of criminal work, but had also to deal with information relating to the upsurge in political unrest. Already the Government of India had decided to restrict certain kinds of political enquiry to the central department[22] because reliance upon the local CID officers was leading to delays in starting investigations.[23]

The inspectors were drawn from the provincial police forces;[24] One was a Bengali, one a Madrassi and one a Pathan. The Director of Criminal Intelligence had difficulty filling the posts, since officers thought their prospects of advancement were better if they remained in the provinces. In 1908 he still had not found a permanent occupant from the Bombay Police for the fourth post. The inspectors differed from one another both according to their province of origin and to their field of work within the DCI. One Inspector was attached to the 'Financial Department' of the DCI, concerned with counterfeit coining and note forgery. In 1908 Stevenson-Moore expected that this aspect of the DCI's work would increase. It had a political aspect, as *swadeshi* coins had been struck in large quantities in Madras, whilst the nationalists had distributed pamphlets throughout India in which they had tried to undermine the stability of government finances.

The Bengali inspector dealt with the arms trade. This was a serious problem at the time, not yet because of Indian terrorism but because quantities of modern rifles were finding their way from sources in the Persian Gulf region to the tribes of the North-West Frontier. In 1907 this officer played an important part in unearthing a revolutionary society in Calcutta. A third officer worked on commercial cases, dealing with the forgery of railway tickets, postal and insurance frauds. The fourth officer was employed on miscellaneous enquiries, particularly those involving drug-smuggling.[25] Thus the growth of political crime was clearly not the main reason for the attachment of this detective staff to the DCI. Of the four inspectors employed, none was entirely concerned with political work, while two were not concerned with it at all.

The DCI's detective staff was improved in September 1908 when a staff of four deputy superintendents and four sub-inspectors replaced the four inspectors.[26] The Police Commission of 1902–3 had laid down a firm ruling that the DCI was not to become an investigative department and even after its acquisition of a detective staff, and the Government of India's decision that it should conduct certain political enquiries, it remained fundamentally a secretariat, collating, not securing, information. No more detectives were placed on the DCI's permanent staff before the First World War. It was able to expand its officer staff to a limited degree by employing officers on secondment from the provincial police forces but no provincial police force could ever spare more than a couple of senior officers at most. Thus the DCI's potential for expansion remained strictly limited.

Despite the outbreak of unrest during 1907 and 1908, political crime did not become by any means the exclusive preoccupation of the DCI. Stevenson-Moore felt that his department's facilities for coping with the nationalist movement were far too restricted. In May 1908 he informed the Home Department that:

> If political crime develops in India (and there is great likelihood that it will) the necessity for central action to link up inter-provincial clues will be very much greater than it is in the case of any other class of crime.[27]

The DCI found that the operations of professional 'agitators' were far more widespread and far better organized than those of professional criminals, and felt that the Local Governments did not have the

69

machinery for dealing with 'sedition which takes the whole of India for its sphere of influence'.[28] Political unrest within India cut across provincial boundaries. For example, the DCI felt certain that unrest in Eastern Bengal was engineered from Calcutta, while Punjabi nationalists sent money to Calcutta, which then found its way into Eastern Bengal and Assam. At the same time certain Hindu hermits or *sadhus* toured India, combining their religious teachings with overtly anti-British political preaching.[29] Moreover, the development of the Indian revolutionary movement overseas was increasingly worrying to the Government of India. Stevenson-Moore wrote that

> it is quite impossible for a group of separate Provincial Secret Services to deal adequately with political conditions of such extent and character as prevail in India. The chief centres of the Indian political movement are Calcutta, Lahore, Poona, New York, Paris, and perhaps Japan. The chief agitators in these places are in close connection with each other and the necessity for secret agents in America and London has recently been brought to notice in letters from London and Dublin.[30]

In response to this political challenge Stevenson-Moore urged the Government of India to allow the DCI to set up a small spy service within India. The Home Department, of which the former Director of Criminal Intelligence, Sir Harold Stuart, was now Secretary, gave him its support.[31] Stuart had already 'employed one or two secret agents' when he was Director, and had found that an agent whom he had kept at Lahore in the Punjab had supplied the DCI with information that was 'of real value'. In May 1908, Stevenson-Moore wrote that he was employing some secret agents 'experimentally' and that 'for the last three years or so a few of my officers in Bengal have been employed almost entirely on [secret service] work'.[32] However, the DCI's secret service arrangements were 'of makeshift character'.[33] Stuart felt that it was dangerous to rely entirely on 'occasional' agents, because they were tempted to report the continuance of disaffection after it had ceased in order to retain their pay.

Stevenson-Moore's and Stuart's proposals did not go very far, despite the deterioration in the political climate. They wanted a secret service staff formed around a nucleus of 25 permanent agents, and expected the cost to be Rs.30,000 or £2,000 a year.[34] Both the Government of India and the DCI agreed that the operation of secret agents and informers by the provincial CIDs left something to be desired; they also agreed that any hypothetical secret service would have to be controlled from the centre and not by the individual provinces.[35] Stevenson-Moore felt that while the local Inspectors-General of Police might be in the best position to secure agents of the class that worked under ordinary police officers, they found it difficult to find what he regarded as the 'higher class' of agents required for political work. Moreover it was 'practically impossible for a European officer of the local police to work directly in secret'. Stevenson-Moore felt that the rank-and-file of the provincial police were not suited to gathering political information because they were either dishonest or known to the agitators. At the same time as proposing the formation of a central secret service controlled by the DCI, Stevenson-Moore also pressed for the creation of provincial secret services 'organized on lines much superior to anything now existing, to watch suspects and fight sedition in its local haunts'.[36]

But the Government of India refused the DCI permission to create a secret service. Sir Harvey Adamson, the Home Member of the Viceroy's Council advising on internal affairs, supported by Minto, informed the Home Department that:

> I am not at all convinced of the expediency of spreading through-out India a body of secret police, working under the immediate orders of the Director of Criminal Intelligence, and unknown to the Local Governments in whose territories they would be stationed. I must confess that I have seen little result from the work as regards sedition of the secret agents already employed in a limited degree by the Director, Criminal Intelligence. There is no check upon their work. So far as I have observed they merely submit sensational reports, very little of which can be believed, none of which can be tested, and which never end even in a prosecution.[37]

Moreover, the Viceroy's Council thought that the establishment of an Indian secret service at this time would bring down the wrath of the India Office's Decentralization Commission, which was then working in India, upon the DCI.[38] The steady devolution of responsibility from the central government to the provinces was another aspect of the Morley-Minto reforms, aimed at making the Raj more palatable to Indian moderate opinion. It was a process intended steadily to lead to the greater association of Indians with the government.[39] This was a clear example of the conflict between Britain's general policy of making the Government of India more responsive to the wishes of the population, and an increased need for political intelligence. Yet the regular secret service which the DCI wanted to create to deal with Indian political unrest throughout the world would have been less than half the size of the political police of Paris, the capital of a state which by any standards was a liberal democracy. At this date the *Service des Garnis*, which performed the registration of all visitors staying in Parisian hotels and lodging houses, had a staff of 25 Inspectors, while the city's political police proper, the *Sûreté Générale*, had a strength of 30.[40]

When the vigour of the political unrest in India temporarily decreased after 1908, the Government of India became even less disposed to permit the DCI to develop the political side of its activities. In 1907 and 1908 the Director of Criminal Intelligence had at his disposal only eight officers, excluding the 'Government expert in handwriting'.[41] In August 1910 the continuance of Ker's three-year appointment as Personal Assistant to the Director was reviewed by the Government of India's Home and Finance Departments. The Finance Department considered axing this political post, but decided to err on the side of caution and to permit Ker to stay on at the DCI, since although there had 'been a great improvement in the general situation . . . our revolutionaries are still active and their proceedings require most careful watching'.[42]

The secret service fund of the DCI grew steadily between 1904 and 1914. The old Central Special Branch of the Thagi and Dakaiti Department had a secret service fund of £380 in 1902, while upon its creation in 1904, the DCI was allotted about £730 a year.[43] By 1912 this had grown to £3,333.[44] However, there was a great difference between the use of such money in the employment of irregular informers, and a regular, permanent espionage service.

The operation of the DCI as an espionage service was not only limited by the restrictions of the central government. On special occasions, because of the growth of Indian revolutionary movement abroad, it used agents of a high quality. Yet there was great difficulty in finding such agents for use abroad. Stuart was reluctant to send young men out on dangerous missions; Stevenson-Moore hoped that opportunities of travel and adventure would attract men into his proposed spy service. However, in June 1913 Sir Reginald Craddock,

72

who was Home Member on the Viceroy's Council between January 1912 and April 1917, wrote:

> The chief difficulty is at present the extreme unwillingness of persons to be informers or spies. They do not regard with confidence assurances of protection, and every informer that is killed makes the role of informer more unpopular.[45]

The religious and social divisions of India did not make the task of finding agents easier. The DCI found it difficult to obtain agents suitable for work in the various social environments created by the differences of caste, race, province and class of different revolutionary groups.[46]

Another problem facing the Department of Criminal Intelligence at this time of political tension in India was its relations with the new CIDs. As already noted, the DCI was carrying out effectively its primary role of collecting and collating information received from the local CIDs, but it was less successful in co-ordinating their political surveillance work.

First, something needs to be said about the development of the CIDs. They grew up to 1911, but relative to the populations of their provinces their numbers remained tiny. The Madras CID increased from 29 in 1907 to 55 in 1910.[47] The Local Government estimated that of these, 15 were employed on political work in 1907 and 23 in 1912.[48] The United Provinces CID grew from 87 in 1907 to 154 in 1910;[49] of these only two were intended to conduct political enquiries in 1907 and seven in 1911.[50] In the Central Provinces the CID likewise almost doubled from 41 in 1907 to 74 in 1911.[51] The CID of the Punjab increased from 34 in 1907 to 47 in 1910,[52] of these six officers were occupied full-time with political work.[53] The strength of the Bombay provincial CID went up from 50 in 1906 to 68 in 1910;[54] that of Bombay City increased from 51 in 1903–7 to 83 in 1911.[55] The total number of officers employed in Bombay on political work, including officers of the ordinary district police and the police of Sind, amounted to 100 in 1906 and 181 in 1912.[56]

Like the DCI, the CIDs were not entirely involved with political crime after 1907. The proportionate increase in the Punjab was significantly less than in the other provinces, which were less affected by political crime. Few of the provinces had special political branches. For example, even at this time the Central Provinces CID had no separate branch concerned solely with political investigations. There were four branches in the Central Provinces' CID: the fingerprint bureau; the Criminal Investigation Office; the Special Branch; and the Investigation Branch. But from 1907 to 1909 'nearly the whole of the Criminal Investigation Branch was employed almost entirely for political work'. The Central Provinces Police, however, regarded the CID basically as 'intended to increase the effective power of police in dealing with dangerous and organized crime'.[57] In other words, it regarded political unrest as just a temporary anomaly in the life of British India. In 1913 none of the CID officers was employed solely for political work, and their chief duties were connected with the investigation of ordinary crime. The Central Provinces relied for political information on the ordinary District Police rather than on the CID.[58] The local police felt that 'the increase in the expenditure on account of political agitation is not a very serious item'. Likewise in the Punjab, in the period 1905–14 there was 'no increase in the staff employed exclusively on . . . special work'. There existed 'no separate and distinct office for dealing solely with political crime'.[59]

What of the working of the new CIDs? How did they cope with the political work for which they had not been primarily intended? The most difficult kind of surveillance for the Indian police to perform, and that which most directly concerned the DCI, was that of 'foreigners' moving around India and crossing different police jurisdictions. This category included the most important Indian 'extreme' nationalists who toured India. In September 1909 Stevenson-Moore informed the Home Department that the arrangements for the surveillance of 'foreigners' in different provinces were 'very defective and cases frequently [came] to notice in which important suspects . . . passed out of observation without apparently any special effort on their part to elude it'.[60] Stuart agreed that the Indian Police were deficient at the lower levels. Surveillance throughout India was entrusted to the 'average police constable'. The only modification in the system which the DCI found practical was that 'instead of using a big character sheet' which made surveillance 'offensively obvious', the shadowing constables should pass special 'advice slips' to one another when the suspect crossed different police jurisdictions.[61] The real remedy was the introduction of a passport system for travellers in India, but the Home Department dismissed this as being 'opposed to British sentiment and practice'.[62] This is an interesting example of the Government of India's application of British practices to Indian conditions. Until after the outbreak of war, passports were not needed in Britain.[63]

It is difficult to generalize about the performance of the CIDs. They were created on the eve of a wave of unrest. As the next chapter will show, the CIDs of Bengal and Eastern Bengal were caught out. The CID of the United Provinces, for example, had time to gain experience of political work.

The DCI held that it was 'on no account desirable that the police should waste time in watching the movements of harmless foreign and American tourists who [visited] India in hundreds every year' but it insisted on the surveillance of 'foreigners who may be suspected of being in the country as military or intelligence spies, political intriguers, revolutionists or anarchists'. Surveillance of the latter group was usually 'initiated on information obtained from Scotland Yard or some other external source'.[64]

The Government of India knew that its police constables could not distinguish between a Frenchman and a Russian. However, they do not seem to have been much worried by either nationality before the First World War. Those foreigners who tried to contact political 'extremists' usually did so openly. The Labour MP Keir Hardie's tour of India in October 1907 was closely followed by the Department of Criminal Intelligence without difficulty.[65] The one-time patron of Indian revolutionaries in New York, Myron Phelps, was one of the few foreigners whose arrival the Home Department viewed with trepidation[66] After eluding the Special Branch in London he arrived in India in June 1910. The Department of Criminal Intelligence, however, managed to keep track of him. They evidently found the task amusing. Ker concluded of Phelps that:

it is not clear whether he poses as a Hindu or as a theosophist, or whether he knows the difference . . . he began to take an interest in Hindu education, particularly in schools for Hindu girls. He frequently goes about in Hindu costume, wearing a white turban. There is some reason to doubt whether he is quite sane. . . .[67]

The seriousness of the deficiencies of the surveillance system only became apparent during the First World War, when the police had to watch large numbers of Japanese visitors to India, many of whom were suspected of having military espionage missions, or of being in touch with Indian nationalists.[68]

The pre-war difficulties which the DCI experienced in organizing the surveillance of foreigners travelling around India were dwarfed by the problems which might arise if it pressed too hard upon the provincial CIDs. In 1908 the very existence of the Department of Criminal Intelligence was called into question. The greatest threat to it before the war arose as the result of a clash between it and a provincial government, not as a result of its performance in combating political crime. In September 1907 Stevenson-Moore asked the CID of the United Provinces to prepare history sheets on the 'prominent agitators' resident there. Sands, the assistant to the Deputy Inspector-General in charge of the CID, replied that there were no 'prominent agitators' in the United Provinces. This claim was undoubtedly wrong. When the DCI insisted, the CID complained to the Local Government about this interference. The latter took the matter up with the Home Department. The Government of India regarded the Government of the United Provinces as 'a peculiarly competent and sensible Local Government, which . . . kept its own province quiet' during the unrest of 1907–8. The Home Department decided that the Director of Criminal Intelligence had 'clearly exceeded his proper functions'.[69]

The Government of India was worried by what the India Office might think about this case. In November 1907 H.H. Risley, the Home Member, wrote that

> the Decentralization Commission, or at any rate some members of it, will make a slashing attack on the entire system of Imperial advisory officers . . . One of the members . . . wishes to abolish the Director of Criminal Intelligence, and all similar officials together.[70]

The critics of the DCI on the Decentralization Commission already thought that it meddled unduly in the affairs of the Local Governments, causing unnecessary friction.[71]

At this time, the members of the Viceroy's Council viewed the existence of the DCI as at best a necessary evil. Even some members of the Indian Police disliked it on ideological grounds. Hastings, the Inspector-General of Police in the Punjab, told the Decentralization Commission that since the establishment of the DCI, the British in India

> seemed to be on the verge of constituting a secret police force, and that no innovation could be more liable to become a weapon of oppression with the material [the poorly paid rank-and-file of the Police] we are obliged to work through.[72]

76

Many educated Indians were hostile to the existence of the CIDs. Even Indian members of the Viceroy's Legislative Council were suspicious of them.[73] They liked the DCI even less. Sir Charles Cleveland, who had succeeded Stevenson-Moore as Director of Criminal Intelligence in 1910, wrote in July 1914 that:

> It will be always difficult for the Criminal Intelligence Department to please advanced Indians and their supporters. We cannot work for popularity. Advanced Indians look upon the Department as a blot . . .[74]

The danger of abolition by the Decentralization Commission proved to be only a passing threat to the Indian intelligence system. But the DCI realized that the chance always existed that its actions might be presented in a bad light to the British parliament. The clash with the United Provinces in 1907 was taken up in the House of Commons two years later, when in May 1909 the Rt. Hon. Sir Henry Cotton, MP, brought Hastings' denunciation of the DCI to the attention of the House, calling for its 'drastic reform'.[75]

The developing feud between the DCI and the government of the United Provinces ensured that the DCI would keep a high profile. At the beginning of 1909, following a request from the Bombay CID, Stevenson-Moore asked the CID of the United Provinces to put a well-known nationalist from central India, Gopal Krishna Deodhar, under surveillance. This they did, but Deodhar complained to the Government of India which caused them embarrassment.[76] The Local Government decided that the Director of Criminal Intelligence was at fault for ordering a watch to be put on Deodhar who, they claimed, had done valuable famine work during his stay in the United Provinces. This time the Home Department ruled that the DCI had given sensible instructions. Evidence from Bombay revealed Deodhar as a prominent member of the nationalist Arya Samaj ('Purity Society') and supporter of the prominent 'advanced' nationalist Lala Lajpat Rai, who were opposed to British rule in India. None the less they were anxious to conciliate the government of the United Provinces and authorized the CID in future to bring any objections it might have about orders received from the DCI to the notice of the Lieutenant-Governor.[77] Thus a Local Government had resisted the Government of India's central intelligence agency on behalf of a man whom all parties believed to be a subversive.

The DCI had to have a vigorous intelligence chief in order to command respect. Yet if the Director did his job too well he was bound to clash with the Local Governments. Sir Charles Cleveland, who became Director of Criminal Intelligence in 1910, was, like his predecessors, an Oxbridge-educated member of the ICS. After leaving Balliol College, Oxford, he came to India in 1885 and had been Inspector-General of the Central Provinces for 10 years before joining the DCI. He served as Director of Criminal Intelligence until his retirement from the ICS in 1919. During his long tenure of office the DCI took firm root as a fundamentally important department of government. But if Cleveland's reign at the DCI was looked back on after the war by the Viceroy, Lord Chelmsford, as a golden age in Indian intelligence, this was hardly to be expected in 1910. The Government of India had originally intended that the Director of Criminal Intelligence should possess the qualities of a diplomat so that he might win the co-operation of the Local Governments. Though eloquent, Cleveland was ill-fitted by temperament for this role. His arrogant and forceful character soon intensified hostility to the DCI. The ill-feeling between the DCI and the government of the United Provinces took on a distinctly personal tone after his appointment.[78] Not until the outbreak of war did the Government of India benefit from Cleveland's caution and resolute attachment to his own judgement.

The system of Indian intelligence which Lord Curzon had set up survived the Morley–Minto reforms, but not unscathed. These reforms were completed at the Delhi Durbar in December 1911, when, amid scenes of euphoria, King George V announced the end of the Partition of Bengal and the transfer of the capital from Calcutta to Delhi. The positive response of the native press and the subsequent decline in political violence led the Government of India 'to the belief that for some time, at all events, any recrudescence of outrages or even any revival of sedition were not to be apprehended'.[79] As a result the new Home Member of the Viceroy's Council, Sir Reginald Craddock, 'was [pressed] on many sides to curtail the expenditure on the CID, [and] to reduce political surveillance to an absolute minimum'. The Government of India asked the Local Governments to make plans for the reduction of the political branches of their CIDs, while Cleveland was put in charge of a commission to put this into effect. The surveillance over many former political suspects was relaxed, in the belief that they had grown tired of politics.[80]

The confidence of the Government of India proved very ill-founded. Not all groups were pleased with the end of the Partition of

Bengal. The most important political development in 1912 was the growth of Muslim unrest. The Muslims of Bengal felt that they had lost privileges with the return of Eastern Bengal and Assam, in which they were the majority, to old Bengal, where they were dominated by the Hindus. As a result the former staunchly pro-British Muslim League drew close to the Indian National Congress. At the same time the defeat of Turkey in the First Balkan War of 1912–13 created great unease among the Muslims. Many felt some sympathy at this time with the Ottoman Empire, as the last truly independent Islamic state, and in particular with the Sultan-Caliph who was the temporal head of Islam. It was clear to Muslims that the British government was at best indifferent to the Ottomans' humiliation in the Balkans. Moreover, while Hindu political unrest apparently lay dormant, the reforms which accompanied the Delhi Durbar did nothing to mollify the hatred for British rule which Hindu revolutionary groups felt, and their organization was developing at this time.

Despite the obvious signs that their optimism about the political situation earlier in the year had been misplaced, several members of the Viceroy's Council were determined to press on with the curtailment of political policing in India. Their target was the Department of Criminal Intelligence. Aziz-ud-Din, who had returned on secondment to the DCI for work on political movements, was allowed to retire, while the Deputy Director was not replaced after he went on leave.[81] In autumn 1912 the size of the DCI's staff came up for discussion by the Government of India. The Home Department wanted to maintain it at full strength, but met opposition from the Finance Department. Sir Guy Fleetwood Wilson, who was then supervising the reform of the Indian provincial administration, proposed the abolition of the DCI and the replacement of the Director by 'a compiler of statistics'. This did not receive much support 'from the other members of the Viceroy's Council. Sir Harcourt Butler, the Education member, wanted to dissociate the Police from political work and instead to attach to each Local Government a special secretary for political work and to make more use of the Indian Civil Service for the control of political movements. This suggestion met with more support.[82]

Only Craddock, the Home Member, urged the continuance of the DCI at full strength. Not for the last time, he showed himself to be the main advocate of an effective intelligence system within the highest ranks of the Government of India. Craddock served as Home Member from 1910 to 1917, when he became Lieutenant-Governor of Burma.

A later India Office official remembers him in glowing terms as the 'most valuable' of the members of Viceroy's Council, who had 'mental vigour and great experience', and was 'conservative in his views and transparently sincere'.[83]

The discussion about the DCI's future was then overtaken by events. The Delhi Durbar was followed by another great symbolic gesture of conciliation. On 23 December 1912 a great ceremony was held in Delhi to mark the restoration of capital status to the city. The elephant carrying the Viceroy, Lord Hardinge, was just passing the buildings of the Punjab National Bank on the Chandni Chawk, Delhi's main street, when a picric acid bomb weighing between half and three-quarters of a pound exploded against the howdah. An Indian attendant was killed instantaneously but Lord and Lady Hardinge, as well as a second servant escaped death, though only Lady Hardinge remained unscathed.[84] At first neither the three CID officers accompanying the elephant nor the crowd realized what had happened, since the procession continued moving, the bomb having made no more noise than a firework.[85] When the alarm was raised a minute later, the detectives rushed off in the wrong direction. By the time Hailey, the Chief Commissioner of Delhi, arrived, the assassins had escaped. It was only 20 minutes later that David Petrie, the DCI's representative at the State Entry into Delhi, arrived on the scene.[86]

Hailey immediately charged Petrie with the enquiry into the bomb outrage.[87] The Government of India ensured that he remained in general charge: the Viceroy's Council insisted that the Director of Criminal Intelligence should have nothing to do with the investigations, beyond giving any assistance that Petrie requested.[88] In the days following the assassination attempt Petrie tried to secure information by contacting the municipal sweepers and the bad characters of Delhi, and by visiting brothels, opium dens 'and other haunts of vice'. Local Indian 'gentlemen of position and influence' formed committees for the purpose of collecting information from people who might be reluctant to approach the police.[89] But these initial investigations had no effect whatsoever.[90]

David Petrie was a 33-year-old Scotsman from Perth. After graduating from Aberdeen University he joined the Indian Police Service in 1900. In 1909 he reached the rank of Assistant to the Deputy Inspector-General of Police in the Punjab. In 1911 he was seconded to the DCI as assistant to the Assistant Director of Criminal Intelligence. He first achieved distinction in that year by winning the Gold Essay prize of the United Service Institution. Thereafter Petrie was to hold several important posts in Britain's imperial intelligence agencies. He was responsible for setting up Indian intelligence in the Far East in the period 1915–19. From 1924 to 1931 he was head of Indian Intelligence.[91] His final job, in the years 1940–46, was Director-General of MI5, the British domestic and imperial counter-intelligence agency. One former MI5 officer gave this description of Petrie at the end of his life:

> Solid in appearance and in mind, he made it his business to know the essentials of his job . . . I doubt if he had more than a B+ mind, but he used it, made few – if any – mistakes, and combined courtesy with firmness.[92]

Petrie's team on the Delhi bomb plot enquiry consisted of CID officers from Bengal, Bihar, Bombay, the Central Provinces and the United Provinces.[93] The first officer to arrive in Delhi, on 25 December, was Stead, a colleague of Petrie's from the Punjab CID. He was followed on 27 December by Denham from the Bengal Intelligence Branch. They were respectively in charge of the Punjab and Bengal ends of the enquiry. Vincent and Guider from the Bombay CID dealt with the parts of the enquiry suggesting a connection with revolutionaries in Western India.[94] The enquiry in the United Provinces was conducted by Richardson. In these officers Petrie had at his disposal some of the best detective talent in India. Including these senior officers of his staff, but excluding the Delhi police, Petrie was in charge of a total of 34 men.

Petrie considered the services of a retired Indian detective, Deputy Superintendent Rai Sahib Daryai Mal, to be an important addition to the work of his team, because he had 'behind him an almost unique record of successes as detective officer, and his knowledge of the Punjab and its political conditions [was] profound'. The Rai Sahib also employed some of his own acquaintances on the case.[95] Petrie engaged as secret agents a member of the staff of the Punjab Bank, whose directors were suspected of complicity with the terrorists, and a local railway official of 'none too good repute', but who knew 'a good deal of local conditions in Delhi'. Petrie also made use of police officers with family connections in Delhi and 'employed besides several secret agents who were fairly representative of the different strata of society they belonged to'.[96]

Petrie did most of his work after the Delhi bomb outrage in Bengal since this was the province most seriously troubled by political unrest, especially in and around Calcutta.[97] In March 1913 he also decided to employ 'a number of private agents in various places in and outside Delhi'.[98] He relied heavily on the sort of informers and secret agents whom the Government of India had so much despised in the past. Not surprisingly the attitude of the government to this was modified. In June 1913 Lord Hardinge encouraged the use of more agents on the case.[99]

The DCI's Secret Service grant was doubled from Rs.50,000 (£3,333) to Rs.100,000 (£6,666) in 1913 because of the bomb plot enquiry. Petrie received his own funds for the enquiry from the Government of India. By August 1913 Petrie had spent Rs.9,500 (£633).[100] This was not a large sum, but the Home Department told Petrie that he could expend any amount of money he wanted on 'Secret Service'.[101]

Despite these desperate remedies, which involved what for British India was the intensive use of agents, Petrie still had no success whatsoever for a long time. He resorted to unusual methods in his application of his secret service funds. In 1913 he contacted old suspects whom he thought to have become less violently anti-British in their opinions and asked them to help. He claimed that this method 'met with a fair amount of success'. He also spoke to relatives of fugitive nationalists for whom he offered pardons in exchange for information.[102]

Throughout 1913 the Government of India subjected the Department of Criminal Intelligence to heavy criticism. The precautions taken by the police at the State Entry had clearly been inadequate, but they had not been below the minimum required by the Government of India's rules for such occasions. However, to his subsequent cost, Cleveland had advised that no special measures were necessary. He only brought special officers to Delhi from Bengal and Bombay in response to advice which he received from Hailey, the Chief Commissioner of Delhi.[103] Cleveland unwittingly made his unpopularity with the Government of India worse by leaving India in 1913 to consult with the officer in charge of the European operations of Indian intelligence. O'Moore Creagh, the Army Member of the Viceroy's Council, complained to the Home Department, saying:

> I am unaware why Sir Charles Cleveland is away all this time, but it seems to me to require some explanation. It is a matter of public astonishment that the head of the CID is away at this most critical moment of its existence . . .[104]

Cleveland had good reasons for his action. He left India because of poor health. In 1910 he had very nearly died of blood poisoning after being mauled by a panther, while in the summer of 1912 he had had a throat infection which put his life in danger. There was no reason why he should remain in India after the obvious vote of 'no confidence' which the Viceroy's Council had passed on him when it put Petrie, his erstwhile subordinate, in sole charge of the enquiry into the bomb plot. Since this happened Fleetwood Wilson had made repeated criticisms of Cleveland's competence, which seem to have been fuelled by a great deal of personal hostility. When at the suggestion of the Home Member, Craddock, Cleveland went to see Fleetwood Wilson, the latter refused even to admit him to his office.[105] As a result of the Delhi bomb plot, the Viceroy's Council passed a formal vote of censure on Cleveland.[106]

It is not easy to see how Cleveland could have prevented the Delhi bomb outrage. An officer charged with the task of curtailing the activities of the CIDs could not reasonably be expected to initiate a massive security operation. On his return to India, Cleveland complained to the Home Department in exasperation that

> . . . the Criminal Intelligence Department are frequently subjected to attacks both from friends and foes; on the one side as to their failure to detect the central organization which is supposed to exist; and, on the other, for alleged needless and excessive attention paid to imaginary and innocent suspects and to societies and religious organizations, which are ostensibly and professedly harmless. They are in fact accused in some quarters of manufacturing anarchists out of good and virtuous citizens by their senseless and irritating attention to innocent men and harmless institutions. With the material that they have to work with, individual stupidity on the part of humbler agents may occasionally justify such criticism; but it is quite impossible to keep a watch over the individuals and institutions that must be watched, and yet avoid at all times the occurrence here and there of some vexatious action by blundering subordinates.[107]

Other members of the Indian Police felt themselves ill-treated by the government. Petrie wrote in June 1913:

> Of the mud with which the Police have been so freely bespattered, a good deal has stuck; it is felt that they have no longer the support of Government behind them, and that in their trial of strength

with the revolutionary party they have come off decidedly second best.[108]

It seems that the dislike for all forms of political policing which many members of the Viceroy's Council had conceived before the Delhi bomb plot, when India's political future looked settled, had been based entirely on theoretical conceptions and not upon sound knowledge of how the police worked in practice. There is a strong element of hypocrisy in the Army Member, O'Moore Creagh's criticism of the police as a whole. He wrote that

> our Indian detective organization . . . has failed after seven months' patient and extensive enquiry to bring to light more than sundry clues of no great matter on a matter of what is in my opinion vital importance to our rule in India.

But at the same time he admitted his complete ignorance of the reasons for the Indian CIDs' ineffectiveness at this time. He continued:

> I do not know what power the CID have of placing suspects under police surveillance, but of one thing I am sure that in India without ample power in this direction no system of espionage is of any avail.[109]

It was, of course, precisely this aspect of police activity which the Government of India had restricted in the past.

In 1909 the Government of India had ordered that the CIDs reduce surveillance of political suspects. Partly this was a response to the improvement in the political climate, partly it was an economy measure. One of the most seriously affected CIDs was that of the new province of Delhi, created in 1912. Hailey claimed at the beginning of 1913 that all intelligence work there had been at a standstill for 'the last few years', and that a good deal of political intrigue existed about which the district police knew nothing.[110] When the province of Delhi was created there was virtually no CID.[111]

At the end of January 1913 Petrie wrote that his enquiries were impeded by what he saw as the Government of India's complacency towards political unrest, which had resulted in the activities of the provincial CIDs being run down. He informed the Home Department that the investigations

> prove very protracted and will require much time and patient labour. Their progress will necessarily be retarded by the fact that

there has been of late a general decline in the closeness of contact maintained with agitators all over India and that much of the ground so lost will have to be regained before it is possible to get to the heart of the present case.[112]

Petrie claimed that the reduction in surveillance all over India had allowed many suspects to disappear, while many of the CIDs were not 'abreast of provincial politics'. The enquiries which Petrie's team conducted soon became part of a general investigation of unrest in northern India.[113]

Following the Delhi bomb plot, the CIDs in every province made systematic enquiries into the activities of political dissidents over the previous two years. Sometimes the location of suspects proved a difficult task; one Bengali suspect, for example, was found as far away as Aberdan in Persia. But by March 1913 Petrie claimed that there was 'scarcely a single person all over India capable of being considered a potential factor in the bomb conspiracy whose doings have not been subjected to careful scrutiny'.[114] Moreover the general clean-up resulted in the successful completion of some other cases unconnected with the Delhi bomb outrage.[115] None the less Petrie regretted that the investigating staff 'had to expend much time and labour on obtaining information that they should have found available in the provinces the moment it was asked for'.[116] Following the enquiries of early 1913, the provincial CIDs made a more extensive use of surveillance than before, though they were still reluctant to introduce blanket surveillance and their work covered only 'the most suspicious suspects'.[117]

In July 1913, Syed Ali Imam, the Native Member on the Viceroy's Council, said that he regarded the failure of the police to solve the Delhi bomb plot as symptomatic of the general failure of the CIDs and the DCI in their political work. He said that 'the officers engaged in the investigation of this case seem to have done their best but have met with the same failure that has attended the detection of so many political crimes committed in recent years in India'. In response, the Education Member, Sir Harcourt Butler, suggested that Scotland Yard lend the Government of India 'a really good detective' and procure for them the services of 'a good French detective' for dealing with the French enclave of Chandernagore, near Calcutta. Butler said:

At the outcome of this and other cases we shall have to organize a special detective service . . . we must have men of real detective ability.[118]

O'Moore Creagh, the Army Member, felt that Scotland Yard should be invited to give assistance on a large scale in order to show Indian detectives how to do their job.

Cleveland, now in England, consulted Sir Edward Henry, the Commissioner of the Metropolitan Police, on the question of sending out English and French policemen to assist the Indian Police in September 1913. Henry, who had been Inspector-General of Police in Bengal, said that he considered local detective talent superior to the English detectives he had at his disposal. He argued that even if English policemen were innately superior to their Indian counterparts, they would be useless in India because of their ignorance of its geography, languages and peoples.[119] Moreover no 'really good' English detective would prejudice a successful career in England by going out to India.[120] Henry's advice proved sound, and the Indian Police were spared the humiliation of a review of their methods by experts from overseas.[121]

During the last six months of 1913 Petrie's team became involved in the investigation of a revolutionary document known as the *Liberty* leaflet which as yet unidentified agitators had distributed throughout the Punjab and the United Provinces.[122] At the end of September Stead, the head of the Punjab CID, obtained information from a secret agent that a revolutionary group based in Delhi, whose leader was one Abad Behari, had produced the leaflet. This statement was only corroborated at the end of January 1914, when a large quantity of *Liberty* leaflets reappeared in Lahore.[123]

At this time work conducted independently of the Delhi bomb plot by the Bengal Police had established a close connection between the construction of bombs used in five separate terrorist acts dating from March 1911 to May 1913, which including the attempt on the Viceroy. On 21 November 1913 Denham led a raid on a house in the Raja Bazar district of Calcutta and arrested four Bengali youths. He found material which proved their participation in one of the five connected bomb cases. He also found copies of the *Liberty* leaflets, and documents which implicated a typesetter at a Calcutta press as a member of the gang.[124] As Petrie concluded:

> Denham's discoveries, therefore, clearly showed the close, though hitherto unsuspected, connection between the production of revolutionary literature and the manufacture of bombs . . . There was thus established a most important link between

the Raja Bazar bomb gang in Calcutta and the society in Delhi of which Abad Behari was alleged to be the head.[125]

The results of Denham's find in Calcutta led to the final unravelling of the Delhi bomb plot. On 16 February 1914, in connection with information obtained about the *Liberty* leaflets, Petrie searched four houses in Delhi. In the house of a man named Amir Chand he found the parts of a picric acid bomb. He also found a list of the original conspirators. This list was headed by the name of Har Dayal, by then in America, whom Petrie believed to be the 'presiding genius of the organization'. Further details of Har Dayal's foundation of the revolutionary Ghadr party in North America are to be found in Chapter VI.

Petrie found conclusive evidence in Amir Chand's house that a character named Rash Behari Bose had brought in the bombs from the place of manufacture in Bengal.[126] Eleven men were put on trial as a result. On the next day, 17 February 1914, Stead from the Punjab CID conducted a series of raids in Lahore. A prisoner taken that day named Dina Nath turned King's evidence and gave details of the revolutionary organization, which further revealed the central role within the bomb plot played by Rash Behari Bose. He had been the link between the Bengal, United Provinces and Punjab branches of the conspiracy.

The leader of the plot, Rash Behari Bose, was a clerk in the Forest Institute at Dehra Dun in Bengal.[127] It is perhaps surprising that the police, who as Petrie claimed, had accounted for almost all the political suspects in India, never gave him consideration. He was a relative of Srish Ghose, who, in Petrie's words, was 'one of the most implacable and most dangerous revolutionaries in Bengal'.[128] Cleveland claimed that he had been screened by his own and his father's positions in Government employment. By far his most famous relative, however, was his nephew, Subhas Chandra Bose, who followed in the family tradition of fighting the Raj by organizing the Indian National Army which served with the Japanese against Britain during the Second World War.

Cleveland admitted that Bose must have been 'a zealous revolutionary for years' and that he was 'intimately related to and associated with some of the very worst members of the . . . gangs in Bengal'.[129] Unfortunately for the British, Rash Behari's home was near Calcutta in the French enclave of Chandernagore. The delays involved in

87

arranging extradition papers thwarted Petrie's chances of catching him,[130] and he was next heard of in Japan.

Even Petrie's success in getting to the bottom of the Delhi bomb plot did not stop criticisms of the Indian Police. In the past, as has been shown, British liberal sentiment at home served as a check on the activities of Indian intelligence. Now, opinion at home, albeit on a limited scale, criticized it for not being efficient enough. On 2 June 1914 the London *Evening Standard* attacked the DCI for not unravelling the conspiracy, pointing out that 'Neither Rash Behari nor the Delhi prisoners are men of substance. The majority are poor students, or schoolmasters and tutors earning probably little more than the wages of a butler'.[131] However, by both Indian and European standards of detective work in the nineteenth and early twentieth centuries, Petrie's team had worked effectively, despite the failure to capture Rash Behari Bose. It is only fair to note, as did the Home Department at the time, that the British and Irish police had in the past been equally slow in solving some major political cases. The Royal Irish Constabulary had taken over a year to solve the Phoenix Park Murders of 1882 when the Fenians had murdered the Lord Lieutenant of Ireland and his Permanent Under-Secretary in broad daylight in the middle of Dublin. Likewise, the performance of London's Metropolitan Police left a good deal to be desired in the investigation of the spate of Irish bombings in mainland Britain which lasted from 1883 to 1887.[132]

Most importantly, Petrie's work had silenced criticisms of the police among the Viceroy's Council. Upon the outbreak of war they gave their full confidence to Sir Charles Cleveland and the DCI, though this by no means led to a fundamental change in their attitudes towards the idea of a political police in India. During the Delhi bomb enquiry the Indian Police had sustained much criticism. On the other hand, the Department of Criminal Intelligence, whose chief suffered most because of the outrage, had never been accused of anything more than failing to protect the Viceroy. All other indications showed that the DCI was working effectively with resources which, given the enormous field over which it worked, were extremely meagre. Despite early problems between the DCI and CID of the United Provinces, the interchange of political information between the Indian provinces and the Central Government had always been carried out smoothly. There is no evidence that the co-ordination of political enquiries was generally defective, and the unravelling of the Delhi bomb plot had been possible only because of close co-operation between the DCI and the CIDs of the northern Indian provinces. Moreover, by 1913 the DCI controlled a small, makeshift, but very effective intelligence service in Europe and North America.

Two months before the outbreak of the First World War, Craddock spoke in praise of the DCI's handling of its agents within India. Upon the outbreak of war, Craddock felt that the only group concerning whom the DCI's sources of information were deficient were the *sadhus* and certain religious societies. Craddock claimed that 'this sort of agent can exercise far more influence on the masses than the educated agitator, and if any real mischief is ever worked among the troops, it will be through this agency'. The *sadhus* were potentially dangerous because they were able to reach a wide audience with nationalist propaganda which they presented in religious terms. Craddock thought:

> There are many . . . *sadhus* disguised in sacred places where *sadhus* congregate and . . . extended espionage in temples and groves in places like Nasik, Benares, Hardwar and many great cities might produce valuable information of the spread of sedition and revolutionary movements, and incidentally put in our hands some valuable chance clues.[133]

Many political suspects had disappeared in the disguise of these hermits.[134] Cleveland, however, replied that the DCI had had a genuine *sadhu* in its pay, who reported on his fellows. He never supplied any useful information whatsoever.

In 1913 Hughes-Buller, the Officiating Director of Criminal Intelligence, drew up a huge and comprehensive scheme for watching *sadhus* all over India by means of police officers who would disappear for long periods. Cleveland wrote that 'in my opinion this was hopelessly impractical and the Provincial Governments found it so and gave it up'. He admitted that the DCI knew little about the stimulation by *sadhus* of anti-British feeling, but he felt that 'they do not . . . deserve an elaborate system of espionage, which in their case would be exceedingly costly, difficult and dangerous'. The enquiries following the Delhi bomb plot had not implicated them.[135] Cleveland's remarks on the *sadhus* are significant in terms of the general attitude of the British in India towards political policing. When given the chance to expand his own intelligence agency, the Director of Criminal Intelligence had refused to do so. None the less, Craddock was correct in his supposition that some political suspects escaped to religious centres in the disguise of hermits. Rash Behari Bose was at that time hiding at the Hindu holy city of Benares. Cleveland summed up the general policy of the DCIs towards espionage thus:

> Our plan is to watch the shores rather than the sea. If *sadhus* are going to get at the troops we ought to hear from our agents and officers near the troops.[136]

By the beginning of 1914 the DCI knew that the revolutionaries, based in the safety of San Francisco, were mounting a full scale propaganda campaign to encourage mutiny among the troops of the Indian Army. Despite this and despite the shock of the Delhi bomb plot, Cleveland assured the Home Department in February 1914 that 'nothing has transpired to make us think that the Indian Army has been touched by the blandishments or incitements of the revolutionaries'.[137]

Cleveland recalled that while he had been Director of Criminal Intelligence 'the worst calamity that befell the Department was its unpopularity with the Government of India in 1912. That almost ruined our work for the time being'.[138] With hindsight it appears that the makers of British policy towards India in the first three decades of the twentieth century were guided by a fallacious belief that reforms could bring complete and lasting political peace to India. This policy had a serious but short-term effect on the operation of the Indian intelligence system in 1913 but, more importantly, prevented the Indian Empire acquiring a large-scale and ubiquitous political police. Whatever the liberal misconceptions about political conditions in India, it remains strongly arguable that the rejection of what would have appeared to be 'Tsarist methods' could only have caused more harm than good. If the Raj had barely adequate police intelligence, at least it generally had Indian public opinion behind it in 1914.

But it would be a mistake to draw too strong a dividing line between what Lord Morley referred to at the time as the 'police mentality' and the outlook of the high officials of the Government of India and of the India Office. The senior officers of the Department of Criminal Intelligence, and the heads of the CIDs in the provinces were not fundamentally different from the members of the Viceroy's Council in class, education or politics. Among both groups the idea prevailed that India must ultimately be held by reason and co-operation rather than by coercion. The only question at issue was whether India should have a political intelligence system at all. The police were hampered in their investigations into the Delhi bomb plot not only by the numerical weakness of their upper cadres, but also by their outlook. In the first months of the enquiry Petrie's team did not look for a link between the assassins and the Bengali Hindu terrorists, who were the most dangerous terrorists in India, and indeed in the British Empire as a whole. One of the most remarkable features of the Delhi bomb plot was the inability of the police to understand how a terrorist would so readily resort to violence. Petrie initially thought that the bomb had been manufactured by Muslim terrorists from Eastern Bengal and Assam, since they alone had come off worse after the termination of the Partition of Bengal. He did not at first realize that Hindu Bengalis like Rash Behari Bose were dedicated to the violent destruction of the British regime and that no reforms could quell their hatred. Sir Charles Cleveland, the man whom liberals saw as the incarnation of the 'police mentality', was astounded at the finds in the Delhi house searches of February 1914. He wrote:

> Perhaps those of us who have had to see the papers and correspondence of the discovered plotters have been more impressed by the savage cruelty and double-faced treachery of the ideas of these educated, philosophical, professedly pious Hindus than by any other features of the discoveries.

After the successful conclusion of the Delhi bomb plot enquiries, the Home Department felt that the DCI was winning its battle with the Indian revolutionary movement. Cleveland boasted that 'real out-and-out revolutionaries make no secret of their opinion that we are their greatest and most implacable enemies'.[139] However, their success was not, as yet, complete. Craddock wrote in June 1914 that 'the blows dealt have . . . only been sufficient to scotch and check, and there is plenty of work before them . . .'[140] He thought that as Indian political movements grew in strength, the DCI would have to be strengthened. The Government of India never returned to the belief that anti-British feeling could be rendered insignificant. Cleveland acknowledged at the beginning of 1914 that 'there has almost certainly been a widespread loss of respect for and fear of the Englishman' in India, though he doubted that the bloodthirsty ideas of Rash Behari Bose and his associates had made any significant headway among the masses of the population. He was, however, concerned that

91

The Sikh or Punjabi immigrant in Canada or America sometimes writes as if the extermination of the English in India were
the desire of his heart.[141]

Cleveland's prediction that trouble would next come to India from the
revolutionary movement abroad materialized in less than a year.

NOTES

1. In the words of one Indian authority: 'Till at least 1903, there can be no doubt that administrative considerations were predominant in all discussions concerning the future map of Bengal.' Sumit Sarkar, *The Swadeshi Movement in Bengal 1903–1908* (New Delhi: People's Publishing House, 1973), p. 12.
2. This is the figure according to the census of 1901.
3. Quoted in Bipan Chandra, *India's Struggle for Freedom* (New Delhi: Penguin, 1989).
4. Valentine Chirol, *Indian Unrest* (London: Macmillan, 1910), p. 107.
5. Ibid.
6. Quoted in N.G. Barrier, *The Punjab Alienation of Land Bill of 1900* (Durham, NC, 1966).
7. Quoted in Bipan Chandra, op. cit., p. 139.
8. See Rumbold, *Watershed in India* (London: The Athlone Press, 1979), p. 1.
9. Quoted in Sir H. Verney Lovett, 'The Rise of an Extremist Party', in H.H. Dodwell (ed.), *The Cambridge History of India. Vol. VI. The Indian Empire* (New Delhi: S. Chand and Company, 1972).
10. James Campbell Ker, *Political Trouble in India 1907–1917*, reprint edited by Mahadevaprasad Saha (Calcutta: Editions India, 1973), pp. 130–31.
11. Letter from Sir Harold Stuart, Secretary to the Government of India, Home Department, to all Local Governments and Administrations except Coorg, 18 Dec. 1909, in *Revision of the system of compilation of the Weekly Secret Police Abstracts*. HDB: Dec. 1909, no. 77, IOLR IOR.POS. 5946.
12. Letter from H.A. Stuart to the Secretary to the Government of India, Home Department, 28 May 1906, in *Question whether the Deputy Director of Criminal Intelligence should be permitted to use the Director of Criminal Intelligence's reserved railway carriage if and when he is deputed by him to undertake an investigation*. HD/Pol: Oct. 1908, no. 145, IOLR P/7889.
13. In 1910 he returned to Bengal as Chief Secretary to the Local Government.
14. Letter from C.R. Cleveland to the Secretary to the Government of India, Home Department, 5 May 1910 and letter from I.G. Lloyd, Under-Secretary to the Government of India, Home Department, 29 June 1910, in *Proposed increase of the Menial Staff of the Office of the Director, Criminal Intelligence*. HD/Pol: June 1910, no. 143 in IOLR P/8447. The DCI first acquired a photographic capability in 1907. Before this private firms in Calcutta produced the half-tone photographs of criminals whom the DCI wanted the CIDs to watch or find. *Indent Submitted by the Director of Criminal Intelligence for a Photographic Apparatus*. HD/Pol: Aug. 1907 in IOLR P/7604.
15. The four clerks initially employed were all Eurasians. Similarly in the Military Intelligence Branch all the clerks were Europeans. Letter from Stuart to the Secretary to the Government of India, Home Department, 4 Nov. 1904, HD/Pol: Dec. 1904, nos. 100–1, IOLR P/6819. Letter from Stuart to the Secretary to the Government of India, Home Department, 21 Sept. 1905, HD/Pol: Dec. 1905, nos. 125–6, IOLR P/7601.
16. *Increase to the Clerical Establishment of the DCI*. HD/Pol: Sept. 1907, no. 151 in IOLR

P/7604. *Revision of the Office Establishment of the Director of Criminal Intelligence.* HD/Pol: Feb. 1909 in IOLR P/8166.
17. Ibid. Letter from I.G. Lloyd.
18. Letter from the Government of India, Finance Department, to the Secretary of State, 20 Dec. 1908. J&P 92/07 in IOLR L/PJ/6/792.
19. At the end of 1907 the Secretary of State for India, Lord Morley, urged the Viceroy, Lord Minto, not to let Stevenson-Moore's 'difficulties' with Aziz-ud-Din block the latter's promotion, because 'that man knows what he is about, and has clues to the doings of evil-doers in Paris and elsewhere'. Morley Papers, Vol. IV, 1909, in IOLR MSS.EUR.D.573/4. Hirtzel Diaries, entries for 13 and 19 July 1909 in IOLR MSS. EUR.D.1090/4.
20. Letter from the Government of India, Home Department, to the Secretary of State, 18 April 1912. J&P 1628/12 in IOLR L/PJ/6/1161.
21. Letter from C.R. Cleveland, to the Secretary to the Government of India, Home Department, 9 June 1910 and letter from the Government of India, Finance Department, to the Secretary of State, 11 Aug. 1910. *Continuance for a further period of two years of the appointment of Personal Assistant to the Director, Criminal Intelligence.* HD/Pol: Nov. 1910, nos. 55–6 in IOLR P/8447. Letter from the Government of India, Finance Department, 13 Feb. 1908, in *Pay of Personal Assistant to the Director of Criminal Intelligence.* J&P 826/08 in IOLR L/PJ/6/854.
22. Letter from the Viceroy in Council, to the Secretary of State, 28 June 1906 and letter from the Director of Criminal Intelligence, to the Secretary to the Government of India, Home Department in *Criminal Intelligence Department: Proposed Additions to Staff.* J&P 2222/06 in IOLR L/PJ/6/7.
23. Ibid. Letter from the Director of Criminal Intelligence, 20 April 1906.
24. Ibid. Letter from the Viceroy in Council, 28 June 1906.
25. Letter from C.J. Stevenson-Moore, to the Secretary to the Government of India, Home Department, 23 May 1908, in *Improvement of the investigating staff employed under the Director of Criminal Intelligence.* HD/Pol: Sept. 1908, nos. 15–21 in IOLR P/7889.
26. They worked in pairs. Stevenson-Moore wrote that 'It is an almost invariable custom for a smart Indian detective to get attached to him a subordinate officer in whose abilities and trustworthiness he has special confidence and without this adjunct he will not give the best work. He requires someone to write notes and look up minor points while he devotes himself to working up the main clues'. Letter from C.J. Stevenson-Moore, Director of Criminal Intelligence, to the Secretary to the Government of India, Home Department, 23 May 1908, HD/Pol: Sept. 1908, nos. 15–21, in IOLR P/7889.
27. Letter from C.J. Stevenson-Moore, 23 May 1908. HD/Pol: Sept. 1908, op.cit.
28. Extract from notes on the Army Department File, 'Watching sedition', signed H.A. Stuart, 13 June 1907, in *Proposed formation of a political service under the control of the Criminal Intelligence Department to furnish information about the spread of sedition.* HDD: May 1908, no. 1, IOLR IOR.POS.10608.
29. *Sadhus* (pronounced sahd-hus or sahd-hoos) are the saints of Hindu tradition, laymen who have given up the worldly existence to seek salvation. Unlike the *swami*, who belongs to an order, the *sadhu* remains independent. They were, and are, an easily recognizable group because of their habit of wandering around half-naked, smeared in dust, with their hair and beard matted, and because of their occasional feats of self-mortification, which rivalled those of the Muslim fakirs.
30. Note by C.J. Stevenson-Moore, Offg. Director, Criminal Intelligence, 13 May 1908. HDD: May 1908, no. 1, IOR.POS.10608.
31. The Home Department reported in September 1907 that 'prominence has been given in the past rather to the criminal than to the political side of the Department's duties.

Recent events have, however, emphasized the need for fuller information on political matters, especially sedition and unrest; and any objections which may have been taken in the past to the employment of a permanent staff of secret agents must give way before the urgent necessity for the fullest and most accurate information about political matters being readily available for the Government of India. Note by G. Fell, 9 Sept. 1907. HDD: May 1908, no. 1, IOLR IOR.POS.10608.

32. Ibid. Note by C.J. Stevenson-Moore, 13 May 1908.
33. Ibid. Extract from notes on the Army Department File, 'Watching sedition', signed H.A. Stuart.
34. Ibid.
35. Ibid. Undated note by H.H. Risley.
36. Ibid. Note by C.J. Stevenson-Moore, 13 May 1908.
37. Ibid.
38. Ibid. Note by H. Adamson, 28 Dec. 1907.
39. Rumbold, op. cit., pp. 17–18.
40. Extract from notes on the Army Department file, op. cit.
41. These officers were: the Director of Criminal Intelligence; the Deputy Director; the Assistant Director; the Personal Assistant to the Director; and the four detective Deputy Superintendents.
42. *Continuance for a further period of two years of the appointment of Personal Assistant to the Director, Criminal Intelligence*, in HD/Pol: Nov. 1910, nos. 55–6 in IOLR P/8447.
43. Note on the *Proposed Establishment of a Central Criminal Investigation Department*, by Sir Andrew Fraser, 25 April 1903, in J&P.493/04 in IOLR L/PJ/6/670.
44. Note by R.H. Craddock, 1 June 1913, in *Attempt to Assassinate His Excellency the Viceroy* on 23 Dec. 1912. Reports Received from the Chief Commissioner, Delhi, the Director, Criminal Intelligence, and Mr Petrie Relative to the –. *Note by Sir R. Craddock, Regarding the CID Matters and Detective Agency*. [Blank present in the original document title.] IOLR HDD: Dec. 1914, no. 11 in IOR.POS.10612.
45. Ibid.
46. For example, note entitled 'Detective to be attached to Scotland Yard' by Stevenson-Moore, 20 Aug. 1909, in *Proposal to depute Sirdar Bahadur Dyal Singh Gyani to London, in connection with the proposed extradition of Vinayek Savarkar. Deputation of Mr Wallinger to London*. HDA: Jan. 1911, nos. 52–64, in IOLR IOR.POS.5949.
47. In 1910 the CID was composed of one Deputy Inspector-General, one Personal Assistant to the Deputy Inspector-General, 18 Inspectors and Sub-Inspectors and 35 Head Constables and Constables. *Question in Council by the Hon'ble Mr Gokhale regarding the strength and cost of the provincial Criminal Investigation Departments*, HD/Pol: Oct. 1911, nos. 66–99, IOLR P/8712.
48. 'Statement showing the strength and cost of the political side of the Criminal Investigation Department of Madras from 1903 to 1912', in *Strength and Cost of the Executive Staff of the Criminal Investigation Department Employed on Political Work in the Various Provinces of India During the Period of 10 Years from 1903 to 1912*, HD/Pol: May 1914, no. 51, IOLR P/9458.
49. In 1912 there were two Superintendents, 55 Inspectors and Sub-Inspectors, 65 Head Constables and Constable and 32 Clerks in the CID. *Question in Council by the Hon'ble Mr Gokhale regarding the strength and cost of the provincial Criminal Investigation Departments*, op. cit.
50. 'Statement showing the strength and cost of the political side of the Criminal Investigation Department of the United Provinces, from 1903 to 1912', in *Strength and Cost of the Executive Staff of the Criminal Investigation Department Employed on Political Work in the Various Provinces of India During the Period of 10 Years from 1903 to 1912*, op. cit.
51. In 1911 there were two Assistants to the Inspector-General, Criminal Investigation

Department, Special Branch, one Deputy Superintendent, 31 Inspectors and Sub-Inspectors and 40 Head Constables and Constables in the CID.

52. This figure represented one Deputy Inspector-General, one Assistant to the Deputy Inspector-General, 18 Inspectors and Sub-Inspectors and 27 Head Constables and Constables. *Question in Council by the Hon'ble Mr Gokhale regarding the strength and cost of the provincial Criminal Investigation Departments.*

53. 'Statement showing the strength and cost of the political side of the Criminal Investigation Department of the Punjab from 1903 to 1912', in *Strength and Cost of the Executive Staff of the Criminal Investigation Department Employed on Political Work in the Various Provinces of India During the Period of 10 Years from 1903 to 1912,* op. cit.

54. This number comprised one Deputy Inspector-General, one Assistant to the Deputy Inspector-General, 30 Inspectors and Sub-Inspectors and 36 Head Constables and Constables. *Question in Council by the Hon'ble Mr Gokhale regarding the strength and cost of the provincial Criminal Investigation Departments,* op. cit.

55. The City CID staff consisted of one Superintendent, 17 Inspectors, Sub-Inspectors, and Jemadars, and 65 Head Constables and Constables. 'Statement of Strength and Cost Submitted by the Commissioner of Police, Bombay', in *Strength and Cost of the Executive Staff of the Criminal Investigation Department Employed on Political Work in the Various Provinces of India During the Period of 10 Years from 1903 to 1912,* op. cit.

56. 'Consolidated statement showing the approximate strength and cost of the Criminal Investigation Department employed on political work in the Bombay Presidency, including Sind and Bombay City', in *Strength and Cost of the Executive Staff of the Criminal Investigation Department Employed on Political Work in the Various Provinces of India During the Period of 10 Years from 1903 to 1912,* op. cit.

57. Copy of note dated 31 Oct. 1912, drawn up by the Inspector-General of Police, Central Provinces, in *Strength and Cost of the Executive Staff of the Criminal Investigation Department Employed on Political Work in the Various Provinces of India During the Period of 10 Years from 1903 to 1912,* op. cit.

58. Letter from the Inspector-General of Police, Central Provinces, to the Chief Commissioner, Central Provinces, to the Chief Commissioner, Central Provinces, 16 Sept. 1913, in *Strength and Cost of the Executive Staff of the Criminal Investigation Department Employed on Political Work in the Various Provinces of India During the Period of 10 Years from 1903 to 1912,* op. cit.

59. Letter from C.A. Barron, Chief Secretary to the Government of the Punjab, to the Secretary to the Government of India, Home Department, in *Strength and Cost of the Executive Staff of the Criminal Investigation Department Employed on Political Work in the Various Provinces of India During the Period of 10 Years from 1903 to 1912,* op. cit.

60. Notes in the Central Criminal Intelligence Office, signed C.J. Stevenson-Moore, officiating Director, Criminal Intelligence, 8 Sept. 1909, in *Arrangements for watching and reporting the movements of foreign suspects.* HDA Series: Dec. 1909, nos. 70–74 in IOLR IOR.POS. 5946.

61. Letter from H.A. Stuart, to the Director of Criminal Intelligence, 10 March 1910, in *Arrangements for watching and reporting the movements of foreign suspects.* HDA: March 1910, nos. 107–8 in IOLR IOR.POS.5947.

62 Letter from E.A. DeBrett, Chief Secretary to the Chief Commissioner, Central Provinces, to the Secretary to the Government of India, Home Department, 17 May 1911, in *Working of the revised methods of watching and reporting the movements of foreign suspects.* HDB: Oct. 1911, nos. 183–201 in IOLR IOR.POS.8972.

63. It is worth recalling the evocative introduction to A.J.P. Taylor's *English History 1914–1945*: 'Until August 1914 a sensible, law-abiding Englishman could pass through

life and hardly notice the existence of the state, beyond the post office and the police-man. He could live where he like and as he liked. He had no official number or identity card. He could travel abroad or leave his country for ever without a passport or any sort of official permission . . . For that matter, a foreigner could spend his life in this country without permit and without informing the police.' A.J.P. Taylor, *English History 1914–1945* (Reading: Penguin, revised edn., 1975), p. 25.

64. DCI Circular to all Superintendents of District, and Railway Police and to the Com-missioner of Police, Calcutta. Ibid.

65. Weekly Reports of the Director of Criminal Intelligence for the weeks ending 5 and 12 Oct. in HDB: Oct. 1907, nos. 88–121 and weeks ending 9 and 16 Nov. 1907 in HDB: Nov. 1907, nos. 2–9, all in IOLR IOR.POS.8959.

66. *Proposed visit of Myron H. Phelps of America to India*. HDB: Aug. 1909, nos. 177–8 in IOLR IOR.POS.8962.

67. Entry entitled 'Myron H. Phelps' in 'Indian Agitators Abroad'. *Containing short accounts of the more important Indian Political Agitators who have visited Europe and America in recent years, and their sympathizers* (Simla, Nov. 1911). IOLR V/27/262/1.

68. See Chapter XI, Part 3.

69. *Complaints of interference on the part of the Director of Criminal Intelligence by the Government of the United Provinces*. HDD: Jan. 1908, no. 3 in IOLR IOR.POS.10608.

70. Ibid. Note by H.H. Risley, 29 Nov. 1907.

71. Note by H. Adamson, 28 Dec. 1907. HDD: May 1908, no. 1, op. cit.

72. Parliamentary Question by Sir Henry Cotton, 18 May 1909. IOLR HD/Pol: Nov. 1909, no. 95 in P/8167.

73. Question by the Hon'ble Babu Bhupendra Nath Basu and proposed reply by the Hon'ble Sir Reginald Craddock to the Hon'ble Bhupendra Nath Basu's question re Criminal Investigation Department in *Question and Answer in the Imperial Legislative Council Regarding the Constitution and Working of the Criminal Investigation Depart-ments*, HD/Pol: April 1912, no. 15, IOLR P/8956. Question of the Hon'ble Raja of Dighapatia and proposed reply by the Hon'ble Sir Reginald Craddock to the Hon'ble Raja of Dighapatia's question re organization and reduction of expenditure on the Criminal Investigation Department, in *Question Regarding Reduction of Expenditure on Criminal Investigation*, HD/Pol: April 1912, no. 103, IOLR P/8956.

74. Note by C.R. Cleveland, 13 July 1914. HDD: July 1914, no. 34 in IOLR IOR.POS. 10612.

75. Parliamentary question and answer regarding the method of working of the Criminal Investigation Department in India. Question no. 5 by Sir Henry Cotton, dated 18 May 1909. HD/Pol: Nov. 1909, no. 95 in IOLR P/8167. On 11 March the Right Honourable Dr Rutherford MP asked whether the DCI was to be afforded 'other facilities for justifying his existence'. Parliamentary question by Dr Rutherford, 11 March 1909, in *Director of Criminal Intelligence. Complaints re encroachment on others' sphere of influence*. J&P 922/09 in IOLR L/PJ/6/926.

76. Notes in the Criminal Intelligence Department, signed C.J. Stevenson-Moore, 22 March 1909, in *Discontinuance of police surveillance over Pundit Gopal Krishna Deodhar and modification in the procedure by which persons are placed under surveil-lance by orders from the Director, Criminal Intelligence to the local Criminal Investiga-tion Department without reference to the Local Governments*. HDB: Oct. 1909, nos. 167–8 in IOLR IOR.POS.8963.

77. Letter from the Home Department, to the Chief Secretary of the Government of the United Provinces, 16 Oct. 1909. Ibid.

78. On one occasion the Secretary to the Government of the United Provinces, W.S. Marris, complained to the India Office that Cleveland 'is a dreadful fellow to work with – ill-balanced, hasty, suspicious, vindictive: and abominably unfair to our CID man, Sands'. Seton Papers, Letters to Seton, op. cit. Letter from W.S. Marris, 5 Oct. 1916.

79. Memorandum by R.H. Craddock, 22 Aug. 1913. HDD: Dec. 1914, no. 11, op. cit.
80. In *Indian Unrest* Sir Valentine Chirol spelt out forcefully that Indian 'advanced opinion' was reacting against western civilization. This was barely comprehensible to contemporary British opinion. However, even Chirol shared the conviction of the Government of India that almost all political groups in India could be reconciled permanently if they pursued a correct policy.
81. Memorandum by R.H. Craddock, 22 Aug. 1913, op. cit.
82. Ibid.
83. Rumbold, op. cit., p. 39.
84. Telegram from Governor-General's Council to Secretary of State, 23 Dec. 1912. CUL Hardinge Papers, Vol.85. This was the second time revolutionaries had made an attempt on the Viceroy. The first occurred on 13 Nov. 1909 when two coconut bombs were thrown at Lord Minto's carriage at Ahmedabad. They failed to explode. Ker, *Political Trouble in India*, op. cit., pp. 310–11.
85. Memorandum entitled 'Enquiry into the Delhi Bomb Outrage', signed D. Petrie, Delhi, 30 Jan. 1913. HDD: Dec. 1914 in IOLR IOR.POS.10612.
86. Note by W.M. Hailey, 24 Dec. 1912. Ibid.
87. From then until the end of the Delhi bomb enquiry, Petrie was officially an Additional Superintendent of the Delhi Police.
88. Memorandum by R.H. Craddock, 5 Oct. 1913. Ibid.
89. Memorandum by Petrie, dated Delhi, 30 Jan. 1913. Ibid.
90. Note by Hailey, 24 Dec. 1912. HDD: Dec. 1914, no. 11, op. cit.
91. Introduction by Mahadevaprasad Saha to the reprint of David Petrie, *Communism in India 1924–1927* (Calcutta: Editions Indian, 1972).
92. Quoted in Christopher Andrew, *Secret Service. The Making of the British Intelligence Community* (London: Heinemann, 1985), p. 479. Similar memories of Petrie as a big, imposing man were related to the author by the late Professor Cheney of Corpus Christi College, Cambridge, who served in MI5 before following a career in Medieval history.
93. Memorandum by Petrie, dated Delhi, 30 Jan. 1913, in HDD: Dec. 1914, no. 11.
94. Note by W.M. Hailey, 2 Jan. 1913. Ibid. They were particularly interested in the activities of the Mahrattas.
95. Particularly important among them was a female detective who made enquiries among the women who had been spectators at the State Entry.
96. Letter from D. Petrie to W.M. Hailey, 21 June 1913. HDD: Dec. 1914, no. 11, op. cit.
97. Copy of a deposition of a witness taken down by V. Connolly, I.C.S., Magistrate, Delhi and Lahore, 24 March 1914, in Reports by Messrs. D. Petrie and C. Stead on the *Delhi–Lahore conspiracy and sedition cases*. HDA: July 1914, nos. 1–2 in IOLR IOR.POS.7147.
98. Progress report by D. Petrie, dated 20 March 1913. HDD: Dec. 1914, no. 11.
99. Note by Hardinge, 3 June 1913. Ibid.
100. Petrie's funds were distributed to him through Hailey and not by the DCI. This was technically because he was then serving as a District Superintendent under the Delhi Administration, and not because the Government of India wanted to reduce the Department of Criminal Intelligence's control over the enquiries.
101. Memorandum by R.H. Craddock, 22 Aug. 1913. HDD: Dec. 1914, no. 11, op. cit.
102. Ibid.
103. They watched for the appearance of suspicious persons belonging to their respective provinces and tried to locate the members of politically active communities, such as Bengalis and Mahratta Brahmins, living in Delhi. They also studied the political records of the Delhi CID. They had many people placed under surveillance.
104. Memorandum by O'Moore Creagh, 1 Aug. 1913. Ibid.
105. Memorandum by R.H. Craddock, 22 Aug. 1913.

106. Letter from Craddock to Hardinge, 19 Feb. 1914. CUL Hardinge Papers; India, Original Letters, Vol. 60.
107. Note by R.H. Craddock, 14 July 1914. HDD: July 1914, no. 34, op. cit.
108. Letter from D. Petrie to W.M. Hailey, 21 June 1913. HDD: Dec. 1914, no. 11, op. cit.
109. Memorandum by O'Moore Creagh, 1 Aug. 1913, ibid.
110. Letter from W.M. Hailey, to H. Wheeler, 1 Feb. 1913. Ibid.
111. 'List of officers belonging to other Provinces who are engaged in the Delhi Bomb Enquiry'. Ibid.
112. Memorandum by Petrie dated Delhi, 30 Jan. 1913. Ibid.
113. Demi-official letter from Sir C. Cleveland, to D. Petrie, 5 Aug. 1914. *Question of the disposal of the police officers employed in connection with the Delhi-Lahore Conspiracy Case. Retention of Mr D. Petrie, Punjab Police, on the investigation in connection with the Delhi Bomb Case.* HDD: Aug. 1914, no. 8 in IOLR IOR.POS.10612.
114. Memorandum entitled 'Enquiry into the Delhi Bomb Outrage', by D. Petrie, 31 March 1913. HDD: Dec. 1914, no. 11, op. cit.
115. The hunting down of P.M. Bapat, an absconder in the Alipore Bomb Case by Vincent of the Bombay CID, was the most important of these subsidiary cases.
116. Letter from D. Petrie to W.M. Hailey, 21 June 1914. HDD: Dec. 1914, no. 11, op. cit.
117. Note by R.H. Craddock, 1 June 1913. Ibid.
118. Note by H. Butler, 27 July 1913, ibid.
119. Note by C.R. Cleveland, Aug. 1913, in *Suggestion that the aid of Scotland Yard or French detectives (with particular reference to Chandernagore) be invoked, either in connection with the Delhi Bomb Case, or generally, to strengthen the detective side of the Indian Police Administration. Correspondence relative to feasibility or training Indian Police Officers in Scotland Yard methods.* HDD: Nov. 1915, no. 33 in IOLR IOR. 10612.
120. Demi-official letter from Sir C. Cleveland to H. Wheeler, dated London, 12 Sept. 1913. Ibid.
121. Some of the early chiefs of the British police and intelligence had served in India. Major General Henry Brackenbury, James Monro and Sir Edward Henry are well-known examples. But it was their length of service and general experience which qualified them for their positions. That they had served specifically in India is of no significance. The Indian Police were not regarded as an elite body by other police forces in the Empire or by the Government of India. Throughout the period, the Indian government felt that its Police Force lagged behind those of Europe. In the first decade of the twentieth century officers of the Indian Police went to Scotland Yard for training, not *vice versa*.
122. Note on the Delhi conspiracy case by D. Petrie, dated Delhi, 14 April 1914, in *Reports by Messrs. D. Petrie and C. Stead on the Delhi–Lahore conspiracy and sedition case. Committal order of the investigating magistrate in the above case.* HDA: July 1914, nos. 1–2 in IOLR IOR.POS.7147.
123. Report by D. Petrie, 8 Nov. 1914. HDD: Dec. 1914, no. 11.
124. Ker, op. cit., pp. 300–3.
125. Note on the Delhi conspiracy case by D. Petrie, 14 April 1914. HDA: July 1914, nos. 1–2.
126. Note by Petrie on the Delhi–Lahore Case, 18 March 1914. *Note by Mr Petrie, outlining the main facts of the Delhi–Lahore sedition and conspiracy case.* HDD: March 1914, no. 7 in IOLR IOR.POS.10612.
127. Petrie's note on the Delhi–Lahore Case, 18 March 1914. HDD: March 1914, no. 7, op. cit.
128. Report by D. Petrie, 8 Nov. 1914. HDD: Dec. 1914, no. 11, op. cit.
129. Cleveland claimed that the police had taken so long to identify Amir Chand as a key suspect because he had been protected by clergymen belonging to the Cambridge

Mission, particularly Charles Andrews, the future supporter of Gandhi, who had 'an exceedingly high opinion of him'. Cleveland on the other hand regarded him as 'a particularly bloodthirsty plotter and debaucher of youths for revolutionary purposes'. Copy of a note outlining the main facts of the Delhi–Lahore Conspiracy case now before a Magistrate at Delhi, signed C.R. Cleveland, 24 March 1914. HDD: March 1914, no. 7, op. cit.

130. Note on the Delhi conspiracy case by Petrie, dated 14 April 1914. HDA: July 1914, nos. 1–2.
131. *Evening Standard*, 2 June 1914.
132. For details and extensive reflections on the Fenians' 'Dynamite War' in Britain see Bernard Porter, *The Origins of the Vigilant State: The London Metropolitan Police Special Branch before the First World War* (London: Weidenfeld & Nicolson, 1987), Ch. 4.
133. Note by R.H. Craddock, 1 June 1913. HDD: Dec. 1914, no. 11, op. cit.
134. Note by R.H. Craddock, 14 July 1914. HDD: July 1914, no. 34, op. cit.
135. Note by C.R. Cleveland, 13 July 1914, ibid.
136. Ibid.
137. Copy of a note outlining the main facts of the Delhi–Lahore Conspiracy case now before a Magistrate at Delhi, signed C.R. Cleveland, 24 March 1914. HDD: March 1914, no. 7.
138. Note by C.R. Cleveland, 13 July 1914. HDD: July 1914, no. 34, op. cit.
139. Ibid.
140. Note by R.H. Craddock, 14 July 1914. HDD: July 1914, no. 34, op. cit.
141. Copy of a note outlining the main facts of the Delhi–Lahore Conspiracy case now before a Magistrate at Delhi, signed C.R. Cleveland, 24 March 1914. HDD: March 1914, no. 7, op. cit.

4

Bengal, 1905–14

Are not ten thousand sons of Bengal prepared to embrace death to avenge the humiliation of their motherland? The number of Englishmen in the entire country is not more than a lakh and half (150,000) and what is the number of English officials in each district? With a firm resolve you can bring English rule to an end in a single day.

Yugantar, Bengali nationalist newspaper, March 1907[1]

After 1905, Bengal was the province of India most seriously affected by nationalist unrest. By 1907, it was also the home of by far the most powerful terrorist movement in the sub-continent. The reasons for the strength of unrest in Bengal were discussed in the last chapter. The enduring strength of hostility to the Raj among sections of the *bhadralok* was the primary reason for the intractability of the terrorist problem, which was approaching crisis point by the time the First World War broke out in 1914. Other factors, which led to the development of this situation were the structure of the provincial administration, the policies of the Local Government, and even the geography of Bengal.

The terrain of Bengal offered great advantages to the terrorist. The communications in the east of the province were worse than in any other part of British India. The many rivers which dissected the region submerged large areas when the rains came, leaving few roads passable. Boats were the ordinary means of transport, and most of the population lived in scattered homesteads.[2] In Western Bengal the problem of communications was not as severe, but was compensated for by the presence of Calcutta, which offered criminals easy shelter, and of the French enclave of Chandernagore, 20 miles upstream from that city, which provided political asylum for terrorists even during the war.

100

The British administration in Bengal had long been undermanned, even in comparison with other parts of India. In fact, the Raj was almost invisible to the majority of people in the countryside. The rapid growth of population in the later nineteenth century greatly increased this problem. At the time of their partition in 1906 the provinces of Bengal, Bihar and Orissa, contained 78 million people.[3] The Dacca Division was a typical area of eastern Bengal: it had an area of 2,777 square miles and a population of three million. In 1908 its police force numbered only 791, while even in 1917, after more than a decade of political unrest, there were still only 1,365 officers and men.[4]

Even before the outbreak of political unrest a more hostile feeling existed between the police of Bengal and the local population than anywhere else in India. There were two reasons for this. First, with the exception of Calcutta, the lower ranks of the police consisted largely of outsiders from the United Provinces and Bihar, who were unable to speak the local language. Second, the revenue system in Bengal had been fixed by Lord Cornwallis's Permanent Settlement of 1793, with the result that the police in Bengal carried out many functions which minor revenue officials performed elsewhere in India, just as elsewhere the latter served as a check on the police. Moreover, in other provinces revenue officials provided information on local conditions. In Bengal the police constituted 'practically the only link between the people and government'.[5] Even by the low standards of the Indian Police in general, the police of Bengal were of particularly poor quality. As one British official later noted:

> They were abominably housed, ill-equipped, under-strength and wretchedly paid. There were cases of constables in hospital with illness due to starvation.[6]

The quality of the already inadequate administration of Bengal actually deteriorated during the first decade of the twentieth century. With the object of decentralization the Police Commission of 1902–3 altered the system by which village watchmen (*chaukidars*) reported to the local police, ordering them instead to report to the local courts (*panchayets*).[7] This further impaired the flow of information from the villages to the central government.[8]

The government of Bengal was unable greatly to improve the native police force because of lack of funds and, after 1906, because of the nationalist intimidation of low-ranking police officers. Thus it needed a specialized force at the centre, capable of improving the flow of information. Since 1888 the local Special Branch had provided political intelligence. Its staff amounted to just four clerks, who depended for information upon the ordinary police, and after 1905, on the provincial and Calcutta CIDs.[9] As we have seen in previous Chapters, the latter were created because of the rapid increase in ordinary crime in the early twentieth century. Initially the provincial CID was composed of 39 officers and 31 men.[10] The separate Calcutta CID had a staff of 61 in the years 1905–12.[11] At the beginning of 1907 a Calcutta Special Branch was set up, consisting of nine officers and 45 men.[12]

Even before the partition there were clear signs of unrest within Bengal. Bengali society was dominated by the high-caste *bhadralok* or 'respectable people'. They had early sought Western education. By the beginning of the twentieth century they felt threatened economically because of the growth of literacy in English among the educated in other Indian provinces, which meant competition for jobs, and because of population growth within Bengal, which resulted in the diminution of their patrimonial holdings. There were also unmistakable signs of ferment in the intellectual climate of Bengal. A spectacular literary renaissance accompanied a movement for the purification of Hinduism. The latter, it proved, could easily be converted to a nationalist cause which wished 'to cleanse' India from its 'foreign occupation'.

Curzon's government announced the partition of Bengal in July 1905. The province was to be divided in three: Bengal proper; Eastern Bengal and Assam (EBA); and parts were to go to Bihar and Orissa. This act provided a focus for the protest of the many discontented groups within Bengal and united Hindus around a new grievance. They had formed the majority in the old province, but the new province of Eastern Bengal and Assam was overwhelmingly Muslim in composition. Its *bhadralok* felt their domination of society threatened.

A vigorous campaign against the partition began in both provinces, which caught the government unawares. Though the malaise within Bengali society was evident from the turn of the century, the Government of India had given no regard to it. Indeed, Curzon did not even consult the local population before dividing Bengal. Likewise the local police provided no warning of the strength of popular feeling on the issue.

The new Viceroy, Lord Minto, who replaced Curzon at the end of 1905, decided to go through with the partition. By this time the Liberals had replaced the Conservative government in London, and were willing to consider abandoning the partition. However, Minto reported to the India Office, sincerely, that the agitation was subsiding, and the debate in the House of Commons came to nothing. The disappointed leaders of the anti-partition movement now intensified the agitation, introducing a *swadeshi* or 'home produce' movement for the boycott of British goods. This was especially fierce in Eastern Bengal, where frequent disturbances occurred as Hindu students and schoolboys picketed shops selling British imports. The anti-partition campaign immediately acquired a nationalist tone.

The Imperial Government split over what policy to take. Sir Bampfylde Fuller, the first Lieutenant-Governor of Eastern Bengal and Assam, determined to meet the *swadeshi* party head on, ordering the police to take firm action against them. When discontent continued to grow, Morley and Minto accused Fuller of fuelling an unrest which would otherwise die down. In March 1906, Minto ordered him to reduce police supervision of *swadeshi* meetings.[13] At the same time Morley worried lest trouble in Bengal should cause difficulties for him in Parliament, at a time when he was steering through his Indian reform legislation.[14] In April 1906 Fuller arrested Surendranath Banerji, the most prominent *swadeshi* leader, when he and his supporters ignored a government warning to keep an anti-partition meeting orderly. Both Morley and Minto felt that Fuller had played into the agitators' hands, and they manoeuvred him into a position which led to his resignation in August 1906.[15] The *swadeshi* campaign continued as before, while the British administration was confused and disgruntled at the Lieutenant-Governor's treatment. Most importantly, Fuller's fall led the future governments in each province of partitioned Bengal to feel circumscribed in the measures at their disposal to curb the unrest, violent or otherwise.

The Department of Criminal Intelligence was unable to organize the unprepared local police, even though they looked to it for assistance, since the Government of India discouraged both its use of agents and its interference in the affairs of Local Governments.[16] However, in August 1907 the Home Department told the DCI to examine reports of *swadeshi* meetings furnished by the local police and administration.[17] In September 1907 Stevenson-Moore, the Director of Criminal Intelligence, submitted a report in which he represented the *swadeshi* boycotters as a much more serious force to be reckoned with than the Local Government had believed hitherto. He reported that while the anti-partition movement lacked a strong central organization, its recruits were drawn from a broad base in Bengali society and were by no means, as the demonstrations made it seem, entirely hot-headed youths. However, Stevenson-Moore shared the common British delusion that the 'non-martial' Bengali had no capacity for violence.[18] This stereotype of Bengali effeteness made it hard for the British to appreciate the seriousness of the impending revolutionary campaign.

Revolutionary activity in Bengal just predated the partition. In 1903 a young Bengali Hindu, Barindra Kumar Ghosh, tried to organize a terrorist group in Calcutta. He made real headway only after 1905. Appealing mainly to youths, he preached a powerful combination of political protest and religious exhortation.[19] Numerous gymnastic societies which existed in the two Bengals provided him with a ready-made base for a revoutionary organization.[20] Revolutionary ideas also caught hold in East Bengal and Assam, where Pulin Behari Das formed the *Anusilan Samiti* or 'Improvement Society' at Dacca, which was quickly ramified into over 500 branches in towns and villages. The *Anusilan Samiti* was at once a religious and political organization.[21]

The party of violence was able to spread its message through the 'extremist' press. Barindra Kumar Ghosh and his brilliant brother, Arabindo, established two of the most vitriolic and influential newspapers, *Yugantar* (New Era) and *Bande Mataram* (Hail Motherland). The Ghosh brothers planned with audacity and ambition. In 1907 Barindra sent a disciple named Hem Chandra Das to Paris to learn bomb-making, under the instruction of Russian revolutionary exiles.[22] It is noteworthy that the Bengali revolutionary movement had such foreign connections from an early date and drew moral support from the existence of the Indian revolutionary movement abroad.

The first serious terrorist act occurred on 6 December 1907 when a bomb derailed the Lieutenant-Governor of Bengal's train. The British were horrified when on 30 April 1908 two women, Mrs and Miss Kennedy, were murdered at Muzaffarpur by a terrorist who had mistaken their carriage for that of the local judge. The bomb had been made by Hem Chandra Das.

The CIDs of Bengal and Eastern Bengal and Assam came into existence simultaneously with the revolutionary movement which was to plague their existence. For many years they remained one step behind the revolutionaries and developed in response to events rather than in anticipation of them. The growth of the CIDs and Special Branches in Bengal and in Eastern Bengal and Assam followed a parallel course, though the two forces remained separate to such an extent that lack of co-operation hindered their efficiency.[23]

In Bengal proper by the end of 1908 the dividing line between ordinary and political crime had become clear and the work involved with the latter was entrusted to a 'Special Officer', first C.W.C. Plowden, then, after February 1909, F.C. Daly.[24] The Government of Bengal acknowledged that they knew little about the revolutionary organization except that it worked 'by very modern methods'. They believed that it was likely to 'gain influence by continually attracting sympathizers and recruits from among the large number of people who are now more or less neutral but would become actively hostile if they dared'. Sir Harold Stuart, the Secretary of the Home Department, foresaw, accurately, that 'the revolutionary movement will gain in influence and strength until, at no distant date, it will become a serious menace to to law and order'. The government concluded that while a 'revolutionary rising is out of the question', an efficient secret service was essential.[25] Thus finally, in September 1909, the Local Government formed an expert Political Crime Branch of the CID, or 'Special Department', which consisted of 23 officers and 45 men. This brought the strength of the whole provincial CID up to 75 officers and 744 constables.[26] At the same time the Government of India sanctioned Rs.227,000 (£15,133) for the introduction of police reforms during 1909–10 in the special and ordinary ranks of the Bengal Police.[27] Yet this remained a very limited attempt to solve the problem of the local police. The fight against the revolutionary movement continued to depend on the expertise of a few individuals. In 1908 there were one Deputy Superintendent, 52 Inspectors and Sub-Inspectors, and 722 Head Constables and Constables working on special political crime duty in various parts of Bengal. But this increase amounted basically to reallocation of the existing police force to new duties, rather than to the formation of a new, specialized force.[28] The activities of the Special Department were, moreover, concentrated in the cities. The increase of the CID was the first sign that political violence, though still on a small scale, had disrupted the administration of the province. By 1909 political work in some districts was proving a serious distraction for superintendents in charge of the regular police, while ordinary crime was increasing.

At the beginning of 1908 the (clerical) Special Branch was placed under Godfrey Denham, an Assistant Superintendent of Police. He worked under the direction of the 'Special Officer' in charge of the political work of the CID.[29] Denham was gifted with a photographic memory and could remember in detail the history of scores of cases.[30] He early distinguished himself by tracking down the Ghosh gang to their house at Manicktolla Gardens in Calcutta. It was serving as a bomb-factory and as a training centre for revolutionaries under the instruction of Hem Chandra Das. On 2 May 1908 Denham led police raids which resulted in the capture of 15 of the gang, including Barindra Kumar Ghosh and Hem Chandra Das.[31]

As a result of the Manicktolla conspiracy case the government of Bengal expanded its Special Branch to a strength of one officer and ten clerks.[32] This amounted to a belated recognition that the revolutionary movement was much stronger than had been estimated. Despite isolated terrorist acts, the government and the police only now acknowledged the existence of a revolutionary conspiracy distinct from the general background of anti-partition unrest. Even then they refused to admit that this 'extended beyond a comparatively low political stratum' of 'degenerate youths'.[33]

The government of Bengal's failure to stem the revolutionary movement in its infancy was repeated in Eastern Bengal and Assam, where the newly-created police force was unable to detect the early spread of revolutionary societies and thereafter unwilling to take them seriously enough. The Special Branch and the CID of East Bengal and Assam came into existence in May 1906. The Special Branch consisted of one Superintendent and five clerks,[34] while the CID had a staff of 28.[35] This strength proved wholly inadequate. By 1908 the temporary strength of the EBA CID had already increased to 39 Inspectors and 67 Constables, and the permanent strength of the CID had risen to one Superintendent, 25 Sub-Inspectors and 32 Constables and Head Constables.[36] But the constant growth of both political and ordinary crime obliged the Local Government in May 1909 to create a Political Branch of the CID, which had a strength of 28 officers and 63 men.[37] F. Brewester, a Superintendent, was put in charge.[38] It cost approximately £10,000 a year.[39] The strengths of the two branches of the CID fluctuated somewhat, but by 1910 the size of the whole EBA CID had risen to its maximum strength of two Superintendents, 51 Inspectors and Sub-Inspectors and 93 Head Constables and Constables, making a total of 147 men, excluding clerks and servants. This was not a large number given the size of the province, the difficulty of the terrain and the scale of the political problems. Moreover, as in western Bengal, much of the rapid expansion of the CID involved no more than assigning local police officers to political duties. They did not perform them well.

When the CIDs were established in 1906, no staff was provided for the conduct of political enquiries outside the cities. But the local police were poorly equipped for dealing with political crime. They were known locally and were 'too fully occupied with their ordinary work to supervise effectively the movements of political agitators or conspirators'.[40] Above all, the local police found political surveillance difficult to effect because they were frequently under the eye of an unsympathetic populace.[41] By 1907 the state of affairs in the hinterland or *mufassil* had become so serious that in both EBA and western Bengal the CID had to send in officers.[42] However, this arrangement did not work well either,[43] since officers from the cities were often shadowed by the revolutionaries from the moment of their arrival.[44]

The British did not trust native Bengali police officers to perform political surveillance. As early as September 1907 Robert Nathan, the Commissioner of Dacca, warned the Local Government that the *swadeshi* movement was putting a severe strain upon the loyalty of Hindu magistrates and police officers, many of whom belonged to the same families as the *swadeshi* agitators, with whom they had much sympathy.[45] British officers too were by no means wholly reliable for political work. According to Nathan, both British and Indian police officers often found spying repugnant.[46]

The pressures on the native police were particularly severe. The nationalist press subjected them to violent abuse. Even more demoralizing was the system of 'social boycott' which the extreme nationalists organized. The government of western Bengal found that police officers were not discouraged by personal danger so much as by the continual harassment which extended to every aspect of their private lives. Priests, washermen and barbers refused to serve them, while friends and relatives shunned them. Worst of all, they found it difficult to marry off their daughters.[47]

The police had great difficulty in recruiting spies and informers from among the local population. On several occasions the two Local Governments of Bengal turned down the central government's offers of extra secret service funds, because they were unable to spend them.[48] In August 1911 the EBA government reported that 'there has never been any difficulty about the secret service fund in the province. Our difficulty has been principally to find agents of a suitable type'.[49] Many spies were Hindus and sympathized with the *swadeshi* movement.[50] By the end of 1908 the EBA government realized that it was 'impossible to trust any but specially selected officers with the highly confidential enquiries that [were] constantly necessary'.[51]

In 1908 it was not the police but two Indian Civil Service officers, Robert Nathan, the Commissioner of the Dacca Police, and H.L. Salkeld, the District Collector, who uncovered the revolutionary *Anusilan Samiti* organization.[52] Nathan distrusted his own police and seems to have helped in enquiries mostly in a personal capacity. At the end of 1908 the Local Government entrusted Salkeld with a general investigation into the activities of the Dacca society.[53] He produced a four-volume report and placed 68 people under surveillance.[54] The ICS investigation continued into 1912. After his early death, from natural causes, Salkeld was succeeded in July 1909 by E.C. Stuart-Baker, another member of the ICS.[55]

After Salkeld's investigations the Local Government suppressed the Dacca *Anusilan Samiti*. But this had little effect, since the society did some of its most important work in the countryside, and about this the ICS and the police still knew little.[56] Moreover, the terrorists in both Bengal provinces had built a powerful organization modelled on that of the Russian revolutionary cells, which meant that discovery of a single branch did not undermine the whole. The leaders concealed their identity from all but their immediate subordinates, and the organization spread with a minimum of communication amongst members.[57] In fact, at the end of 1909, the police of Bengal and EBA could not say for certain whether the terrorist campaign had a centre or whether it was made up of independent groups.[58]

In 1908 political crime in western Bengal amounted to eight dacoities, seven attempted murders and bomb explosions, 11 murders and two conspiracy cases (at Alipore and Midnapore). At the end of 1908 the terrorists began a new phase of their campaign, aimed at assassinating police officers and their families, and intimidating the judiciary.[59] In Autumn 1908 they murdered a man who had turned King's evidence in the Alipore conspiracy case and a Sub-Inspector of the CID, Nanda Lal Banarji, who had arrested one of the murderers of Mrs and Miss Kennedy. On 10 February 1909 the Public Prosecutor who had acted in the Alipore case was shot dead. By the standards of terrorism in the late twentieth century and of violent crime in certain contemporary Western countries, such as Russia and the United States, the scale of terror in Bengal was not high. But it cannot be stressed too strongly that the British perceived the terrorist campaign and the unabated *swadeshi* agitation as a serious threat to their rule, which was founded upon relatively weak forces of order and upon the co-operation of Indian society. Any step to strengthen the former brought the danger of weakening the latter.[60]

By the beginning of 1910 the situation in both Bengal provinces threatened to become critical. The government of Bengal informed the central government:

> It is easy to produce a reign of terror in Bengal. A few instances of successful action by the terrorists would confirm the impression that there is everything to fear from them and nothing either to hope or to fear from the Government and would deprive us of all chance of assistance and support from the public.

> [A] very few successful assassinations would produce a more paralysing effect on the administration than perhaps in any part of India and the Government might easily be reduced into a condition of practical impotence.[61]

Just as seriously, the police were becoming demoralized. Junior officers frequently complained that nothing was done to protect them, while, thanks to the intimidation of juries, murderers were escaping scot-free.

The Viceroy's Council came to two conclusions: first, the detective police in India had not long been organized and lagged behind those of other countries, including Great Britain; second, they regretted that 'we have to deal with [terrorists] on lines that commend themselves to English sentiment and not on the lines that suggest themselves as natural to the people and police in this country'.[62] The Council did not realize that its conclusions were contradictory. The terrorist movement could only be broken decisively if the government was willing to run a serious risk of alienating Indian 'moderate' opinion, with possibly long-term results. The Government of India escaped from this dilemma by laying undue emphasis on the failure of the provincial CIDs. Sir Charles Cleveland defended their performance, stressing that conditions in India were different from those elsewhere.[63] Unlike the European anarchists with whom the Viceroy's Council made a facile comparison, Indian terrorists could count on the sympathy of a broad strata of the population.[64]

On 11 December 1908 the Government of India passed Criminal Law Amendment Act XIV, which provided that certain offences might be tried without jury. However, it was impractical to use this act on a large scale for fear of alienating both Indian and British public opinion, and its application was restricted to the prosecution of proven terrorists. The most obvious remedy for the terrorist problem was the deportation of suspects. Yet, as the deportation from the Punjab in 1907 of two prominent agitators, Lala Lajpat Rai and Ajit Singh, had shown, this was certain to cause a storm in Parliament and to meet opposition from the India Office.[65] None the less, in January 1910 the government of Bengal pressed the Government of India for permission to deport Noni Gopal Sen Gupta, who was a proven terrorist though he had not been caught in the act. The Government of India replied that it did not wish to give the impression that it regarded deportation 'as a proper and permissible substitute for good police administration'.[66]

Just as much as they feared the wrath of Parliament, so the central and local governments were loath to take any steps which might alienate Indian moderate opinion. The ICS in EBA opposed the increased use of ordinary police even in the districts most troubled by the *swadeshi* movement, because

> The constant imposition of additional police at the expense of the people would soon become a weapon in the hands of the agitators, who would represent it to the masses as the action of an oppressive Government.[67]

The government was distressed at the lack of public support which it obtained in its struggle with terrorism. It was particularly alarmed that the nationalist press constantly complained about police methods, though it never condemned the terrorists.[68] In February 1910 the government of Bengal stated:

> The general public practically never takes any positive attitude unless vigorously worked upon and readily submits to any show of force. Throughout the history of the movement extremely little information has been obtained from voluntary sources; the great bulk of it has come either from informers or from persons who have been arrested and prosecuted for offences against the law, by far the greater part from the latter.[69]

Before the war the government's unwillingness to risk alienating Indian 'moderates' hindered even the effective exercise of police surveillance. In 1912 one Krishna Kumar Mitra complained to Lord

110

Crewe, the Secretary of State for India, about the watch the police of Bengal were keeping on his son, Sukumar.[70] Crewe took this criticism seriously, and the Local Government felt obliged to explain its action, even though Sukumar had been a member of the *Yugantar* gang.[71]

Yet the police proved much more effective than either the provincial or the central governments had expected. In 1910 the police of western Bengal successfully brought 50 revolutionaries to trial under the Criminal Law Amendment Act. This put a stop to *bhadralok* dacoities in the area around Calcutta, though not in the city itself until 1914. At the same time the police of EBA brought 44 terrorists to trial in the Dacca conspiracy case, though this had little effect in reducing political crime.

The terrorist campaign against the judiciary and the police continued. On 24 January 1910 Deputy Superintendent Shamsul Alam was murdered while assisting in the Alipore bomb case. In 1911 Sub-Inspector Rajkumar was shot at Mymensingh; and Inspector Man Mohan Ghosh was murdered at Barisal – he had been 'conspicuously active in various political enquiries and had appeared as a witness in the Dacca conspiracy case'. On 21 February 1911 Head Constable Srish Chandra Chakrabarti, attached to the CID, was shot dead in Calcutta. On 2 March 1911 a bomb was thrown into the car of an Englishman named Cowley, whom the assassin had mistaken for Godfrey Denham, the head of the Special Branch.

In 1911 King George V was to visit India with the object of bringing about reconciliation. The success of his visit depended to a considerable extent on the ability of the Bengal police to preserve law and order. Its effect would be greatly reduced if the terrorist party could increase the level of violence in Bengal, or assassinate a prominent political figure.

In December 1910 the specialization of the political section of the police in EBA was increased with the appointment of a Special Officer to assist the Deputy Inspector-General in charge of the CID.[72] This led to an improvement in co-ordination of police activities and greater professionalism.[73] However, in the middle of 1911 the government felt that it still did not have 'a reasonable police force at its disposal'.[74] Early in the year it formed a special force of one Sub-Inspector, and 397 Head Constables and Constables, which would be able to keep every suspected terrorist under constant surveillance during the royal visit.[75] Like previous measures to improve the control of political crime, this involved weakening the ordinary police. A large number of

111

officers were called in from the districts to carry out surveillance in Dacca.[76] The Government of India cricitized the crudeness of the EBA government's security measures, pointing out the difficulties of keeping 226 suspects under surveillance with the force proposed.[77]

At the same time the Local Government began a drive to improve the efficiency of the ordinary police. The rivers were better patrolled.[78] Some improvements were made in arming of the police. In July 1911 it reintroduced the 'circle system' which restored police local control of the villages.[79] It also took measures to improve the performance of senior officers.[80] The reforms still did not get to the root of the problem – the low pay of the police force and local sympathy for or fear of the 'extremists'.

The government of western Bengal made similar plans to defend the royal visitors by the heavy surveillance of all suspected terrorists.[81] The Local Government approved a 120-man special surveillance section for Calcutta and a 361-strong unit for the hinterland. At the same time it alloted a surveillance force of 68 policemen to Chandernagore. Nineteen Constables and Head Constables were sent into French territory, taking up various trades as a cover. The remainder were placed around the French enclave in order to shadow any suspect crossing into British India.[82]

The surveillance scheme was a great success. There was only one terrorist outrage in Bengal in December when a policeman was murdered. Most importantly this showed what could be achieved if Indian opinion was disregarded. But there was no question of the scheme being extended beyond the duration of the royal visit. For one thing, neither the Government of India nor the Local Government would risk antagonizing their Indian subjects, and for another 'the scheme provided so drastic and expensive a system of surveillance as could not be maintained except in very special circumstances and for a very limited time practically confined to the period of the royal visit'.[83] The expenses came to Rs.8,343 for Calcutta and Rs.34,814 for the *mufassil* and Chandernagore.

Cleveland noted that there had been little Indian opposition to the security measures. He attributed this to the wholehearted public support which the Local Government, for the first time since Fuller's resignation, had given to its police.[84]

However, the success of the police during the royal visit can be exaggerated. It turned out that though the police had been able to prevent violence, they still did not know of the whereabouts of some of the most important suspects. Worst of all, they had no idea that the most dangerous revolutionary in India, Rash Behari Bose, was working quietly in the forestry department at Dehra Dun.

At the Delhi Durbar in December 1911, King George V announced the reunification of Bengal. As a result, the CIDs of Bengal and EBA were merged. The Local Government felt optimistic about the future, but it was not complacent. The cuts which were introduced in the staff of the political police throughout India were the least marked in Bengal. The Calcutta Special Branch was reduced by the removal of eight Head Constables and three Constables, while the government of Bengal did not replace its Head when he went on leave in January 1912. The Government of India thought the retrenchments excessive.[85] But talk of reducing the political police in Bengal was largely academic. The renewal of terrorism in 1912 did not take the government entirely unawares, though it had not expected that it would reappear on the same scale as in the past.

Though still restricted in its powers of arrest, the political police in Bengal were now established as an essential element of the administration. The government of Bengal informed the Home Department in June 1912 that no 'responsible government' could afford to be without some means of collecting and co-ordinating the information which it received from its own officers, from other provinces and from abroad. It concluded that 'the nucleus of the special departments must be permanent'.[86]

By mid-1912 the Local Government looked at the political situation in post-partition Bengal with concern. In an appraisal sent to the Government of India it remarked that Calcutta was the centre from which terrorist schemes emanated; Chandernagore remained an ever-present source of danger; while the *bhadralok* were still committing dacoities in eastern Bengal.[87]

The police continued to score successes over individual terrorist gangs. On 28 November 1912 they found a collection of weapons and revolutionary documents in a box belonging to Girindra Mohan Das. Girindra's father, who was a magistrate, induced him to become an informer. As a result the police greatly increased their knowledge of the Dacca *Anusilan Samiti*, and 26 were put on trial in the Barisal conspiracy case. But, on the other hand, the terrorist movement was now well-established and had no shortage of recruits to make good its losses. Moreover, in 1912 the weaponry of the revolutionaries improved as they began to use powerful picric acid bombs.

By 1913 the terrorists were acting more audaciously than ever. In that year two police officers were murdered,[88] while a series of successful robberies increased revolutionary funds. In that year the enquiry into the Delhi bomb plot took place. This 'outrage', coupled with the increased ferocity of the terrorist groups in Bengal, awakened the local police and the DCI to the full scale of the danger that was looming in the province. At this time the police and the Government of India came to view the French enclave of Chandernagore as a grave threat to the security of Bengal.

In December 1913 the Political Branch of the Bengal CID was renamed the Intelligence Branch (IB). It numbered 50 officers and 127 men. It was divided into four sections: a 100-strong headquarters staff also carried out miscellaneous enquiries and acted as reserve; 34 men staffed the *dakaiti* section; 22 were in the bomb and explosive section; and 20 in the assassination section.[89] Two senior officers led the IB: Superintendent Sneyd-Hutchinson dealt with the Eastern Provinces and the hinterland of Calcutta, while Deputy Commissioner Tegart dealt mainly with enquiries in Calcutta and its neighbourhood.[90] At the same time the Calcutta CID continued its independent existence.

At this time effective political police work depended heavily on strong leadership. In this sense the appointment of Charles Augustus Tegart proved to be of considerable importance. Tegart is probably the most famous of all the officers of the Indian Police. He was the son of an Irish Protestant clergyman from County Meath. After leaving Trinity College, Dublin, he joined the Indian Police in 1901. By 1906 he had attained the rank of Deputy Commissioner in the Calcutta police, where he was in charge of the CID. He worked closely with Denham during the investigations into the Manicktolla conspiracy.

Tegart was a charismatic leader of outstanding courage. During the height of the terrorist campaign during the First World War he indulged a passion for automobiles by driving around the city freely, accompanied only by his Staffordshire bull terrier. He was particularly skilful at building up a network of agents and informers, who were the most important sources of information available to the police. His friend Petrie wrote after his death:

> The proper use of agents is one of the hardest and most difficult tasks an intelligence officer can undertake, and it is only the ablest and most experienced that are likely to do it to full advantage. Bad and unreliable agents can be far worse than none at all . . .

There was no one more alive to this danger than Tegart and his pains to cross-check all that was brought to him were unremitting.[91]

Tegart met agents himself, often at night. Some were known only to him. He also operated as a secret agent in his own right. In the words of his wife:

Tegart never once disguised himself as a Bengali. His features were strongly marked, he was tall and muscular, his eyes were dark blue and his tan had a warm, reddish tinge. Whatever aids might be brought to disguise him he could not appear other than a remarkable Bengali. At night, wearing a beard and puggaree [a light turban], he could pass as a Sikh taxi-driver, but even in the daytime he could go unnoticed as a Kabuli or Pathan. These men from the North are tall, there is often a warmish tinge in their cheeks and their noses are prominent and sometimes hawk-like; Tegart's nose was also well-defined with a touch of aquiline in its shape. He and Mr F.G. Lowman, an officer of the Special Branch, used a Pathan disguise on more than one occasion when they wished to watch the movements of certain suspects or check a report given them by a source.

Tegart's first duty in his new job was to assist Denham and Petrie with their enquiries into the connection between Chandernagore and the terrorist group which had committed the Delhi bomb outrage. They set 'private informers' and 'French informers' to work in French territories. The enquiries showed that the terrorists had planned bomb plots and murders from Chandernagore and produced conclusive evidence that the first of the series of picric acid bombs had been in Chandernagore.[92] The IB and the Home Department concluded that after the exposure of the Manicktolla Garden conspiracy in Calcutta in 1908, Chandernagore became the main centre of the terrorist party.[93] It was also the main source from which Bengali revolutionaries acquired arms in the period up to August 1914.

Chandernagore had a population of 26–30,000. There were few French officials and they were underpaid. Except for the Brigadier of Police, whose pay was scarcely larger than that of a Deputy Superintendent in British India, there was not a single European in the police service. The French officials had very little authority over their Indian subjects. When the Mayor of Chandernagore, M. Tardivel, tried to deal firmly with the revolutionary party in 1908 they attempted to blow him up. According to Tegart those officials who were not intimidated by the terrorists were in their pay.[94]

The climate in Chandernagore thus favoured the terrorists. The population returned an extreme socialist member to the French Chamber of Deputies. From 1913 onwards the Government of India, which took the problem of Chandernagore very seriously, ran into great difficulties in negotiations for a political solution to the problem. The British wanted to annexe Chandernagore in exchange for British territory, preferably around the French enclave of Pondicherry in the south of India. But the Government of India found the French unco-operative. The exchange of Chandernagore would be fiercely resisted by the local population, and no French government was willing to face the storm which this would cause in the Chamber of Deputies. More-over, the French felt great pride in the two tiny remnants of their Indian empire and were unwilling to part with either of them. Indeed, in their dealings with British complaints, the French conducted them-selves as a power of equal status in India.[95]

The Home Department debated various solutions to the problem but found none satisfactory. All that could be done was to improve its sources of intelligence within Chandernagore. The watchers whom the French grudgingly allowed to enter Chandernagore and Pondi-cherry at the time of the royal visit stayed put.[96]

By the eve of the First World War the Government of India had managed to hold the terrorist movement in check in Bengal, and had been able to do so without taking harsh action which might alienate moderate opinion both in Bengal and elsewhere in India. But they had failed to eradicate any of the root causes of terrorism, such as the asylum offered by Chandernagore, the poor quality of the lower ranks of the police or the sympathy felt by juries with young revolutionaries. Nor had had they been able seriously to damage the terrorists' organi-zation. Moreover, even the limited success which had been achieved had put the Bengal police under great strain. This pressure was greatly to increase with the coming of the war.

NOTES

1. Quoted in *Terrorism in India*, a speech delivered before the Royal Empire Society in 1932 by Sir Charles Tegart.
2. See the comments of the Bengal District Administration Committee of 1913–14, quoted

in the Rowlatt Report, Ch. 2, *The Beginnings of the Revolutionary Movement in Bengal*, para. 26.

3. Ibid.

4. Additions to the CID and Special Branch accounted for only a tiny fraction of this increase. The Mymensingh Division had an area of 2,649 square miles and a population of over four million. Cited by J.H. Kerr, Chief Secretary to the Government of Bengal, in a letter to the Home Department, dated April 1917. In *Sanction to an increase to the District Intelligence Staff in Bengal for a period of one year*, IOLR HD/Pol: July 1917, nos. 132–3, P/10136.

5. From Craddock to Carmichael, 28 June 1915, CUL Hardinge Papers, Vol. 65; India, Original Letters, IXii, pp. 422–6.

6. Sir Algernon Rumbold, *Watershed in India 1914–1922*, (London: Athlone Press, 1979), p. 15.

7. Note signed B.N. Mitra, H.G. Stokes, G.F. Wilson, dated 25 May 1911, in 'Increase in Police in Eastern Bengal and Assam for the Surveillance of Political Suspects', HDA: May 1911, nos. 93–5, IOLR IOR.POS.6048. The chaukidars were proverbial for the neglect of their watch duties. See paragraph 11 of letter from R.B. Hughes-Buller, Inspector-General of Police, Eastern Bengal and Assam, to the Secretary to the Government of Eastern Bengal and Assam, Revenue and General Department, dated 1 June 1911, in *Conference at Simla with certain officers from Eastern Bengal and Assam on the subject of the prevention of political crime in that province*, HDA: Sept. 1911, nos. 126–7, IOLR IOR.POS.6048.

8. Sir Edward Henry, a former Inspector-General of the Bengal Police claimed that after the reforms of the Police Commission, the British attempted 'the impossible task of governing Bengal without a reasonable and necessary amount of information'. Demi-official letter from Cleveland to Wheeler, dated London, 12 September 1913, in *Suggestion that the aid of Scotland Yard or French detectives be invoked . . . to strengthen the detective side of the Indian police administration*, HDD: Nov. 1914, no. 33, IOLR IOR. POS.10612.

9. Letter from F.W. Duke, officiating Chief Secretary to the government of Bengal, to the Secretary to the Government of India, Home Department, dated 30 July 1909, in HD/Pol: Sept. 1909, nos. 37–8. IOLR P/8167. A.V. Knyvett, a Deputy Inspector-General of Police was placed on special duty in connection with railways and crime. In mid-1906 he was succeeded by C.W.C. Plowden. At the end of 1908 Plowden was ordered to supervise some political trials, and was replaced by F.C. Daly in his special functions.

10. The exact figures were: three senior officers, 36 Inspectors and Sub-Inspectors, and 31 Head Constables and Constables. 'Statement showing the number of men employed in the Criminal Investigation Department and Special Department in Bengal and their cost', in *Question in Council by the Hon'ble Mr Gokhale regarding the strength and cost of the provincial Criminal Investigation Departments*, HD/Pol: Oct. 1911, nos. 66–9. IOLR P/8712.

11. More precisely, the Calcutta CID consisted of one Superintendent in charge, 12 Inspectors and Sub-Inspectors, and 48 Head Constables and Constables. *Statement showing the cost actually incurred on account of Criminal Intelligence Department from April 1908 to December 1910*, ibid.

12. The breakdown of the CID's strength was: one Deputy Superintendent, eight Inspectors and Sub-Inspectors, 45 Head Constables and Constables and clerical establishment of five. Letter from C.J. Stevenson-Moore, Chief Secretary to the Government of Bengal, Political Department to the Secretary to the Government of India, Home Department, in *Continuance of the Special Branch of the Calcutta Police and of the five Sub-Inspectors previously sanctioned for political crime work up to 30 June 1912*, HD/Pol: May 1912, no. 97, IOLR P/8956.

13. Minto to Morley, 29 March 1906, Morley Papers, IOLR MSS.EUR.D.573/7.
14. Morley to Minto, Vol.I, 19 April 1906, Morley Papers IOLR MSS.EUR.D.573/8.
15. M.N. Das, *India Under Morley and Minto* (London: George Allen & Unwin, 1964), pp. 36–41.
16. Note by R. Nathan, dated 12 June 1907; and note by C.J. Stevenson-Moore, dated 3 July 1907, HDD: July 1907, op. cit.
17. The DCI's brief was to prove that, contrary to the claim of some 'agitators', the aims of the *Swadeshi* movement were political, not just economic. *Note by the Director of Criminal Intelligence on the origin and character of the 'Swadeshi' movement*, HDD: Oct. 1907, no. 18, IOLR IOR.POS.10608.
18. He reported that while Bengali physical education societies provided organizational bases for the *Swadeshi* movement their role should not be exaggerated. He said that the 'martial races' of the Punjab did 'not require to be trained in those pursuits which beget manliness'. *Memorandum on the National Volunteer Movement in the Provinces of Bengal and Eastern Bengal and Assam*, by C.J. Stevenson-Moore, 11 Sept. 1907, HDD: Oct. 1907, no. 19, IOLR IOR.POS.10608.
19. J.C. Kerr wrote: 'The main doctrine of the Samiti was revolution on a religious basis, the English being the demons who were to be driven out of the country by the gods with the help of the incarnation of Kali. Political assassinations were looked upon as a sacrifice to Kali'. 'Notes in the Criminal Intelligence Office', signed J.C. Ker, dated 28 July 1909, in *Report by Mr H.L. Salkeld, ICS, regarding the proceedings of the 'Anusilan Samiti' in Dacca*, HDD: Aug. 1909, no. 21, IOLR IOR.POS.10609.
20. For the Bengali gymnastic societies, see John Rosselli, 'The Self-Image of Effeteness', in *Past & Present*, No. 86 (Feb. 1980).
21. Conditions in the two Bengals differed. Sir Harold Stuart wrote in October 1908 that: 'conditions in the two Bengals are not altogether similar . . . while sedition in Bengal is largely concentrated at Calcutta, in Eastern Bengal and Assam it is more scattered throughout the districts'. Letter from Sir Harold Stuart, Secretary to the Government of India, Home Department, to the Chief Secretary to the Government of Eastern Bengal and Assam, in *Scheme for the formation of a political branch of the police force in Eastern Bengal and Assam*, HD/Pol: March 1909, IOLR P/8166.
22. James Campbell Ker, *Political Trouble in India 1907–1917*, edited by Mahadevaprasad Saha (Calcutta: Editions Indian, 1973), pp. 130–31.
23. In August 1911 the government of Eastern Bengal reported that: 'we find greatest difficulty in getting information from the Calcutta police'. Note on the questions raised by the Government of India in Mr Earle's note of 10 June, by R.H. Hughes-Buller, op. cit.
24. HD/Pol: Sept. 1909, nos. 37–8. IOLR, P/8167.
25. Letter from the Government of India, Finance Department, to the Secretary of State, dated 27 Jan. 1910, in *Reorganization of the Special Branch of the office of the Inspector-General of Police, Bengal, and the formation of a department to deal with political crime*, HD/Pol: Jan. 1910, no. 181.
26. The exact make-up of the Special Department was: one Deputy Superintendent, one Assistant to the Deputy Inspector-General, 21 Inspectors and Sub-Inspectors, and 53 Head Constables and Constables. Letter from F.W. Duke, dated 30 July 1909, HD/Pol: Sept. 1909, IOLR P/8167, op. cit. 'Bengal Special Department' in *Question in Council by the Hon'ble Mr Gokhale Regarding the Strength and Cost of the Provincial CIDs*, op. cit. As of September 1909, the Political Branch and the Special Branch were lodged at 7 Kyd Street, Calcutta. The former residence, 41 Park Street, had proved too public. It remained at Kyd Street until 1 January 1917, when it moved to Elysium Row. Letter from J.H. Kerr, Chief Secretary to the Government of Bengal, to the Secretary to the Government of India, Home Department, dated 21 July 1917, in *Grant of a house allowance of Rs.150 a month to the Deputy Commissioner of Police in charge of*

Special Branch, Calcutta, with effect from 1 January 1917, until free quarters are provided for him, HD/Pol: Aug. 1917, nos. 79–80.

27. No. 21 of 1910. From Government of India, Finance Department, to the Secretary of State, dated 27 Jan. 1910: Schedule C, *Estimate of expenditure of Rs.227,000 sanctioned for the introduction of police reforms during 1909–1910 in the Bengal Police*, J&P 470/10 in IOLR L/PJ/6/987.

28. Letter from F.W. Duke, dated 30 July, op. cit. HD/Pol: Sept. 1909, nos. 37–9, IOLR P/8167.

29. Letter from F.W. Duke, Officiating Chief Secretary to the Government of Bengal, to the Secretary to the Government of India, Home Department, in *Extension of the period of deputation of Mr Denham to hold charge of the Political of the office of the Inspector-General of Police*, Bengal, HD/Pol: March 1909, IOLR P/8166.

30. Denham was also known for his ability to recite the minutest details of railway time-tables. Mentioned in *Charles Tegart, Memoir of an Indian Policeman*, by K.F. Tegart, Vol. I, Ch. 2, p. 15, IOLR MSS.EUR.C.235/1.

31. Tegart Papers, op. cit., Ch. 7, 'The Growth of Terrorism'.

32. Two of the ten clerks were temporary. The Government of Bengal wrote that: 'Both [Daly and Denham], and especially the latter, have accumulated a great mass of knowledge about the conspirators and the secret societies in Bengal. Some of it is contained in rough notes and diaries, and in disconnected items in reports and statements of witnesses. It is of the utmost importance that this information should be classified and recorded as early as possible'.

33. Letter from F.W. Duke, Chief Secretary to the Government of Bengal, to the Secretary to the Government of India, Home Department, dated 1 February 1910, *Proposals for putting an end to the revolutionary activity in Bengal*, in HDA: March 1910, nos. 33–40, IOLR, IOR.POS.5947.

34. The Personal Assistant to the 'Deputy Inspector-General in charge, Crime, Rivers and Railways' controlled both the Special Branch and the CID. The work of both was seriously hampered in the early stages of the fight with the revolutionaries by the Inspector-General of Eastern Bengal and Assam, Bonham-Carter, who complained that the Deputy Inspector-General, Crime, Rivers and Railways was attaching too much importance to Special Branch work to the detriment of the ordinary work of the police. Memorandum entitled 'For Simla Conference. Delegation of powers', by H. Le Mesurier, dated 29 August 1911, in *Conference with certain officers from Eastern Bengal and Assam on the subject of the prevention of political crime in that province*, HDA: Sept. 1911, nos. 126–7, IOLR IOR.POS.6048.

35. The breakdown was: one Deputy Inspector-General, 12 Inspectors and Sub-Inspectors and 15 Head Constables and Constables. 'Statement Showing the Strength and Cost of Officers and Men of Criminal Investigation Department, Eastern Bengal and Assam, Since its Constitution in 1906' in HD/Pol: Oct. 1911, nos. 66–9 in IOLR P/8712.

36. Letter from H. Le Mesurier, Officiating Chief Secretary to the Government of Eastern Bengal and Assam, the Secretary to the Government of India, Home Department, dated 31 October 1908, *Scheme for the formation of a political branch of the police force in Eastern Bengal and Assam*, HD/Pol: March 1909, no. 37. IOLR P/8166.

37. The details were: one Superintendent, one Deputy Superintendent, 26 Inspectors and Sub-Inspectors, 55 Constables , two Clerks and six servants. Letter from R. Nathan, Officiating Secretary to the Government of Eastern Bengal and Assam, to the Secretary to the Government of India, Home Department, dated 19 August 1910, in *Further retention up to the 31st March 1912 of the temporary staff for the Political Branch of the Criminal Investigation Department in Eastern Bengal and Assam*, HD/Pol: Oct. 1910, nos. 78–80, IOLR P/8447.

38. Letter from H. LeMesurier, Chief Secretary to the Government of Eastern Bengal and

Assam, to the Secretary to the Government of India, Home Department, dated January 1910, in *Extension of the period of deputation of Mr Brewester to hold charge of the office of the Political Branch of the Police Force in Eastern Bengal and Assam for a further period of six months*, from 28 Oct. 1909, HD/Pol: Jan. 1910, no. 2, IOLR P/8446.

39. Letter from H. LeMesurier, Officiating Chief Secretary to the Government of Eastern Bengal and Assam, to the Secretary to the Government of India, Home Department, dated 31 October 1908, in *Scheme for the formation of a political branch of the police force in Eastern Bengal and Assam*, HD/Pol: March 1909, no. 37, IOLR P/8166. Bonham-Carter, the Inspector-General, noted: 'The original intention was to create a further post of Deputy Inspector-General for political crime as was done in Bengal, but eventually it was decided to give this idea up, because I believed importance was attached to keeping at the head of the department the connection between ordinary and political crime and to the avoidance of any tendency to form two separate and possibly mutually jealous services in the Police'. Memorandum entitled 'For Simla Conference. Delegation of powers', by H. LeMesurier, op. cit.

40. Letter from H. LeMesurier, dated 31 Oct. 1908, op. cit.

41. Mr Hart, the Superintendent of Police, Backarganj, wrote in his Diary on 9 June 1907: 'I think very few of the local police are reliable, while they are really all known and closely watched'.

42. It was the policy of the government of Eastern Bengal and Assam to get District Officers to co-operate in dealing with political crime. On the other hand, the government of 'West' Bengal complained that: 'District Officers do not give much assistance in respect of the detection of criminal organizations or of reporting the general state of feeling in their districts'. Memorandum by R.B. Hughes-Buller, entitled 'Note on the questions raised by the Government of India in Mr Earle's note of 10 June', op. cit.

43. Letter from J.H. Kerr, Officiating Chief Secretary to the Government of Bengal, to the Secretary to the Government of India, dated 13 March 1917, in *Sanction to an increase in the District Intelligence Staff in Bengal for a period of one year*, HD/Pol: July 1917, nos. 132–6, IOLR P/10136.

44. Letter from F.W. Duke to the Secretary to the Government of India, Home Department, dated 30 July 1909, op. cit.

45. Letter from R. Nathan, Officiating chief Commissioner of the Dacca Division, to the Chief Secretary to the Government of Eastern Bengal and Assam, 17 September 1907, in *Proposals to combat the seditious movement in Eastern Bengal and Assam*, HDA: Nov. 1907, no. 12, IOLR IOR.POS.5942. Note by R. Nathan, 12 June 1907, in *Proposed Deputation of a few good selected officers to conduct confidential enquiries in the Barisal District with reference to the suspected communication through medium of Calcutta between the agitators of Barisal and those of the Punjab*, HDD: July 1907, no. 67, IOLR IOR.POS.10608.

46. Hughes-Buller, the District Magistrate of Backarganj had at his disposal a Special Branch Inspector with ten men under him. However, the men disliked the 'work of spying' and the results of surveillance were not as good as they might have been had they had their hearts in the job. Letter from R. Hughes-Buller, District Magistrate at Backarganj, to the Commissioner of the Dacca Division, dated 31 August 1907, in *Proposals to combat the seditious movement in Eastern Bengal and Assam*, HDA: Nov. 1907, no. 12, IOLR IOR.POS.5942.

47. Letter from F.W. Duke, Officiating Chief Secretary to the government of Bengal, to the Secretary to the Government of India, Home Department, 30 July 1909, op. cit.

48. Letter from C.R. Cleveland to the government of Bengal, 15 March 1910, in *Proposed Deportation of Noni Gopal Sen Gupta, Head of a Dacoiti Gang. Proposed Improvement of the Criminal Investigation Department*. IOLR HDA: April 1910, nos. 59–62 in IOR.POS.5947. Secret Service money was controlled by Superintendents of Police. It

was mainly spent on the salary of and rewards for informers. The government of Bengal advised that 'agents should be treated liberally but not extravagantly'. *Draft rules regarding the expenditure of Secret Service money in Bengal*, IOLR HD/Pol: Jan. 1913, nos. 98–9, IOLR P/8957.

49. Memorandum entitled 'Note on the questions raised by the Government of India in Mr Earle's note of 10 June and in postscript to the note of 13 June, together with certain suggestions put forward by this Department for matters to be considered by India', by R.B. Hughes-Buller, Inspector-General of Police, Eastern Bengal and Assam, HDA: Sept. 1911, nos. 126–7, op. cit.

50. Diary for the week ending 8 June 1907, by R.B. Hughes-Buller, HDD: July 1907, no. 67, op. cit.

51. Letter from H. LeMesurier, dated 31 Oct. 1908, op. cit.

52. Memorandum entitled 'For Simla Conference. Delegation of powers', by H. LeMesurier, 29 Aug. 1911, op. cit.

53. Letter from P.C. Lyon, Secretary to the government of Eastern Bengal and Assam, to the Secretary to the Government of India, Home Department, in *Extension of the deputation of Mr H.L. Salkeld, ICS, to work up the case against the Anushilan Samiti of Dacca*, HDB: Aug. 1909, nos. 14–15, IOLR IOR.POS.8962.

54. Demi-official letter from H. LeMesurier to A. Earle, dated 26 June 1911, in *Scheme for the surveillance of political suspects in Eastern Bengal and Assam*, HDD: Aug. 1911, no. 13, IOLR IOR.POS.10611. *Report by Mr H.L. Salkeld, ICS, regarding the proceedings of the Anushilan Samiti in Dacca*, HDD: Aug. 1909, no. 21, IOLR IOR.POS.10609.

55. Letter from H. LeMesurier, Chief Secretary to the government of Eastern Bengal and Assam, to the Secretary to the Government of India, Home Department, dated 13 October 1909, in *Deputation of Messrs. Stuart Baker and Veitch to work up the case against the Anushilan Samiti*, HDB: Nov. 1909, nos. 93–/4, IOLR IOR.POS.8963. *Extension of the deputation of Mr E.C. Stuart Baker on special duty for a further period of six months from 16 April 1910*, HDB: July 1910, no. 53, IOLR IOR.POS.8964. *Extension of the deputation of Mr E.C. Stuart Baker in connection with the Dacca Conspiracy Case*, HDB: Aug. 1911, nos. 111–19, IOLR IOR.POS.8971.

56. Letter from P.C. Lyon, to the Secretary to the Government of India, Home Department, op. cit. Notes in the Criminal Intelligence Office by J.C. Ker, 28 July 1909, *Report by Mr H.L. Salkeld, ICS, regarding the proceedings of the Anushilan Samiti in Dacca*, HDD: Aug. 1909, no. 21, IOLR IOR.POS.10609.

57. Letter from F.W. Duke, Chief Secretary to the government of Bengal, to the Secretary to the Government of India, Home Department, 14 December 1909, HD/Pol: Jan. 1910, no. 181, IOLR P/8446, op. cit.

58. Sir Harold Stuart wrote in December 1909: 'We are at present very much in the dark about the constitution, strength and doings of the physical force party. We know nothing of their organizations, we do not know who the leaders are; and we do not know what funds they have or where their money comes from'. Note by H.A. Stuart, 31 December 1909, in *Increased activity that is visible among the National Volunteers of Calcutta. Legislation for the purpose of securing a greater degree of control over the press*, HDA: July 1910, nos. 5–32, IOLR IOR.POS.5962.

59. Ibid.

60. Note by G. Fell, 10 Oct. 1907, op. cit. Already in September 1907, Robert Nathan complained that all his District Officers were 'absorbed in questions relating to the suppression of sedition and the maintenance of the peace', and that it was 'impossible for them to give anything like adequate attention to the ordinary work of their Districts'. In August 1907 the government of Eastern Bengal and Assam reported: 'We run our administration on a dangerously narrow margin of officers. Most responsible officers are overworked more or less in ordinary times. When abnormal conditions prevail, as

at present, the machine is bound to break down'.

61. Letter from F.W. Duke to the Secretary to the Government of India, Home Department, 1 Feb. 1910, op. cit.
62. Ibid.
63. As a sign of its lack of confidence in the police, the Government of India had sent Cleveland to examine the records of the police in Bengal and EBA. *Deputation of Mr C.R. Cleveland on special duty to examine the information collected in Bengal and Eastern Bengal and Assam regarding the revolutionary movement*, HDB: Jan. 1910, nos. 114–21, IOLR IOR.POS.8963.
64. Ibid. Letter from C.R. Cleveland, Officiating Director of Criminal Intelligence, to the Government of Bengal, 15 March 1910.
65. Letter from the Government of Bengal, dated 1 February 1910, HDA: March 1910, nos. 33–40, IOLR IOR.POS.5947. Fear of Parliamentary opposition to too strong a police action hampered the government of Eastern Bengal and Assam. In 1907 the Local Government singled out Aswini Kumar as a nationalist rabble-rouser. However, Aswini Kumar had made a good impression on the Labour MP Keir Hardie who toured India that year, and the Local Government was afraid of taking any 'step which would certainly be challenged in Parliament'. Note by H.H. Risley, 24 Oct. 1907, HDA: Nov. 1907, no. 12, IOLR IOR.POS.5942, op. cit.
66. Note by the Home Department on Letter from the Government of India, no. 91-P, dated 8 January 1910, recommending the deportation of Noni Gopal Sen Gupta, HDA: April 1910, nos. 59–62, op. cit.
67. Letter from R.B. Hughes-Buller, District Magistrate at Backarganj, to the Commissioner of the Dacca Division, 31 Aug. 1907, op. cit.
68. On 9 June 1909 the *Amrita Bazaar Patrika* wrote: 'The state of panic prevailing in Dacca on account of the open and secret doings of the police is the talk of the two Bengals just now. The official disclaimer as to the system of espionage being regularly followed in the town has not improved matters in the least. For everyone feels the vague dread of being shadowed and watched ceaselessly. No greater torture can be conceived than being a prey to such a shadowy fear'. This was written just after the house of the brother of an informer had been blown up, killing the owner, though not the informer. HDB: Aug. 1909, nos. 21–2, IOLR IOR.POS.8962. *Enquiry regarding a visit paid to Babu Rajani Kanta Gupta by the District Superintendent of Police, Dacca, in company with an informer on the night of 4 June 1909*.
69. Letter from the government of Bengal, 1 Feb. 1910, HDA: March 1910, nos. 33–40, IOLR IOR.POS.5947, op. cit.
70. Letter from Babu Sukumar Mittar, 15 February 1912, in *Surveillance exercised over Babui Sukumar Mitter*, HDB: May 1912, nos. 26–7, IOLR IOR.POS.9831.
71. Letter from C.J. Stevenson-Moore, Chief Secretary to the government of Bengal, to the Secretary to the Government of India, Home Department, 16 Jan. 1912, in *Complaint made to Mr Montagu regarding the surveillance alleged to be exercised over Babu K.K. Mitra and his son*, HDB: Feb. 1912, nos. 19–22, IOLR IOR.POS.9830.
72. W.M.C. Dundas was the first to hold this office. He was succeeded by Superintent Sneyd-Hutchinson at the end of 1911.
73. Letter from J.F. Gruning, Secretary to the government of Eastern Bengal and Assam, Revenue and General Department, to the Secretary to the Government of India, Home Department, in *Proposed employment, for a further period of two years, with effect from 24 December 1911, of a Superintendent of Police, to assist the Deputy Inspector-General in charge of the Criminal Investigation Department of Eastern Bengal and Assam*, HD/Pol: Jan. 1912, nos. 20–1, IOLR P/8956.
74. Note by A. Earle, 25 May 1911, in *Increase in police in Eastern Bengal and Assam for the surveillance of political suspects*, HDA: May 1911, nos. 93–5, IOLR IOR.POS.6048.
75. Ibid., note signed B.N. Mitra, H.G. Stokes, and G.F. Wilson, 25 May 1911.

76. 'Note on the questions raised by the Government of India in Mr Earle's note of 10 June' by R.B. Hughes-Buller, op. cit.

77. Note by W.H. Clark, 25 May 1911; note by A. Earle, 26 May 1911, HDA: May 1911, nos. 93–5, IOLR IOR.POS.6048.

78. Since October 1909 there had existed a system of boat patrols of armed police. Demi-official letter from the Hon'ble Mr Beatson-Bell to A. Earle, 13 July 1911, HDA: Sept. 1911, nos. 126–7, IOLR IOR.POS.6048. In the reform of 1911 stop boats placed on all the principal rivers. Letter from J.F. Gruning, Secretary to the government of Eastern Bengal and Assam in the Revenue and General Department, to the Secretary to the Government of India, Home Department, 16 May 1911, HDA: May 1911, nos. 93–5, IOLR IOR.POS.6048. But it proved impossible to register all the half a million boats in the province. Ibid. Memorandum entitled 'Registration of boats' by L. Hare, 19 Aug. 1911.

79. Proceedings of a meeting held at Gorton Castle on Saturday 9 Sept. 1911, op. cit.

80. The Government of India had complained of the short touring and lack of local supervision of investigations by superior officers. As part of its reforms of 1911, the Local Government prepared to remove inefficient officers.

81. Suspects were placed in three categories, ranging from the most dangerous characters who were alloted 'three stars', to the least, who were given 'one star'. Groups of four Head Constables, with one Sub-Inspector to every 28 Head Constables were to watch the 3-starred suspects. Two Head Constables or Constables were to serve each 2-starred suspect. A Deputy Superintendent supervised the surveillance. Letter from C.J. Stevenson-Moore, Chief Secretary to the government of Bengal, to the Secretary to the Government of India, Home Department, 14 March 1912, *Report on the surveillance exercised over political suspects in Bengal*, in HDB: April 1912, nos. 144–5, IOLR IOR.POS.9831.

82. Ibid.

83. Ibid. Note by R.H. Craddock, 14 April 1912.

84. Cleveland wrote that: 'For some time the watched and their friends thought, or pretended to think, that the new scheme was the unauthorized effort of the tyrannical CID. Then I think they understood Gov. was behind it and there was therefore no open attack in Council. The relaxation of the system has, on the whole, I think, been wisely and tactfully carried out'.

85. Letter from C.J. Stevenson-Moore, to the Secretary to the Government of India, Home Department, 27 June 1912, in *Revision of the Special Branch of the Calcutta Police in consequence of its permanent retention as a separate staff from the Criminal Investigation Department*, Calcutta, HD/Pol: Sept. 1912, nos. 19–20, IOLR P/8957.

86. Letter from C.J. Stevenson-Moore, Chief Secretary to the government of Bengal, Political Department, to the Secretary to the Government of India, Home Department, in *Criminal Investigation Department and Special Department staff for the Bengal Presidency*, IOLR HD/Pol: Dec. 1912, nos. 101–2, IOLR P/8957.

87. Ibid.

88. On 29 September 1913 Head Constable Haripada Deb was shot dead in Calcutta. On 30 September 1913 Inspector Bankim Chandra Chaudhuri was murdered when a picric acid bomb was thrown into his house at Mymensingh. He had been prominent in investigations against the Dacca *Anusilan Samiti*.

89. Letter from J.G. Cumming, Officiating Chief Secretary to the government of Bengal, to the Secretary to the Government of India, Home Department, dated 30 January 1914, in *Waiving of the restrictions imposed by Article 78-A of the Civil Service Regulations in favour of Mr Hutchinson or any other officer appointed to fill the temporary post of Deputy Inspector-General in charge of the Intelligence Branch, Bengal*, HD/Pol: May 1914, no. 117, IOLR P/9458.

90. Letter from J.H. Kerr, Officiating Chief Secretary to the government of Bengal, to the

Secretary to the Government of India, Home Department, in *Grant of a conveyance allowance of Rs.150 a month with effect from 22 July 1915 to Mr Tegart*, HD/Pol: Jan. 1916, nos. 117–18, IOLR P/9957.

91. Tegart Papers, op. cit., Ch. 8.
92. A plot to blow up the train of Sir Andrew Fraser, the Lieutenant-Governor of EBA, had been worked out in Chandernagore, as was the successful plot to murder an important police informer, Gosain, in Alipore jail.
93. Memorandum by R.H. Craddock, 28 Aug. 1913. This in fact mouthed a report from Tegart which the Department of Criminal Intelligence had sent to him. HDD: Dec. 1914, no. 11, IOLR IOR.POS.10612, op. cit.
94. Ibid.
95. Sir Reginald Craddock summed up the situation in these words: 'Held by the French entirely on sufferance, constituting a small enclave within a few miles of the largest city in India, with an incompetent and underpaid police in the pay of the anarchists, it offers the easiest possible Alsatia to all these political criminals. The head of the anarchist gang is a professor in the only college, and an influential citizen. In this sanctuary exists unchecked a gang whose object in life is to compass the assassination of high officers of the British Government'. Ibid.
96. Ibid.

5

The Surveillance of Indian Revolutionaries in Great Britain and Europe, 1905–14

On the evening of 1 July 1909, as the audience was leaving a lecture at the Imperial Institute in London, Madan Lal Dhingra, an Indian student, shot down Sir William Curzon Wyllie, the Political Aide-de-Camp to the Secretary of State for India. An Indian doctor, Cowasji Lalcaca, who rushed to Wyllie's aid was mortally wounded. Dhingra tried unsuccessfully to take his own life but was seized and taken into police custody.

Wyllie's murder broke the long lull in political violence in Great Britain which had existed almost uninterrupted since the Fenian bombing campaign in the 1880s. England had escaped the wave of anarchist assassinations which terrified the rest of Europe and the United States at the turn of the century.

By the outbreak of the First World War there were Indian communities throughout the Pacific, North America and Western Europe, every one of which might provide a base for Indian revolutionaries.[1] This danger was first revealed by events in London between 1905 and 1910. The original organizer of Indian dissent in London was Shyamji Krishnavarma, a wealthy merchant from the west of India. He had fled to Britain in 1897 after the imprisonment of his mentor, Tilak. In January 1905 he started printing the *Indian Sociologist*,[2] which was the prototype for all anti-British newspapers published by Indians abroad. In February 1905 Krishnavarma formed the Indian Home Rule Society and in July bought a mansion in Highgate, which he called India House, as a hostel for nationalist students. However, before 1908, though nationalist ideas found strong support among Indian

125

students abroad, only a handful were willing to engage in terrorism.[3] That a few young Indians living in London took up political violence was largely the result of the powerful influence established over them by a young law student named Vinayek Damodhar Savarkar.[4]

There were close links between Indian unrest in England and the sub-continent at a very early date.[5] On the other hand, before 1910 insufficient integration existed between the intelligence and police agencies of the British Empire, which proved incapable of handling adequately a terrorist threat at an imperial level. With hindsight, the Indian police held that by 1908 some of the most dangerous branches of the revolutionary movement existed abroad and not in India.[6] The main burden of watching Indian nationalists in London fell upon the Special Branch of the Metropolitan Police at Scotland Yard. It was a task for which it was not well prepared. The years following the end of the Fenian 'Dynamite War' in the mid-1880s had lacked action for the Branch. At the beginning of 1909, the year of the Wyllie murder, sections 'B' and 'D' of the CID, which made up the Special Branch in London, had a combined strength of 34 men.[7]

Apart from its limited manpower, the Special Branch was severely impeded by the absence of any speaker of Indian languages within its ranks, and by a fundamental failure to understand Indian attitudes.[8] The Commissioner of the Metropolitan Police, Sir Edward Henry, did not perceive the threat to London's peace posed by Indian revolutionaries. At first sight this appears surprising; Henry's family had a long connection with India and he had been Inspector-General of Police in Bengal from 1891 to 1900. However, though Henry has an impressive reputation – based upon his pioneering work with fingerprints – he was considered lethargic by both the India Office and Indian intelligence.

The British government and British law effectively protected the Indians in London from the justice administered by the Government of India, a strange anomaly which was largely attributable to a strong attachment to 'liberal' values within British governing circles. This was the single most important cause of the failure by the authorities to respond to the threat which the nationalists posed. Furthermore, Scotland Yard regarded London as its own patch which it would not willingly share with any spies or with the officers of other police forces, including those of the Indian police.

The Special Branch carried out the surveillance of Indians as part of its general brief to watch 'anarchists' in London.[9] It did not deal directly with the activities of Indians in the rest of Great Britain or on the continent of Europe.[10] There was no separate Indian section of the Special Branch until after the Wyllie murder. Moreover, the past non-violent record of anarchists resident in England cannot have encouraged the police to take the Indians too seriously.[11] Indeed, there was no significant link between anarchists living in London and the Indian nationalists. The habitual description of the Indian revolutionaries as 'anarchists' by both the British and some members of the Indian police is thus seriously misleading.[12]

The Department of Criminal Intelligence on occasion asked Scotland Yard to keep a watch over certain Indian arrivals in England, sending such instructions through the India Office. It helped Scotland Yard by furnishing 'history sheets' of the main suspects.[13] By 1909 Scotland Yard was sending weekly reports on Indian agitators to the DCI. The frequency of these reports was probably much less in 1906 and 1907 when most of the information which India received about events in London came from the pages of the *Indian Sociologist*.[14] The distance between the DCI and London, and the DCI's initial dependence upon Scotland Yard's own information, precluded its playing a direct advisory role, even if this had been politically advisable.

Sustained pressure for better control of Indian agitators in London came from the bureaucrats of the India Office. Some of them performed a limited surveillance on their own account, by occasionally attending the public meetings held by the Indians.[15] The most positive attitude was that of Sir William Lee Warner, the senior member of the India Council, which was a body of ex-Indian officials set up to advise the Secretary of State. Lee Warner was ahead of Scotland Yard in making contacts within Indian circles. It seems that he received information from a Muslim named Fazlbhoy, 'a student of mature years'.[16] But there is nothing to suggest that before the Wyllie murder the India Office was ever in receipt of anything more than rumours of Indian plots.[17]

Lee Warner and Arthur Hirtzel, the Private Secretary to Lord Morley, then Secretary of State for India, were not happy about the lack of police control of Indians in London. Hirtzel was particularly concerned that a continual protective watch should be kept over Morley. Unfortunately, Morley himself was strongly opposed to measures intended either for the surveillance of Indians or for his own safety. His main concern was to secure the passage through a

Conservative-led House of Lords of his Indian Councils Act, which gave Indians a limited amount of self-government. He felt that there should appear to be no need for repression at home just when liberal measures were being introduced into India itself. However, Morley disliked what he called the 'police mentality' on purely personal and ideological grounds.[18] Even as Gladstone's Irish Secretary he had believed that police measures for his safety had been generally unnecessary. By August 1908 this attitude had produced a near farcical situation, whereby Hirtzel gave Scotland Yard orders of his own for Morley's protection in defiance of those of the Secretary of State. As a result a detective followed Morley to work every day, spent the whole day sitting with the India Office messengers and finally followed him home, being let out of a private door just after Morley had left.[19]

Given the lack of sustained support and direction from Indian intelligence or the India Office, it is not surprising that the Special Branch generally underestimated the potential danger from London Indians, though the proportion of their time spent on watching Indians increased between 1905 and the Wyllie murder. The earliest record of Special Branch activity in connection with Indians is for 11 May 1907, when some officers attended a meeting at India House where 'seditious' pamphlets were distributed.[20] There is evidence that from an early date a detective going by the name of O'Brien had been making friends with the Indians. In September 1907 he visited Krishnavarma, posing as an Irish-American. He acted with so little subtlety that, according to a DCI report, Krishnavarma fled to Paris in a fright. He was never to come within British jurisdiction again.[21]

The Metropolitan Police, however, were not unscrupulous in their treatment of the Indians. Only in May 1909 when information was received that a bomb plot was being organized against the India Office did Henry suggest to Morley that Indians' letters should be opened.[22] Postal censorship even of the most important suspects was not introduced until after the Wyllie murder. Because of the special difficulties of keeping the Indians under surveillance, however, it would be difficult to generalize about the Special Branch's general level of competence. Morley recognized this when in June 1908 he wrote a general critique of Scotland Yard's abilities and performance to the Viceroy, Lord Minto:

> Experts from the Home Office and Scotland Yard pointed out that their men are wholly useless in the case of Indian con-

spirators. They have no sort of agency able to distinguish Hindu from Mahomedan, or Verma from Varma. The whole Indian field is absolutely unfamiliar, in language, habits, and everything else. In short, both you and I can easily understand that the ordinary square-toed English constable, even in the detective branch, would be rather clumsy in tracing your wily Asiatics.[23]

At a conference between the India Office, Scotland Yard and the Home Office on 3 June 1908 it was decided that an ex-Indian policeman, almost certainly one of Lee Warner's acquaintances, should 'try to get in touch with the suspects'.[24]

In August and September 1908 the significance of London as a centre of Indian nationalism within the Empire increased. A group of prominent nationalists made an exodus to London. The most famous in 1908, though not openly committed to violence, were Bepin Chandra Pal and G.S. Khaparde.[25] At the same time as these 'extremists' arrived in London, if not before, the Special Branch succeeded in securing an informer within India House. There is no reason to suppose that he was other than one of Lee Warner's agents. The police were now able to ascertain something of what was going on, particularly at the regular Sunday meetings, to which Europeans came by invitation only. The first report about one of these events is for 2 September 1908.[26]

More importantly, in November 1909 a young law student from Poona, Vinayek Damodhar Savarkar, came to the notice of the police as a particularly dangerous suspect. He gave a Sunday speech advocating an immediate uprising in India.[27] Soon afterwards he formed his Free India Society from a few selected men. In the last week of November Lee Warner's informer reported that there was much talk of assassination in Indian circles, though he himself was not one of Savarkar's inner circle.[28]

At the beginning of 1909 the Special Branch had not only been unable yet to secure a first-rate source of information within India House but they were also unable to keep a protective watch over politicians. The first act of violence by Indians that year came on 12 January, when a Bengali named Kunjalal Bhattacharji obtained an audience with Lee Warner at the India Office and slapped his face. At the end of January another Indian, who had already disclosed his hatred of Lee Warner to a Special Branch Officer, assaulted him in a London park.[29]

Shortly after this second assault on Lee Warner, and probably because of it, Scotland Yard seems to have increased its surveillance of Indian suspects. On 2 March 1909 an MP asked in the House of Commons whether the Secretary of State was aware that Indian students in London were being shadowed by Scotland Yard detectives and as a consequence had been forced to leave their lodgings.[30]

At some time around the beginning of 1909 the DCI started to receive information from its own secret agent, 'C'.[31] His presence is the first indication that the Indian authorities were dissatisfied with Scotland Yard's performance. The Director of Criminal Intelligence wrote that 'C' 'only began to be of real use after he had lived a false life for over a year and won the confidence of the men he was hunting'.[32] Thus 'C' began to operate effectively only in the months immediately preceding the Wyllie murder. His existence was not known to Scotland Yard.[33] It seems that 'C' was the first agent whom the DCI had sent abroad on a long-term basis. However, the DCI still remained true to the principle that they should not interfere in the jurisdiction of local investigation agencies. 'C's' information was at first all but useless because the DCI could not move Scotland Yard to take greater precautions without not only losing their full control of 'C', but also revealing their 'deviousness' in putting him in London in the first place.

At the end of June 1909 the DCI received a report that the situation in London was more dangerous than they had hitherto suspected. Some of the India House party were practising revolver shooting at a range near Tottenham Court Road and were using an air-gun in the rifle-range at the back of India House. If this information came from Scotland Yard's sources they did nothing about it. The owner of the rifle-range told a police court after the Wyllie murder that Dhingra had been there for a practice session on the evening of the murder.[34] Scotland Yard certainly did not know that Savarkar's 'lieutenant', V.V.S. Aiyar, was training a destitute Madrassi, Tirumal Acharya, in the 'art of martyrdom'. The DCI, on the other hand, reported that Acharya had become very careless of his life and had announced 'with a ring of suicidal insanity' that his end was very near.[35]

Further danger signals were picked up from London on the eve of the Wyllie murder. On 9 June 1909 news from India reached London that Vinayek Savarkar's brother, Ganesh, had been sentenced to transportation for life because of his revolutionary activities. On 20 June, at a public meeting at India House, Vinayek Savarkar swore vengeance on the British.[36] On 22 June Savarkar was informed that his call to the bar had been postponed because of his 'seditious' behaviour. Nine days later Wyllie was murdered at the Imperial Institute. At least one police officer was present in the audience, but the police were not watching Sir William, who was a high-profile figure to the Indians and who along with Special Branch officers had been responsible for blocking Savarkar's call to the Bar; nor were they keeping more than a general watch on the Indians in the audience.[37]

In reports dated 8 and 16 July Scotland Yard reported to the Department of Criminal Intelligence that there had been no Indian conspiracy in London.[38] This was contradicted by reports received from 'C' after the murder. V.V.S. Aiyar said that there was one among the Indian nationalists 'who was the real *guru*, the *Avatar* of Krishna, who had produced a man like Dhingra', and he hinted that this was Savarkar. Another of Savarkar's intimates told 'C' that Dhingra was the product of Savarkar's teaching, and that he had been hunting for Lord Morley, Lord Curzon and Sir William Curzon Wyllie for the last seven months. Savarkar even hinted that he was planning a murder in India when he said of Wyllie's murder: 'It is an initial step, I have still to avenge my brother's life'.[39]

After the murder Scotland Yard's general attitude towards the Indian problem in London was taken to task. The Viceroy, Lord Minto, made the general point that not just Scotland Yard but the British governing circles as a whole were in a sense responsible for the murder. He wrote to Morley on 2 July expressing a hope

> that people at home will at last realise the dangers of allowing the hatching of sedition in their midst – not only for themselves, but for us in India . . . Nothing has been done to destroy the sources of so much iniquity. I am afraid the exaggerated worship of so-called freedom has led the British public to ignore hard facts.[40]

Morley and Hirtzel were more specifically critical of Sir Edward Henry. On 12 July they agreed that 'so far Henry has been useless'.[41] Morley wrote to Lord Minto:

> I much fear that Henry has no real grasp of a situation that has taken him entirely by surprise . . . On the whole the police frame of mind strikes me as extremely casual; either making needless fuss or else not making serious fuss enough.[42]

Scotland Yard's immediate response to the crisis was to place Morley and Curzon under protective surveillance, though even after the murder Morley did not encourage effective police action, continuing to travel to work on the underground from Wimbledon. But by 17 July there were three men watching him.[43] He wrote to Minto on 6 August:

> It may amuse you (though the topic is not without a gruesome side) to hear that the Strangers' Gallery contained a certain number of swarthy men, but I observed also scattered among them plenty of unmistakable 'plain-clothes' police officers.[44]

By 8 July there was still no Indian section of the Special Branch, though Lord Morley suggested that one should be brought into being.[45] Discussions took place between the India Office and Henry on 13 July, leading to the creation of a special Indian section of the Branch sometime later in the month. The Branch's strength was increased by the addition of four officers, which brought its London-based strength up to 38.[46]

Despite its small personnel the Special Branch's performance was markedly improved in the weeks after the murder in terms of the resources which it allotted to the Indian problem, though not in terms of the sophistication and meticulousness of its surveillance. The Director of Criminal Intelligence, Charles Stevenson-Moore, wrote in September 1909 that:

> the London police may be trusted henceforward to utilize all the resources at their command in order to keep in touch with the movements of the more dangerous extremists in London.[47]

David Garnett, an Irish sympathizer of the Indian nationalists, said that after the murder:

> My friends were kept under a close watch by Scotland Yard, and there was usually a detective hanging about, watching their lodgings or following them in the street.

Though he noted contemptuously that:

> It was an easy matter to shake these detectives off in the tube railways.[48]

The pressure of the police upon the Indian students seems to have followed them into their homes. In one case two Indians left their lodgings because their landladies were informing upon them.[49] From the end of 1909 there was an obvious tension within India House because the Indians knew that there were informers within their ranks.[50]

It is difficult to argue with the criticisms of Scotland Yard made by the India Office and the Department of Criminal Intelligence. It is noticeable, however, that those which the DCI made about Scotland Yard's performance within London were written after the murder. Despite the despatch of agent 'C' to Europe, the DCI itself clearly did not regard the doings of Indian nationalists in the capital with nearly so much concern before the murder as it did afterwards. There is a remarkable difference in tone between two *Memoranda on the Anti-British Agitation Among Natives of India in England*, which the DCI submitted to the Government of India respectively before and after the Wyllie murder. The first of these circulars, dated 15 June 1909, was somewhat mocking towards the India House group and concluded that Indian agitation in Europe would soon die away because of divisions among the Indians. In the second circular dated 28 October 1909 the DCI presented the evidence mentioned above which it had obtained from 'C' before the murder indicating that there was a terrorist conspiracy in London which had been largely ignored by the Metropolitan Police. The DCI therefore claimed an omniscience over past events in London which it did not possess. It took the Wyllie murder to make the DCI see the threat posed by Indian nationalists abroad, which in turn led it to reconsider its function as an imperial intelligence agency.

Savarkar's assassination plans were more ambitious than the British authorities had expected. Their success in India itself reveals the inadequate level of co-operation existing between the various police and intelligence agencies of the British Empire. At the beginning of 1910 the Bombay police arrested two former residents of India House, H.K. Koregaonker and Chatturbhuj Amin, who had returned to India. They confessed that in 1909 Savarkar had sent Chatturbhuj to India carrying 21 Browning pistols concealed in the false bottom of his trunk. Savarkar intended the pistols as a revenge insurance for his brother Ganesh, who was then under trial in Bombay. Mr Jackson, the Magistrate who condemned Ganesh to transportation was killed with one of the revolvers on 21 December 1909.[51] This episode reveals how imperfect was the Special Branch's knowledge of the inner workings of the India House group before Wyllie's murder. They made no effort to have Chatturbhuj examined on his departure from England. Remarkably, the DCI had received information that Chatturbhuj was trying to smuggle revolvers into India[52] but no sustained surveillance of him seems to have been undertaken by the local Bombay CID or encouraged by the Department of Criminal Intelligence. Chatturbhuj freely handed the pistols over to another conspirator in Bombay.

Immediately after the Wyllie murder the first impulses towards direct Indian intervention in England came not from the DCI itself, but from the India Office and Scotland Yard. Scotland Yard admitted its inability to handle adequately the Indian agitators in London, and took the unprecedented step of asking the DCI to provide it with the 'services of one or two reliable persons to watch suspected Indians in London'.[53] The Indian Home Department noted on 30 August 1909 that the agents requested had left for England.[54]

However, even before Wyllie's murder, the Indian government had intended to send a native Indian police officer out to England. Throughout June 1909 the DCI, the Home Department and the Government of Bombay had the proposed extradition of V.D. Savarkar under discussion. The case against him was not strong.[55] They proposed therefore to collect evidence in London in connection with the case prepared in India. Not only was the deputation to be for one case only but, at the suggestion of the Indian authorities themselves, the officer selected was to work strictly under the supervision of Scotland Yard.[56] However, Morley felt that there was no point in seconding an officer to the Metropolitan Police for the short-term enquiry into the Savarkar case, but that a 'general and continuous aid to Scotland Yard' was worthy of consideration.[57] Furthermore, the India Office wrote to the Indian Home Department in August that a native Indian officer would draw more attention to the action of the police than was desirable; because of his colour an Englishman obviously would not be as conspicuous in the London of 1909 as an Indian. It seems that the India Office thought a European officer would avoid the attention of two specific groups: the Indian nationalists themselves; and more generally, the majority opinion in British governing circles, which might object to the presence of a secret policeman spying on British subjects.[58]

The pressures towards direct but limited Indian intervention in London came from the obvious need for help on the part of Scotland Yard and the Indian government's need to work up the case against Savarkar. But the Department of Criminal Intelligence viewed these pressures along with a third impulse towards their intervention in Europe: the complete failure of Scotland Yard to provide information from abroad. That better links with the French police were necessary was brought into relief as a result of Scotland Yard's improved performance in the second half of 1909. By September it had become clear to the Director of Criminal Intelligence that the main centre of Indian agitation in Europe had moved to the safer soil of France in order to escape the vigilance of the London police.

The DCI had first perceived the potential threat from Indians living in Paris in 1907. In December of that year revolutionaries tried to derail the train of Sir Andrew Fraser, the Lieutenant-Governor of Bengal. Due only to the seriousness of what had happened, the Paris police informed the British authorities that a Russian anarchist named Nicholas Safranski was teaching some Bengali students in Paris how to make bombs. The French said that the attempt to wreck Fraser's train was the result, though on enquiry by the British authorities the evidence for the statement proved insufficient.[59] This episode did not lead to an increase in co-operation between the French police and Scotland Yard, whose relations sometimes bordered on animosity. The main source for what went on in Paris remained the *Indian Sociologist*, supplemented by some French newspapers. However, the situation in Paris was always potentially dangerous. Though the Indian community there numbered only about 250, it included a group of wealthy Indian pearl merchants, some of whom furnished the younger revolutionaries with funds.[60]

It was only after Wyllie's murder that the DCI itself gave sustained attention to the threat from France. Stevenson-Moore, the Director of Criminal Intelligence, wrote in 1909:

> While we have succeeded in getting valuable information from Scotland Yard about the doings of anarchists in London, we have signally failed to obtain from that source any knowledge of their doings elsewhere.[61]

When Henry requested the assistance of the French police in the surveillance of Indians in 1909 they told him to apply through the 'official channels'. But no French government would risk the political storm which might result if they authorized such a breach of French political asylum.[62] The problem went deeper than this. Lord Morley wrote in 1909:

> It occurs to some people that we might ask the French government to deal with Krishnavarma, who is deluging us with villainous

leaflets. But it is quite hopeless and we should certainly be asked to remember John Bull's shelter and encouragement to Poles, Hungarians, Italian Carbonari and all other swarms of political refugees for the last eighty or a hundred years.[63]

Henry informed the Indian government in April 1909 that he would not place officers abroad for any length of time, though he was ready to send them over on short missions.[64] The DCI resented this decision as it had found out from sources in India that the Paris revolutionaries were planning to smuggle arms into India.[65] Stevenson-Moore concluded that the threat posed by Indian agitation abroad was now so serious as to necessitate the despatch of an Indian police Officer to London. However, he was not to be attached to Scotland Yard, because he would not then be free to operate outside London. Stevenson-Moore concluded that the officer would have to remain in direct subordination to the DCI.[66]

Thus, five years after its creation, the Department of Criminal Intelligence advised the Government of India that one of the fundamental rules laid down at its creation should be broken. The DCI asked not only that it should be allowed to acquire *investigation* functions to add to its *intelligence* functions, but that it should conduct investigation on the territory of a police force not under the control of the Government of India.

Until Stevenson-Moore's note of 21 September 1909, all the parties concerned with the surveillance of Indians in Europe, the DCI, the India Office, Scotland Yard and the Paris police, had been reacting to events started by the Indian revolutionaries. Stevenson-Moore now intended to create a secret service network centred on the DCI in India and controlled by a deputy of the Director based in the India Office. In a limited sense the DCI already had experience of imperial intelligence because it served as a repository for information received from other agencies abroad that were not under its direct control. These regular overseas sources of information were Scotland Yard itself and the British Home Office's agency in New York which was subsidized by India. The latter was a small establishment whose main function was to watch Irish republican plotters in New York, but which since 1905 provided the Indian authorities with information about the doings of the Fenians' Indian allies.[67] The existing system of international intelligence based on the DCI was distinctly makeshift in character; the elements comprising it were under the Director's control to varying degrees. It was only with the creation of the London agency that the DCI became a regular intelligence bureau at the imperial level.

In his note of 21 September, Stevenson-Moore gave details of the new Indian secret service establishment for the continent of Europe. The work abroad was to be done entirely through secret agents, including 'C' and the two others recently despatched to London. The DCI intended now to employ 'a stationary officer' in each important centre of Indian agitation in Europe; he believed that there were probably less than half a dozen such centres. By far the most important part of the scheme was the 'itinerant officer' himself, based at the India Office. His initial role was to secure agents from among those already resident in the main centres for 'a small remuneration', and then to control them along with those already deployed. Neither of these tasks was easy for the Director of Criminal Intelligence because he was too far away to exercise effective control. The 'itinerant officer' was also to perform secret service duties in person. He had the important task of visiting less important centres which were outside the scope of the stationary agents; and he was to give special personal attention to tracing any contacts between the Indian and the continental 'anarchists'. He was also concerned with watching for the spread of Indian nationalist and revolutionary propaganda in Europe.[68]

Although Stevenson-Moore's decision to establish an Indian secret service network in Europe was a very important step in the development of the Department of Criminal Intelligence, it was not a deliberate move taken to expand the DCI into a permanent imperial intelligence agency, but a limited response to what the Indian government still saw as the short-term problem of Indian agitation abroad. The 'itinerant officer' was to be appointed on secondment to the India Office for one year only.[69] Furthermore, despite its geographical scope, the success of the network was entirely dependent upon the abilities and good fortune of that officer. The other elements in the scheme, the 'stationary officers', were no more than informers. Moreover, the DCI, unlike the London-based intelligence agencies, lacked the ability to generate a secret service run by regular British Officers. The experienced detectives needed to work on intelligence operations abroad had to be taken from the cadres of the Local Governments' CIDs. Even during the First World War, when the defence of India obliged the DCI to set up intelligence operations in the Far East, this could lead to clashes between central and local governments.[70]

The 'itinerant officer' had to be one of the best detectives in India. The Director of Criminal Intelligence's choice for the job fell upon Superintendent John Arnold Wallinger of the Bombay police. Early in 1909 he had distinguished himself by his detective ability in working up evidence against a revolutionary conspiracy in one of the Native States. The DCI believed it important that he possessed a considerable linguistic aptitude, speaking three Indian languages.[71] He was intimately acquainted with many Gujarathi merchants, which was useful for operations in Europe, since the main leaders there, and the majority of the Paris pearl merchants, had close connections with Gujarat. Last, but to the eyes of the DCI not least, Wallinger was socially acceptable as the DCI's representative to Scotland Yard and the Paris police. Stevenson-Moore wrote:

> Having started, I think, as an Inspector, he has a specially intimate knowledge of detective work, but he is gentlemanly and tactful and seems to have succeeded in escaping the acquisition of those defects which often adhere to police officers who have risen from a subordinate rank.[72]

On 15 January 1910 Wallinger sailed from Bombay.

On arrival in Britain, Wallinger was attached to the Judicial and Public Department at the India Office, which corresponded to the Government of India's Home Department dealing with British India's internal affairs. In many ways his arrival had been poorly prepared by the Indian authorities. The DCI had not even bestowed a title upon him before sending him out to England, which Wallinger found involved him in many inconvenient explanations. It was only in June 1910 that he was designated 'Special Assistant to the Director of Criminal Intelligence in India'.[73]

Scotland Yard at first resented his working independently. Wallinger recalled in a letter to the Director of Criminal Intelligence that:

> I should have had to return to India as soon as I arrived here, had it not been for [Lee Warner, who used] his great personal influence and abilities in our favour.

Despite Lee Warner's efforts it took Wallinger nearly three months 'to get to work' after his arrival because of friction with Scotland Yard. Even after this relations between them remained cold for several months more.[74] Wallinger was perhaps lucky that during this period

138

when he could not 'get to work', Scotland Yard finally arrested Savarkar and deported him to India after he rashly returned to London from Paris, where he had gone to stay in January 1910.[75]

None the less, the Government of India wrote that at the end of his first year's work Wallinger had brought about a genuine improvement in India's relations with Scotland Yard.[76] By the beginning of 1911, if not before, he was working in close connection with Special Branch officers; in June 1911, for example, he went to Rotterdam with one of them to investigate the printing of 'seditious' Indian publications.[77] Throughout the period of his secondment to the India Office, Wallinger was dependent upon Scotland Yard to carry out surveillance of Indians in London. The Special Branch, indeed, continued to send its own reports to India, just as it had done before Wallinger's arrival.[78] The DCI had no further complaints about the Metropolitan Police until Summer 1914, when the Director of Criminal Intelligence recorded that 'for some time past the information given by Scotland Yard about the doings of Indian agitators in England had been rather meagre', because 'the officers of Scotland Yard were so fully occupied with the Suffragette movement that they had very little to devote to Indians'.[79] On the other hand, Indian nationalism in Great Britain outside London was Wallinger's own concern. He extended the surveillance of Indians to 'new centres', principally Oxford, Cambridge and Edinburgh. He found students there to be nationalist, but articulate, a quality which he seems to have admired.[80]

Wallinger brought about an improvement in relations between the Indian and French police in an even shorter time. However, he had an initial problem in establishing cordial relations with them. For one thing, he proved to be anything but a capable linguist. The Indian Home Secretary, Sir H. Wheeler, wrote:

> One of the worst French scholars I have ever known was Wallinger at the beginning of his term of special duty, and I do not think he knew German or other Continental languages. When I travelled with him in France in 1913 his accent was abominable and his French vocabulary very poor.[81]

On 26 February 1910 the Director of Criminal Intelligence wrote that 'The French police give us very little assistance in the surveillance of Indian suspects in Paris'. But just two months later he reported that 'valuable assistance is being obtained from the chief police officers of Paris'.[82] The reason for this remarkable change in the attitude of the

French was that 'Wallinger was able to work arrangements in France in hearty co-operation with the Paris police'.[83]

The most important aspect of Wallinger's mission was his ability by personal contacts in Great Britain and in France to overcome the official difficulties brought by each country's tradition of political asylum. When assessing his role as 'itinerant officer' in a letter to the DCI of September 1911, Wallinger said that

> you can put proposals and carry on work through [me] which it would be impossible to do officially – either direct with the India Office or Scotland Yard, as both, in most cases are unwilling to act owing to political considerations . . . [I] can visit any of the Government officials and do what is necessary, without it being interpreted as an official act.

Wallinger felt that the same applied in France:

> The Continental police dare not correspond officially on matters political, except through the recognized channels; which would really mean a waste of everyone's time.

Wallinger believed that 'it is very essential that [the DCI] should have an officer in England while the present unrest continues in India', and listed further reasons for his being in London: the censorship of newspapers going out to India would not be done by the India Office or by Scotland Yard; and there would be no means of getting information of Indian agitation from areas in England outside London, unless special arrangements were made with the Home Office, which would be impossible under Asquith's Liberal government. Wallinger believed that if his mission were at any time discontinued it would be very difficult to start it up again because 'Scotland Yard would fight hard against the proposal'.[84]

By the end of 1910 Wallinger had secured at least one informer within the Paris Indian group.[85] In 1910 for the first time the Director of Criminal Intelligence provided detailed information about Indian affairs in Europe. However, the first years of Wallinger's mission coincided with what the DCI saw as a sharp decline in the danger of violence from Indians in Europe. Wallinger reported that links between the revolutionaries in Europe and those in India were almost non-existent.[86] The main source of concern to the Indian police in the period 1910–14 was not so much what the Indians in Europe were capable of on their own account, but that they might make common cause with the many Egyptian nationalists in Europe. It was particularly because of this potential threat that Switzerland, a favourite residence of Egyptians, became a centre of interest to Wallinger.[87]

Despite the seeming weakness of the Indian revolutionary movement in Europe, Wallinger's mission showed signs of becoming permanent before the war. There was never any question of it being folded up when it came up for review in India every year, though had it not been for the war, Wallinger himself would have returned to India. However, the value placed on the mission by the Indian government was shown when they singled out no less than Charles Tegart of the Bengal Intelligence Branch, as a replacement for Wallinger, describing him as 'an Elisha to Mr Wallinger's Elija'.[88] In February 1914 Cleveland wrote:

During the past 12 months Wallinger's work has been more valuable than ever as his system has developed and fuller results have been secured.[89]

This indicates how far the attitude of the DCI had changed since the time before the Wyllie murder when both its own reluctance and the rules guiding its operation had prevented its playing an active imperial role in combating the Indian revolutionary movement. The importance of the Indian secret service network in Europe had not been fully appreciated by the Indian authorities at its creation. Its success lay partly in Wallinger's own abilities, which were much appreciated in India, and partly in the continued smouldering of Indian unrest in Europe. Partly also, the emergence in 1913 of a strong Indian revolutionary movement in North America, in the form of the Ghadr Party, led the Indian authorities to view Indian agitation abroad with caution.

NOTES

1. V.N. Datta, *Madan Lal Dhingra and the Revolutionary Movement* (New Delhi, 1978) is the best account of the Indians in London.
2. *Memorandum on the Anti-British Agitation Among Natives of India in England, with Appendix*, CID Circular, no. 7 (Simla, 15 June 1909) in IOLR L/PS/19/168.
3. Ibid., pp. 3–4.
4. Already in 1904 Savarkar had set up the revolutionary *Abhinav Bharat* society in Poona. See Ch. 3.
5. For the influence of the *Indian Sociologist* within India see Weekly Report of the Director of Criminal Intelligence (henceforth referred to as 'Weekly Report') dated

10 August 1907 in HDB: Aug. 1907, nos. 135–45, in IOLR IOR.POS.8959.

6. J.C. Ker, *Political Trouble in India* (Reprint, Calcutta: Editions Indian, 1973), 'Introductory'.

7. Bernard Porter, *The Origins of the Vigilant State. The London Metropolitan Police Special Branch before the First World War* (London: Weidenfeld & Nicolson, 1987), p. 154.

8. Cf. the situation in New York, where the British Home Office's agent also complained about his inability to disguise himself as an Indian or to understand Indian languages. In *Employment of Agents in America*. HDD: July 1911, no. 17 in IOLR IOR.POS. 10611.

9. Note by Stevenson-Moore, dated 21 September, in *Proposal to Depute Sirdar Bahadur Dyal Singh Gyani to London in Connection with the Proposed Extradition of Vinayek Savarkar. Deputation of Mr Wallinger to London*. HDA: Jan. 1911, nos. 52–64 in IOLR IOR.POS.5949.

10. J&P 4600/08 in IOLR L/PJ/6/908.

11. Sir Charles Cleveland, Director of Criminal Intelligence, 1910–19, wrote in March 1910: 'In London the police deal very well with the "anarchists" as far as I know. But the anarchists in London are not really on the war-path; they are a small distinct element with the Londoners against them as a class.' Letter from C.R. Cleveland to the Government of Bengal, 15 March 1910. HDA: April 1910, nos. 59–62, in IOLR IOR.POS. 5947.

12. *Weekly Report* dated 17 April 1909 in HDB: June 1909, nos. 108–114 and *Weekly Report* dated 18 September 1909. HDB: Oct. 1909, nos. 110–17 in IOR.POS.6942. Sir Charles Cleveland wrote in March 1910: 'the situation in India is vastly different from that elsewhere. I absolutely agree with Arabindo Ghose [a famous Indian nationalist] that "anarchical" is not the proper description of the movements, organizations and crimes which have been troubling us. The situation more closely resembles that in Ireland in the eighties and I do not think "anarchical" was ever considered applicable to the Irish developments'. Letter from C.R. Cleveland to the government of Bengal, dated 15 March 1910, op. cit.

13. See for example the enquiries about one Sundar Lal. Letter from H.H. Risley to Sir Charles Lyall, Secretary, Judicial and Public Department, 26 Sept. 1907. J&P 3549/07 in IOLR L/PJ/6/631.

14. Proposals for obtaining more complete information about the doings and dealings of political extremists and their correspondents and sympathizers residing in London, Paris, and other Socialist centres and proposed authorization of the East Bengal and Assam government to correspond direct through the DCI with the Commissioner of Police, London. HDD: April 1909, no. 26. IOLR IOR.POS.10609.

15. Minto to Morley, 7 July 1909 in IOLR MSS.EUR.D.573/21. Letter from Sir William Curzon Wyllie to Sir Charles Lyall, 5 Nov. 1908. J&P 4223/08 in IOLR L/PJ/6/903.

16. Letter from Lee Warner to Stuart, dated 20 August 1907 in *Papers connected with the employment of Pinkerton's Detective Agency*. HDD: June 1909, no.30, in IOLR IOR. POS.10609.

17. Hirtzel Diaries, 5 June 1907, IORL MSS.EUR.D.1090/2. It seems that Lee Warner knew an ex-Indian policeman as well as Fazlbhoy.

18. See, for example, his letter to Minto dated 6 January 1909, and criticism of Stuart and Plowden in letters dated 13 January and 11 February 1909, all contained in Morley Papers, IOLR MSS.EUR.D/573/3.

19. Hirtzel Diaries, entry dated 22 June 1906, IOLR MSS.EUR.D.1090/1; entry dated 31 May 1907, IOLR MSS.EUR.D.1090/2; and entries dated 5 August and 26 November, OLR MSS.EUR.D.1090/3.

20. Hirtzel Diaries, entry dated 11 May 1907, IOLR MSS.EUR.D.1090/2. Statement of Detective Inspector Edward John Parker in the Nasik Conspiracy Trial, January 1911.

J&P. 847/10 (with 778/11) in IOLR L/PJ/6/994.
21. O'Brien was posing as a member of the staff of the New York *Gaelic American*. Weekly Report for 28 Sept. 1907. HD(B): Oct. 1907, nos. 40–9 in IOLR IOR.POS.8959.
22. Hirtzel Diaries, entry dated 13 May 1908, IOLR MSS.EUR.D.1090/3.
23. Lee Warner wrote similarly to the Indian Home Department on 20 August 1907: 'It was observed at Scotland Yard that they have no one in London capable of dealing with Indians and distinguishing between Hindu and Mahomedan, harmless and dangerous agitators'. in Papers Connected with the Employment of Pinkerton's, op. cit. Morley to Minto, dated 4 June 1908, Morley Papers, IOLR MSS.EUR.D.573/3.
24. Hirtzel Diaries, entry dated 3 June 1907, IOLR MSS.EUR.D.1090/2.
25. *Weekly Report* dated 29 August 1909 in H.D.(B): Sept. 1908, nos. 49–58 and *Weekly Report* dated 10 October 1908. HD(B): Oct. 1908, nos. 1–8 in IOLR IOR.POS.8960. See the personal histories of the prominent agitators contained in *Memorandum on the anti-British agitation among natives of India in England* C.I. Circular no. 11. HDD: Nov. 1909, no. 32 in IOLR IOR.POS.10610.
26. It seems that on this date the Special Branch first learned that the India House group had links with Indian revolutionaries in North America. At the meeting they distributed copies of *Free Hindusthan*, which was printed at Seattle. J&P 3264/08 in IOLR L/PJ/6/890.
27. *Weekly Report* dated 23 January 1909. HDB: Jan. 1909, nos. 106–12 in IOLR IOR.POS.8960.
28. Hirtzel Diaries, 24 Nov. 1908, IOLR MSS.EUR.D.1090/3.
29. *Assault on Sir W. Lee Warner by a Hindu Student – B. Bhattacharyya*, in J&P 318/09, IOLR L/PJ/6/920.
30. Question by Mr O'Grady in J&P 758/09 in IOLR L/PJ/6/924. On 11 March the Rt. Honourable Mr Claude Hay, MP, also referred to this obtrusive police presence. J&P 924/09 in IOLR L/PJ/6/926.
31. Memorandum by Stuart, dated 20 July 1909, in *Deputation of Mr Wallinger to London*. HDA: Jan. 1911, nos. 52–64 in IOLR IOR.POS.5949.
32. *Dissemination in Siam of the seditious Indian newspaper 'Ghadr'*. Note by C.R. Cleveland of 12 July 1915. HDB: Aug. 1915, nos. 414–39 in IOLR IOR.POS.9840.
33. Disturbing information had reached India at least a month before the murder. The news that Tirumal Acharya was being coached for martyrdom was received on 25 June 1909, while the report that Indians were doing target practice was printed up in May 1909. See HDB: June 1909, op. cit., and *Weekly Report* dated 17 July 1909. HDB: Aug. 1909, nos. 47–54 in IOLR IOR.POS.8962.
34. CID Circular no. 11, dated 28 October 1908, op. cit., p. 7.
35. *Weekly Report* dated 17 July 1909. HDB: Aug. 1909, nos. 47–54 in IOLR IOR.POS. 8962.
36. CID Circular no. 11, dated 28 October 1909, op. cit., p. 5.
37. As early as October 1907 the *Indian Sociologist* had singled out Curzon Wyllie and Lee Warner as 'old unrepentant foes of India who have fattened on the misery of the Indian peasant every since they began their career'. *Weekly Report* dated 9 November 1907. HDB: Dec. 1907, nos. 2–9 in IOLR IOR.POS.8959. For the moves of the India Office and Scotland Yard to stop Savarkar's call to the Bar see J&P 1849/09 in IOLR L/PJ/6/939.
38. *Weekly Reports* dated 31 July 1909 in H.D.(B): Aug. 1909, nos. 47–54 and 7 August 1909. HDB: Sept. 1909, nos. 47–54 in IOLR IOR.POS.8962.
39. CID Circular no. 11, dated 28 October 1909, op. cit.
40. Minto to Morley, dated 7 July 1909. Morley Papers, IOLR MSS.EUR.D.573/21.
41. Hirtzel Diaries, op. cit., 12 and 14 July.
42. Morley to Minto, 15 July 1909. Morley Papers, IOLR MSS.EUR.D.573/4. In March 1910 the Director of Criminal Intelligence wrote: 'The London police seem to me to

have been quite overcome by the difficulties of the Indian question directly it came to them in an acute form. They failed to protect Sir William Curzon Wyllie and their detection was confined to a single murderer caught red-handed. The Indian police have done much better than that on the whole'. Letter from C.R. Cleveland to the Government of Bengal, 15 March 1910, op. cit.

43. Hirtzel Diaries, op. cit., 17 July 1909.
44. Morley to Minto, dated 6 August 1909. Morley Papers, IOLR MSS.EUR.D.573/4.
45. Hirtzel Diaries, op. cit., entry for 8 July 1909. Letter from Morley to Minto, 8 July 1909. Morley Papers, IOLR MSS.EUR.D.573/4.
46. Bernard Porter, op. cit., pp. 164–5.
47. Memorandum by Stevenson-Moore, dated 20 September 1909, in HDB: Jan. 1911, nos. 52–64, op. cit.
48. David Garnett, *The Golden Echo*, p. 148.
49. Special Branch report, signed J. McBrien, 16 Aug. 1909. J&P 3280/09 in IOLR L/PJ/962.
50. *Weekly Report* dated 30 October 1909. HDB: Nov. 1909, nos. 33–41 in IOLR IOR. POS.8963.
51. *Savarkar Case, trial and conviction and question of extradition in case of failure at The Hague.* File 476/11 in J&P 778/11 in IOLR L/PJ/6/1069.
52. History Sheet of Chatturbhai Javerbhai Amin, contained in CI Circular no. 11, dated 28 October 1909, op. cit., p. 40.
53. Telegram from Sir Richmond Ritchie to the Director of Criminal Intelligence, 16 July 1909, in HDA: Jan. 1911, nos. 52–64, op. cit.
54. Note from Stuart to Risley, 30 August 1909, in HDA: Jan. 1911, nos. 52–64, op. cit. In the early part of the twentieth century the Indian government opposed the indiscriminate use of spies on purely humanitarian grounds. Sir Harold Stuart, the Indian Home Secretary, wrote on 25 March 1910: 'It must be remembered that our "conspirators" are mostly boys and that the office of spy is a very dangerous one. There is therefore a good deal of natural reluctance to ask a boy to take a role which must put his life in danger.' Memorandum by H.A. Stuart, dated 25 March 1910, in HDA: April 1910, nos. 59–62, in IOLR IOR.POS.5947.
55. Note by H.G. Stokes, dated 3 June 1909, in HDA: Jan. 1911, nos. 52–64, op. cit.
56. Note by Stevenson-Moore, dated 7 July 1909, in HDA: Jan. 1911, nos. 52–64, op. cit.
57. Telegram from Morley to Minto, dated 3 July 1909. A week later Stevenson-Moore had singled out three candidates for the mission from among the Native police officers. Memorandum entitled *Detective to be attached to Scotland Yard*, dated 20 August 1907, in HDA: Jan. 1911, nos. 52–64, op. cit.
58. Letter from Sir Charles Lyall to Sir Harold Stuart, dated 27 August 1909, in HDA: Jan. 1911, nos. 52–64, op. cit.
59. Ker, *Political Trouble in India*, op. cit, pp. 143–5. The Commissioner of the Paris Police had been told that Safranski referred to the Indians as his *camarades noirs*. Since he was under the impression that the natives of other provinces of India were not 'black', he described the suspects as 'Bengalis'. Ker, *Political Trouble in India*, op. cit., p. 145.
60. *Weekly Report* dated 23 January 1909. HDB: Feb. 1909, nos. 2–11 in IOLR IOR.POS.8960.
61. Memorandum by Stevenson-Moore, dated 21 September 1909, in HDA: Jan. 1911, nos. 52–64, op. cit.
62. Foreign Office, General Correspondence: France, 1909: FO371/1968, pp. 93–5.
63. Morley to Minto, 26 Aug. 1909. Morley Papers, IOLR MSS.EUR.D.573/4.
64. Letter from Sir E. Henry to Sir R. Ritchie, dated 1 April 1909, in *Proposal to obtain information regarding Natives of India residing in Europe.* HDD: May 1909, no. 21 in IOLR POS.10609. The Foreign Office was even less willing than Scotland Yard to

conduct enquiries on the Continent on behalf of the Government of India. Charles Hardinge, the Permanent Under-Secretary at the Foreign Office, wrote that 'Experience has shown that in enquiries of this sort through our Embassies abroad little or no assistance is ever given to us by foreign governments.' Letter from Sir C. Hardinge to Sir R. Ritchie, 27 March 1909.

65. Memorandum by Stevenson-Moore, dated 21 September 1909, in HDA: Jan. 1911, nos. 52–64, op. cit.
66. Ibid.
67. See Ch. 6.
68. Memorandum by Stevenson-Moore, dated 21 September 1909, op. cit.
69. At the end of his first year's work Wallinger himself was uncertain whether his mission would be continued. Memorandum by H.C. Woodman, dated 14 September 1910, in HDA: Jan. 1911, nos. 52–64, op. cit.
70. See, for example, letter from Cleveland to Wallinger, dated 4 September 1915, in correspondence on the subject of the deputation of Hector R. Kothavala, Deputy-Superintendent, Bombay Presidency, to the Straits Settlements government. HDB: Nov. 1915, nos. 389–406.
71. Wallinger had passed the exams for the Higher Certificate of the Government of India in Gujarathi and Marathi. These details were obtained from a curriculum vitae of Sir John Wallinger compiled after his retirement, which was kindly provided to me by his nephew, Mr J.D.A. Wallinger.
72. Note by Stevenson-Moore, dated 24 November 1909. HDA: Jan. 1911.
73. Letter from Sir H.H. Risley to the Hon'ble Mr A. Earle, dated 9 June 1910, in HDA: Jan. 1911, nos. 52–64.
74. Letter from Wallinger to Cleveland, dated 22 September 1911, in *Extension of the Deputation of Mr Wallinger in England*. HDA: Nov. 1911, no. 87 in IOLR IOR.POS. 6048.
75. By the beginning of 1910 the Government of India were very worried by the presence of Savarkar in Paris which meant that he could not be imprisoned once and for all after the statements made in India by Koregaonkar and Chatturbhuj Amin, which implicated him in the Jackson murder. A member of the Viceroy's Council even suspected that the Indians were operating their own system of Intelligence: 'It is significant that the members of this group seem to know precisely the legal value of the evidence against them. Against those who remain in London . . . the evidence is not strong, while the moment the evidence against Savarkar was complete he escaped to Paris. The inference is obvious that they have a well-organized system of intelligence.' Note by W.C. Woodman, dated 27 January 1910, in *Note by the Director, Criminal Intelligence on the Revolutionary Group, India House, London*. HDA: May 1910, nos. 133–5 in IOLR IOR.POS.5947.
76. Memorandum by H.C. Woodman, dated 14 September 1910, in HDA: Jan. 1911, nos. 52–64, op. cit.
77. Letter from F.H. Lucas, 7 July 1911, in CUL Hardinge Papers, Vol. 92.
78. The *Weekly Reports* of the Director of Criminal Intelligence distinguish between the material provided by the DCI's own officer in London, i.e. Wallinger, and information provided in Scotland Yard reports.
79. *Weekly Report* dated 28 July 1914. HDB: Aug. 1914, nos. 259–62 in IOLR IOR.POS. 9837.
80. Memorandum by H.C. Woodman, dated 14 September 1910, in HDA: Jan. 1911, nos. 52–64, op. cit. *Weekly Reports* dated 4 and 12 July 1910, in HDB: Aug. 1910, nos. 18–25, IOLR IOR.POS.8965, and *Weekly Report* dated 16 August 1910, in HDB: Sept. 1910, nos. 51–59, ibid.

In *Weekly Report* dated 5 May 1914, in HDB: June 1914, nos. 142–5, IOLR IOR. POS.9837, Wallinger reported that: 'In the debates on national subjects, especially at

Oxford and Cambridge, Indian students advance solid arguments backed up by facts and figures. They no longer talk at random as they used to.'

In *Weekly Report* dated 20 October 1914, in HDB: Dec. 1914, nos. 218–22, IOLR IOR.POS.3837. Wallinger seems sympathetic to the policies of the British Liberal Party towards India. 'The failure of the British government to grant concessions will bring disillusionment and strengthen the position of the nationalists.'

81. Hon'ble Mr Wheeler's note, dated 7 June 1915 in *Appointment of Mr Vickery, Assistant Superintendent of Police, Punjab, as an assistant to Mr Wallinger*, in HDA: Nov. 1915, nos. 88–92 in IOLR IOR.POS.7296.

82. *Weekly Report* dated 26 February 1910, in HDB: June 1910, nos. 1–8, and *Weekly Report* dated 3 May 1910, in HDB: Aug. 1910, nos. 1–9, IOLR IOR.POS.8965.

83. Cleveland's letter dated 21 August 1915, in *Spread of the Ghadr Movement in the Far East*. HDB: Oct. 1915, nos. 369–74, IOLR IOR.POS.9840.

84. Letter from Wallinger to Cleveland, dated 22 September 1911, in *Extension of the deputation of Mr Wallinger to Europe*, in HDA: Nov. 1911, no. 87, IOLR IOR.POS. 6048.

85. The first reference to conversations within the Paris Indians' 'inner circle' is made in *Weekly Report* dated 6 December 1910, in HDB: Jan. 1911, nos. 17–19, IOLR IOR. POS.8966.

86. *Weekly Report* dated 6 June 1911, in HDB: July 1911, nos. 1–4, IOLR IOR.POS. 8969.

87. 'Switzerland' became a regular feature in the *Weekly Reports* of the Director of Criminal Intelligence, after 1910.

88. Note by C.W.E. Cotton, dated 29 January 1915, in *Extension of the Deputation of Mr Wallinger in Europe for one year from 1 April 1915*, in HDA: March 1915, nos. 14–16, IOLR IOR.POS.7151.

89. For example, Cleveland's letter, dated 20 January 1915, ibid.

6

North America, 1905–14

Indian agitators abroad before the First World War generally feared the efficiency of the overseas intelligence system of the British Empire. In the United States their fears were strengthened by the past experience of their Irish-American sympathizers. After the Civil War the latter built up a military organization with which they hoped to conquer Canada. Yet their most secret plans fell into British hands thanks to the famous informer, 'Henri Le Caron'.[1] Despite their reputation, however, British intelligence arrangements in North America were not extensive. Neither the War Office nor the Admiralty ran networks of agents there before the First World War, and were represented solely by the Military and Naval Attachés in Washington. The activities of the British Secret Service Bureau, which was founded only in 1909, were directed almost entirely against Germany.[2] It did not operate in the Western hemisphere.

New York, the first centre of Indian unrest in the United States, was also the stronghold of Irish nationalism. The violently anti-British Clan-na-Gael organization welcomed the first Indian agitators to arrive in New York in 1905 with open arms. The Irish-American leader George Freeman had hoped that the Clan-na-Gael would provide the backing for a revolt in India.[3] Though the British were anxious lest the Irish provide Indians with firearms or with experience of bomb-making, they did not over-react to this potential menace.

Since the 1860s the British Home Office had run agents inside Irish-American circles. In 1905 the Home Department of the Government of India arranged with the Home Office that its New York agency should also provide India with intelligence. In 1910 India was paying a yearly subsidy of £300 for this service, in return for which it received a weekly report on Indian affairs.[4]

147

The Home Office agency was not extensive. Its activities were restricted almost entirely to New York, and it provided next to no information on Indians elsewhere in the United States. In 1905 the agency had only one full-time officer, Francis Cunliffe Owen.[5] The Home Office agent obtained information on Indians 'partly through personal investigation of [his] own, and partly through specially selected newspaper reporters'.[6] Cunliffe Owen himself, or one of his hired reporters, posed as a member of the Clan-na-Gael, and became intimately acquainted with George Freeman and with Myron Phelps, an American lawyer who, at the end of 1907 formed his own association for Indian students, the Society for the Advancement of India. By May 1909 he was one of only five or six whites attending the meetings of New York's main Indian club.[7]

In a general review of the Home Office agent's performance in 1911 the Government of India listed the kind of tasks he had performed.[8] He had read the American newspapers on India's behalf. He had traced some notable 'seditionists' for the Department of Criminal Intelligence, and gathered some quite detailed information about a few of them. More importantly, he had warned India that some of the nationalists in America had international connections. At times this intelligence gave cause for real concern. At the end of 1908 he mentioned a rumour that the SS *Moraitis*, carrying thousands of Mauser pistols, had sailed from New York for the Persian Gulf. This news stimulated considerable Foreign Office activity, which came to a farcical conclusion when the Consul at Smyrna (now Izmir) discovered that the ship was carrying only bicarbonate of soda.[9]

Despite the occasional scare, the Home Department and the DCI felt that Cunliffe Owen's reports furnished little of interest. Largely this was because of the slump in the activity of the Indian and Irish nationalists in the United States in 1909. Both the two main Indian nationalist societies in New York failed within a short time of their foundation. They attracted little support from the Indians in New York, and almost none from American whites. Cunliffe Owen, however, attributed the revolutionaries' lack of success to his own ability in invoking against them 'quiet influences of one kind and another, especially on the part of powerful people'. [10]

In April 1910 a meeting of a short-lived Indo-American Society was held in order to wind it up. The Clan-na-Gael leadership believed that the movements of the Indian agitators had been reported to the British authorities by one of the English or American members of the society, and that the Indians would be safer if they formed an exclusively Oriental society.[11] When the Indians followed this advice the Home Office agent complained that it was very difficult to provide information about them. The Home Office backed Cunliffe Owen, writing that the employment of at least one native Indian agent in New York was 'very essential', as English and Irish agents were 'practically useless' in Indian circles.[12] This request met with no response from the the DCI.

On rare occasions the DCI or the local CIDs persuaded Indians leaving for America to send back reports on the state of Indian opinion there. Likewise they encouraged natives of India to persuade their relatives abroad to supply information. These practices were a far from reliable way of gathering information.[13] A more regular means of supplementing the Home Office agency's information was to employ Pinkerton's, the famous American private detective agency. Lord Minto, who had formerly been the Governor-General of Canada, particularly favoured this method.[14]

The DCI despatched its own native Indian agent on a short mission to the United States and Canada in 1910. It was noted that the reports submitted by the Home Office agent compared very unfavourably with those of 'his coloured rival'. The latter reported that a large number of Indians in North America were 'full of anti-British and revolutionary ideas', but that they had not formed themselves into effective organizations; rather they were 'dotted about in many places in Canada and America'. This intelligence persuaded the Government of India that there was no foreseeable need to employ a permanent agent in North America.[15]

Far from finding the situation in America dangerous, in 1911 the DCI and the Home Department even considered stopping the subsidy to the Home Office agent. But the DCI was reluctant to cut itself off from its sole regular source of information in North America. The Indian government was still subsidizing the Home Office agency on the outbreak of the First World War.[16]

The reports of the Director of Criminal Intelligence give a good indication of how American intelligence was interpreted in India from week to week. From 1907 to 1911 the DCI seems to have been uncertain whether the Indians in New York were mainly concerned with politics, with money or with chasing white women.[17] By the end of 1908 it felt that the two latter factors generally predominated. The weekly reports cited many cases where Indians were allegedly only posing as freedom fighters in order the better to acquire donations from the American public.[18] The Indian authorities saw the vast majority of Indian agitators abroad as moral degenerates of one kind or another.[19] They held the often unsavoury personal habits of Indian agitators to be an extension of what they considered the immorality of their political opinions, namely their opposition to the Empire. This contempt, combined with the basic uneventfulness of Indian and Irish affairs on the East Coast, discouraged the Indian authorities from over-reacting to the far more dangerous situation among the Indian settlers on the West Coast which had developed by 1913.

Before the First World War both the affairs of Indians on the Pacific Coast and their surveillance by the imperial authorities were conducted in near independence from the East Coast. Until the out-break of war the only links between the intelligence agents in the two areas were the India Office in London, and the Department of Criminal Intelligence itself, thousands of miles away in India. By 1913 India was already the beneficiary of various ill-assorted methods of surveillance on the East Coast: the Home Office Agency, informers controlled from India, a DCI spy sent on a 'round trip' to America, and Pinkerton's. Pre-war events on the West Coast were not to break this *ad hoc* pattern.

THE WEST COAST

Sikhs from the Punjab and Hong Kong began to enter British Columbia in large numbers from 1905 onwards and were confronted by the wide-spread white hostility to Asians already experienced by British Columbia's Chinese and Japanese communities.[20] The situation in Canada soon became disturbing from an Indian as well as a Canadian point of view. In September 1907, while the Punjab was going through the most active period of unrest which it experienced before the First World War, a serious race riot broke out in the Asian quarter of Vancouver. This led to a Canadian government investigation from May to June 1908,[21] and to a secret mission by T.R.E. McInnes, the personal agent of the Minister of the Interior who enquired into the whole question of Asiatic immigration into British Columbia.[22]

McInnes singled out several agitators among the Sikhs, the most important of whom was the young Bengali, Tarak Nath Das. Like the Indian authorities, McInnes despised the 'seditionists' as extortionists and confidence tricksters, and denied their claim that there would be serious danger to the Empire if Indians were shut out of Canada. None the less, in July 1908 Ottawa instructed the Vancouver police to make enquiries about Indians who were collecting money to be sent to revolutionaries in India.[23] At the same time Canadian military intelligence also showed a fleeting interest in Indian affairs.[24]

The most positive action against Indian nationalists in British Columbia came not from the intelligence service but from an officer of the Vancouver Immigration Department, William Hopkinson. Though in the Canadian service, Hopkinson was an Englishman born in India, who was acutely aware of the potential danger to India of events in Canada. His father had been one of the military escort of Sir Louis Cavagnari massacred at Kabul in 1879, leaving him and his mother stranded at Lahore in the Punjab.[25] In effect Hopkinson was born into the service of the Empire. He spoke Punjabi and other Indian languages fluently. He had served in the Indian Police since the age of 16, first in the Punjab, and then in Calcutta from 1901 to 1907. There he attained the rank of sub-inspector. At the end of 1907 he went to Canada on two years' leave, unconnected with the Indian police, and was employed by the Vancouver Immigration Department as an interpreter soon after his arrival.[26] Hopkinson was annoyed to discover that Tarak Nath Das had set up a press near Vancouver. He reported this to the London *Times*. *The Times* published an article on Das, who as a result fled to the USA.[27]

At the beginning of November 1907 the Canadian government tried to encourage its unwanted Sikh population to emigrate to British Honduras. A delegation of Canadians and Indians went there, with Hopkinson acting as its interpreter. The scheme failed amid mutual recrimination, and the Indians accused Hopkinson of trying to bribe them.[28]

Canada's Governor-General, Albert Grey, and Prime Minister, Sir Wilfrid Laurier, thought that because of the current unrest in India they ought to watch for events in Canada which might be exploited by 'agitators' in India. They ordered the Department of the Interior to keep them informed on Indian affairs in British Columbia.[29] It is noticeable that the initiative in the surveillance of Indian agitators on the Pacific Coast at this time came entirely from the Canadian side and not from India, let alone from the British government in London.

The Canadian Department of the Interior employed Hopkinson as 'Dominion Police Officer on special duty at Vancouver' for an enquiry into the Sikh unrest there. At Canada's request he was put in communication with the Calcutta police. However, in the course of 1909 he resigned from the Indian police, and in February was formally engaged by the Department of the Interior on a salary of $100 per month. For the next two years he was officially a member of the Immigration Department at Vancouver. He did not receive a commission in the Dominion Police until January 1911.[30]

From 1909 to 1914 Hopkinson to all intents and purposes constituted India's intelligence system on the Pacific coast. His role was in many ways anomalous. Not only did he cease to be an Indian officer when he took up his duties in the Government of India's cause, but also the Canadians did not immediately inform the DCI of his appointment as special agent of the Ministry of the Interior. Indeed, the DCI had turned down his services in the past.[31] His reports were sent by the Governor-General's office to the Colonial Office in London, not direct to the India Office. Moreover, Hopkinson's mission, though secret, was not entirely concealed from the Indian agitators. Hopkinson and Tarak Nath Das were already personally acquainted in 1908, when Hopkinson had forced Das to resign a post as Indian interpreter with the US immigration service by giving the Americans details of his 'seditious' activities. In return Das denounced him as a secret agent in a Canadian newspaper even before he had become one.[32]

The employment of a Canadian agent in India's interests suited the DCI's policy of avoiding direct involvement in investigation as far as possible. The discovery of extensive British or Indian secret service activity within the United States would have had serious diplomatic consequences. The British Ambassador in Washington, Sir Cecil Spring-Rice, wrote in May 1914 that even official representations against a proven Indian revolutionary would at once galvanize anti-British sentiment and the Irish press.[33]

Hopkinson's one-man intelligence agency worked to the satisfaction of the Canadian Department of the Interior, the India Office and the Government of India. Because he had a 'good knowledge of Indians',[34] and spoke Indian languages, he found it easy to make contacts within Indian circles, unlike the Special Branch of the Metropolitan Police and the Home Office Agency in New York. India was thus spared additional irritating requests for assistance from Canada for the loan of its limited number of secret agents. Hopkinson had already made friends among the Sikhs before his appointment as special agent.[35] From 1908 to 1914 he built up an effective system of informers which was a recognizable faction within the Sikh community by 1914. There is some evidence that Hopkinson personally infiltrated Indian circles. His main assistant, Bela Singh, declared before a Canadian court in 1914 that 'he used to dress in a turban with a false beard and moustache and old clothes and go to the temple'.[36]

Hopkinson performed the dual role of imperial intelligence agent and agent of the Ministry of the Interior, besides working as immigration inspector. He reported regularly to the Canadian Deputy Minister of the Interior, W.W. Cory, upon 'sedition' among the Indians, their economic wellbeing, and all attempts to break the Canadian immigration laws. His reports show clearly that as a Canadian citizen he personally approved of his new country's strict immigration policy, which the Government of India wished to see relaxed.

Though he received no directives from the DCI, Hopkinson seems regularly to have contacted the Indian police. He reported that Tarak Nath Das's colleague, G.D. Kumar, held a meeting at which he denounced Hopkinson as being responsible for all the house-searches which the police had made at the homes of the audience's relatives in India.[37] Hopkinson was hated by the 'disloyal' Sikhs all the more because they realized that he upheld the immigration laws. His informers reported that at a meeting in Vancouver in June 1910 he was held personally responsible for Sikh immigration problems and for keeping Sikh women out of Canada.[38]

Despite his efficiency in securing informers inside Canada, Hopkinson felt frustrated at the end of 1911 by his inability to find Indians sufficiently trustworthy to operate within the United States. His main immediate concern was to prevent Tarak Nath Das's naturalization as a US citizen lest he take advantage of this status to return to India and cause trouble at the forthcoming coronation of George V.[39] In the autumn of 1911 Hopkinson made a 19-day tour of the US Pacific Coast. In San Francisco he met Inspector Ainsworth of the US immigration service to discuss Das's activities. Ainsworth professed his astonishment that the British government had never taken notice of the activities of the Indian students at Berkeley University. Hopkinson was particularly disturbed when he discovered that knowledge of explosives was widespread among the Indians on the Pacific coast, and that some of them were connected with the revolutionary societies in Bengal.[40]

The substance of the report submitted by Hopkinson found its way back to the recently appointed British Consul-General in San

Francisco, Alexander Carnegie Ross. He countered Hopkinson's implied criticism of his office by saying that its staff was too small to make a detailed investigation among Indians and that:

> As Mr Hopkinson points out his enquiries were of a superficial character . . . It seems unfortunate that when he called at the Consulate he was unable to produce any document showing that he was a Government Official of any sort . . .[41]

But Hopkinson's mission to America of 1911 had positive results. At Seattle, an American immigration inspector, Hunter, agreed to state on oath what he knew of Tarak Nath Das. Das was not granted naturalization as a US citizen until 1914. More importantly, Hopkinson started a network of informers within the United States; from this time onward the Indian 'agitators' on the Pacific coast were never to be free of British informers.

Hopkinson's informers came from widely different backgrounds. Upon his first arrival in San Francisco, Hopkinson called on the priest of the local temple, Swami Trigunatita, whom Das had once threatened and one of whose protégés he had beaten up. Hopkinson offered him protection, and thus secured the support of a very well-placed member of the Indian community.[42]

When Hopkinson returned to San Francisco in January 1913 Ross introduced him to two Indian students of Berkeley University, Surendra Nath Guha and Edward Pandian, who volunteered reports that at the end of December 1912 one Har Dayal held a dinner at the university to celebrate the recent assassination attempt upon the Viceroy, Lord Hardinge.[43] This event prompted the British authorities in Delhi and in London to view Indian agitation in America in a much more serious light than before.

In 1913 Indian agitators on the Pacific coast became more united and better organized. This was largely because Har Dayal provided them with charismatic leadership. He was the first Indian leader in North America to see that the ill-educated Sikhs of the United States and Canada could provide mass support and funds which the nationalist movement in exile needed. His cause was given vital assistance by the unremitting severity of the Canadian immigration laws which damned the Empire in the minds of the Sikhs. The first major step towards uniting Hindu intellectuals and Sikh farmers was taken when the Hindu Association of the Pacific Coast was formed in May 1913. By the Autumn, Har Dayal had started a revolutionary newspaper in San

154

Francisco together with a revolutionary party, which took its name from the paper *Ghadr*, or revolt.[44] By the outbreak of the First World War, *Ghadr* was being despatched throughout the British Empire, printed in numerous Indian languages.

The increasing virulence of the Indian agitation on the Pacific coast was accompanied by a strengthening of Hopkinson's ability to provide intelligence. In 1913 he was given greater assistance by the Foreign Office and by the Indian authorities, while by his own efforts he extended the contacts with informers and with US immigration officials which he had started in 1911. On 12 February 1913 the Foreign Office ordered Ross to co-operate with Hopkinson.[45] Ross by now was content to be guided by Hopkinson's expert knowledge of Indians and India, and put loyal Indians who volunteered information in contact with him.

In January 1913 Hopkinson attended two meetings in Seattle at which Har Dayal lectured on anarchist subjects. Hopkinson's relationship with the immigration officials at San Francisco and Seattle became very close in 1913. They were much more favourably disposed to Britain's desire to control Indian agitators in the United States than were the authorities in Washington. Hopkinson's personal contacts with them enabled the British to secure American assistance without approaching the State Department. Hopkinson was so trusted by the American immigration officials that in 1913 they employed him as the official US Hindu interpreter at Vancouver, and allowed him to send his informers on missions across the border.[46] The San Francisco officials also assisted Hopkinson's efforts to remove Har Dayal from the United States. The assistant commissioner at the Seattle immigration station promised him that if he was given documents implicating Har Dayal with anarchism, then the Immigration Department would investigate his case with a view to deportation.[47] Hopkinson was even allowed to hire a clerk inside the San Francisco post office, so that he could intercept Har Dayal's mail.[48] When Har Dayal gave his lecture on anarchism at Seattle in January US immigration officers attended, at Hopkinson's request.

Hopkinson eventually secured the agreement of the Washington administration to Har Dayal's deportation because it regarded him as far more obnoxious than other Indian nationalists. Har Dayal was one of the few Indian agitators abroad for whom the word 'anarchist' was not merely a term of British opprobrium, but an objective statement based on his own speeches in support of the Industrial Workers of the

World organization. Moreover, his supporters occasionally threatened US officers with violence if he was deported.[49]

By April 1913 Hopkinson claimed that he had only to give the word and the US immigration authorities would effect Har Dayal's deportation. Even though Har Dayal was a special case in American eyes, it is unlikely that the State Department would have responded so favourably to British wishes had it not been for Hopkinson's skill in winning the support of local American officers on the West Coast and in assiduously building up the case against him. Vital to the success of the case was Hopkinson's official status in Canada. Because he was not an agent of the Indian government neither the Indian agitators nor their sympathizers within the American administration were readily able to represent him as the henchman of a 'repressive colonial regime'.

The campaign against Har Dayal was devised and instituted by Hopkinson in complete independence of the Indian government. However, unknown to the Americans, Hopkinson was finally given discreet support by the Indian government in 1913. The question of the deportation of Har Dayal was too important an issue for a junior officer to bring to conclusion on his own. This was particularly so now that the authorities in India had become aware of Har Dayal's involvement in the assassination attempt on Lord Hardinge in December 1912. This precipitated discussion about employing Hopkinson as an agent by the Indian authorities. In April Hopkinson travelled to London in order 'to get his position in Vancouver placed on a satisfactory basis'. At the India Office Wallinger briefed him on the worldwide situation of Indian 'agitation'. Wallinger was 'favourably impressed with Hopkinson', while the Director of Criminal Intelligence found his reports of 'increasing value'. As a result, in April the Home Department granted Hopkinson an allowance of £60 a year as a 'retainer' and another £60 a year to spend on acquiring information.[50] The money was paid out of the Department of Criminal Intelligence's secret service fund. As a result the DCI started to receive a large number of reports from Hopkinson, while through Wallinger, the Director of Criminal Intelligence was able to recommend action to Hopkinson and provide him with advice.[51]

The improvement of the links between India and intelligence-gathering in North America came precisely three years after the Government of India had sent Wallinger on his mission to Europe. Such control as he had over American intelligence before 1913 was probably confined to receipt of information from the Home Office agency in New York.[52] By putting Wallinger in touch with Hopkinson, the Government of India was not yet consciously moving towards the creation of a truly imperial intelligence system under which the DCI controlled a heterogeneous but worldwide network of agents. Though the intelligence from the DCI's agents abroad solely concerned Indians and their plots, Wallinger's system of intelligence on the continent of Europe was not much smaller in scale than that of Britain's foreign intelligence agency, the Secret Service Bureau, which had been founded in 1909. Moreover, the quality of Indian intelligence from North America was certainly better than that at the disposal of the British secret service. However, the DCI did not intend to continue its imperial role. It employed both Wallinger and Hopkinson on a short-term basis; as in the case of the Home Office agency in New York, the continuation of their work and the maintenance of their subsidy was subject to review every year by the Home Department. The Government of India were so uneasy about employing agents in the United States that it even proposed spying on Hopkinson's work. In May 1913 the Director of Criminal Intelligence suggested getting in touch with someone who was going to America to check up on him.[53]

The *ad hoc* nature of the Indian intelligence system was epitomized by the relations between Wallinger and Hopkinson. Despite his superior rank, Wallinger acted not as Hopkinson's chief but as his adviser. The two men still served different viewpoints. In June Hopkinson forwarded a secret DCI circular to the Canadian government. Wallinger complained that he had no right to do so as the document was secret and the property of the Government of India. Hopkinson replied to Wallinger that he had circulated the DCI's formula with a view to keeping the Canadian government in touch with all information received, from whatever source.[54] But their relationship generally worked smoothly.[55]

Wallinger instructed Hopkinson to ask the US authorities to deport Har Dayal.[56] They arrested him in February 1914 but he immediately broke bail and fled to Switzerland. This did not at first weaken the Ghadr Party in North America, but the lack of a strong leader was later to prove disastrous to their cause.[57]

The Secretary of State for India, Lord Crewe, wrote in April 1914 to the Viceroy, Lord Hardinge, arguing that a better intelligence organization was needed for the Pacific coast.[58] The Governor-General of Canada, the Duke of Connaught, informed the Colonial Office in

May that, though Hopkinson was 'an energetic and excellent official',

> It is, however, highly undesirable that this work should be dependent on the existence of a single individual. In the first place, Mr Hopkinson has to cover the entire country from San Francisco to New York and from the Canadian to the Mexican frontiers. In the second place, the entire system – if system it can be called – is dependent on one man. If anything happened to Mr Hopkinson, the work would automatically collapse.[59]

Canada was not willing to pay for any improvements to the system. The Governor-General argued that Hopkinson ought to be transferred back to the Indian police. He felt that his work was of imperial rather than Canadian interest; yet despite the subsidies paid to him by India, the major part of Hopkinson's salary and his costly trips to the United States were met from Canadian funds. The Duke of Connaught's main worry was the danger that this expenditure might become known to members of the Canadian Parliament, and cause complaints which would severely compromise Hopkinson's work.

Wallinger persuaded the India Office not to take the Governor-General's advice. He argued that

> . . . the permanent transfer of Mr Hopkinson to the Indian Government would entirely destroy Mr Hopkinson's usefulness. He is now, by very reason of his multifarious offices . . . in a position to do some delicate work for us without having suspicion drawn upon himself. Once he is removed from these offices he would be a marked man.[60]

In August 1914 the Canadian Deputy Minister of the Interior, W.W. Cory, met Wallinger and Malcolm (later Sir Malcolm) Seton, the Secretary of the Judicial and Public Department, in London. He convinced the India Office that some expansion of the Pacific coast intelligence system was necessary because of the strength of the Ghadr Party. He did not feel that Hopkinson was suitable to be put in sole charge of an agency in America and Canada, though he recommended him as a 'very suitable worker under superior guidance'.[61] For five years Hopkinson had, of course, been such a one-man agency. However, he was a junior officer, only 35 years of age. Moreover, he probably lacked the sort of 'clubbability' which seems to have been considered an essential part of the make-up of senior secret service officers.[62]

Wallinger was certainly mistaken when he said that Hopkinson's 'multifarious duties' kept him out of the limelight. The conflict between his duties as intelligence agent and as immigration officer was in the end fatal for him. On 23 May 1914 a Sikh entrepreneur from Singapore, Gurdit Singh, challenged the Canadian immigration laws, arriving at Vancouver with 376 Sikhs from Asian ports on board the *Komagata Maru*. They were refused permission to land, and did not leave until 23 July. As interpreter at the Immigration Office, Hopkinson naturally handled the negotiations with Gurdit Singh. He acted as a very important restraining influence upon the more bellicose Canadians. Hopkinson stopped their plan to rid themselves of the Indians on the *Komagata Maru* simply by starving them.[63] When the Canadians finally decided to seize possession of the ship before dawn on 19 July, Hopkinson tried courageously but unsuccessfully to parley with the Sikhs 15 minutes before the assault. The attempt to board the ship failed ignominiously before a barrage of missiles from the *Komagata Maru*. Hopkinson came into public prominence during the affair. A journalist claimed that the Sikhs were particularly aiming for him when they fired on the boarding party. Hopkinson, it was said, only avoided serious injury when someone pulled off his immigration officer's cap.[64] The *Komagata Maru* left Vancouver only when warships were brought up.

The two-month wait of the *Komagata Maru* in Vancouver whipped the Vancouver Sikh community into a frenzy and gave a great fillip to the Ghadr Party. The first victims of Sikh vengeance were the Sikhs loyal to Hopkinson, led by Bela Singh. One Harnam Singh of Patiala was found with his throat slit.[65] On 3 September another of his faction, Arjan Singh, was shot by a member of the Sikh Temple Committee, which was the centre of 'sedition' among Vancouver Sikhs. The 'seditionists' trapped Bela Singh himself as he was praying for one of his dead friends inside the Vancouver Sikh temple. Bhag Singh, the priest, advanced towards him with an unsheathed holy sword, but Bela Singh drew out a revolver, shot the priest and another Sikh dead, wounded seven others, and made his escape from the temple. He then gave himself up to the police.[66]

The Vancouver press expected the trial of Bela Singh, whom one paper described in complimentary terms as the 'Hindu Adonis', to be a sensational one. But they got a different cover story from the one they had expected. On 21 October 1914 Hopkinson was waiting outside the court room at Victoria to testify in favour of his friend when a Sikh named Mewa Singh shot him at point-blank range in the chest. Hopkinson fell to his knees, catching his assailant round the thighs. Mewa Singh then struck him on the head with a revolver, Hopkinson released his hold, and Mewa Singh shot him five more times with a second pistol. He died five minutes later.[67]

From August to the end of 1914 the Ghadr leadership put into effect plans to send bands of revolutionaries to cause mutiny and revolt in the Punjab. Their failure will be described in the next Chapter. The Consulate at San Francisco and the Canadian immigration authorities had no trouble in passing to the Indian authorities information about the large numbers of Indians leaving. The Director of Criminal Intelligence credited the success in detecting the Ghadr exodus to the small intelligence system built around Hopkinson. Cleveland wrote:

> As the result of the existing agency in Canada and the United States of America, and of the co-operation of . . . [diplomatic] representatives in Japan and Singapore, we knew a lot of Indians were returning to India with some firearms. We also knew that at one time a proportion of the returning had been seriously tainted with the 'Ghadr' propaganda . . . practically we had all possible information about these people. The most extended intelligence agency abroad could not have told us more than we had been told, as no agency could have correctly foretold their state of mind on arrival in India.[68]

The Indian authorities were not sure what the effect of the death of Hopkinson would be. Wallinger wrote to Cleveland on 30 October 1914:

> The blow delivered by the terrorists may be said to be both morally and materially a very serious one. For the present we shall be left without any information from America whatever, which I think is a most deplorable thing.[69]

The Secretary of State for India wrote: 'I do not know of anyone who could fill the place of Hopkinson'.[70] But the Indian authorities soon concluded that for the time being they did not need anyone to replace Hopkinson in all his many functions. The whole situation in America changed upon the outbreak of the First World War. Within months of its beginning many of the most active leaders from North America were either in Germany – in particular Har Dayal and Tarak Nath

Das – or were involved in the plot in India, or were in British custody. Cleveland wrote to the Home Department:

At the present stage the practical question is not the intelligence abroad, but how to deal with seditious activities in India. If we can deal with the 'Ghadr' people already in India and with those who come to India during the next few months we shall have won our big fight. Intelligence from abroad may be useful to us during the next few months but it will not by any means be the most important factor. We have enough to go on and enough to tackle for the decision of the fight. The doings of the returned and returning 'Ghadr' people in India itself are now our primary objects of watch and action.[71]

The Home Department concluded that it was now the whole Pacific and the Far East rather than just the West Coast of North America which needed to be watched.[72]

NOTES

1. For Fenian activities in America in the nineteenth century see J.A. Cole, *Prince of Spies: Henri Le Caron* (London 1984), and K.R.M. Short, *The Dynamite War* (Dublin, 1979).
2. C.M. Andrew, *Secret Service. The Making of the British Intelligence Community* (London, Heinemann, 1985), Ch. 2.
3. For the importance of George Freeman in Irish-Indian affairs see Weekly Reports of the Director, Criminal Intelligence (Weekly Reports), Report for the Week Ending 9 March 1915 in HDB: April 1915, nos. 412–15, IOLR IOR.POS.9838.
4. The first reference to the Indian subsidy comes from March 1908. *Employment of Agents in America*. HDD: Aug. 1911, no. 17 in IOLR IOR.POS.10611.
5. In 1912 Cunliffe Owen became Military Attaché serving with the Greek forces during the First Balkan War. For his career in the Balkans see Richard Popplewell, 'British Intelligence in Mesopotamia, 1914–1916' in Michael Handel (ed.), *Intelligence and Military Operations* (London: Frank Cass, 1990).
6. Letter from F. Cunliffe Owen, New York, to Spring Rice, Washington, 26 Nov. 1915, in PRO FO115/1908 (113). Letter from P.S. Bullen, journalist, to Clive Bayley, 3 March 1908 in P&S 3000/08 in IOLR IOR.POS.438.
7. Weekly Report for 17 April 1909, in HDB: June 1909, nos. 108–14, IOLR IOR.POS. 8969. The association was by this date called the Indo-American Club.
8. *Employment of Agents in America*, op. cit.
9. P&S 3000/08, in IOLR L/PS/3/438. Telegram to Viceroy, 28 April 1908, P&S 3101/08, ibid. Letter from Foreign Office to Political and Secret Department, India Office, P&S 3150/08, ibid.
10. Letter from F. Cunliffe Owen, op. cit.
11. Weekly Report for 23 April 1910, in HDB: June 1910, nos. 17–25, IOLR IOR.POS. 8964.
12. *Employment of agents in America*, op. cit., quoted by H.H. Risley in letter to DCI of

March 1911.

13. An informer named Mahomed Husain provided details from Chicago. His reports were soon found useless and discontinued. Later Mahomed Husain went mad and in July 1911 started shooting indiscriminately with a magazine-rifle at passers-by outside the Chicago Opera House. He claimed on arrest that he had been prompted to do this by the 'tyranny of the British government'. He was so obviously insane that the Government of India escaped compromise. *Weekly Report* for 12 Sept. 1911, in HDB: Oct. 1911, nos.46–9, IOLR IOR.POS.8972.

14. For example, in 1911 the Foreign Office made enquiries through Pinkerton's when the Home Office informed them that an anarchist in Bessemer, Michigan, intended to sail to England and assassinate George V. PRO FO371 1270 (787).

15. The Director of Criminal Intelligence, Sir Charles Cleveland, concluded in July 1911: 'It would mean our employing several Indian agents if we wanted to keep in close touch with all that is going on among Indians over there but for the present it is sufficient to know the general trend of things as, I think, we do know it. When we have reason to suspect anything immediately dangerous we can adopt measures of our own'. Note by C.R. Cleveland, 8 July 1911, in *Employment of Agents in America*, op. cit.

16. *Home Office Secret Agent*. HDB: Feb. 1913, nos. 53–5 in IOLR IOR.POS.9835. *Home Office Secret Agent*. HDD: Dec. 1913, no. 8 in IOLR IOR.POS.10612.

17. For example, the DCI made sure that the Government of India and the Local Governments learned the full details of a scandal concerning the old suspect, Swami Abhedananda: 'Swami Abhedananda has at last been exposed in New York by a Mrs Beauley of Manhattan, and a considerable number of his feminine admirers have left the Vedanta Society in consequence. Mrs Beauley's grievance is that the Swami has been captivated by "a certain young woman" – a "Chinese blonde" – too fat for her height, ignorant, and not even prepossessing in appearance', and she regrets, in a strange language used by the followers of the cult, that 'the discordant woman got a hold on the Swami's psychic soul'. Weekly Report for 27 June 1911, in HDB: July 1911, nos. 1–4, IOLR IOR.POS. 8970.

18. For example, in the *Weekly Report* for 27 June 1911, op. cit., the DCI claimed that by telling tales of British oppression in India 'it is said to be very easy to reap a rich harvest . . . from credulous Americans of the class that provides recruits for the Vedanta Society'.

19. In the DCI's compilation of History Sheets, *Indian Agitators Abroad. Containing short accounts of the more important Indian Political Agitators who have visited Europe and America in recent years, and their sympathizers* (Simla, 1911), IOLR V/27/262/1, few offenders are accused of purely political offences.

20. For a general discussion of Indian immigration into British Columbia see T.G. Fraser, 'Canada and the Sikh problem, 1907 to 1922', in *Journal of Imperial and Commonwealth History*, Vol. 7, No. 1 (Oct. 1978).

21. Letter from Grey to Elgin, 15 Nov. 1907, in PRO CO42/914.

22. Ibid. McInnes's existence was so secret that the Governor-General did not know of it until the trouble with the American Exclusion Leagues.

23. *Note by the DCI on the anti-British movement among natives of India in America*. HDD: Nov. 1908, No. 6, in IOLR IOR.POS.10608.

24. Lieutenant W. MacLeod, Sub-Divisional Officer, Vancouver, forwarded the mailing list of the *Free Hindusthan* to his superior, Major Rowland Brittain, district intelligence officer. J&P 1309/09 (4452/08) with IOLR L/PJ/6/930. For other references to Canadian Military Intelligence see PRO CO42/929 (2904, 3723, 10826). The Canadians informed the British military attaché at Washington that Tarak Nath Das was receiving military training at a college in Vermont. The attaché transmitted this information to the War Office, and to the United States General Staff at Washington. The Americans instituted enquiries through a training officer at the college, who reported that Das had no

military ability and was not to be feared in any way. *Information regarding Tarak Nath Das who is receiving military training at the Norwich University, Vermont.* HDA: Feb. 1911, nos. 98–101 in IOLR IOR.POS.5949.

25. Extract from the *Daily Province* contained in HDA: Jan. 1915, nos. 3–6 in IOLR IOR.POS.7150. Hugh Johnson, in *The Voyage of the Komagata Maru* (Oxford: OUP, 1979), claims that Hopkinson was a Eurasian. However, this fact did not come out when the Government of India vetted him in 1913. They had full access to his police CV. Moreover, none of his colleagues commented on his race. It is in any case unlikely that a non-white would have been employed in the Canadian government service at this time.

26. Note by Cleveland, 7 December 1914, in *Murder of Mr Hopkinson.* HDA: Jan. 1915, nos. 3–6, op. cit.

27. Memorandum by Mackenzie King (undated), in PRO CO42/920. Undated report on sedition and immigration in Canada by Col. Swayne. J&P 320/09 in IOLR L/PJ/6/930.

28. Colonial Office to Governor General, Sept. 1908. J&P 320/09 in IOLR L/PJ/6/930. Ibid. Report by Col. Swayne. Ibid. Governor General to Colonial Office, 11 Dec. 1908. Telegram from Governor General to Colonial Office, 8 Dec. 1908. J&P 1309/09 (4591/08) in IOLR L/PJ/6/930.

29. Governor General to Sir Wilfred Laurier, 3 Dec. 1908. J&P 320/09 with IOLR L/PJ/6/930.

30. Hopkinson to Cory, 11 Jan. 1911. J&P 568/11 in IOLR L/PJ/6/1064.

31. On 19 April 1909, Stevenson-Moore for the second time argued against using his services. But he was informed in July by Ottawa's Commissioner of Police that Hopkinson had been employed by the Department of the Interior since the beginning of the year. HDA: Jan. 1915, nos. 3–6, op. cit.

32. Quoted by Mackenzie King in confidential memorandum, dated August 1908. PRO CO42/920.

33. Sir Cecil Spring-Rice to Sir Edward Grey, in *Question of Placing the 'Ghadr' on the List of Publications Prohibited from Transmission by Post to India.* HDA: Dec. 1914, nos. 96–8 in IOLR IOR.POS.7149.

34. Note by W.S. Marris in *Indian Agitation in California and Proposals to Check it.* HDB: June 1913, nos. 5–17 in IOLR IOR.POS.9835.

35. Undated Memorandum of Mackenzie King in CO42/920, op. cit.

36. Letter from Hopkinson to Cory, 17 Nov. 1910. J&P 568/11 in IOLR L/PJ/6/1064. Hopkinson was not, however, a master of disguise. When the Sikh temple at Victoria was dedicated he told Cory that he doubted whether any whites would be allowed to attend the ceremony, but that since he had sent his Indian agents to attend he would know what had happened all the same. Letter from Hopkinson to Cory, J&P 4161/12 in IOLR L/PJ/6/1137.

37. Letter from Hopkinson to Cory, 28 June 1912. J&P 2818/12 in IOLR L/PJ/6/1064.

38. Letter from Hopkinson to Cory, 17 Feb. 1911. J&P 1133/11 in IOLR L/PJ/6/1064. Letter from Hopkinson to Cory, 1 April 1912. J&P 1794/12 in IOLR L/PJ/6/1137. Letter from Hopkinson to Cory, 6 June 1912. J&P 2551/12 in ibid.

39. Letter from Hopkinson to Cory, 29 June 1911. J&P 3001/11 in IOLR L/PJ/6/1137. Letter from Hopkinson to Cory, 25 Oct. 1911. J&P 4803/11 in ibid.

40. From British Embassy, Washington, to Foreign Office. J&P 1257 in IOLR L/PJ/6/1137.

41. Letter from Hopkinson to Cory, 5 Oct. 1911. J&P 4355/11 in IOLR L/PJ/6/1137.

42. Letter from Hopkinson to Cory, 13 Oct. 1911. J&P 4530/11 in IOLR L/PJ/6/1137.

43. Letter from Hopkinson to Cory, 11 Jan. 1913. PRO CO42/968 (7054).

44. See E.C. Brown, *Har Dayal: Hindu Revolutionary and Rationalist* (University of Arizona Press, 1975).

45. Telegram from Sir E. Grey to Ross, 13 Feb. 1913. PRO FO115/1731.

46. Letter from Hopkinson to Samuel Barkus, Commissioner of US Immigration, San Francisco, 20 July 1914. PRO CO42/980 (29650).

47. Letter from Clayton Harrington, Special Agent in Charge, Department of Justice, Bureau of Investigation, San Francisco, to Hopkinson, 16 June 1913. PRO CO42 970 (25503).
48. Letter from Hopkinson to Cory, 17 Feb. 1913, in HDB: June 1913, nos. 5–17, op. cit.
49. Report by Samuel W. Backus, Commissioner of Immigration, San Francisco, to Commissioner-General of Immigration, Washington DC, 23 Jan. 1914. J&P 871/14 in IOLR L/PJ/6/1302. Letter from Hopkinson to Cory, 13 Feb. 1914. PRO CO42 978 (8778) In January 1913 the Department of Justice even granted a request from the Foreign Office that Clayton Herrington, its 'Special Agent' at San Francisco should assist Hopkinson. As a result Hopkinson was given a list of the Hindu students attending Berkeley and an account of the events leading up to Har Dayal's expulsion from his teaching post at Berkeley University for over-zealous advocacy of free love.
50. *Indians on the Pacific Coast. Proceedings of Har Dayal in the United States of America.* HDB: Nov. 1913, nos. 62–3 in IOLR IOR.POS.9836.
51. *Question of Placing 'Ghadr' on the List of Publications Prohibited from Transmission by Post to India*, in HDA: Dec. 1914, nos. 96–8, op. cit.
52. Note by C.J. Stevenson-Moore, dated 21 September 1909, in *Deputation of Mr Wallinger to England*, in HDA: Jan. 1911, nos. 52–64, IOR.POS.5949.
53. Note by R. Hughes-Buller, dated 21 April 1913, in HDB: June 1913, nos.5–17, op. cit.
54. Letter from Cory to Governor General's Secretary, 1 Oct. 1914. PRO CO42/981 (41409).
55. Wallinger described Hopkinson's work as 'of a most meritorious and useful character'. Letter from Wallinger to Cleveland, 30 October 1914. HDA: Jan. 1915, nos. 3–6, op. cit.
56. Wallinger's letter of 4 April 1913. HDB: June 1913, nos. 5–17, op. cit.
57. See Ch. 7.
58. No. 249a from Secretary of State. CUL Hardinge Papers; Telegrams, Secretary of State, Vol. 97.
59. Governor-General to Harcourt, 20 May 1914. HDA: Dec. 1914, nos. 96–8, op. cit.
60. Ibid. Undated memorandum by J.A. Wallinger.
61. Ibid. Wallinger to Cleveland, 28 Aug. 1914.
62. See in various places, Andrew, *Secret Service*, op. cit.
63. Letter from Hopkinson to Samuel Backus, 20 July 1914. PRO CO42 980 (29650).
64. Letter from Hopkinson to Cory, 16 July 1914. PRO CO42 980 (29647).
65. For the events leading up to the Sikh Temple shooting case see Weekly Report for 27 Oct., in HDB: Dec. 1914, nos. 227–229 in IOR.POS.9837.
66. J&P 5372/14 (5166) with IOLR L/PJ/6/1341. See also Weekly Report for 27 Oct., op. cit. The Director of Criminal Intelligence, like some members of the India Office, wondered whether Bela Singh needed to shoot nine men with two revolvers in pure self-defence. However, on the basis of this story Bela Singh was acquitted of the charge of murder by a Canadian court.
67. Letter from Malcolm Reid to W.D. Scott, 22 Oct. 1914. J&P 4987 in IOLR L/PJ/6/1341.
68. Note by Cleveland, dated 2 October 1914, in HDA: Dec. 1914, nos. 96–98, op. cit.
69. Letter from Wallinger to Cleveland, 30 Oct. 1914, HDA: Jan. 1915, nos. 3–6, op. cit.
70. Telegram from Secretary of State to Viceroy, 3 Dec. 1914. HDA: Dec. 1914, nos. 96–98, op. cit.
71. Letter from Cleveland to Home Department, 8 Dec. 1914, in ibid.
72. Ibid. Note by C.R. Cleveland, dated 8 December 1914.

7

India, 1914–18

When the First World War broke out in August 1914, the Government of India was greeted by a wave of support for Britain from the Indian middle classes and the princes. At this time the leaders of all the belligerents expected that the war would be a short one. It seemed that India would hardly be affected at all, apart from the need to deploy the Indian Army in anticipation of hostile action from the still neutral Ottoman Empire. Throughout the war there was never any serious threat of invasion by the Central Powers. The only possible routes into India which the Turks and the Germans might take lay through Afghanistan, which was neutral, and through Persia, which was jointly controlled by the British and the Russians. The Ottoman Empire remained on the defensive throughout the war, despite British reverses at the end of 1915, and despite the collapse of Tsarist Russia at the end of 1917.

The main threat to India came from the well-armed tribes of the North-West Frontier and from Afghanistan. The question of Afghanistan's neutrality was of key strategic importance to the Government of India in the years 1914–16. In that period the Raj's powers of control within India were considerably reduced. The administration and the police were stripped of men, whose services were required by the war effort in Europe. At the same time the bulk of the Indian Army was deployed on the Western Front, and against the Turks. By March 1915 there were only eight battalions of British regulars in India, who were fully occupied in defending the North-West Frontier.[1]

The worst possible situation which the Government of India feared during the first three years of the war was a combination of war with Afghanistan and some form of internal unrest. There were no doubts that such an event would put a major strain on the British war effort on a global level. Which sections of Indian society might create serious internal unrest? First and foremost, were the *bhadralok* of Bengal. The terrorist campaign which had already started before the war gained new vigour after 1914. One of the main achievements of British intelligence was in keeping the Bengali terrorists isolated from the Central Powers. Yet even without material aid from abroad, Bengali terrorism threatened to make the province ungovernable at the end of 1915. Bengal and its problems will be discussed in the next chapter.

The second potential source of unrest within India were the Indian Muslims. Upon the outbreak of war, the Government of India had some concern that sections of the Muslim community might sympathize with their Ottoman co-religionists. As will be seen, this threat was never more than potential throughout the war. The third source of unrest was the Ghadr Party, which had been formed in North America in 1913. Ghadr's initial plan was to cause revolution in the Punjab, a province which was of key importance to India's war effort. The initial Ghadr campaign had fallen through by the beginning of 1915. Thereafter, the Ghadr movement continued to exist throughout the war in its foreign bases. The activities of the Ghadr revolutionaries in the Punjab are one the subjects of this chapter. The Ghadr campaign against the Raj, which continued throughout the war from bases in the Far East and North America, will be dealt with separately.

Overarching the subversive activities of disparate Indian groups were the plans of the German government. From early on, the German General Staff had a fair understanding of the problems facing the British Empire. From the end of 1914 onwards they unleashed a series of plots with which they intended to destabilize India. Colonial subversion was a novel form of warfare at this time. The Germans failed in all their schemes largely because of their over-ambitious implementation. What was more apparent to the British at the time was the resourcefulness of German intelligence and the breathtaking geographical scope of its subversive campaign.

During the First World War the Department of Criminal Intelligence, the provincial CIDs, and a number of intelligence agencies based on London soon came to play a vital role in defending the Empire behind its front lines. Yet, as will be argued below, the war did not lead to a significant increase in the strength of the political police within British India.

Upon the outbreak of war then, the most immediate threat to the security of India came from the revolutionaries of the Ghadr Party who, from the end of August 1914, had started to return from North America and the Far East in order to cause mutiny and revolt in the Punjab.

A series of errors by the police in dealing with violent crime in the year before the intended uprising ironically had the effect of leaving them better prepared for the Ghadr plot than they would otherwise have been. The first of these salutary humiliations was the Delhi bomb enquiry. Before this the Punjab police had not appreciated how strong the base of the revolutionary movement was in their province. Though the extent of hostility to British rule was not nearly as widespread there as it was in Bengal, and the revolutionary movement was correspondingly much weaker, Additional Superintendent of Police Petrie believed that Rash Behari Bose had had 'marvellous success . . . as a political missionary in the Punjab'.[2] Rash Behari started work in the province in October 1910 at the latest. He found the nucleus of a revolutionary society among the followers of Har Dayal. Petrie wrote:

Collecting the remnants of Har Dayal's society around him, Rash Behari in October 1912 visited Lahore and found the time right for the inception of a campaign of violence.[3]

As a result of this information Stead, the Deputy Inspector-General in charge of the local CID, conducted a 'general "clearing up"' in the Punjab at the same time as he handled the Punjab end of the bomb plot enquiry.[4]

On the other hand, the seriousness of the threat posed by the returning Ghadr revolutionaries, which was greater than that from the home-grown revolutionary movement outside Bengal, became clear when the *Komagata Maru* arrived in Bengal, carrying the Sikhs who had been refused entry into Canada.[5] Cleveland chaired discussions between the Government of India and the Local Governments of the Punjab and Bengal about what to do with the returning Sikhs.[6] On 5 September 1914 the Government of India promulgated the Ingress into India Ordinance, which allowed it to restrict the liberty of anyone entering India after 5 September 1914, if such action was necessary to protect the State.[7] The government decided to apply the Ordinance to the passengers of the *Komagata Maru*.

When the *Komagata Maru* arrived in Bengal at the mouth of the

Hooghly river on 27 September 1914 she was met by a group of 29 Punjab police officers, including Petrie, and by Sir William Duke, a senior member of the government of Bengal. On 29 September, near the village of Budge-Budge, the British ordered the Sikh passengers to board a special train which was to take them back to the Punjab. The Sikhs refused and set off on the road to Calcutta, but were forced back by troops. At nightfall the British asked to see Gurdit Singh, the entrepreneur who had organized the voyage to Vancouver. Petrie recalled that at this point the Sikhs 'suddenly became very excited, and without warning hot revolver fire was opened on police and officers, while others charged them with staves, knives and even one or two swords'. Several of the British were wounded. Petrie was shot in the leg and arm. Troops then moved up and dispersed the Sikhs.[8] By the end of October, 202 passengers of the *Komagata Maru* had been interned under the Ingress into India Ordinance. Gurdit Singh and 28 others escaped.

The police had not searched the boat for arms, since the Government of India wanted to conciliate the Sikhs. It was anxious about the effect which their story might have on Indian opinion and genuinely sympathized with their predicament.[9] A *Weekly Report* of the DCI which indicated that the Sikhs might be dangerous arrived too late.[10] But the mishandling of the *Komagata Maru* passengers, like the enquiries into the Delhi bomb plot put the CIDs on the alert. The British took a much firmer line with the returning Ghadr revolutionaries.

The Ghadr revolutionaries had started to return to India in the first half of September 1914. The services of Hopkinson and Ross were of great benefit to the police in controlling them. The Punjab CID was waiting for the revolutionaries when they arrived at Hong Kong. Though they did not immediately take action, police officers mixed with the Ghadr supporters.[11] By this means they found out the full scale of the Ghadr Party's plans, and that Har Dayal had gone to Germany.[12]

On arrival in India, all returning emigrants were questioned by the police and checked against lists of revolutionaries sent by Hopkinson and by the authorities in Hong Kong. Furthermore, all travellers returning home from abroad to the Punjab or the North-West Frontier Province were ordered to report to the District Superintendent of Police at Ludhiana in the Punjab within six days.[13]

The majority of the Ghadr leaders had set out for India in only two ships, and made little secret of their revolutionary intentions en route.[14] The first boat, the *Tosa Maru* sailed for Calcutta and the second, the *Mishima Maru*, for Colombo. When the *Tosa Maru* arrived at Calcutta on 29 October 1914, police and troops were waiting for it; 173 were interned and despatched to the Punjab without being allowed to stop in Bengal.[15] Of the eight original Ghadr leaders, five were now in prison. The DCI later noted that 'the Ghadr movement in the Punjab possessed at the outset some fine material so far as men were concerned'.[16] Many of these men were now in custody. In his memoirs, Sir Michael O'Dwyer, the Lieutenant-Governor of the Punjab, reflected on the importance of this initial victory of imperial intelligence over the Ghadr movement:

> What the state of the Province would have been if all this gang had remained at large one shudders to imagine. The internment of the responsible leaders seriously disorganised the original plan of campaign, the success of which turned mainly on the secrecy and suddenness of their attacks. Before they were able to devise another plan and replace the leaders interned, we knew much more about their nefarious designs and were in a better position to cope with them.

Though many of the intended leaders of the rising were arrested, the number of Ghadr supporters who succeeded in getting through to the Punjab was still substantial. As will be seen, the Ceylon police were not fully prepared for the arrival of the *Mishima Maru* at Colombo. Moreover, a second major group left the USA at the end of October and assembled at Hong Kong at the end of November.[17] One of the problems facing the Indian police in dealing with Ghadr was that the CIDs were just too small to prevent every revolutionary from slipping through. Partly this was the result of the war, which had disrupted and overstretched the Indian administration as personnel were recalled to Europe. But the problems of the police also reflected the internal security policies which the Government of India had followed before 1914. The disadvantages of restricting the DCI's pre-war operations in the provinces and abroad now began to show. Cleveland informed the Home Department that 'The geographical information of my Department is . . . insufficient to enable me to say exactly where ships containing Indians are likely to come from'.[18] On the other hand, further clashes took place between Cleveland and the United Provinces CID on the eve of the war. The Lieutenant-Governor of the United Provinces criticized the DCI to the Viceroy, claiming that Cleveland had given the local CID no help, and blamed the DCI for its failure to conduct searches in the town of Benares where, indeed, Rash Behari Bose was hiding.[19]

Another problem the Indian police faced in dealing with Ghadr stemmed from their failure to appreciate the scale of the revolutionary movement, despite the warnings from Hopkinson and Ross, and despite the work of the Punjab CID at Hong Kong. The Indian authorities assumed too readily that all the revolutionaries would enter India through Calcutta. As a result, they had taken few precautions except in Hong Kong, Bengal, and the Punjab. But the passengers on board the *Mishima Maru* had joined the ship at Shanghai, whence they sailed to Ceylon without arousing suspicion.

The weakest link in the police organization against the Ghadr plot was precisely in the south of India. In 1914 F. Slocock of the Punjab police was deputed to the DCI 'on special duty in connection with the return of Indians from the Far East'.[20] Cleveland sent him to Ceylon. Slocock discovered that Indians were landing at Colombo and then crossing to India from the port of Dhanushkodi. The Colombo police guaranteed that no Sikhs would land with arms, but they would not guarantee that they could not pick up weapons on the way to Dhanushkodi. Slocock informed Cleveland that 'Neither the Inspector-General, Colombo, nor the Colombo Chief Secretary seemed to know anything of what was going on in India'. They were not even in receipt of the *Weekly Reports* of the DCI.[21] By December 1914 when Slocock arrived in Ceylon, many Indian revolutionaries had already penetrated India by this route.

The police in the south of India were no better prepared for the arrival of the revolutionaries. In crossing the Madras Presidency, Punjabi suspects were watched by detectives. The government of Madras was not confident that the railway police would be able to perform this task well. This was a province where there had been very little political unrest, and the police were unfamiliar with the techniques for dealing with it. The Local Government felt it necessary to stress that 'the police surveillance should be unobtrusive and should be carried out by men in plain clothes'. Moreover, the government of Madras was late in passing this order.[22] It seems that, as in the case of the Ceylon police, neither the DCI nor the Punjab CID had informed the Madras government of the seriousness of the threat from the Ghadr Party. The fact was that despite Hopkinson's information, the

DCI and the government of the Punjab had been taken by surprise by the sheer rashness of the revolutionaries' plans.

Another fact which hampered the police in dealing with Ghadr was a reluctance to appear to be using indiscriminate 'repression' against Indian citizens. The Ingress into India Ordnance gave the government a power over returning suspects which it did not have over resident revolutionaries until the Defence of India Act was passed in 1915. But within the British administration there was debate about how extensively the Ordnance should be applied. The Bombay government thought that returning Punjabis should be shipped direct to Karachi, while the Ceylonese government felt that Punjabis should at least not be allowed to enter Ceylon. But it was Cleveland who spoke for moderation, commenting: 'I do not think it advisable that the Government of India should forbid the landing of returning emigrants at any port to which ships are bringing them'.[23]

The impact of the Government of India's measures to stop the return of revolutionaries to India in the first months of the war did not become fully clear until several years later. The number of active revolutionaries who penetrated to the Punjab may be gathered from the results of the three Lahore conspiracy cases in which they were tried. A total of 212 were charged; of these 36 were sentenced to death, 77 to transportation for life and 15 to imprisonment. By this reckoning 128 were involved in the insurrection and caught. The DCI believed that considerably more must have wished to participate but thought better of it when they saw that the police and army were vigilant.[24] Further statistics indicate how great was the role played by returning emigrants. In the second Lahore case 90 were accused, of whom 50 were returned emigrants.[25] The cautiousness of the government in acting against its citizens is also revealed by police and immigration statistics. By 1917 about 8,000 Punjabis had returned home from abroad. In 6,000 cases no police action was taken, while 1,534 were temporarily restricted to their villages.

The Punjab was in an unsettled state at the end of 1914. There were various causes, amongst them religious revivalism, suffering caused by plague and rising grain prices, and rumours that the war was not going well for Britain, as well as the Sikhs' irritation caused by immigration policies within the British Empire, which had recently culminated in the *Komagata Maru* affair. But there was no broadly based opposition to the Raj of the kind which had emerged in 1907. The conciliatory measures which the government had taken since then had had their effect, and the Ghadr revolutionaries grossly mis-calculated when they assumed that the Punjabi population would welcome them with open arms.

The aims of the revolutionaries were to subvert Indian regiments in the Punjab, and to gather arms and money by a series of robberies. Their activities were at first unco-ordinated, and they wandered around either singly or in small gangs, attempting to collect recruits. They very quickly made themselves unpopular with the peasantry when they started to conduct dacoities from December 1914, which led to the deaths of a number of villagers. The revolutionaries were only marginally more successful in their plans to win over the Indian Army to their cause.

At the end of November 1914 the Ghadr Party made two attempts to start a rising. A group of revolutionaries had won over some troopers from the 23rd Cavalry, stationed at Amritsar. Their plan was to attack the magazine at Lahore. On 26 November a small group of mutineers marched against Jhar Sahib, a small town near Lahore. News of the plot leaked out and they were arrested on arrival. A second group planned to rob the treasury at Ferozepore on 30 November but a Native Sub-Inspector stopped them. They shot him dead and the police chased them, killing two and capturing seven.[26]

Despite these feeble attempts to shake the government, the majority of the Ghadr conspirators remained at large. Their plans to subvert the army continued as emissaries were sent to military canton-ments all round the Punjab and the United Provinces. In many cases they met with no success at all; in others a few men said they were prepared to help, but nowhere did they succeed in causing any serious trouble. The revolutionaries' main success was with the soldiers of the 26th Punjabi regiment who had just returned from Hong Kong, where they had become familiar with the Ghadr movement. Rebellion was being openly preached in the regiment by the beginning of 1915. The revolutionaries also still had hopes of the 23rd Cavalry, as well as elements in the 12th Cavalry and the 128th Pioneers. Moreover, the Ghadr Party had also taken steps to improve its command structure. At the beginning of November 1914, the Punjabi revolutionaries got into touch with Rash Behari Bose, who was hiding at Benares and in early February 1915 he set up a headquarters at Lahore from where he took command of the campaign.[27]

The police were already aware of a link between the Bengali and Punjabi revolutionaries by the beginning of December 1914.[28] Stead, the head of the Punjab CID, was in charge of the police operation against the Ghadr 'invaders' of the Punjab.[29] Another member of Punjab CID prominent in the counter-subversive action was a Muslim officer, Superintendent Liaqat Hayat Khan. At the beginning of February 1915 the police succeeded in penetrating the revolutionary leadership in the Punjab. The method which they used was remarkably simple. Hayat Khan sent for a Sikh whom he knew to be loyal, and asked him to find a man who would be willing to provide him with information. Two days later the Sikh came up with Kirpal Singh, the cousin of a revolutionary member of the 23rd Cavalry. Thanks to this family connection, Kirpal Singh quickly worked his way into the Ghadr leadership. They put him in charge of the work with his cousin's regiment.[30]

Ghadr plans were proceeding quickly by this time. Rash Behari Bose planned that on 21 February 1915 the revolutionaries should seize the weapons of the 23rd Cavalry while they were at roll call, and then kill the officers. Mutiny was to follow in the 26th Punjabis, which would be the signal for a general rising. British troops would be massacred and the revolutionaries would advance on Delhi and Lahore.

Since Kirpal Singh was organizing the revolutionaries' initial move by co-ordinating the action which was to take place in the 23rd Cavalry, the British should have had no problem whatsoever in crushing the plot. Rash Behari Bose, however, caused problems for the police by moving forward the date of the rising. Kirpal Singh found out the projected date of the uprising just in time. On 19 February, he returned to Lahore from his work among the 23rd Cavalary and discovered not only that the rising was to take place that evening but also that he was under suspicion as a spy. It is hard to understand why the revolutionaries both told a suspect police agent their plans and did nothing to restrain him. Kirpal Singh's next visit was to the Punjab CID, to inform Liaqat Hayat Khan of what was afoot. The only stake now at issue was how many of the Ghadr leaders the police would be able to capture.

Liaqat Hayat Khan ordered Kirpal Singh to return to the headquarters, and to give a signal when the revolutionaries had assembled. Only now did the revolutionaries take the precaution of confining Kirpal Singh to their house. None the less, they were still reluctant to restrain the call of nature, and when he asked to relieve himself in the afternoon they let him go out onto the roof. Kirpal Singh immediately signalled the police, who rushed in. Seven revolutionaries were captured, only one of whom was a major figure.[31]

The significance of the police action in Lahore on 19 February 1915 should not be overestimated. By now there was little chance that the rising would succeed. Thanks to Kirpal Singh's earlier information, the army command was already alerted to the possibility of unrest in the Indian regiments in the Punjab, and they imposed strict discipline. From the British point of view the big loss which might have been caused by the precipitate collapse of the Ghadr organization in the Punjab was Rash Behari Bose, the most wanted man in India, because of the attempt on the Viceroy in 1912. Bose escaped, and the British next located him in Japan, from where they were never able to extract him.[32] The Ghadr campaign in the Punjab continued with a few sporadic robberies, but even these had petered out by August 1915.

One notable feature of the Ghadr campaign was the reluctance of both the Government of India and the Punjab Local Government to overreact to the threat from the revolutionaries. One consequence of this restraint was the failure of the Indian police to stop all the Ghadr revolutionaries returning to the Punjab. But it is strongly arguable that the overall effect of British caution was positive. Despite a degree of concern about the internal security of India, which Ghadr and above all the terrorist campaign in Bengal were causing, the Raj stuck to its pre-war security policy. This amounted two rules: first, the overwhelming priority was to maintain the support of Indian moderate opinion; second, heavy-handed police action had to be avoided in order to avoid offending public opinion.

One notable feature of the Indian political scene throughout the war was the absence of any sort of spy scare. At the beginning of the war the British government and the British public were gripped by a fear of German espionage, which led to a major development of the counter-intelligence agencies at home. Despite an awareness of the German government's plans to subvert the British Empire, neither the Government of India nor the Indian police suggested that German or Turkish agents were involved on the spot with the political trouble in Bengal and the Punjab.

Notwithstanding its general restraint, by early 1915 the Government of India felt the need to equip itself with greater legal powers in order to counter any development of unrest within India, and help the fight against the Bengali terrorists. In March 1915 the Defence of India Act, which was modelled on the Defence of the Realm Act in

Britain, was introduced. Its key provisions were for the detention of political suspects without charge or trial, and for the appointment by provincial governors of commissions of three judges to try political cases without jury. To many of the British at the time, the introduction of the Act was a major step. Lord Crewe, the Secretary of State for India, stated on 6 March 1915:

> As long as the war lasts, I am not prepared to be at all particular about the liberty of the subject or about the need for legal proof before suspected persons are interned for such time as may be necessary.

It is important to note just how uneasy Crewe felt about introducing such measures, even when the Indian administration was stretched to the limit by the war, and faced by genuine revolutionary threats at home. Moreover, the implementation of the Defence of India Act depended to a considerable degree on the will of the Local Governments in India to apply it.

A good deal of the pressure for the introduction of the Defence of India Act had come from Sir Michael O'Dwyer, the Lieutenant-Governor of the Punjab, and as such it was partly a response to the Ghadr movement. From his point of view, the Act was very much in the way of insurance. It was not applied wholesale in the Punjab, particularly since the revolutionaries' plans had collapsed. The government of Bengal, on the other hand, was reluctant to put it into effect, even though the terrorist unrest which they faced was far greater than that in the Punjab, even at the height of the Ghadr campaign.

One group whose contribution was conspicuously lacking from the Ghadr campaign in the Punjab was the German General Staff. Before the outbreak of the First World War, the Germans had not established links with Indian revolutionaries. According to the Rowlatt Committee, which investigated the problem of Indian unrest in 1918, Har Dayal had founded the Ghadr Party as the result of conversations with German agents in Europe before 1911. This conclusion was based on evidence provided by the Indian Police.[33] However, there is no evidence to support this claim. At the time when the Ghadr Party was active in the Punjab, police reports did not point to any connection between the revolutionaries and the Germans. But for the Germans, their failure to associate themselves with the Ghadr movement at an early stage was a missed opportunity. It by no means reflected a lack of interest on their part in stirring up unrest in India.

German interest in the possibilities for subverting the British Empire extended to the highest levels of the German government. A month after the war broke out, Bethmann Hollweg, the German Chancellor, stressed the strategic importance of weakening Britain through a campaign of colonial subversion. As he told the German Foreign Office:

> England appears determined to wage war to the bitter end . . . Thus one of our main tasks is gradually to wear England down through unrest in India and Egypt, which will only be possible from there . . .[34]

The immediate problem for the Germans was that with the collapse of its plans in February 1915, the Ghadr Party ceased to be a serious revolutionary force in India. But for several reasons the Germans were convinced of the practicability of hitting the British in their colonial underbelly. First, though Ghadr had been defeated in the Punjab, it still had supporters in North America and throughout the Far East. Second, the British were facing mounting difficulty in containing the terrorist movement in Bengal. Finally, there was the question of the loyalty of India's Muslims. If the Ottoman Empire entered the war, the Muslims might provide backing for subversion. Even more importantly, the Central Powers might be able to stir up the tribes of the North-West Frontier and to shake Afghanistan from its neutrality.

Though the Germans had shown interest in the possibilities of subverting the British Empire before the war, they had no clear plans for doing so in August 1914, nor had they formed organizations for carrying out any such schemes once they were made. None the less, with the coming of war, the Germans moved very quickly to formulate a policy towards fomenting unrest in India and elsewhere. For its implementation they drew on the material nearest to hand – a collection of diplomatic staff, explorers and expatriates.

The formulation of the plans for the subversion of the Indian empire and its Persian and Egyptian satellites fell to the 'Intelligence Bureau for the East', attached to the *Auswärtiges Amt*, the German ministry of foreign affairs. This was created just on the eve of the war. It was headed by Baron Max von Oppenheim, who took up his position on 2 August 1914. Oppenheim's early career had embraced service in the German Consulate-General in Cairo, and archaeological research into the ancient Near East. In 1893 he had toured the region, and in the process acquired the nickname of 'the Spy'. This was an accurate description, since he seems to have combined his scholarly researches with intelligence-gathering.[35] A British archaeologist who knew him at this time gave him the even less flattering epithet of that 'chattering egotistical Jew'.[36] The Indian side of the eastern bureau's work fell to Otto Günther von Wesendonck, a junior official of the *Auswärtiges Amt*.[37]

One of the first tasks of the Intelligence Bureau for the East was to set up an Indian revolutionary centre in Germany itself. This they had succeeded in doing by the end of August 1915. The problem was that there were very few Indians, revolutionary or otherwise, living in Germany at this time. The Germans did, however, procure the services of Virendranath Chattopadhyaya, who had been a prominent if ineffective figure in pre-war revolutionary circles in London and Paris. The situation improved in January 1915 when Har Dayal arrived in Berlin, along with the prominent Muslim member of the Ghadr Party, Maulvi Barakat Allah.

Despite the name of the central organization, it would be misleading to speak at this time of a German secret service organized for the destruction of the British Empire. The Intelligence Bureau for the East gathered suitable officers wherever it could find them. The Germans who worked for it mostly combined their intelligence functions with their original jobs.

The most senior official involved with the Bureau was Franz von Papen, an aristocratic diplomat then serving as military attaché at Washington. Von Papen was the principal German intelligence officer in the United States until his expulsion in December 1915. His political career ended in 1933 when he was the last Chancellor of the Weimar Republic before Hitler came to power. Von Papen's liaison officer with the Indians was Ernst Sekunna.

In China, there was an Indian colony at Shanghai. Here, the German plans were in the control of the Consul-General, Knipping. In the Netherlands East Indies, the main German agents were two expatriate brothers, Emil and Theodor Helferrich. Here there was no strong Indian community, though there were many German residents. In Siam, on the other hand, there were numbers of both Indian and German engineers working on railway construction projects. In the Bureau's plans, the Germans were to provide the leadership for an incursion into India.

By Spring 1915, the Bureau's plans to cause havoc in the British

Empire had crystallized. The centrepoint of the campaign was a bold plan to arm the revolutionaries of Bengal. Von Papen was to acquire arms in the United States and ship them to India via the Netherlands East Indies. The Ghadr organization was to come into play in a second line of attack on the Indian empire. From Siam, Indian revolutionaries were to subvert the Raj's security forces in Burma. But the use of Indian revolutionaries did not stop in Asia. Other Indian groups were operating in Europe. Nor were the Bureau's plans confined to undermining India directly. A vital part of the Bureau's work involved the Near East. German agents were sent to work in Persia and in Afghanistan. The intention was to create instability on India's frontiers and, if possible, to instigate an Afghan invasion.

Though outside the scope of the Intelligence Bureau for the East, even Africa became part of Germany's plans to harass the British behind their front lines. The Germans had no chance of holding their pre-war colonies in Africa when faced by British naval power and the armed forces of South Africa, but they had no intention of quitting Africa without a fight. In East Africa, General von Lettow-Vorbeck succeeded in raiding Kenya. His guerrilla operations continued until the end of the war, and at one point the German General Staff even sent a Zeppelin to keep him supplied.[38]

Von Lettow-Vorbeck's operations in East Africa were only a side-show in the war. The Germans generally, and Oppenheim in particular, intended to cause major unrest against Britain in the Muslim world. The Germans' hopes received a great boost when the Ottoman Empire entered the war on the side of the Central Powers on 5 November 1914.

Since the late eighteenth century, the Ottoman Sultan had claimed a religious authority over all Muslims, whether were his subjects or not. This was because they were also Caliphs, or successors to the Prophet Muhammad in his social and political functions. By the end of the nineteenth century, these claims had found resonance among some Muslims, who looked with respect upon the Ottoman Empire as the last powerful Muslim state. It was also the only truly independent Muslim state with the exception of Afghanistan. After Abd ul-Hamid became Sultan in 1876, the Ottomans used the caliphate much more vigorously as a diplomatic weapon against those European powers which ruled over large numbers of Muslims, namely Russia, France and Britain.[39] Caliphate propaganda did not amount at this time to a threat to subvert the British Empire but the Ottomans did see it as a kind of insurance policy, for use should trouble arise with the colonial empires.

British concern about the Ottoman government's fostering of Pan-Islamic loyalties came after Abd ul-Hamid had been deposed, during the First Balkan War of 1912–13. In this conflict, the British maintained a strict neutrality. None the less, large quantities of Ottoman propaganda found its way into India, calling on Muslims to support their Turkish co-religionists in their struggle against the Christian powers of Serbia, Bulgaria and Greece. Numerous documents of the Government of India's Home Department show the concern with which the British saw this development. Indian Muslims had always looked outside India for cultural inspiration, above all to the Persian court. By the beginning of the twentieth century, there were clear signs that they were concerned both about the weak state of the Muslim powers and about their own decline in importance within India. The revocation of the Partition of Bengal in 1912 had encouraged these feelings, when the British appeared to be courting Hindu support at Muslim expense. Indian Muslims felt that Britain's lack of sympathy for the Ottoman Empire during the Balkan wars paid little respect to their religious feeling.

When war broke out with Britain, the Turks were quick to play the pan-Islamic card. In November 1914 the Ottoman government issued five religious pronouncements or *fatwas* in which they called upon all Muslims to wage *jihad*, or holy war on the Allies. At this time the danger of Muslim unrest in Egypt, Persia, Afghanistan, and India seemed more of a threat to the British than Ottoman military strength.[40] On top of this, there was the danger that pan-Islamic sentiment might spread to the Indian Army, about a third of which was composed of Muslim troops.

But British concern about pan-Islamism within India should not be exaggerated. In 1914 the DCI started to issue general reports on Muslim opinion to the government. No one in the DCI could speak Turkish or Arabic. They had difficulty in translating the *fatwas*. In 1910–12 there were no files in the DCI on 'Muhammedan agitation'. In fact the Government of India was probably less worried by Muslim support for Turkey at the beginning of the war than it was during the Balkan wars. Thus in 1913 there were 124 files on Muslim 'agitation' (compared with 283 on 'Political Agitation'). In 1914 this figure decreased to 93 (compared with 291 on 'Political Agitation' and 294 on 'Indians Abroad').[41]

Fear of the Indian Muslims' reaction to Turkey's entry into the war soon died away. At the beginning of 1915 Sir George Roos-Keppel, the Chief Commissioner of the North-West Frontier Province which faced Afghanistan, reported that most of the warlike Pathan population of his province were 'unmoved by Pan-Islamic agitation', and were likely to remain so. The only Pan-Islamic threat he perceived came from a small pro-Turkish party of young men, which existed mostly in the cities. This totally lacked popular support and the Local Government was unwilling to make martyrs of them.[42]

During the Ghadr campaign in the Punjab, O'Dwyer had had remarkably little to say about the condition of the local Muslims, who gave no support to the Ghadr Party.[43] In December 1914 he informed Lord Hardinge that the British victories over the Turks in Mesopotamia had impressed the Muslims, and recruiting among them was going very well.[44] O'Dwyer later claimed that during the war the government of the Punjab had had to take the Pan-Islamic movement 'seriously' even though it was confined to a very small group, and had little chance of mass support.[45]

The Government of India had no difficulty in stemming such pan-Islamic agitation as there was in India with mild police measures. The more extreme pan-Islamic journals were censored, while news about the war with the Turks was strictly controlled. The main pan-Islamist leaders, Shaukat Ali and Mohamed Ali, were found in correspondence with persons in Afghanistan about a *jihad*, but this came to nothing. In June 1915 the government had confined them to their home village under the Defence of India Act.[46]

The main Muslim threat to the Raj throughout the war came not from within India, but from Afghanistan and the tribes on the North-West Frontier. Even here the Government of India was surprised by the end of 1914 that no tribal incursion had taken place.[47] The Afridis were the most dangerous of the tribes, whose territory faced the central part of the North-West Frontier Province, including the strategically-important Khyber Pass. They were well-armed, well-organized and numerous. They had been quiet since Curzon's day, and the British had kept them sweet through regular subsidies. The improvement in relations with the Afridis had been particularly marked since 1908. Roos-Keppel remarked that 'if we can hold the Afridis throughout the war, they will prevent any frontier conflagration from becoming national or general'. Many of the less friendly frontier tribes were either dominated by the Afridis or were feuding among themselves.

180

The main threat from the North-West Frontier came from Afghanistan, where conditions were unsettled and the central government was far from being in complete control of all its subjects. Roos-Keppel stated in early 1915:

> The position is a curious one, as we are practically at war with an Afghan province, the war being so one-sided that the enemy can prepare a stroke at leisure, safe from our observation and can strike when and where he likes in great force, while we are bound to a very strict defensive and are debarred even from the tactical offensive to our very great disadvantage.[48]

The Germans thought that they would be able to exploit this situation to great effect.

Afghan tribal raiding was no more than a nuisance to the British. The real danger lay in the possibility that the Amir of Afghanistan might be forced into declaring a *jihad* on the British because of popular pressure or at the instigation of the Central Powers. The worst possible situation for the British in 1915–16 would be if they were faced with war with Afghanistan, and the Muslim unrest in India which this might stimulate, together with an escalation of the terrorist campaign in Bengal. If this situation had come about, as seemed possible, in the years 1915–16, there is no doubt that the Raj would have been faced with a serious military threat, and that the British war effort in general would have been undermined as a consequence. This threat was by no means fanciful. In these years, the internal situation in Bengal approached crisis, while in 1919 the Afghan government did launch a surprise invasion of India, even though the Raj was in a stronger military position than it was at the outset of the war.

From the beginning of the war, the Germans were very much alive to the possibilities of creating unrest in the Muslim world, as were the Turks. The Ottoman Empire's war leader, Enver Pasha, had divided the Islamic world into four areas for the purposes of the holy war which he hoped to create: the Arabian peninsula; Persia; Afghanistan and India. Each was under the direction of an officer of the Ottoman General Staff. An Indian revolutionary headquarters was set up in the Arabian city of Medina, headed by one Moulvi Mahmud Hassan.[49]

The British became aware that the Turks were planning to stir up India's Muslims even while the Ottoman Empire was neutral. In August 1914 they arrested a young man who had arrived in India through the Khyber Pass. Sewn into the linings of his clothes the police found messages to Indian Muslim leaders, warning them the Caliph would declare a *jihad* if he went to war with Britain.[50]

Despite Enver's initial plans, the Ottoman Empire played only a subsidiary role in the fomenting of Muslim unrest after the outbreak of war. By the middle of 1915, the Turks were not even making a serious attempt to spread propaganda among the troops of the Indian Army.[51] During their unsuccessful campaign against Egypt at the beginning of 1915, the Turks had brought with them quantities of Pan-Islamic propaganda, but this element was notably lacking from their subsequent campaigns. British military intelligence in Mesopotamia, for example, never commented on Turkish propaganda, and expressed little concern about the loyalty of the Muslim soldiers. There were, after all, only a very few desertions to the Turks.

By the beginning of 1915 the main thrust behind the Central Powers' subversive campaign in the Islamic world was provided by Oppenheim and the German Intelligence Bureau for the East. The Bureau was involved with the early Turkish plans, but its relations with the Turkish General Staff were poor.[52]

German operations in the Near East fell into three general areas: attempts to secure recruits from among Indian prisoners of war; a scheme to cause unrest in Persia; and a mission sent to Afghanistan to try to cause an Afghan invasion of India.

Little need be said about the attempt to recruit Indian POWs captured in Mesopotamia. The Germans sent a small group of Indian revolutionaries to Baghdad. The expedition was a shambles. Even after the British defeat at Kut at the beginning of 1916, the Indians had little success, since they were preoccupied by their squabbles with one another. As one of them complained to Berlin, one of the leaders of the mission, Dr Mansur, had created a 'licentious atmosphere' and was 'governed by people who have absolutely no morals and lead a dissipated and debauched life'.[53]

There is no evidence that the British were at all concerned about the Indian revolutionary group at Baghdad. They were far more worried when they discovered German agents operating among the tribes in the south of Persia at the beginning of 1915. In the early twentieth century, Persia was a state almost in name only. The authority of the Shah barely extended beyond a handful of cities. Much of the country was desert and was in the hands of nomadic tribes who had great military and political power inside the country. Both the British and the Russians were concerned about the presence of this unstable land on the borders of their respective empires. In 1907 they acted in concert to divide Persia into two spheres of influence, with the Russians taking the north, and the British the south. As a consequence, Persian sentiment was often hostile to the British, who were seen as occupiers, although their presence in Persia was low-key. Russia, on the other hand, was the historic enemy which Persians generally hated. Persians, from the Shah downwards, could be expected to sympathize with whichever power was fighting Russia. In Persia, then, there existed ample fuel for the Germans to stoke up unrest. This was of concern to Britain for two reasons: first, their army in Mesopotamia was small and could not afford trouble behind its lines; second, serious unrest in Persia might well cause a chain reaction affecting Afghanistan and the tribes of the North-West Frontier and, ultimately, even the Muslim population in India.

German subversion in the south of Persia was in the hands of Wilhelm Wassmuss, the former Consul at the port of Bushire. His exploits were to earn him the admiration both of his own side and of the British, together with the title 'the German Lawrence'. Wassmuss arrived in Persia in the middle of February 1915 along with another German and two Indian revolutionaries. The British were aware of their presence and intercepted them at the beginning of March 1915. Wassmuss managed to escape, but he left his possessions behind him. These included several thousand subversive documents written in various Indian languages, [54] among them a code book which was to be of tremendous importance to Britain in reading German diplomatic correspondence.[55] But the loss of Wassmuss was serious. As early as the beginning of March 1915, troops from the Mesopotamian Expeditionary Force had to be detached to deal with tribal unrest behind the front line. Wassmuss was able to work effectively among the tribes until the end of the war. He undoubtedly contributed to the instability in Persia, which at times led to fears that it might enter the war on the German side.[56] These fears only abated when the British finally began their successful campaign against the Turks in Mesopotamia at the beginning of 1917.

The Germans' third line of attack was through Afghanistan. Their intrigues in Kabul in 1915 were unsuccessful, but for a time they caused the British just as much concern as Wassmuss's operations in Persia. The Germans' main plan to strike at India from the north revolved around Kunwar Mahendra Pratap, the deposed ruler of a tiny Native state. He arrived in Switzerland in March 1915. By a magnificent feat of showman-ship Pratap convinced the Germans that he was an important Indian Prince. He refused to treat with the German officials in Switzerland and demanded an audience with the Kaiser himself. This, in the opinion of the Germans, was how an Indian prince ought to behave.[57]

On 10 April Pratap set out for Afghanistan, accompanied by a German consular official, Werner von Hentig, and a Turkish officer, Kasim Bey. The German Chancellor, Bethmann Hollweg, gave Pratap three illuminated addresses to the Indian princes, in which he promised German support for Indian freedom, as well as a letter to the Amir of Afghanistan in which he promised him India as far as Bombay if he would join in the 'jihad war' against the Raj.[58] At Constantinople, Enver Pasha, Turkey's war leader, wrote him a letter of introduction to the Amir of Afghanistan.[59] In Mesopotamia, Pratap was joined by the Muslim revolutionary Barakat Allah, and by an army officer, Oberstleutnant Oskar von Niedermayer, who was the leader of the expedition. The mission reached Kabul on 2 October 1915.

The mission failed to shake Habibullah, the Amir of Afghanistan from his neutrality. He informed the Viceroy of the presence of the Germans and Indians and promised to keep the peace with India.[60] But the British were aware that Habibullah was under pressure to side with the Central Powers. First, he had to keep in mind the Muslim passions of many of his subjects; as it was, he was unable to restrain Afghan raids against India from the south of the country. Second, he was under pressure from a court faction led by his brother, Nasrullah, which included his son, Amanullah. They were anti-British and pro-Turkish and wanted to join the Central Powers. They were supported by the Kabul press. The chance that Habibullah might die worried the Government of India. These fears were not unfounded. The Third Afghan War did indeed break out when Amanullah became Amir in 1919, after Habibullah's death in suspicious circumstances.

The combined threat from Afghanistan and Persia was particu-larly serious at this time because of the strain put on India by the war and because of the terrorist problems in Bengal. At this time, the Government of India was critically short of troops for its internal defence, since so many men had been sent to Mesopotamia and France. What was worse, the British were suffering reverses at the hands of the Turks. At the end of 1915 the evacuation from Gallipoli started, while in April 1916 a British army surrendered with its colours at Kut in Mesopotamia, after a siege lasting five months.

From the Government of India's point of view, a particularly disturbing feature of the developments in Afghanistan was their lack of information about intrigues at the Amir's court and about the operations of German intelligence. The Indian secret service in Europe only received information that the expedition had set out in October 1915.[61] The Russians tried unsuccessfully to intercept it in Persia but they were a month too late, since Pratap and his party had already arrived at Kabul. The British had no guarantee at this time that they could stop the free flow of German and Turkish emissaries into Afghanistan.

A second problem was that there was great difficulty in obtaining information from Kabul. Roos-Keppel noted at the beginning of 1915 that 'News from Afghanistan is scanty'.[62] There was always an Indian Muslim, or agent, representing the Government of India in Kabul. His reports were supplemented by often unreliable information picked up at Peshawar by tribal informers.[63] But obtaining information was never easy, not least because of the ruthless nature of the Afghan regime. The first reference to the DCI in Kabul was dated January 1916, when an agent codenamed 'X' arrived there. He reported on the German–Turkish–Indian mission and his reports supported apprehensions that Afghanistan's neutrality was very fragile.[64]

By the middle of March 1916, the German-Indian mission to Kabul started to break up because of Habibullah's persistence in maintaing neutrality, and because of its own internal squabbles.[65] The failure of Germany's immediate plans in Afghanistan was only a limited reassurance to the British. Habibullah did not deport Pratap who, on 1 December 1916, founded the 'Provisional Government of India'.[66] From the British point of view a particularly alarming feature of the situation was the re-emergence of the Wahabi threat.[67] A number of Indian exiles gathered round Pratap, the most prominent of which was the Wahabi 'Home Minister', Obeidullah, a former teacher at the Islamic fundamentalist Deoband School in the United Provinces. He had gone to Afghanistan to encourage a *jihad* against the British.[68]

During the war enquiries in India showed 'a considerable revival of activity' amongst the Wahabis, as well as 'a revival of interest in the Colony of Hindustani Fanatics'. Fifteen young men from Lahore went to join them. Four of them went to Kabul, where they were favourably received by the Amir's brother, Nasrullah. Some of the 'Hindustani Fanatics' were involved border skirmishes in 1915.[69] At the end of 1916 the police found that the Hindustani Fanatics had recently received 'increased supplies of money and very material additions to their numbers'. Two Bengali Wahabis were captured transferring money collected in Bengal to the Hindustani Fanatics. The DCI still felt at the end of the war that 'a close connection still exists between the Fanatics and the descendants of the old Wahabi leaders, a combination which must always be regarded as a possible danger'.[70]

British fears about the Wahabis reached a climax at the end of 1916 in the so-called 'Silk Letter Plot'. The 'provisional government' at Kabul wanted help from the Turks in order to fulfil their grand strategy. O'Dwyer recalled:

> It was designed to unite all the forces of Islam, the Turks, the Arabs under the Sherif of Mecca, the Afghans, the Frontier tribes, and the Mohammedans of India, in a combined effort against British rule. This was to take the form of an attack by the Frontier tribes, incited by the Hindustani Fanatics . . . supported by a general Mohammedan rising in India. It was hoped that the revolutionary Hindus and the America-returned Sikhs would at once join in.[71]

With the aim of contacting the Turks, Obeidullah tried to get in touch with the headmaster of the Deoband School, Mahmud Hassan, who was a fellow Wahabi. Obeidullah intended that Mahmud Hassan should find a pilgrim on his way to Mecca who would deliver to the Turks two letters written on yellow silk. However, the messenger carrying the letters from Kabul to Deoband showed them first to a Muslim in the Punjab who was a friend of O'Dwyer's and who contacted the police.[72]

It seems that the British had not been aware of the ambitions of the 'provisional government' until then. One of the 'silk letters' claimed that the 'provisional government' 'has commenced to establish centres in India and to make alliances with other powers, in which work initial success has been gained'. The letter also referred to the formation of 'The Army of God' within India.[73] Cleveland feared another terrorist surprise, such as had been inflicted on the Bengal police in 1907. He wanted to make widespread arrests in the United Provinces. The Local Government would not agree to this, having come to the conclusion that the letters were 'really a confession of failure'. The Inspector-General of the United Province, Sir William Marris, expressed the hope that the local Muslim population would 'be so busy with their Congress and League proceedings as not to have much leisure for Pan-Islamism or desperate remedies'.[74] The Local Government placed about 20 of the most active conspirators under house arrest.

By 1917 the British no longer perceived a threat from Indian revolutionaries in Afghanistan. The Arab revolt against the Turks which started in June 1916 had made communications between India and Turkey via the pilgrimage routes to Mecca and Medina very difficult. The DCI noted:

In Afghanistan there is a party in favour of war against Britain which has powerful leaders and adherents, though there is reason to believe that opinion in that country has lately veered round to the view that things are not now going so well for the Central Powers of Europe, and that the Amir has been well advised to remain neutral.[75]

In fact, by the beginning of 1917 German plans to subvert the British Empire had failed completely. Their greatest success was through the work of Wassmuss in Persia, though even this had only a limited effect on hampering the British war effort against the Ottoman Empire. The Germans had not succeeded in causing unrest in the Muslim world and had notably failed to assist the terrorist campaign in Bengal, which the British now at last had under control. None the less, it is too easy to dismiss German plots as ill-founded, if not farcical. It is important to look not just at the material effects of German intrigue, but also at its psychological impact. Undoubtedly the Germans created fear in the minds of the British about what their intrigues might lead to and this had a significant effect on two important areas of imperial policy: first, the strategy adopted in the war against the Ottoman Empire in the period 1915–16; second, the internal security policy followed by the Government of India after the war. In both cases the British overreacted to the threat which they perceived and this over-reaction was a direct result of their lack of intelligence about their adversaries both within India and abroad.

A key factor guiding Britain's strategy against the Turks was the need to impress Muslim opinion in Afghanistan and in India. At the end of 1914 a small expeditionary force was sent to Basra. For over a year it won spectacular victories against the Ottoman armies, but by the end of 1915 it found itself depleted and faced by superior forces. With the benefit of hindsight, the British army in Mesopotamia ought to have retreated. In fact, the Government of India demanded that it should stay put and prepare for an advance on Baghdad. This decision appears irrational, unless the enormous political difficulties caused by German intrigues in Persia and Afghanistan, and the virulence of terrorism in Bengal are taken into account. In November 1915, the Viceroy, Lord Hardinge, informed Austen Chamberlain, the Secretary of State for India, that:

> To regard the capture of Baghdad as impossible would be to give up our best means of countering the German intrigues in Persia and Afghanistan against India and should therefore be dismissed from our calculations. Our success hitherto in Mesopotamia has been the main factor which has kept Persia, Afghanistan and India itself quiet . . .[76]

Far from advancing on Baghdad, the Mesopotamian Expeditionary Force found itself besieged by the Turks in the town of Kut, shortly after Hardinge wrote his telegram. The result was the greatest British military humiliation of the First World War. In April 1916, the Mesopotamian Expeditionary Force surrendered with its colours to the Turks, the first time a British army had done this since the battle of Yorktown in 1781, during the American War of Independence.[77] Even after the disaster, the India Office still justified the logic behind the Mesopotamia campaign, or the 'mess pot' as it was now often called. It claimed that the presence of the expeditionary force in Mesopotamia

> probably arrested a pan-Islamic movement on a large scale throughout Mesopotamia, Persia and Afghanistan, which might easily have developed into *jihad* on the Indian frontier. It may justly be asserted that this timely offensive stroke saved India from being involved in a great war on its own borders, the consequences of which would have been a serious strain on the vital resources of the whole British Empire.[78]

The second area where German intrigues and the existence of the Indian revolutionary movement contributed significantly to British anxiety was in their post-war policy for dealing with internal unrest. In July 1918, the Government of India published the Rowlatt Report, by which it marked its intention to continue the application of the war-time powers of arrest contained in the Defence of India Act into peacetime. This fuelled the wave of unrest which shook the Raj under Gandhi's leadership after 1919. It will be argued in Chapter 12 that the Indian police were directly responsible for the preparation of the

Rowlatt Report. This was the result of the fear which the Indian revolutionary movement and German intrigues had created in the minds of the Government of India. It did not foresee that it would alienate moderate opinion since it was intended purely for application to political criminals and not as part of a general plan of coercion. Throughout the war the British tried to rally Indian moderate opinion to the war effort.

From a position of hindsight, it appears that the main long-term threat to the Raj which developed during the war years came from the increasing demands of the Indian National Congress. The Congress split into two factions of 'moderates' and 'extremists' in 1907. After 1915, however, unity was restored under the leadership of Tilak and the English Theosophist leader, Annie Besant, who had a wide following among Hindus. The Congress claims to represent the Indian population increased at the end of 1916 when it united with the Muslim League in the Lucknow Resolution, and called for a 'a proclamation that it is the aim and intention of British policy to confer self-government on India at an early date'. However, at this time the British by no means saw the Congress as an immediate danger to their power nor as a violent threat, likely to incite breaches of the peace. Because of this it was not an intelligence target. The Congress leaders came under police surveillance when they were suspected of conniving with Indian revolutionaries,[79] but such police interest, as the numerous compilations of history sheets show, was exceptional. The activities of most politicians were overt and police intelligence coverage would have been superfluous. Though she set up a strong Home Rule League, Annie Besant was by no means an unmitigated problem for the Raj. It seems that she became interested in Congress politics as a means to provide young men with an alternative to terrorism. When Gandhi, who was to be the most dangerous enemy of the Raj after 1920, returned to India in 1915 the DCI regarded him as 'neither an anarchist nor a revolutionary', but as 'a troublesome agitator whose enthusiasm has led him frequently to overstep the limits of the South African laws relating to Asiatics',[80] though they did start to see him as a 'dangerous agitator' after he forced the government's hand in his social work campaigns at Champaran, Kaira and Ahmedabad in 1917–18.

The government arrested certain prominent nationalists, such as Annie Besant and the Pan-Islamist Ali brothers. However, its attitude to the Congress was characterized by a restraint which was most noticeable in the absence of police interference with moderate nationalists.

The Ali brothers, as mentioned earlier, fell foul of the Defence of India Act when they called for a *jihad*. The government only interned Besant in 1917 because, as the DCI said in the only reference to her in their official record of the war, she had published a theory that 'any attack on what was called bureaucracy was permissible so long as it was accompanied by a perfunctory expression of loyalty to the Crown and the British connection'.[81]

Lord Hardinge perceived during the war a tendency for extremists in the Congress to become moderates. His government went to great lengths to foster this tendency. An interesting example of this attitude is shown by the case of Chirol vs. Tilak. In writing his book *Indian Unrest* in 1910 Sir Valentine Chirol, the head of the Foreign Department of *The Times*, drew on Indian CID documents.[82] He painted a very black picture of Tilak, who was then in Mandalay jail. On his release he started a libel action against Chirol.[83] The government of Bombay felt unable to give Chirol the police documents for his defence, for fear of alienating such a powerful leader of the Indian National Congress as Tilak had become. The government held it vital to keep the activities of its CID hidden even though they had been directed against an obvious offender several years before.[84] During the war the DCI remained genuinely a criminal intelligence department, concerned overwhelmingly with Indian nationalists who broke the law and posed an armed threat to the Raj. The ideological restraints upon its activities continued.

Lack of resources also meant that the police had to concentrate on physical threats to the Raj. During the war there was a chronic shortage of trained manpower for the fighting services and the police. None the less the government consciously planned to refrain from coercion. In Bengal the forces of law and order were for a long time allowed to exist at a dangerously low level. At an all-India level, the central government did not allow the Department of Criminal Intelligence and the CIDs to grow significantly.

Precise figures for the size of the CIDs are available for 1914 only. However, the lists containing them were drawn up under the authority of the Home Department in October 1916 and there is no indication that the CIDs had grown at all since 1914. During the war, all sections of the Indian administration, including the police, complained of a chronic shortage of trained manpower. In Madras, the CID had 55 men in 1914, just as it had in 1910.[85] In the United Provinces, the strength of the CID either fell or remained the same throughout the war.[86] In the Bombay Presidency, Bombay City and Sind, there was a very slight increase in the numbers of all the CIDs, which increased to 202.[87] In the Punjab, the CID grew from 45 in 1910 to 55 in 1914.[88]

The DCI's permanent staff of officers did not grow at all during the war. There remained only five of them – the Director, the Deputy Director, the Assistant Director, the Personal Assistant to the Director,[89] and the Government Expert in Handwriting.[90] In October 1915 they cost, excluding the salary of the Personal Assistant, Rs.14,965. Likewise the detective staff remained fixed at four Superintendents and four Sub-Inspectors.[91] The DCI's strength did not grow significantly through the secondment of officers from the provincial police forces either. In June 1915, there were three senior police officers serving on special duty with the DCI: Petrie, Denham and Sempkins.[92] Petrie was soon to be sent on a mission to the Far East. F.A.R. Sempkins was a police officer from the Central Provinces who was attached to the Delhi administration in July 1914 in connection with the investigation and prosecution of the Delhi bomb plot.[93] From 1 April 1915 he was deputed to the DCI to take charge of counter-espionage work.[94] Until the middle of 1916 Denham was the only officer to reinforce the DCI's staff involved with the Indian revolutionary movement inside India, acting as the DCI's reserve 'available for any urgent job that may arise'.[95] He acted primarily as the DCI's link with Bengal. He was joined in 1916 by Satish Bannerji, a Deputy-Superintendent of the Calcutta Police.[96]

On the eve of 1914, the political side of the DCI's work already predominated. When war came the DCI lost any hope that its political role would decrease, let alone that this role was only a passing burden. Cleveland wrote that after the end of the war the Government of India would 'always find it necessary to expect from this Department an amount of political work which has hitherto been regarded as called for only by passing emergencies'. None the less the DCI in 1914 was still performing criminal work. It was divided into two sections: Section A dealt with the political work and religious movements; Section B dealt with ordinary crime. The following table shows the distribution of cases handled by Sections A and B.

	1910	1911	1912	1913	1914
Section A	962	792	412	792	1254
Section B	357	312	253	416	602

Thus, by a rough calculation, the proportion of the DCI's time spent on Indian political crime cases was 73 per cent in 1910, 72 per cent in 1911, 62 per cent in 1912, 66 per cent in 1913, and 68 per cent in 1914. In fact the overall amount of time which the DCI spent on political work in 1914 was greater than this figure, since of the 602 files in Section B, 150 fell into the category of non-criminal foreigners, as opposed to 44 in 1913.[97]

Section A on the other hand, was not exclusively concerned with political matters. In 1910 21 per cent of files in Section A were entirely non-political; in 1911, 21 per cent in 1912, 25 per cent; in 1913, 18 per cent; in 1914, 13 per cent. Significantly, there was no category entitled the 'Indian National Congress'. In 1914, the DCI still handled any matters which impinged on the criminal sphere, be they religious or political. Thus it dealt with both Hindu and Muhammedan perverts, of whom the latter outnumbered the former, and with the killing of cows, sacred to Hindus.

During the War DCI had a clerical staff of only 19. Seven served in the political section and three in the criminal section. The others served both criminal and political functions. They were the superintendent in charge of the clerical office, the 'record section', the 'issue section' responsible for putting out the DCI's publications, and the 'miscellaneous section'. All but two of the clerks were British, the others being Eurasians. Many were ex-soldiers. Besides them there was a fingerprint bureau consisting of one superintendent in charge and 15 fingerprint experts, and a 'menial establishment' composed of 40 Indian servants.[98]

In 1916 the DCI's origins as an almost entirely criminal department showed to its detriment. Though no one now saw it as such, it still functioned as if it were a temporary political intelligence department. Its staff was inadequate for coping with both political and criminal work. The clerks and the detectives were underpaid.[99] The average clerk's salary was under Rs.180 a year. Cleveland noted in October 1915 that 'my office staff have been for a long time past in an ever increasing state of unhappiness and discontent' because of the pressure of work and low pay.[100] The clerks did not have time to read up on specialized subjects. According to Cleveland, on several occasions they disregarded their pledge of secrecy.[101] What they divulged remains unclear.

Cleveland wanted to increase his clerical staff from 19 to 29 and to pay them better. He submitted proposals to the Government of India which would have involved an overall annual increase of Rs.30,790 from Rs.44,120 to Rs.74,910.[102] The Government of India allowed him to incur a maximum of 50 per cent of this sum.[103] Thus the clerical staff increased from 19 to 25 at the beginning of 1916.[104]

To a remarkable degree the same political and ideological restraints continued to restrict the expansion of the DCI and the CIDs as they had done before the war. In holding a delicate balance between the suppression of armed threats to the Raj and the conciliation of Indian moderate opinion, the Government of India always tried to err on the side of moderation. Yet a serious terrorist problem existed in Bengal which drew moral strength from bases abroad. Ironically, while the British had infinitely greater legal powers for dealing with the revolutionaries at home in India, it was left for their agents abroad – in Europe, in the Far East and in North America – to strike them down before they reached India. The DCI was to inflict as great a blow upon the Indian revolutionary movement in the United States as it ever did in India.

NOTES

1. Hardinge informed Sir Valentine Chirol, that: 'there is no disguising the fact that our position in India is a bit of a gamble at the present time'. Hardinge to Chirol, 19 November 1914, CUL Hardinge Papers; Letters and Telegrams: England, Vol. 93.
2. Note on the Delhi conspiracy case by D. Petrie, Additional Superintendent of Police, dated Delhi, 14 April 1914, in *Reports by Messrs. D. Petrie and C. Stead on the Delhi–Lahore Conspiracy and Sedition Cases.* HDA: July 1914, nos. 1–2 in IOLR IOR.POS. 7147. Sir Michael O'Dwyer, *India as I Knew It* (London: Constable & Co., 1925).
3. Report by D. Petrie, dated 8 November 1914, in *Attempt to Assassinate His Excellency the Viceroy on the 23rd December 1912.* HDD: Dec. 1914, no. 11 in IOLR IOR.POS. 10612.
4. Progress report by D. Petrie, dated 20 March 1913. Ibid.
5. A detailed account of the activities of the revolutionaries of the Ghadr Party, from the time they left their homes in North America and the Far East until the failure of the Punjab uprising, is contained in T.G. Fraser, *The Intrigues of German Government and Ghadr Party.* An account of the Ghadr Plans was prepared in the DCI by F.C. Isemonger and J. Slattery, entitled *An Account of the Ghadr Conspiracy, 1913–1915* (Lahore, 1919). IOLR V/27/262/9.
6. Komagata Maru Report, Vol. 3, Exhibit 116, Narrative of Mr D. Petrie, p. 282. J&P 1524/15 in IOLR L/PJ/1338.
7. Telegram from Hardinge to Crewe, 2 Oct. 1914. CUL Hardinge Papers, Telegrams to and from the Secretary of State, Vol. 98.
8. Telegram from the Viceroy to the Secretary of State, 1 Oct. 1914. CUL Hardinge Papers, Vol. 88. Ker, *Political Trouble in India* (Reprint, Calcutta: Editions Indian, 1973), pp. 239–42.
9. The Government of India had even wanted to send an officer to greet the returning

Sikhs at Singapore. They had been unable to do so because the war had dislocated shipping routes. They also proposed to provide financial assistance for the destitute passengers. Telegram from Viceroy to Secretary of State, 2 Oct. 1914. CUL Hardinge Papers, Vol. 98.

10. Letter from Lord Carmichael, Governor of Bengal, to Hardinge, 10 Oct. 1914. CUL Hardinge Papers, India, Original Letters, Vol. 63.

11. Letter from L.L. Tomkins, officiating Deputy Inspector-General of Police, Criminal Investigation Department, Punjab, to the Superintendents of Police, Amritsar, Lahore and Lyallpur, October 1914, in *Deportation from Shanghai of One Harnam Das, Son of Kanchi Ram, and his Internment in the Punjab under the Ingress into India Ordinance, 1914* (V of 1914). HDA: Jan. 1915, nos. 188–97 in IOLR IOR.POS.7150.

12. Copy of a report by an officer of the Punjab Criminal Investigation Department, 19 Oct. 1914 in *Deportation from Shanghai of One Harnam Das, Son of Kanchi Ram, and his Internment in the Punjab under the Ingress into India Ordinance, 1914* (V of 1914). HDA: Jan. 1915, nos. 188–97 in IOLR IOR.POS.7150.

13. O'Dwyer, op. cit., p. 196.

14. At Hawaii the first group of Indians, travelling on the *Korea* advertised their planned rising in India. The British Consul-General sent a complete list of passengers to India. Crewe to Hardinge, 11 Sept. 1914, CUL Hardinge Papers, Telegrams to and from the Secretary of State, Vol. 98. A second group of about 60 left the USA on 5 September. F.C. Isemonger and J. Slattery, *An Account of the Ghadr Conspiracy 1913–1915* (Lahore, 1919), IOLR V/27/262/9 in IOR.NEG.5022 p. 44. Lahore Conspiracy Trial, B – The Return to India, p. 3, J&P 4095/15 in IOLR L/PJ/6/1405. Two groups left from Canada. One left from Manila. Isemonger and Slattery, p. 46.

15. 100 were later released. O'Dwyer, op. cit., p. 195.

16. Ker, op. cit., p. 372.

17. The DCI admitted that: 'The possibility of other emigrants returning in any number through the ports of Madras and Colombo was not considered at first'. Isemonger and Slattery, op. cit., p. 63.

18. Letter from C.R. Cleveland to Home Department, 27 Nov. 1914 in *Request by the Government of India to be Informed by the British Authorities at Singapore, Hong Kong, Manila and Batavia, of Particulars Regarding Indians Returning from the Far East.* HDA: Jan. 1915: nos. 126–33 in IOLR IOR.POS.7150.

19. Letter from Meston to Hardinge, 24 March 1915. CUL Hardinge Papers; Printed Letters and Telegrams, Vol. 89, p. 230.

20. *Discussion as to the Best Means of Exercising Effective Control over Indians Returning from America and the Far East via Colombo.* HDA: April 1915, nos. 296–300 in IOLR IOR.POS.7151.

21. Letter from Slocock to Cleveland, dated Madras, 25 December 1915 in *Discussion as to the Best Means of Exercising Effective Control over Indians Returning from America and the Far East via Colombo.* HDA: April 1915, nos. 296–300 in IOLR IOR.POS.7151.

22. General Order of the [Madras] Judicial Department, no. 2983, dated 20 December 1914 in *Discussion as to the Best Means of Exercising Effective Control over Indians Returning from America and the Far East via Colombo.* HDA: April 1915, nos. 296–300 in IOLR IOR.POS.7151.

23. Note by Cleveland, dated 2 February 1915 in *Discussion as to the Best Means of Exercising Effective Control over Indians Returning from America and the Far East via Colombo.* HDA: April 1915, nos. 296–300 in IOLR IOR.POS.7151.

24. Ker, op. cit., pp. 364–5. According to Isemonger and Slattery between 646 and 1,000 revolutionaries entered the Punjab between August and 1 December. O'Dwyer claimed in November 1915: 'Over 6,000 emigrants returned to the Punjab from America and the Far East since the war began. It is believed that at least half of these were more or less deeply involved in the revolutionary movement. They probably found an equal

number of adherents in men who had returned from abroad earlier or whom they succeeded in infecting with their views. I take it that early this year there were from 6,000 to 10,000 men in the Punjab, who given the arms, the direction and the opportunity, were ready to raise the standard of revolution'. Letter from O'Dwyer to Hardinge, 8 Nov. 1915. CUL Hardinge Papers; Printed Letters and Telegrams, Vol. 90, p. 369.
25. Letter from O'Dwyer to Hardinge, ibid.
26. Ker, op. cit., p. 366.
27. He was known to his followers as 'the fat babu'. Ker, p. 367.
28. Letter from Hardinge to Chirol, 10 Dec. 1914. CUL Hardinge Papers; Letters and Telegrams, England, Vol. 93.
29. Letter from Craddock to Hardinge, 19 March 1915. CUL Hardinge Papers; India, Original Letters, Vol. 64, p. 575.
30. Fraser, op. cit., Ch. 4.
31. O'Dwyer wrote: 'The rebel headquarters in four separate houses at Lahore were raided by our police that afternoon headed by that very brave and able officer Khan Liyakat Haiyat Khan [who ran Kirpal Singh], and Mr L.L. Tomkins, the efficient [officiating] head of the CID. Thirteen of the most dangerous revolutionaries were captured with all the paraphenalia of the conspiracy, arms, bombs, bomb-making materials, revolutionary literature, and four rebel flags (one of which I claimed and hold as a souvenir)'. O'Dwyer, op. cit., p. 202.
32. Ibid.
33. Isemonger and Slattery argued that 'the leaders knew beforehand of Germany's intention to go to war'.
34. Bethmann Hollweg to *Auswärtiges Amt*, 4 September 1914, GFM 397/00326, quoted in German in T.G. Fraser, 'The Intrigues of German Government and the Ghadr Party Against British Rule in India, 1914–1918' (University of London, unpublished PhD thesis, 1974). Translation by the author.
35. H.V.F. Winstone, *The Illicit Adventure* (London: Jonathan Cape, 1982), p. 8.
36. Ibid., p. 133.
37. T.G. Fraser, 'Germany and Indian Revolution, 1914–18', in *Journal of Contemporary History*, Vol. 12, No. 2 (1977), p. 257.
38. Keith Robbins, *The First World War* (Oxford: Oxford University Press, 1985), pp. 62, 102.
39. M.E. Yapp, *The Making of the Modern Near East 1792–1923* (Harlow: Longman, 1987).
40. For a discussion of Britain's appraisal of Turkish war potential see Richard Popplewell, 'British Intelligence in Mesopotamia, 1914–1916', in Michael Handel (ed.), *Intelligence and Military Operations* (London: Frank Cass, 1990).
41. 'Statement of files in "A" Section for 1910 to 1914' in *Proposed Revision of the Pay and Prospects of the Clerical Establishment of the Office of the Director, Criminal Intelligence*. HD/Pol: Feb. 1916, nos. 99–101 in IOLR P/9957.
42. Letter from Roos-Keppel to Hardinge, 13 Feb. 1915. CUL Hardinge Papers; Printed Letters and Telegrams, Vol. 89.
43. His comments on this subject are notable by their absence from the Hardinge Papers.
44. Letter from O'Dwyer to Hardinge, 6 Dec. 1914. CUL Hardinge Papers; Printed Letters and Telegrams, Vol. 88.
45. O'Dwyer, op. cit., Ch. XI, 'Pan-Islamist Movement'.
46. Sir Algernon Rumbold, *Watershed in India 1914–1922* (London: The Athlone Press, 1979), p. 31.
47. Letter from Hardinge to Chirol, 10 Dec. 1914; CUL Hardinge Papers; Letters and Telegrams, England, Vol. 93.
48. Letter from Roos-Keppel to Hardinge, 13 Feb. 1915, CUL Hardinge Papers, op. cit.
49. Winstone, op. cit., p. 165.

50. Ibid., p. 165.
51. See, generally, the 'Weekly Summaries of Intelligence' of the British army in Mesopotamia contained in PRO WO157.
52. The Turkish General staff refused to participate in German subversion in Persia. Winstone, op. cit., p. 137.
53. Quoted in Fraser, *Plots of German Government*, op. cit., p. 277.
54. Ker, op. cit., pp. 299–300.
55. C.M. Andrew, *Secret Service* (London: Heinemann, 1985), pp. 107, 110.
56. For example, Letter from Hardinge to Sykes, 21 April 1915. CUL Hardinge Papers; Printed Letters and Telegrams.
57. See Weekly Report, dated 21 December 1915, HDB: Dec. 1915, nos. 709–11, IOLR IOR.POS.9841.
58. Letter from Bethmann Hollweg to the Maharajah of Jodhpur. Chelmsford Papers, IOLR MSS.EUR.E.264/52. Ker, op. cit., p. 302.
59. Mahendra Pratap, *My Life Story of Fifty-Five Years* (Dehra Dun, 1947), pp. 44 and 50.
60. Winstone, op. cit., p. 168.
61. See Ch. 9.
62. Letter from Roos-Keppel to Hardinge, 13 Feb. 1915, CUL Hardinge Papers; Printed Letters and Telegrams, Vol. 89, p. 69.
63. Rumbold, op. cit., p. 22.
64. Undated, unsigned letter. CUL Hardinge Papers; Printed Letters and Telegrams, Vol. 91, p. 21.
65. Winstone, op. cit., pp. 168–9.
66. Pratap, op. cit., p. 51.
67. It should be noted that the Chief Commissioner of the North-West Frontier Province, Sir George Roos-Keppel, was far from convinced of the danger from the Wahabis/'Hindustani Fanatics'. He wrote in his general summary of the state of affairs on the Frontier in February 1915: 'Further down the Indus are our old friends of Mutiny times the Hindustani fanatics, who have shown themselves in my time merely to be what I may call "professional fanatics", as, on many occasions in my recollection, when the frontier has been disturbed, they have loudly beaten the drum of Islam, but simultaneously sent messengers to assure me that they had no intention of doing anything more serious, and that it was necessary for them occasionally to make a noise in order to keep up the supply of presents from the Amir and of offerings from dupes in India. Now they will probably play the same game'. Letter from Roos Keppel to Hardinge, 13 Feb. 1915, op. cit.
68. O'Dwyer, op. cit., p. 179.
69. Ker, op. cit., p. 307.
70. Ibid., p. 315. Cleveland's fears of the Wahabis are summarized in 'Summary of proceedings of a conference held at Lahore in the office of the Inspector-General of Police on 21 October 1916', in Chelmsford Papers; Letters to and from Secretary of State, IOLR MSS.EUR.E.264/2.
71. O'Dwyer, op. cit., p. 178.
72. Ibid., pp. 179–80.
73. Ker, op. cit., p. 311.
74. Letter from Marris to Seton, 5 Oct. 1916. Seton Papers, IOLR MSS.EUR.E.276/6.
75. Ker, op. cit., p. 287.
76. Hardinge to Chamberlain, 30 Nov. 1915, CUL Hardinge Papers, Vol. 90.
77. See Richard Popplewell, 'British Intelligence in Mesopotamia', op. cit.
78. Quoted in Rumbold, op. cit., pp. 26–7.
79. A good example is provided by the activities of the DCI informer in London who was watching, inconclusively, the Bengali leader Surendranath Banerjea. *Memorandum on the Anti-British Agitation Among Natives of India in England,*

CID Circular No. 11, 28 Oct., 1909, refs. to Surendranath Banerjea, pp. 4, 10, 11, 17, 18, 19, 30, 31.

80. *Indian Agitators Abroad*, first edition, November 1911, in IOLR V/27/262/1.
81. Ker, op. cit., p. 63. Gandhi gets no mention at all in this work, which was published in 1917, while Surendranath Banerjea gets only one.
82. Gerald Barrier, *Banned. Controversial Literature and Political Control in British India 1907–1947* (Columbia: University of Missouri Press, 1974), p. 73.
83. Letter from Chirol to Lord Willingdon, 12 Jan. 1916. CUL Hardinge Papers; Printed Letters and Telegrams, Vol. 91, pp. 16–24.
84. Letter from Willingdon to Hardinge, 1916. CUL Hardinge Papers; Printed Letters and Telegrams, Vol. 91, p. 54.
85. Its staff now consisted of one Deputy Inspector-General, one Personal Assistant to the Deputy Inspector-General, three Deputy Superintendents, 22 Inspectors and Sub-Inspectors, and 28 Head Constables. Thus it was better supplied with officers than it had been in 1910. 'Statement showing the strength and cost of the Criminal Investigation Department of the Madras Presidency (excluding the Fingerprint Bureau), during the financial years 1906–1907, 1911–1912, 1912–1913, 1913–1914', in *Statement Showing by Provinces the Total Strength and Cost of the Criminal Investigation Department (Officers and Men, Excluding the Fingerprint Bureau) for Each of the Years 1904–1905, 1911–1912, 1912–1913 and 1913–1914*, in HD/Pol: Oct. 1916, nos. 60–73, IOLR P/9955.
86. According to one estimate made by the Local Government in 1914, its strength was down to 103. 'Statement showing the total strength and cost including allowances of the officers and men employed in the Criminal Investigation Department, United Provinces (excluding the Fingerprint Bureau) for the years 1904–1905, 1911–1912, 1912–1913 and 1913–1914'. Ibid.
87. The two CIDs consisted of one Deputy Inspector-General, one Assistant Deputy Inspector-General, one Deputy Commissioner, one Superintendent of Bombay City, 56 Inspectors, Sub-Inspectors and Jemadars, 138 Head Constables and Constables, and a 'temporary establishment' of three. 'Statement B: Showing the strength and cost of the Criminal Investigation Department (excluding the Finger-print Bureau) in the Bombay Presidency, including Sind and Bombay City'. Ibid.
88. In 1914 the staff of the CID included one Deputy Inspector-General, two Assistant Deputy Inspectors-General, one Deputy Superintendent, 18 Inspectors and 33 Head Constables and Constables. 'Statement showing separately for each of the financial years 1904–1905, 1911–1912, 1912–1913, 1913–1914, the total strength and cost, including allowances of the officers and men employed in the Criminal Investigation Department, Punjab, excluding the Fingerprint Bureau. Ibid. In November 1915 Sir Harcourt Butler, the Lieutenant-Governor of Burma, informed the Viceroy that he intended 'to strengthen the Criminal Intelligence Department and extend the secret service system'. Letter from Butler to Hardinge, 18 Nov. 1915. CUL Hardinge Papers; Printed Letters and Telegrams, Vol. 90, p. 385.
89. In January 1914 J.W. Nelson, an officer of the Bengal Civil Service, replaced Kerr as Personal Assistant to the Director of Criminal Intelligence. *Refusal of the Request Made by Mr J.W. Nelson, Personal Assistant to the Director, Criminal Intelligence, that he Should Benefit in Accordance with the 'Next Below' Rule.* HD/Pol: Oct. 1915, nos. 116–17 in IOLR P/9722.
90. F.A.M.H. Vincent was appointed Deputy Director of Criminal Intelligence on 1 February 1913. Letter from the Director of Criminal Intelligence to the Secretary to the Government of India, Home Department, 3 March 1914, in *Sanction to the Grant of Increments of Salary to Mr F.A.M.H. Vincent while he Holds the Post of Deputy Director of Criminal Intelligence.* HD/Pol: Aug. 1914, no. 75 in IOLR P/9459. F.C. Isemonger became officiating Assistant Director of Criminal Intelli-

gence in January 1913. Telegram from Secretary to the Government of India, Home Department, to the Chief Secretary to the Government of the Punjab, 3 January 1913, in *Deputation of Mr D. Petrie, Assistant Director, Criminal Intelligence, Mr C. Stead, Mr G.C. Denham, and Mr F.A.M.H. Vincent in Connection with the Enquiry into the Outrage on His Excellency the Viceroy.* HD/Pol: April 1913, no. 100 in IOLR P/9210. At the beginning of October 1914 F.C. Isemonger relinquished and V.P. Vivian, Superintendent of Police, Sialkot, assumed charge of the office of Assistant Director of Criminal Intelligence. Letter from the Director of Criminal Intelligence to the Secretary to the Government of India, Home Department, 14 Oct. 1914, in *Relinquishment by Mr Isemonger and Assumption by Mr Vivian, a Superintendent in the Punjab Police, of the Charge of the Office of Assistant Director, Criminal Intelligence, on 1 October and 12 October 1914 Respectively.* HD/Pol: Nov. 1914, no. 160 in IOLR P/9459.

91. Letter from the Director of Criminal Intelligence to the Secretary to the Government of India, Home Department, 29 June 1917 in *Sanction to the Appointment of Sub-Inspector Sant Singh on Special Duty under the Director, Criminal Intelligence.* HD/Pol: Sept. 1907, nos. 155–9 in IOLR P/10176.

92. Letter from Lieutenant Colonel C. Kaye, Offg. Director, Central Intelligence, to the Secretary of State to the Government of India, Home Department, 3 Jan. 1920 in *Proposed Extension for a Period of Two Years, of the Deputation of an Officer under the Director, Central Intelligence, to Deal with the Subject of Contre-Espionage against Suspicious Foreigners.* HD/Pol: Feb. 1920, nos. 222–4 in IOLR P.10839.

93. Letter from the Director, Central Intelligence, to the Secretary to the Government of India, Home Department to the Secretary to the Government of India, Home Department, in *Grant of 3 Months' Privilege Leave to Mr F.R. Sempkins, Officer on Special Duty under the Director, Central Intelligence, with Effect from 21 November 1918.* HD/Pol: Dec. 1918, nos. 159–74 in IOLR P/10373.

94. Letter from Lieutenant Colonel C. Kaye, Offg. Director, Central Intelligence, to the Secretary of State to the Government of India, Home Department, 3 Jan. 1920 in *Proposed Extension for a Period of Two Years, of the Deputation of an Officer under the Director, Central Intelligence, to Deal with the Subject of Contre-Espionage against Suspicious Foreigners.* HD/Pol: Feb. 1920, nos. 222–4 in IOLR P.10839.

95. Note from Cleveland to Wheeler, 7 Aug. 1914, in *Question of the Disposal of the Police Officers Employed in Connection with the Delhi-Lahore Conspiracy Case.* HDD: Aug. 1914, no. 8 in IOLR IOR.POS.10612.

96. Note by C.R. Cleveland, 8 June 1916, in *Proposals for dealing with the political situation in Bengal. Questions relating to the efficiency of the Bengal Police*, HDA: June 1916, no. 298, IOLR IOR.POS.7297.

97. 'Statement of files in "A" Section for 1910 to 1914' and 'Number of files in "B" Section during the years 1910–1914', in *Proposed Revision of the Pay and Prospects of the Clerical Establishment of the Office of the Director, Criminal Intelligence.* HD/Pol: Feb. 1916, nos. 99–101 in IOLR P/9957.

98. Letter from the Director, Criminal Intelligence, to the Secretary to the Government of India, Home Department, 19 Oct. 1915, ibid.

99. Letter from the Director of Criminal Intelligence to the Secretary to the Government of India, Home Department, 29 June 1917 in *Sanction to the Appointment of Sub-Inspector Sant Singh on Special Duty under the Director, Criminal Intelligence.* HD/Pol: Sept. 1907, nos. 155–9 in IOLR P/10176.

100. Letter from the Director, Criminal Intelligence, to the Secretary to the Government of India, Home Department, 19 Oct. 1915, in *Proposed Revision of the Pay and Prospects of the Clerical Establishment of the Office of the Director, Criminal Intelligence.* HD/Pol: Feb. 1916, nos. 99–101 in IOLR P/9957.

101. Letter from the Director of Criminal Intelligence to the Secretary to the Government of India, Home Department, 13 March 1916 in *Reorganization and Strengthening of the Office Establishment of the Director, Criminal Intelligence*. HD/Pol: May 1916, no. 5 in IOLR P/9957.
102. Letter from the Director, Criminal Intelligence, to the Secretary to the Government of India, Home Department, 19 Oct. 1915, in *Proposed Revision of the Pay and Prospects of the Clerical Establishment of the Office of the Director, Criminal Intelligence*. HD/Pol: Feb. 1916, nos. 99–101 in IOLR P/9957.
103. Letter from H. Wheeler to the Director of Criminal Intelligence, 3 Feb. 1916, in *Proposed Revision of the Pay and Prospects of the Clerical Establishment of the Office of the Director, Criminal Intelligence*, ibid.
104. Letter from the Director of Criminal Intelligence to the Secretary to the Government of India, Home Department, 13 March 1916 in *Reorganization and Strengthening of the Office Establishment of the Director, Criminal Intelligence*. HD/Pol: May 1916, no. 5 in IOLR P/9957.

8

Bengal during the Great War

On the outbreak of the First World War, the plans of Indian revolutionaries based in North America to raise the Punjab represented the most dangerous immediate threat to the Raj. But, overall, the protracted terrorist campaign in Bengal was a far more serious challenge to British rule. Bengali terrorists enjoyed far greater popular support than the Punjabi revolutionaries and their war of attrition was far more effective than Ghadr's attempt at open revolt. The Ghadr Party survived the war, but was never again a serious threat to the Empire. On the other hand, while the British defeated Bengali terrorism during the war, they could neither eradicate its causes nor its organization.

In August 1914 the Government of India feared that political violence might spread from Bengal to other parts of India. It knew that Rash Behari Bose had successfully formed terrorist cells in the Punjab, while the Benares conspiracy case at the end of 1915, showed that other Bengali revolutionaries had been active in the United Provinces.[1] Despite Bose's participation in the attempted insurrection in the Punjab in Spring 1915, the other provinces of India never experienced revolutionary violence on anything like the scale of Bengal.[2] In fact the co-ordination between the revolutionaries in Bengal and the Punjab never went beyond the personal contribution of Rash Behari Bose. Throughout the war the Bengali revolutionaries worked independently of the Ghadr Party, which made little impact upon them.

The Bengali revolutionaries seized the opportunity offered by the war, and started a campaign of unprecedented violence. They were better armed than ever after 26 August 1914, when they raided a Calcutta arms dealer, Rodda & Co., seizing 50 Mauser pistols and 46,000 rounds of ammunition. In 1917 the British found that few if any political crimes had taken place in Bengal during the war in which the stolen pistols had not been used.[3] A new feature at the beginning of

1915, which caused much alarm and was indicative of the growing sophistication and boldness of the terrorists, was the use of taxi-cabs to commit robberies in and near Calcutta.[4]

The Rodda raid contributed to a marked increase in the crime rate from 1914 to 1916. The figures for major terrorists acts such as murder, dacoity and bomb outrage had been more or less steady in the years 1913–14, with 13 occurring in 1913 and 14 in 1914. In 1915 the number of such acts shot up to 36, while in the first half of 1916, there were 25 'outrages'. Statistics alone do not reveal the seriousness of the terrorist campaign in Bengal. After 1914 the revolutionaries were quickly able to launch a reign of terror in both the cities and the countryside. The terrorist campaign reached its height at the end of 1915 and the beginning of 1916. From October 1915 to the end of the year not a fortnight passed in Calcutta without some revolutionary crime being committed, while dacoities continued in the hinterland and throughout eastern Bengal. At the same time revolutionary violence spread to northern Bengal which had been hitherto peaceful. The terrorists' aim was not just to kill and to rob. Their key goal was to paralyse the overstretched administration. This they had come close to doing by the end of 1915.[5] This general atmosphere of fear encompassed not only the ordinary people, but also the police and the law courts.[6] Even the CIDs and Intelligence Branch (IB) were becoming demoralized, while the legal system had almost broken down as a result of the terror. In the whole of 1915 only six terrorists were successfully brought to trial.[7]

By 1915 the Germans were aware of the difficulties which the British administration was facing in India. They planned to fuel the unrest in Bengal until it reached revolution, sending large quantities of arms to the Bengali terrorists from the United States. The German plans failed partly because of problems in their implementation, partly because of the vigilance of British intelligence in North America and the Far East. Details of these events outside India are given in Chapters 10 and 11. However, the British not only succeeded in foiling German plots near their source; they also destroyed the facilities which the Germans had set up for distributing the arms in India.

The Germans had taken great care in selecting a trustworthy revolutionary, Jotindra Nath Mukherji, to carry out the Indian end of their schemes. Jotin had led the Rodda raid and by March 1915, when the Germans selected him, he was the most prominent revolutionary in Bengal.

Negotiations between the Germans and the Bengali revolutionaries were carried out by a youth called Norendra Nath Bhattacharji. He is better known by his alias of M.N. Roy under which he achieved fame as the leading Indian agent of the Soviet Comintern in the 1920s. In the early years of the First World War, however, he styled himself 'C.A. Martin'. In 1915 he met the German Consul at Batavia (Djakarta) in the Netherlands East Indies. He arranged for money to be sent to a gramophone shop named 'Harry and Sons', which the revolutionaries had set up as a 'front' in Balasore, a coastal town south of Calcutta.[8] But the plan was compromised from the outset. The British Consul-General at Batavia was running an agent who had access to the Germans' plans. Thus the British were soon aware of the presence of an Indian revolutionary emissary going by the alias of C.A. Martin. By the beginning of September the Indian police knew both that 'C.A. Martin' was receiving large remittances from Batavia,[9] and that he was connected with 'Harry and Sons'.[10] Tegart, the head of the Calcutta Intelligence Branch, started enquiries. When he searched the store he found revolutionary literature and learned that 'Martin' had gone to a remote place in the jungle. Local villagers searching for 'Martin' discovered a party of young Bengalis, who shot one of them. On 9 September Tegart and a squad of armed police tracked the gang down.[11] In fact, the police had not discovered the emissary, but the leader of the gang himself, namely Jotindra Nath Mukherji. A shoot-out ensued in which Jotindra was fatally wounded and his followers surrendered. Over ten years later a young revolutionary claimed that it was a bullet from Tegart's gun which had killed Jotindra.[12] N.N. Bhattacharji, alias C.A. Martin, was not one of the party and turned up next in America.

The death of Jotindra Nath Mukherji was a serious blow to German plans, but the loss of important leaders had not reduced the virulence of Bengali terrorism in the past. The killing of a revolutionary leader was not as serious a blow to the terrorists as the assassination of an efficient officer was to the police. Equally, the failure of German plots to send arms and money to Bengal did not amount to a decisive British victory. Revolutionary 'outrages' had increased yearly since 1906 without the support of other provinces in India and without material aid from abroad.

On the other hand, it was vital for the security of both the British administration in Bengal and, ultimately, in India as a whole, that weapons should be kept away from Bengali revolutionaries. Throughout the war the Government of India was anxious lest the Germans should finally succeed in supplying the terrorists. A crucial task of the British secret service and of Indian intelligence in the Far East and North America was to isolate Bengal from the Germans. It is important to note, however, that part of the British success was the result of German misplanning. In the hope of causing a full-scale revolution the German arms suppliers in the USA over-reached themselves by trying to send arms to Bengal in bulk shipments which were relatively easy to detect. As the Rodda raid showed, the supply of even a small number of weapons might have had disastrous consequences for the British.[13]

Important stakes were at issue in the terrorist campaign in Bengal during the First World War. Yet the struggle there has been largely forgotten, even by historians of the Indian revolutionary movement.[14] This lacuna is easily explained. After they had beaten the terrorist party by 1917, the British were not disposed to make public how serious the situation had been in Bengal in 1915–16.[15] Likewise, the papers of Viceroys Lord Hardinge and Lord Chelmsford say more about their dealings with the Local Government than they do about the real concern which Hardinge in particular felt about conditions in Bengal. A very different picture emerges from the *Proceedings* of the Home Department. By the beginning of 1916 Bengal threatened to become ungovernable and the Local Government seemed likely to fall. This would have had disastrous consequences at a time a British army had surrendered in Mesopotamia and an insurrection had broken out in Ireland. The maintenance of law and order in Bengal rested on the ability of the Intelligence Branch to resist the terrorists. In so doing they fulfilled a vital role in protecting the Empire behind its front line. The small number of men involved on either side, which was minute in comparison with the vast armies at the front, belies the true importance of the issue.

Even without German help, the Bengali terrorists were causing alarm within the British administration by the end of 1915. Cleveland concluded that

we are actually, I fear, losing ground week by week. The revolutionaries have been foiled in their attempts to do really great things with the assistance of German leaders, money and arms, but are being far too successful in their internal schemes for hampering the administration of the country, for extending widely

203

their own numbers and for checkmating the plans of government and for their repression of conciliation.[16]

Ironically while the terrorists were winning by the end of 1915, the British always had the power to defeat them. The large-scale use of police surveillance which had proved so successful during the Royal visit of 1911 was not reintroduced until the end of the war. But the problem lay deeper than just the extension of intelligence arrangements. These were of relatively limited use when the legal system was not working properly and terrorists were regularly being acquitted. The British gave the terrorist campaign time to gain momentum and continuously lost ground against it because they were reluctant to impose harsh laws which might alienate moderate opinion not only in Bengal but throughout India at a time when the Government of India was attempting to create a general Indian commitment to the war effort.

There were two broad problem areas with the legal system. First, existing laws were not functioning properly. Second, the British were reluctant to introduce harsher but more effective legislation to counter the terrorist threat. A key problem was the difficulty of securing convictions in the courts under the ordinary judicial system. There were many reasons for this. First and foremost, there were the threats which the terrorists made against witnesses. Linked to this was the sympathy which juries clearly felt for the idealist young revolutionaries in the dock. Then there was the problem of administrative rivalry within the British administration, which the war had done nothing to reduce. Traditionally there had long been hostility between the Calcutta High Court, where terrorist cases were tried, and the central government. This was reflected in the very high standard of evidence demanded by the High Court. The incompetence of the Bengal police only gave fuel to the defence. There were several cases of the police fabricating evidence and this made the courts suspicious of all their evidence. The significance of this to the counter-terrorist effort was clear. In the period 1906–17, 1,038 people were known to have been implicated in 210 acts of terrorism and 101 attempted acts. There were only 205 convictions.[17]

Cleveland lamented the state of the legal system in Bengal, when he complained to the Home Department on 1 December 1914:

It is very dangerous to keep on setting the Criminal Investigation Department and the Police on to these people [the terrorists] without a reserve power in the background.[18]

But there was already some 'reserve of power', if only the British had been able and willing to use it. This was Regulation III of 1818, which allowed the Government of India to detain political suspects without trial. The problem was that extensive use of Regulation III, and detention without trial generally, was offensive to British public opinion, to the India Office, and to many members of the Indian administration, including members of the government of Bengal. Even the desperate situation caused by the war was slow to break down these ideological objections to imperial defence.

At the beginning of the war the Government of India proposed that the most dangerous suspects should be deported under Regulation III. The India Office refused permission. The Home Member of the Viceroy's Council, Sir Reginald Craddock, with Cleveland's firm backing, responded with a furious letter to the Government of India, in which he complained:

> Surely when the Government of India have denuded the country of their best troops in order to give every assistance in their power to the British Government and the Empire, this is a powerful argument for the British Government in its turn to refrain from hampering our action, and to allow us to use the law that we have in order to ensure the internal security of India.[19]

Thus a confusion of authority between the India Office, the Government of India and the Local Government encouraged delay in passing laws against terrorism. The Defence of India Act, which gave the police the powers which the Home Department and the DCI wanted, was passed only in March 1915, eight months after the analogous Defence of the Realm Act was passed in Great Britain. It authorized the arrest and internment of dangerous persons and the introduction of trial by Special Tribunals.[20] This immediately eased the strain on police manpower imposed by the need to maintain a large number of watchers over a large number of suspects. By the end of June 1916 the government of Bengal had placed 233 Bengalis in compulsory domicile.

Success against terrorism depended not only on the existence of effective laws, but also on the will to impose them. This will did not exist when the Defence of India Act was introduced because the police lacked the whole-hearted support of the Local Government and above all of the provincial governor, Lord Carmichael.

Carmichael, a Scottish laird, became governor of the reconstituted

province of Bengal on April Fool's Day, 1912. He was a distinguished
art collector and entomologist. He had written the definitive mono-
graph on the centipede and while in India had the biggest species of
daddy-long-legs yet discovered named after him.[21] His career as a
statesman was less happy, and his previous career as governor of an
Australian state left him ill-equipped for the far harsher problems of
Bengal. Many British officials in India remembered him with disgust
long after his period of office had come to an end in 1917.[22]

Carmichael arrived in India in 1912 with a brief to conciliate
Indian moderate opinion. He listened to the complaints of Indian
politicians about the CID and passed them on forcefully to the
Government of India. In May 1915 he wrote:

> I have never yet met an educated Indian who trusts the police.
> I doubt if I have met one who does not hate and despise them.
> They are evidently in terror of them and think them capable of
> any wickedness.[23]

Carmichael was undoubtedly popular with Indians. None the less,
there is no doubt that he left the government of Bengal, and the police
which followed its directives, all but deprived of leadership on counter-
terrorist policy. Craddock found that the government of Bengal was
divided within itself since 'one member of the government is always
deprecating what the government itself has done, and throws the
responsibility on some other'.[24] At the height of the terrorist assassination campaign Carmichael complained that the police were too
secretive.[25] He made no secret of his dislike for his senior police
officers.[26] He claimed that

> Calcutta criminals . . . have an intelligence branch so to speak
> which is at least as capable as the police intelligence branch.[27]

The divisions within the Bengal government had an immediate impact
upon the way the police worked. With no firm direction from above,
different branches were often at odds with one another. Disorganiza-
tion continued even into 1916 as the terrorist campaign reached its
height. There was friction between the District and the Calcutta police,
as well as between the Inspector-General of police and the Local
Government.[28] Even Carmichael felt that the police effort needed
greater co-ordination.[29]

The attitude of Carmichael's administration encouraged the
increasing demoralization of the police. The government of Bengal

deprived them even of adequate protection. It was not until November 1915 that it authorized armed guards for officers of the Intelligence Branch and ordered that all officers should be trained in the use of revolvers.[30]

The question remains why the Government of India allowed Carmichael to ignore the mounting terrorist threat in Bengal. Even before the start of the war, Hardinge had decided to push Carmichael into more vigorous action against terrorism. He insisted that the government of Bengal should use Regulation III against 24 suspects against whom there was hard evidence even in the eyes of the Calcutta High Court. In response, Carmichael went straight to Lord Crewe, the Secretary of State for India. Crewe then informed the Cabinet of what was going on. The Cabinet decided the issue in Carmichael's favour, since they were afraid of a public outcry in Britain at the Government of India's harsh action.[31]

Even in the second year of the war, the government of Bengal was still reluctant to take vigorous action against the terrorists. In March 1915, the Defence of India Act permitted them to confine suspects to their villages. This was a milder sanction than Regulation III which allowed for the jailing of suspects. None the less, Carmichael was unwilling to put it into effect.

By July 1915 the Government of India were aware that the Germans intended to send arms to Bengal, though they did not yet know how completely the Germans plans were failing. This made it more urgent than ever, in the eyes of the Government of India, that Carmichael should use the law against the terrorists. During 1915 conflict developed between Carmichael and Cleveland. In August, Cleveland wanted to carry out a series of arrests in Bengal under the Defence of India Act. The basis of the arrests lay in secret intelligence that the DCI had received from Singapore, which Cleveland felt could not be disclosed to the Local Government.[32] Distrusting the word of the DCI and of his own police officers, Carmichael objected to implementing the arrests until a full case was established, and asked the Government of India to assure him that each case was 'really serious'.[33] The central government supported the DCI.

With the backing of the Home Department, Cleveland spearheaded an attack on Carmichael which gained force at the beginning of 1916. In a memorandum to the Home Department Cleveland argued that both the policies of repression and conciliation were failing in Bengal.[34] The moderates whom Carmichael supported would not back the government against terrorism. On the contrary, Indian politicians 'hotly criticized' increased expenditure on the police in the press.[35] To Carmichael's argument that conciliation had not gone far enough, he replied that any relaxation of surveillance was out of the question. Cleveland demanded that the Government of India should overule and ignore the wishes of Carmichael's administration, since 'Imperial interests may be seriously affected before life in Calcutta or Bengal becomes badly inconvenienced'.[36] He demanded increased powers for jailing suspects, a less divided police administration and stiff penalties for those found carrying firearms.

The offensive against Carmichael was taken up by the Government of India. Lord Hardinge went on visit to Bengal, doubting that the situation there was as serious as the Home Department and the DCI claimed. He came back seriously shaken and converted to their point of view. He even considered taking the drastic step of sacking Carmichael.[37] Instead, the government of Bengal was put under steady and effective pressure to make a stand against terrorism.

By this time, events in Bengal were reaching crisis point. By the beginning of 1916, the province seemed to be reaching the point where it would become ungovernable. Craddock wrote in despair about the situation:

> The policy of murdering informers and zealous Criminal Investigation Department officers has been grimly pursued, and has now been supplemented by the murder of schoolmasters who have faithfully done their best to suppress sedition in the schools under their charge.

> But it is not only the actual outrages that have to be considered. Threatening letters are causing panic among respectable citizens and colleges and schools are permeated with a spirit of indiscipline which manifests itself in strikes, and threatened strikes, on the most ridiculous of pretexts.[38]

One of the most serious developments at this time was the deterioration in the morale of the rank and file of the police, and even the Intelligence Branch. The ordinary police were so demoralized that there were difficulties in implementing the Defence of India Act even when Carmichael was willing to apply it. Frequently police constables carrying out the surveillance of suspects confined to their villages were threatened by the terrorists still at large. Just as frequently, the revolutionaries were able to bribe them to turn a blind eye to their charges.[39] Cleveland informed the Home Department:

> The posts which involve 'political' work have become so distasteful that the present occupants wish to leave them while new men do not wish to join them. Enquiries are becoming half-hearted and information is not being checked. The British officers are disheartened but not in the least afraid while the Indian officers are both disheartened and afraid. The difference means no disparagement to the latter as so far it is they and not the British officers who have been murdered, ostracized and threatened.[40]

Intimidation and assassination had even begun to wear down the Intelligence Branch. On 16 January 1916 Sub-Inspector Madhusan Bhattacharji was murdered in Calcutta. On 30 June 1916 the Dacca *Anusilan Samiti* murdered Sub-Inspector Jogendra Gupta, who was learning too much about its members. A crisis in morale occurred when one of the most able Intelligence Branch officers, Superintendent Basanta Kumar Chatterjee, was murdered on 30 June 1916. The murder took place in broad daylight in Calcutta. All the witnesses were too afraid to come forward to give evidence. By this time 11 officers of the Intelligence Branch, or 20 per cent of its strength, had been killed. On top of all this, the Intelligence Branch had come under heavy criticism from the nationalist press in Bengal. As a result of Chatterjee's murder, Tegart summoned all his important Indian officers and gave them permission to leave the Intelligence Branch if they wished. Without exception they said that they wanted to stay put.[41]

By now, the Intelligence Branch was a very different body from the inexperienced and untrustworthy CIDs which had confronted the revolutionary movement in its early stages. It was an elite body with a strong *esprit de corps*. Many of its members displayed a high degree of courage. Tegart told his wife an interesting story which is indicative of this. She recorded:

> Some of the IB men even began to be faintly blasé about unexploded bombs. A small cast-iron bomb which had been brought in from Midnapore was used for some time as a paperweight on Tegart's desk on the assumption that the contents had deteriorated and it was harmless. One day, when engaged in a

friendly rag with Denham and another friend, Tegart picked it up and threw it across the room at a map, saying 'Let's have a shot at Bogra' (a particularly unpleasant up-country station). Instantly there was a shattering explosion; part of the wall blew out, dust and debris littered the room and more IB men came rushing in, convinced that yet another assassination had taken place.[42]

The revolutionaries did not break the police. The second quarter of 1916 began the turning of the tide in the terrorist campaign in Bengal, partly as a result of police successes. On 3 March 1916 the police made arrests in Barisal and Baranagore which cleared away two hitherto successful terrorist gangs. The police conducted extensive searches which led to the end of the hitherto powerful Dacca *Anusilan Samiti*'s activities in Calcutta.

A second reason for the defeat of the terrorists was a change in attitude of the Local Government. By now the pressure from both the Government of India and the India Office had begun to work. In August 1916, the government of Bengal started to apply Regulation III and the Defence of India Act on a wide scale. Calcutta now became free of political crime. Those terrorists who had not been arrested by the police were rounded up. By June 1917, 99 were imprisoned under Regulation III, while 705 were confined to their homes under the Defence of India Act.

An outstanding feature of what for the British was unusually harsh action in India was the lack of public outcry, either in Britain or in India. It is difficult to criticize Carmichael and the liberal officials both in India and in London who had opposed 'repression' in the past. In 1914, very few expected the war or the Bengali terrorism which it fostered to last. The attitude of the public in 1916 might well have been very different from that of 1914. It will be seen that the British badly miscalculated Indian public opinion when they tried in 1919 to extend wartime powers of arrest into peacetime.

An offshoot of the vigorous application of anti-terrorist legislation was a general improvement in the performance of the police. Large numbers of arrests allowed the police to secure information from the captives. Moreover, with large numbers of terrorists out of action, the general atmosphere in Bengal improved, and members of the public were much more willing to step forward as witnesses. As a result, police knowledge of the terrorist organizations increased greatly.[43]

Another reason for the rapid improvement in the situation in

Bengal was a change in leadership. After Austen Chamberlain became Secretary of State for India in 1915, London started to apply a firmer hand on security issues than that given by the rather squeamish Lord Crewe. In March 1916, Lord Chelmsford became Viceroy. Before going out to India, Chamberlain had insisted that he should take a firmer line with the terrorists. His first official visit was to Calcutta. Early 1917 saw perhaps an even more significant change in personnel at the top, when Lord Carmichael finally sailed for home. He was succeeded by Lord Ronaldshay who brought with him a determination to combine conciliation of the moderates with firm action against the terrorists.

The new determination to fight back against the terrorists was also reflected in improved police intelligence arrangements for Bengal. One of the most decisive results of the pressure which the Government of India placed on the Local Government was the formation of the Bengal District Intelligence Branch in August 1916. Tegart's Central Intelligence Branch had never had enough men to spare for the countryside. Despite the impressive start made by ICS officers in the Dacca district, District Officers generally regarded the control of political unrest as the preserve of the Intelligence Branch.[44] The new plan which the Bengal Police devised involved maintaining a central agency in Calcutta, which was to exercise a general control over the IB work in the districts, collate all information regarding terrorist activities from whatever source and supply it to District superintendents.[45] The District Intelligence Branch was big enough to keep up constant pressure on suspects. It numbered three Superintendents, 45 Inspectors and Sub-Inspectors, 275 Head Constables and Constables and 36 clerks. In mid-1919 the strength of the District Intelligence Branch had increased to three Superintendents, 71 Inspectors and Sub-Inspectors, 432 Head Constables and Constables and 36 Clerks, or a total of 542 men.[46] At the same time the Central Intelligence Branch had a staff of one Deputy Inspector-General, ten Superintendents, Assistant and Deputy Superintendents, 45 Inspectors and Sub-Inspectors, 258 Head Constables and Constables and 41 Clerks, or a total of 355.[47] This was reduced to a strength of 150 in January 1920. No instance of friction between the Central Intelligence Branch staff and the District Intelligence staff occurred.[48]

Thus the number of revolutionary outrages diminished considerably. Action under the Defence of India Act contributed to this improvement but the government relied on information collected by the District intelligence staff in passing orders under the Act. There were 36 cases of political crime in Bengal in 1915; 24 in 1916; eight in 1917, six in 1918, and only two in 1919. However, the organization responsible for revolutionary crime was still in existence.[49] At the beginning of 1917 100–150 men had been convicted; about 100 'more desperate men' were in detention under Regulation III; while about 50–100 men of this category had fled the country or were in hiding. A further 800 were being 'held in varying degrees of restraint under the Defence of India Act'. The government of Bengal estimated that from 5,000 to 10,000 Bengali youths still sympathized with the terrorists, though the revolutionaries themselves claimed 80,000 adherents.[50]

In the war the government had always possessed the physical power to suppress the Bengali terrorist movement. However, it never wanted to appear to be applying coercive measures to its Indian subjects. The strength of British commitment to a belief that Indian moderate opinion would rally to their cause is indicated by how long it took them to control the Bengali terrorists.

Throughout the war the key British success was in preventing the revolutionaries of Bengal acquiring any more large quantities of arms. The importance of Indian intelligence activity abroad, as we shall see, lay in the way it reduced the government's need to use force at home.

NOTES

1. Sir Reginald Craddock believed that: 'With education extending day by day, with more railways, more telegrams, and more newspapers, any hope that this revolutionary movement can be kept permanently isolated in a watertight compartment in Bengal is illusory'. Note by R.H. Craddock, 16 Feb. 1914, in *Proposal to appoint a mission with special powers to deal with political crime. Measures for coping with the political situation in Bengal*, HDA: Nov. 1914, nos. 39–40, IOLR IOR.POS.7148.
2. On 6 August 1914 the British prepared against such an event in Bengal by improving co-ordination between the police and the army. Superintendent J.S. Wilson was appointed an intelligence officer in liaison with the military authorities at Calcutta. He was particularly involved with postal and telegraphic censorship. In March 1916 F.D. Bartley succeeded Wilson. Letter from J.H. Kerr, Officiating Chief Secretary to the Government of Bengal, to the Secretary to the Government of India, Home Department, in *Retention of the appointment of a Special Intelligence Officer in Calcutta for 3 months after the War*, HD/Pol: Nov. 1916, nos. 21–5, IOLR P/9955.
3. Sedition Committee of 1918 Report (Reprint, New Delhi, 1973).
4. Between February and December 1915 there were four such dacoities, in the course of which one chauffeur was killed and cash and ornaments of the value of Rs.90,000 were looted. Letter from J.H. Kerr to the Secretary to the Government of India, Home Department, 17 July 1916, op. cit.
5. Letter from J.H. Kerr, Officiating Chief Secretary to the Government of Bengal, to the

Secretary to the Government of India, Home Department, in *Proposed Retention for a further period of one year up to 31 December 1916 of the temporary staff employed in the Intelligence Department*, Bengal, HD/Pol: Feb. 1916, nos. 68–70, IOLR P/9957.

6. On 19 October 1915 they killed a senior officer, Deputy Superintendent of Police Jatindra Mohan Ghosh, who was sitting facing the door of his house with his little child upon his knee when four or five youths came to his door and fired at him, killing both him and the child. On 21 October 1915 a Sub-Inspector was killed in Calcutta.
7. Notes in the Criminal Investigation Department by C.R. Cleveland, 4 Feb. 1916, in *Proposals for dealing with the political situation in Bengal*. HDA: May 1916, no. 172, IOLR IOR.POS.7296.
8. J.C. Ker, *Political Trouble in India* (Reprint, Calcutta: Editions Indian, 1973), pp. 251, 254.
9. Telegram from the Viceroy, dated 15 Sept. 1915, PRO FO371/2495 (133092).
10. K.F. Tegart (ed.), *Charles Tegart, Memoir of an Indian Policeman* (Tegart Papers), Ch. 9: 'Germany takes a Hand'. IOLR MSS.EUR.C.235/1.
11. Telegram from Viceroy, dated 15 Sept. 1915, PRO FO371/2495 (133092).
12. Tegart Papers, Ch. 9, op. cit.
13. The Sedition Committee of 1917 noted that: 'If the supply had been sufficient to give every gang an ample and separate supply, we think that the conspiracies might have produced, especially in the event of a rising in some other parts of India such as was planned for February 1915, a calamity of a terrible character in Bengal'.
14. This is a fundamental flaw in T.G. Fraser's thesis, *Intrigues of German Government and the Ghadr Party* (London, 1974) and in his subsequent articles, in that he underestimates both the strength of the Indian revolutionary movement and, in consequence, fails to understand British responses to it. Likewise Don Dignan's *The Indian Revolutionary Movement in British Diplomacy, 1914–1919* (New Delhi, 1983) discusses British diplomacy and Indian revolutionaries abroad, but fails to mention the terrorist campaign within India itself.
15. The strength of the Bengali terrorist movement is, for example, underrated in the DCI's compilation, *Political Trouble in India* (Simla, 1917).
16. Notes in the Criminal Investigation Department, by C.R. Cleveland, 4 Feb. 1916, op. cit.
17. Sir Algernon Rumbold, *Watershed in India 1914–1922* (London: Athlone Press, 1979), p. 16.
18. Note by C.R. Cleveland, dated 1 Dec. 1914, in *Attempt to bomb Deputy Superintendent of Police, Basanta Chatterjee, on the evening of 25 November*, HDA: May 1915, nos. 302–7, IOLR IOR.POS.7151.
19. Memorandum by R.H. Craddock, 13 Oct. 1914, HDA: Nov. 1914, nos. 39–48, IOLR IOR.POS.7148. Cleveland, who wrote that the Government of India should tell the Secretary of State his job: 'There is absolutely nothing to be done, in my opinion, but to tell the Secretary of State a fairly extensive use of Regulation III has now become necessary and to use it promptly'. Note by C.R. Cleveland, 1 Dec. 1914, op. cit.
20. Notes in the Criminal Intelligence Office by C.R. Cleveland, 4 Feb. 1916, in *Proposals for dealing with the political situation in Bengal*, HDA: May 1916, no. 172, IOLR IOR.POS.7296.
21. 'Mystery of the "Medina"', in *The Observer* Colour Supplement, 12 July 1987.
22. See, for example, the comments on Carmichael in Rumbold, op. cit.
23. Carmichael to Hardinge, 20 May 1915, CUL Hardinge Papers, Vol.66; India, Original Letters, Xi, pp. 286–9.
24. Memorandum by R.H. Craddock, 26 Feb. 1916, op. cit.
25. Carmichael claimed that: 'If there were more knowledge [of police activities] there would be less distrust and less hatred, and our police would be more efficient'. Carmichael to Hardinge, 24 March 1913, CUL Hardinge Papers, Vol. 56; India,

Original Letters, Vii.
26. Carmichael to Hardinge, CUL Hardinge Papers, Vol. 59; India, Original Correspondence, VIii.
27. Carmichael to Hardinge, 15 August 1915, CUL Hardinge Papers, Vol. 66; India: Original Letters, Xi, pp. 225–6.
28. Carmichael wrote to Hardinge on 1 Dec. 1915 that 'the relations between the CID of the Bengal police and the special branch of the Calcutta police ought to be altered'. Note by H. Wheeler, 21 Feb. 1916, in *Proposals for dealing with the political situation in Bengal*, HDA: May 1916, no. 172, IOLR IOR.POS.7296. Carmichael also complained to Hardinge that: 'There is a certain amount of distrust of each other's judgement, perhaps also of jealousy, among officers which rather hampers one'. Carmichael to Hardinge, 25 Aug. 1915, CUL Hardinge Papers, Vol. 66; India, Original Letters, Xi, pp. 322–8.
29. Carmichael to Hardinge, CUL Hardinge Papers, Vol. 67; India, Original Letters, Xii, pp. 240–43.
30. *Supply of 39 Colt .450 bore pistols with ammunition and leather holsters to the police employed in the Intelligence Branch of the Criminal Investigation Department, Bengal*, HD/Pol: March 1916, nos. 88–93, IOLR P/9957.
31. Rumbold, op. cit., p. 17.
32. See Ch. 11, part 1.
33. Wheeler to Hardinge, 30 Aug. 1915, CUL Hardinge Papers, Vol. 66; India, Original Letters, Xi, pp. 387–8.
34. He complained about Carmichael's administration: 'the conciliation policy has involved careful and sympathetic discrimination in arrests and internments and a degree of moderation in coercive measures that is considered by most Englishmen in India to have been far in excess of the requirements of the situation'. Notes in the Criminal Intelligence Office, by C.R. Cleveland, 4 Feb. 1916, op. cit.
35. Note by W. Booth-Graveley, 19 July 1916, HDA: March 1917, nos. 225–32, op. cit.
36. Notes in the Criminal Intelligence Office by C.R. Cleveland, 4 Feb. 1916, op. cit.
37. Hardinge complained that: 'Lord Carmichael seems quite content to allow the present situation to continue and when I last saw him he seemed to regard it as regrettable without being in the least perturbed'. Memorandum by Lord Hardinge, 13 March 1916, HDA: May 1916, no. 172, IOLR IOR.POS.7296.
38. Memorandum by R.H. Craddock, 26 Feb. 1916, HDA: May 1916, no. 172, IOLR IOR.POS.7296, op. cit.
39. Letter from J.H. Kerr, Chief Secretary to the government of Bengal, to the Secretary to the Government of India, Home Department, dated 17 July 1916, in *Proposals for dealing with the political situation in Bengal and in other parts of India*, HDA: March 1917, nos. 225–32, IOLR IOR.POS.8614.
40. Notes in the Criminal Investigation Department, by C.R. Cleveland, 4 Feb. 1916, op. cit.
41. Tegart Papers, op. cit. Ch. X: 'Law and Order Win a Round'. Letter from J.H. Kerr to the Secretary to the Government of India, Home Department, 17 July 1916, op. cit.
42. Tegart Papers, Ch. X, op. cit.
43. Rumbold, op. cit., p.44.
44. Letter from J.H. Kerr, Chief Secretary to the government of Bengal, to the Secretary to the Government of India, Home Department, HD/Pol: July 1917, nos. 132–6, IOLR P/10136.
45. Letter from J.H. Kerr, Chief Secretary to the government of Bengal, to to the Secretary to the Government of India, 13 March 1917, op. cit.
46. Letter from J.H. Kerr to the Secretary to the Government of India, Home Department, Feb. 1919, op. cit.
47. Letter from J.H. Kerr to the Secretary to the Government of India, Home Department,

27 Oct. 1919, op. cit.
48. Letter from J.H. Kerr to the Secretary to the Government of India, Home Department, February 1919, in *Further continuance of the temporary staff employed on District Intelligence work in Bengal*, HD/Pol: July 1919, nos. 93–7, IOLR P/10597.
49. Letter from J.H. Kerr to the Secretary to the Government of India, 27 October 1919, in *Reduction in the temporary portion of the staff employed in the Central Intelligence Agency Branch of the Bengal Criminal Investigation Department and the continuance of this reduced staff and that of the temporary staff employed in the district intelligence work up to 31 December 1920*, HD/Pol: March 1920, nos. 96–9, IOLR P/10839.
50. Memorandum by R.H. Craddock, 11 April 1917, HDA: March 1917, nos. 225–32, IOLR IOR.POS.8614.

9

British Intelligence and the Indian Revolutionary Movement in Europe, 1914–19

With the outbreak of the First World War the Indian intelligence network set up by Superintendent Wallinger as described earlier might have been expected to play an important role within the general structure of British intelligence in Europe. In scale it was not much smaller than the European intelligence operations of the Secret Service Bureau, let alone those of the War Office.[1] Moreover, John Wallinger already controlled agents operating in Switzerland, which was to become an important centre of German intrigue, and was an obvious point of entry for Allied agents into Germany. There were few, if any, secret service officers in 1914 whose experience of the Continent could match that of Wallinger, or who, like he, had cultivated friendly relations with the Paris political police, the *Sûreté*.

Soon after the outbreak of war Wallinger proceeded to France, and at some time in 1914 he was made a temporary Major on the Imperial General Staff, as a member of which he performed both 'his own duties and those connected with the war'.[2] He was at first largely concerned with preventing Indian nationalists residing in France from contacting the large number of Indian troops who began to arrive in the country from September 1914 onwards.

Wallinger's activities on the Continent, however, were soon no longer confined to Indian agitators. John Wallinger had a younger brother named Ernest who, after being severely wounded in France in September 1914, was appointed to a senior position on the Intelligence Section of the General Staff at British General Headquarters in France. In March 1915 Ernest Wallinger suggested that John Wallinger should run one of two intelligence systems in Switzerland, which the Army Intelligence Section were setting up.[3] By December 1915 John Wallinger had set up his headquarters in Paris.[4]

Though John Wallinger was officially a part of the network of British Military Intelligence he remained primarily an officer of the Indian Department of Criminal Intelligence. According to the Indian Civil List his services had been 'placed at the disposal of the War Office'.[5] In 1916 the head of the Special Branch still referred to him as 'the Indian secret service officer'.[6] At the end of 1915 Sir Charles Cleveland wrote that

> 'W' works in Europe partly under the India Office and partly under myself, and the cost of his Agency, including his pay and travelling allowance, is defrayed by the India Office.[7]

Surprisingly, Cleveland did not mention the control which the War Office exercised over Wallinger. Without doubt his duties were confined to purely Indian intelligence only in the very early stages of the war. But even if J.A. Wallinger's field of action had been so limited it would still have been placed under the general authority of Military Intelligence, because this decreased the problems of overlapping jurisdictions. Army intelligence already ran one network in Switzerland which operated alongside another set up by Mansfield Cumming's Secret Service.[8]

The DCI were pleased with John Wallinger's work at the end of the first six months of the war. On 20 January 1915 Sir Charles Cleveland informed the Home Department that his work had 'continued to be most satisfactory and valuable'.[9] Had it not been for the war, Wallinger would have returned to his post on the CID of the Bombay Presidency, but in August 1915 Cleveland decided that a change of personnel in the DCI's European agency was undesirable.[10] By this time Wallinger had requested the DCI to send him help. Cleveland decided that because the 'scope of Wallinger's work' had 'been so greatly widened by the war' he should have 'a second officer of the Indian Police Department to work with him'. This officer did not arrive in Europe until October 1915.[11]

Though the DCI were able to spare only one officer for work in Europe, they wanted this to the best man they had. David Petrie had had to return to Britain to get rid of fever which he had contracted after his wounding in the Budge Budge affray. However, Petrie turned down the post. Instead the DCI selected P.C. Vickery, an Assistant

Superintendent, on the recommendation of both the Inspector-General of Police and the Lieutenant-Governor of the Punjab. Vickery was at that time working in the non-political crime section of the DCI and before that had spent three years as Personal Assistant to the Deputy-Inspector General of the Punjab CID. He was suited for the post because he had 'a fair knowledge' of French and spoke German well. Vickery's relatively high rank is obscured in documents relating to his work in Europe which he signed using the temporary rank of Lieutenant which he held within British Military Intelligence.[12]

If by the beginning of 1915 John Wallinger had ceased to be concerned only with Indian 'sedition' in Europe, so too Indian 'sedition' in Europe became no longer the sole preserve of John Wallinger. Indian revolutionary activity around the world had become so widespread that the resources of the Indian police proved inadequate to control it. At some time between December 1914 and January 1915 an interdepartmental committee was formed in London on which all the departments of the British government concerned with the Indian revolutionary problem sat. The Foreign Office was represented by Rowland Sperling, the head of its American Department, because North America was by this time the main centre of the Indian revolutionary movement abroad. The India Office was represented by Malcolm (after 1919 Sir Malcolm) Seton, the head of the Judicial and Public Department, who for the previous five years had worked closely with Wallinger. The Political and Secret Department of the India Office also participated on the committee.[13] Throughout the war John Wallinger himself was also an important member, representing the India Office. At the beginning of 1916 the representatives of MI5 were Vernon Kell, its head, and two ex-Indian officers, Nathan and Stephenson. MI1(a), which carried out 'the distribution and registration of intelligence' and which served as a liaison office for the various intelligence departments, naturally played an important role on the committee. MI1(a)'s chief, Colonel C.N. French, seems to have had a particularly influential voice in its deliberations. The Admiralty was represented by Rayment, an officer of its Intelligence Division. It had a particular interest in the Indian problem because its vessels, in the last resort, kept Indian and German gun-runners away from the coasts of India. The Colonial Office, like the Admiralty, was particularly interested in Indian activities in the Pacific. There is no evidence that the Secret Service participated on the committee. This is surprising, since from the end of 1915 Cumming came to have general control over the operations of British intelligence in North America as well as running a network in Switzerland. Possibly Cumming's interests were represented by the Foreign Office.[14]

Of the departments other than the India Office which were represented on the Committee, Britain's domestic counter-intelligence agency, MI5, was the most directly concerned with the control of the Indian revolutionary movement in Europe. MI5 was known as Section MO5g of the War Office in August 1914, acquiring its modern designation in January 1916. Upon the outbreak of war, the department's head, Vernon Kell, had a total staff of only 19. In November 1918, when the war ended, MI5 was 844-strong.[15] From early in the war the department had Indian experts on its staff. Gradually it came to see itself as responsible for counter-espionage at an Imperial level and this was recognized in September 1916 when a special section – MI5(d) – was formed to co-ordinate counter-espionage measures throughout the British Empire. Another section, MI5(b), was formed in January 1917 'to deal with questions affecting natives of India and other Oriental races'. The official title of the department dealing with the Indian problem in Europe during its most serious phase from 1915 to mid-1916 was MO5(g)A, and it had the general duty of investigating 'espionage and cases of suspected persons'. In 1916 it became known more simply as MI5(g).[16]

MI5 was reinforced over the course of the war by an influx of officers from India. In February 1917, out of 27 officers working on the staff of MI5(g) alone, eight had served in India. It is not known how long they had worked for MI5. This concentration of Indian intelligence officers is remarkable, particularly at a time when there was a chronic shortage of officers to perform intelligence duties in India and the Far East upon which the security of the Indian empire depended. Within the general scheme of British intelligence in the First World War, overriding priority in the allocation of men and money was given to the main European theatre of the war. As will be seen in Chapter 11, the protection of the Empire in the East was conducted with very scanty resources.

In the early years of the war Robert Nathan was the most important of the Indian officers who served under Kell. He was the former Chief Commissioner of the Dacca District who had helped track down the Dacca *Anusilan Samiti* in 1907.[17] In 1915 he had retired from the Indian Civil Service after 26 years' service. In India he enjoyed a reputation for efficiency and had just been appointed Vice-

Chancellor of Calcutta University when, at the end of January 1914 he was forced to return home through ill-health.[18] By October 1914 at the latest he was the leading Indian officer working in MI5.

The Special Branch acted as the covert executive arm of MI5 but became involved in MI5 cases only when surveillance was necessary. Relations between MI5 and the Special Branch were often fraught. MI5 resented the way in which Basil Thomson, the head of the Special Branch, publicly took the credit for actions for which they were responsible yet, being officially non-existent, could not avow.[19] Robert Nathan was the only officer of MI5 whose assistance Thomson recognized in his memoirs, *The Scene Changes*.[20] He acknowledged Nathan's close involvement in all his dealings with Indians who came to him for interrogation. However helpful Thomson may have been in interrogating and in changing the loyalties of Germany's Indian agents, the real work of counter-espionage was conducted by Nathan and MO5(g)/MI5(g) in concert with John Wallinger who, at this time, operated mainly abroad. Basil Thomson had had no experience of India and Indians in his career before he became head of the Special Branch in 1913. Significantly, he did not sit on the interdepartmental committee.

In the first year of the war the main concern of Indian intelligence in Europe was not with the Indian revolutionary movement, which was thought to have gone into hibernation for the duration of the conflict, but with the Indian soldiers who came to France to fight for the Empire. The first Indian division left India on 8 August 1914 and arrived at Marseilles seven weeks later. Altogether 138,000 Indian troops served on the Western Front in the course of the war. By the end of 1915, after 14 months' service in Flanders, the bulk of the Indian contingent left to fight the Turks.[21]

'Sedition', in the sense of support for the revolutionary movement, gained no hold whatsoever on the minds of the Indian troops in France. Their morale had deteriorated by the end of 1915, by which time the British censor was worried that the men had started to write poetry, which he considered to be 'an ominous sign of mental disquietude'.[22] But Indian morale was not significantly worse than that of English soldiers. Equally, the censor at Boulogne intercepted only a very small quantity of anti-British propaganda sent to the troops by Indian nationalists overseas. None the less fears of an outbreak of unrest among the Indian Army contingent preoccupied the British, despite the increased supervision of Indian revolutionaries by the

French authorities. As late as January 1916 the Indian government feared that Indian agitators might get in touch with native troops at the front and at Marseilles, where they disembarked.

The assistance rendered by the French authorities was complete. In Autumn 1914 the Department of Criminal Intelligence supplied the French military authorities with a list of Indians who might attempt to go to the front to subvert the loyalty of the Indian troops.[23] Many but by no means all the prominent Indian nationalists fled the Allied countries on the outbreak of war. Madame Cama was an old Parsi lady who had figured prominently in the DCI's reports since 1907. Though Wallinger regarded her as 'brainless', the DCI seems to have had some admiration for her tenacity. After war broke out, she lost no time in attempting to persuade the Indian troops of the error of their ways in fighting for the Empire.[24] On 27 October 1914 she was ordered to leave Marseilles.[25] The *Sûreté Générale* warned her of unpleasant consequences if she did not stop her nationalist activities during the war.[26] A worse fate overtook S.R. Rana, the other old leader of the Paris Indian group. The French expelled him, his German wife and his dying son to Martinique. The British feared the effect that such aged revolutionaries might have on the troops, and uncompromisingly opposed the Ranas' return to France, even when the French government itself pleaded with them to permit on humanitarian grounds the return of Mrs Rana to France for a cancer operation.[27]

By October 1914 the *Sûreté* was watching Indian nationalist propaganda 'with the greatest care'.[28] But this did not satisfy the British. In January 1916 they put forward far-reaching measures, which the French Ministry of the Interior and the *Sûreté* approved. These gave the British military authorities the power to deport not only Indian agitators who had penetrated into the camps, but also any British subjects whose presence the military authorities considered a danger to the army.[29]

These measures coincided with the introduction of a greater degree of Indian police control over the Indian troops. In August 1915 the War Office asked that a few officers of the 'Indian Criminal Investigation Department' be placed at the disposal of the Base Commandant at Marseilles. The Government of India agreed to send a staff of three or four Indian police officers together with a British officer, whom they judged necessary for the supervision of the Indian staff. For the senior position they chose Superintendent R.H. Hirst of the Bihar and Orissa police. He left for France on 7 November 1915, with the task of determining the number and class of Indian police officers required.

Despite the growth of Indian police activity in Europe in 1915, the Department of Criminal Intelligence did not have the ready possibility of expanding its network abroad. The war did not remove past restraints which prevented the DCI's growth overseas as well as at home. Its expansion was blocked by its relationship with the Indian Local Governments, upon whom it was dependent for experienced personnel, and by the enduring aversion of the British government to the operation of an Indian imperial secret police, particularly in Europe and America, where a strong 'liberal conscience' continued to exist, despite the rigours of the war.

Wallinger had not prepared for a war with Germany, since he had not expected any increase in the activities of Indian revolutionaries in Europe. In June 1914 the Department of Criminal Intelligence reported on 'The future of Indian nationalist agitation in Europe'. They concluded that terrorism had lost ground while constitutional nationalism had gained in strength.[30] In August 1914 Wallinger reported to the DCI that the war had practically put a stop to 'extremist' propaganda and had temporarily rendered Indian malcontents on the Continent innocuous.[31] Wallinger realized that 'the sympathies of Indian nationalists, among whom almost all Indian students are to be classed, are with the Germans so far as the war in Europe is concerned . . .'[32] Though the British were apprehensive of Indian nationalists contacting the troops, they were far less worried about Indian terrorism in Europe than they had been in 1910, when Savarkar roamed free. However, Germany now took up the cause of the Indian revolutionaries on an international scale.

Wallinger was aware that in September 1914 a prominent Indian revolutionary, Chempakaraman Pillai, approached the German Consul in Zurich and gave him an outline of the strength and plans of the Indian revolutionary movement.[33] He also knew that Pillai had left Zurich not long afterwards for Berlin where he was to work under the German Foreign Office.[34] However, before the war Wallinger's network had been devoted to the needs of the Indian government. He had not set up a network of agents inside Germany, where the Indian nationalist movement had barely existed before September 1914, when the Indians and the Germans established an Indian revolutionary committee, attached to the German General Staff in Berlin. British intelligence only learned that this had happened in May 1915.[35]

The four leading members of the committee upon its foundation were Chempakaraman Pillai, Virendranath Chattopadhyaya, Dr Prabhakar and Dr Abdul Hafiz. They were later joined by other prominent pre-war revolutionaries including Har Dayal and Tarak Nath Das. One important Punjabi nationalist, Ajit Singh, made his escape from right under the noses of John Wallinger and the Paris Sûreté. At the beginning of September 1914 he left Paris without even informing his landlady which, as the DCI pointed out, was 'considered a low trick by agents of the secret service in any country'.[36]

But there was nothing that Wallinger could have done to prevent the majority of the Indians who reached Berlin getting through since they came from two neutral states, the USA or Switzerland. Wallinger's sources of information about Indian activities in Switzerland were good. He was aware that Chattopadhyaya visited Switzerland in the middle of May 1915 and established agencies at Geneva and Zurich and also that he went to Lucerne where he met the Egyptian nationalist Farid Bey.[37]

The DCI had been concerned about the danger of a combined effort by the Indian and Egyptian nationalist groups since 1910. By July 1915 it had received information that the German Foreign Office had recruited a number of Egyptians who were helping the 'Indian National Party' to distribute anti-British propaganda. Among them was a medical student named Ali Eloui, whom the DCI already knew to be on particularly intimate terms with Virendranath Chattopadhyaya.[38]

There is no evidence that the Egyptian intelligence was running any network of agents in Europe at this time. The surveillance of Egyptian nationalists abroad fell largely to John Wallinger. But even in 1917 he seems not to have been working in close association with Egyptian intelligence. In January 1917 Wallinger requested that Egypt provide him with 'the names of suspicious Egyptians going to America from Egypt'. It is remarkable that he was not already in receipt of this information.[39]

The British received early information that the Germans and the Indians were plotting assassination from Switzerland. Dr Parodi, the Director of the Egyptian School at Geneva, had worked for the British since before the war.[40] Leading Egyptian nationalists trusted him. In Autumn 1914 Dr Mansur Rifaat, the former editor of the leading Egyptian nationalist journal abroad, La Patrie Egyptienne, left Switzerland for America in a hurry. The Swiss police seized some of his papers which, however, they allowed Parodi to read, though they

223

denied access to the British authorities. These papers revealed what the British Ambassador at Berne saw at this time as 'a somewhat vague and wild scheme of action against British India including the assassination of officials and extensive propaganda'. The papers also gave the British an early indication that 'an intelligence bureau' had been formed at Berlin, namely Oppenheim's organization, which was discussed in Chapter 7.[41]

Parodi's information did not arouse any interest among the British. On the part of the Indian authorities this was understandable. Earlier fears that Egyptians and Indians might collaborate in an assassination plot had proved unfounded. In September 1911 Wallinger had received information from both Paris and London that an attempt was to be made on the life of Lord Kitchener, who was 'evidently extremely unpopular with the Egyptian nationalists and the Indian conspirators [were] at one with them in desiring his removal'.[42] But this plot never materialized.

On 20 March 1915 Gobind Behari Lal, Har Dayal's right-hand man, arrived in Liverpool from New York. The British authorities were worried lest he try to contact Indian soldiers and he was closely watched. But they allowed him to return to America unmolested in April 1915. They did not realize their mistake until two months later, when the US secret service suggested that Behari Lal had intended to cause explosions at the docks.[43] Nathan and Thomson only learned at the end of the year that Behari Lal had come to England in connection with a plot to murder Lord Kitchener. The DCI claimed that he failed in his mission because he was unable to find anyone willing to commit the murder.[44]

It was not until Autumn 1915 that the British had an idea of the full scale of the European plot which the Germans and Indians had evolved. After the obliteration of their spy network in the first days of the war by MO5, the Indians provided the Germans with potential agents in England. The Germans realized that an even more promising field for the use of Indian nationalists lay in Italy, where high-caste Indians were not always distinctive because of their skin-colour.

Though Behari Lal's mission failed, the Germans had managed to establish a small revolutionary cell in England. Soon after the Indian National Party in Berlin was constituted, Virendranath Chattopadhyaya attempted to get in touch with some of the remaining members of the old 'India House'. The existence of the English branch of the European conspiracy was revealed by the British censor.[45]

The first arrest was only made on 15 June 1915. Examination of Chattopadhyaya's correspondence led British counter-intelligence to a Swiss girl named Meta Brunner, who acted as the messenger between Switzerland and the English group. The small band of conspirators whom Brunner revealed included an Indian named Vishna Dubé and his common-law German wife, Anna Brandt. Hilda Howsin, the daughter of a Yorkshire doctor, was known to have knowledge of their plans.[46] They were arrested and interned until the end of the war.[47] That they were not executed proves that they had supplied no information of any worth to the Germans.

The main strength of the German–Indian plot did not lie in the imprisoned English group. The existence of a large-scale assassination conspiracy was only confirmed late in August 1915, when, once again, the censor seized certain incriminating documents. Thomson wrote:

> The plan was to bring about the simultaneous assassination of the leading men in the *Entente* countries. These included the King of Italy, the British Foreign Secretary, Lord Grey, and the War Minister, Lord Kitchener, the French President, Poincaré, and Prime Minister, Viviani, as well as the Italian Prime Minister, Salandra. The bombs had been manufactured in Italy and were tested by the German military authorities at a military testing ground near Berlin.

It was not clear whether the plot was devised by the Germans or by the Indians themselves.[48]

In their *Weekly Report* for 29 June 1915 the Department of Criminal Intelligence reported that they had received information 'from a trustworthy source' that German agents in Switzerland, including Dr Abdul Hafiz, one of the leaders of the 'Indian National Party', were plotting to assassinate Italian government ministers.[49] By August the DCI was in possession of full details of the plot. On 22 July Hafiz had come to Zurich and arranged for ten time-bombs to be sent to the German Consul there. Ali Eloui and an Italian anarchist named Bertoni were to take charge of the bombs. The Germans expected Bertoni and other Italian anarchists in their pay to be useful in smuggling the bombs over the Italian border. However, the plot 'miscarried as it was not kept sufficiently secret'. Hafiz was thrown out of Switzerland by the local police.[50]

Despite these alarming reports it was only on 29 November 1915 that Robert Nathan sent a request through the Foreign Office to the

Italian government for all Indians to be stopped from crossing from Italy to Switzerland and, if possible, deported to England. If the German assassination plot was handled ineptly by the conspirators, Italian security measures appear to have been hardly more competent. Nathan noted that 'it would seem to be greatly to the interest of the Italian government to stop any such [Indian] traffic, since, as they know, one of the plots in which the Indian party in Berlin and Switzerland is concerned has been directed against high personages in Italy'. Nathan himself was by this time very impressed with the destructive capabilities of the Indo-German plotters. In a letter dated 4 December 1915 he informed Rowland Sperling of the Foreign Office that recent attempts to blow up the Turin arsenal and the railway tunnel of the Turin–Paris line were probably connected with their activity.[51]

On 1 December 1915 Sir Rennell Rodd, the British Ambassador at Rome, reported that 'an informer paid by India' had produced evidence which resulted in the arrest in Italy of 'three British subjects'.[52] This is the first reference to direct British secret service activity in Italy in connection with the Indian plot. A senior Indian officer was only stationed in Italy in January 1916. On 31 January 1916 Nathan wrote that Major Gabriel, an officer of the Indian Civil Service who was home on leave, had been appointed to the British Military Mission in Rome.[53] Gabriel advised the Italian government on the security measures which it finally undertook at this time against Indian suspects.[54]

At the same time that the plot in Italy was developing, in March 1915, the German and Indian plotters sent out a mission to the Suez Canal with the task of distributing seditious leaflets among Indian soldiers there. The mission included Tarak Nath Das and Tirumal Acharya. The British knew, after the event, that Das reached Constantinople at the end of 1915, and that by March 1916 he was back in Zurich.[55] Yet the plan to subvert the loyalty of Indian troops in Egypt never materialized. At the beginning of September 1915 the Intelligence Department of the Egyptian War Office found copies of 'various Indian proclamations' in the Canal, which they assumed had been left by 'enemy individuals coming across the Sinai Peninsula'. No more than this was discovered about the German–Indian plot in Egypt. There was little more to learn, since the Indians called off their propaganda campaign almost as soon as it started. They had soon lost spirit when they realized that the call for the establishment of an

Islamic state in India contained in their pamphlets was likely to have little appeal to the largely Hindu garrison of Egypt.[56]

Basil Thomson admitted that the British only came into possession of 'very definite evidence . . . of the extent of the German–Indian conspiracy' in October 1915.[57] In that month the London Special Branch arrested an Indian named Harish Chandra who had recently returned from America. Thomson recorded that on 23 October 1915 his 'long investigations' with Nathan into the Indian assassination plot culminated with Harish Chandra's confession, which took four hours to record in shorthand.[58] Harish Chandra gave full details of the formation of the 'Indian National Party' in Berlin. The Indians' initial plans had been to subvert the loyalty of Indian POWs and to conduct a propaganda campaign from Berlin. The Germans looked down on them until the arrival of Mahendra Pratap together with his secretary, Harish Chandra. The details of Mahendra Pratap's mission have been given in Chapter 7. Were it not for Harish Chandra's confession the British might not even have known its existence. Though a failure, it was potentially the most dangerous of the German–Indian plots based in Europe. Harish Chandra gave further reliable information that at least two other missions had been sent off – one to Japan and one to Singapore – and also gave some information about the activities of the Ghadr Party in California.[59]

Despite his impeccable revolutionary credentials – his father was the founder of a school devoted to educate the youth of India on purely Hindu lines – Thomson and Nathan persuaded Harish Chandra to work for them as a secret agent.[60] In December 1915 he arrived in Switzerland posing as the secretary to a (genuine) Prince who had recently been in England. The revolutionaries freely gave him details of German–Indian plots which Nathan and Thomson found that other sources confirmed.

In January 1916 Harish Chandra's mission in Switzerland was complete and he was examined by Major Wallinger. Chandra provided numerous addresses of Indians sympathetic to, or aiding Germany; the British were already familiar with some of them.[61] Chandra provided a list of members of the Indian revolutionary committee at Berlin and gave details of the German secret service in French Switzerland. The importance of the link between Switzerland and unrest in the British Empire in the minds of the Germans was obvious. According to Harish Chandra, two of the most important German agents there were primarily concerned with Eastern affairs. The man 'in charge of the espionage arrangements in French Switzerland', Jacoby, had been in Persia for some years and had been ordered to watch Orientals visiting Switzerland, particularly Persians and Egyptians. Harish Chandra claimed that the Germans were 'anxious to find some person of rank who will proclaim a revolution in India'. In dealing with Egyptians Jacoby employed an Irishman married to a German who had served in the British Army in Egypt.[62] On leaving Switzerland Harish Chandra received from the German Consul at Geneva a typewritten plan for a military rising in India led by German officers.[63]

In May 1916 Harish Chandra carried out a second mission in Switzerland. By this date not only had the German–Indian plans for assassination in Europe and for a rising in Afghanistan failed, but also ambitious schemes to cause mutiny in Burma and to supply arms to the revolutionaries of Bengal had fallen through completely. But Harish Chandra provided evidence that the Indian Committee in Berlin still had some support from the German government. The Indian revolutionaries in Switzerland gave him two glass tubes which he was to carry into India. The first tube contained a letter from the Kaiser to the Indian Princes; and the second contained a summary of the Berlin Indian Committee's aims. This document showed that the Germans were now concentrating on a vain project of inciting the Indian Buddhists. By the end of 1916 at the latest the London inter-departmental committee which dealt with German–Indian plots had concluded that it would be rash to disregard these schemes altogether, and that the best policy was to encourage the Germans to waste as much money as possible upon them for, given a minimum degree of vigilance, they now had no chance whatsoever of success.[64]

Harish Chandra was not the only Indian agent whom the British successfully used in Switzerland in 1916. In correspondence relating to the assassination plot of 1915 seized by the British censor there were many references to an Indian named Thakur Jessrajsinghji Sessodia. He had already come to the notice of the DCI in 1911 when he started a short-lived nationalist paper, *The Rajput Herald* in London. He had never been influential with Indian nationalists, who, none the less had propitiated him because he was related to Rajput noble families.[65] When, at the beginning of October 1915, Nathan and Thomson interrogated Sessodia about the assassination plot, they found him to be 'a good-humoured-looking person with easy manners'. But on searching his room the police found 'letters addressed to notorious rebels and fomenters of assassination'. Sessodia admitted that his sympathies lay with the Indian nationalists, but that he was only 'coquetting' with the revolutionaries. He truthfully pointed out to Thomson that he had already given some details of the Indian plot to the India Office. Thomson encouraged him to become a British agent and released him.[66] According to Thomson he soon 'succumbed' and was put 'on our regular pay list'.[67]

On 3 August 1916 Sessodia was sent to Switzerland, styling himself, to his great satisfaction, 'His Highness Prince Jessrajsinghji Sessodia of Jodhpur, Marwar' in order to attract the Germans.[68] He returned from Switzerland at the end of October 1916 with information which confirmed the impression created by Harish Chandra's second mission that the German–Indian plots were no longer dangerous. The Germans instructed Sessodia to arrange by now fantastic plans for a native rising involving the landing of German armies on the west coast of India.[69]

Despite the success of his mission Sessodia's career in British intelligence was short. On 16 November 1916 Thomson entered in his diary that he had finished with him because he had shown himself to be 'leaky' by asking the Indian Member of the Viceroy's Executive Council for letters of introduction to Indian Rajahs in order to carry out the tasks which the Germans had set him.[70]

Not all the operations of Indian intelligence in Switzerland were successful. At the end of 1915 Thomson and Nathan encouraged a plan the boldness of which was matched only by that of the Indian conspirators themselves. Donald Gullick was a 24-year-old marine engineer suffering from a serious illness which led him to believe that he had only a few months to live. He had met Anna Brandt, the German mistress of the Indian nationalist Dubé, in a sanatorium and had fallen in love with her. He proposed to Thomson 'a daring scheme for the capture of Chattopadhyaya by luring him into France, on the understanding that, if he was captured, Anna would be set at liberty'. Gullick impressed Thomson, as being 'resolute and powerful'. He was therefore allowed to proceed with his plan.[71] Gullick succeeded in getting Chattopadhyaya to come to Berne. Anna Brandt had mentioned Gullick in her correspondence with Chattopadhyaya who, according to Gullick, trusted him. Thomson claimed that 'Chattopadhya was quite ready to cross the French frontier, but just as they came to details, Swiss detectives ran up and arrested them both on a charge of espionage'.[72]

Despite their early failure to keep pace with Indian plots in Europe, Nathan and J.A. Wallinger succeeded remarkably well in their surveillance of Indian revolutionaries in Europe during the critical period between late 1915 and early 1916. However, by the middle of 1915 John Wallinger's work for Military Intelligence was in disarray after the arrest of most of his European agents by the Swiss police. The Secret Service had fared little better in Switzerland. Wallinger tried to re-establish his network, recruiting among others, the writer Somerset Maugham. However, at the end of May 1916 his Swiss operations were again, according to Kirke, the head of the Intelligence Section at GHQ, close to collapse. Kirke concluded that 'JAW's show so far as we are concerned is a waste of money . . .' John Wallinger later tried to develop contacts with Germany through Denmark and Holland, which Kirke dismissed in turn as respectively a total failure and 'poaching' on his younger brother Ernest's territory. On 28 July 1916 Kirke recorded in his diary the 'parting of the ways with Wallinger'.[73]

Yet there is no evidence that Wallinger ever lost the respect of the Indian DCI and Home Department. There is little doubt that he operated primarily as an Indian officer. He continued to be seen as the mouthpiece of the DCI on the interdepartmental committee throughout the war. The main successes of Indian intelligence in Europe during the First World War – the capture of Harish Chandra and of Sessodia – owed something to chance, but far more to the knowledge of the Indian revolutionary movement and of its activities in Switzerland, which Indian intelligence had acquired since John Wallinger first arrived in Europe at the beginning of 1910.

It remains unclear whether J.A. Wallinger's failed agent networks in Switzerland, which he ran for Kirke, constituted the main part of his work. It is probable that they did not, and that John Wallinger was largely responsible for Indian operations in Switzerland. This would account for the presence of three British networks in Switzerland.[74] There is no evidence that any Asian agent in British employ was ever captured by the Swiss or by the enemy. Dr Parodi was still working for the British at the end of the war, while in 1917 Harish Chandra was sent on a successful mission to the United States, where he was put in charge of an enquiry into the revolutionary party's finances. In January 1917 Wallinger claimed that the British had also had recent success in sending agents into Germany from America.[75]

Wallinger did not cease to perform the duties of military intelligence after his 'parting of ways' with Kirke in July 1916. His operations seem to have been placed under the control of Mansfield Cumming and the Secret Service on 1 August 1916. He was still working in Cumming's office at the end of 1917, training an officer to go into Switzerland.[76] In 1917 and 1918 Austen Chamberlain, the Secretary of State for India, sent John Wallinger letters of thanks and appreciation. His operations in Switzerland continued to be important, since the activities of Egyptian nationalists there grew in importance in 1919, when serious civil unrest broke out in Egypt and when Switzerland became the scene of the negotiations which ended the Ottoman Empire. In 1919 Wallinger was placed on special duty in connection with the Egyptian political situation in addition to his own duties. Even then he did not have direct contact with all the agencies dedicated to the control of Egyptian unrest.[77] By 1919 Wallinger had so much experience of Eastern nationalism in Europe that the Government of India no longer thought of replacing him. He remained the head of Indian intelligence in Europe until he retired in 1926.[78]

NOTES

1. See, generally, C.M. Andrew, *Secret Service* (London: Heinemann, 1985), Ch. 2.
2. *Curriculum vitae* of Sir John Wallinger kindly given to me by his great-nephew, Mr J.D.A. Wallinger.
3. See Andrew, op. cit., pp. 146–7. The Wallingers' sister's diary shows that 25 meetings took place between them in the first eight months of 1915. This information was kindly supplied by Mr J.D.A. Wallinger.
4. In December 1915 John Wallinger's address was 'Intelligence anglaise, 31 Boulevard des Invalides, Paris'. In 1916 it was c/o Cassia, 282 Boulevard St Germain.
5. Note signed 'A.L.', dated 25 May 1916, in *Correspondence on the subject of Hector R. Kothavala, Deputy Superintendent, Bombay Presidency, to the Straits Settlements Government*. HDB: Nov. 1916, nos. 389–406, in IOLR IOR.POS.10511.
6. Basil Thomson, *The Scene Changes*, (London: Doubleday, Doran & Co., 1939), p. 260.
7. Letter from C.R. Cleveland to Home Department, dated 29 October 1915, in *Sedition in the Far East. Proposed deputation of Mr Petrie, Superintendent of Police, Punjab and Criminal Investigation Department, as Indian Intelligence Officer in the Far East*. HDA: Feb. 1916, nos. 496–514, in IOLR IOR.POS.7296.
8. Likewise, when an Indian intelligence system was re-established in North America in 1916 it officially formed part of Mansfield Cumming's operations, although all concerned recognized that its operations were directed by the India Office.
9. Demi-official letter from M.C. Seton to Sir Charles Cleveland, dated 6 November 1914, in *Extension of the deputation of Mr Wallinger in Europe for one year from 1st April 1915, and decision that he shall be paid a fixed salary during that period instead of pay according to the next below rule*. HDA: March 1915, nos. 14–16, IOLR IOR.POS.7151.
10. On the termination of his mission to London, the Government of India had hoped to

send Wallinger 'abroad to examine the position and to draw up considered proposals for the future'. Note by C.R. Cleveland, dated 2 June 1915. HDA: Nov. 1915, nos. 88–92, in IOLR IOR.POS.7295.

11. Ibid. Telegram from Secretary of State to Viceroy, 19 Aug. 1915.

12. Ibid. Note by C.R. Cleveland dated 11 Oct. 1915.

13. The Judicial and Public Department was the India Office's department which corresponded to the Home Department of the Government of India. It was, therefore, concerned with the Indian police and with the domestic and foreign intelligence operations of the DCI. The designation of the Political and Secret Department has misled historians into believing that it was India's secret service. In fact it dealt with the Government of India's foreign affairs and corresponded to the Foreign and Political Department of the Government of India. It was largely concerned with the Indian Princes and with the Persian Gulf, since India's relations with most parts of the world were handled by the Foreign and Colonial Offices.

14. Note by Secretary, Judicial and Public Department, on Interdepartmental Conference held at the India Office on 10 March 1916. *Deputation of Mr D. Petrie as Intelligence Officer for the Far East in connection with Indian sedition.* HDA: June 1916, nos. 285–95, IOLR IOR.POS.7297. Much of the information at the disposal of the interdepartmental committee has been preserved in Foreign Office Series 371, 'Hindu Agitations'. Reports from the Secret Service in this compilation are notably absent.

15. Andrew, op. cit., p. 174.

16. PRO WO9944-A-3.

17. See Ch. 4.

18. Letter from Harcourt Butler to Hardinge, dated 30 January 1914 in CUL Hardinge Papers, India: Original Correspondence, VII i, Vol. 60.

19. Andrew, op. cit., p. 193. However, the events related by Thomson in *The Scene Changes* and *Queer People* (London: Hodder & Stoughton, 1922) are all confirmed by Foreign Office and Indian sources.

20. By 1939, when Thomson printed his war diary in *The Scene Changes*, Nathan had been dead for over ten years. This may have encouraged Thomson to refer to a man who had served not only in MI5, but also as head of the political branch of the Secret Service.

21. The cavalry divisions remained, serving on the Western Front throughout the war. Boris Mollo, *The Indian Army*, (Poole: Blandford Press, 1981), Ch. 5, 'Kitchener's Army, 1903–1922'.

22. Rozina Visram, *Ayahs, Lascars and Princes* (London: Pluto Press, 1986), quoting E.B. Howell's report dated 23 January 1915, L/Mil/5/825, part I, ff. 1–185, extracts from censored mails.

23. *Weekly Report* of the Director of Criminal Intelligence (henceforth 'Weekly Report'), 3 Nov. 1914. HDB: Dec. 1914, nos. 223–6, in IOLR IOR.POS.

24. Ibid. *Weekly Report*, 17 Nov. 1914.

25. *Weekly Report*, 1 Dec. 1914. HDB: Dec. 1914, nos. 227–9, IORL IOR.POS.9837.

26. Ibid. *Weekly Report*, 8 Dec. 1914.

27. Letter from Bertie to Grey, 31 July 1915, in PRO FO371 2494 (104416). Minute Paper on letter from India Office, 5 Aug. 1915, in PRO FO371 2494 (107584).

28. Letter from Bertie to Foreign Office, 28 Oct. 1914, in FO115 1907, no. 2.

29. Suspects were to be handed over to the local French civil authorities, who, in turn, were to hand over the suspect to the British military authorities for deportation. Letter from Cambon to Bertie, 28 Jan. 1916, in PRO FO371 2784 (20898).

30. *Weekly Report*, 15 Sept. 1914. HDB: Dec. 1914, nos. 216–17 in IOLR IOR.POS.9837.

31. *Weekly Report*, 29 Sept. 1914. HDA: Dec. 1914 in IOLR IOR.POS.9837.

32. *Weekly Report*, 20 Oct. 1914. HDB: Dec. 1914, nos. 218–22. IOLR IOR.POS.9837.

33. This meeting with the German Consul was reported in the *Weekly Report*, 20 Oct.

1914. HDB: Dec. 1914, nos. 218–22 in IOLR IOR.POS.9837.
34. James Campbell Ker, *Political Trouble In India, 1907– 1917* (Reprint, Calcutta: Editions Indian, 1973), p. 241.
35. Ibid., pp. 265–6.
36. Ibid., p. 244. *Weekly Report*, June 1915. HDB: June 549–52, in IOLR IOR.POS.9840.
37. Ibid., *Weekly Report*, 22 June 1915.
38. *Weekly Report*, 27 July 1915. HDB: July 1915, nos. 516–17 in IOLR IOR.POS. 9840.
39. Letter from Seton to Sperling, 24 January 1917. PRO FO371/3064 (19618).
40. Parodi reported to the Consul at Geneva, who in turn reported to Berne. The British Embassy then sent on Parodi's reports to the Foreign Office. It is not clear whether Parodi had been recruited by John Wallinger or whether he had been sent out from Cairo by the Arab Bureau.
41. Letter from Evelyn Grant Duff, Berne, to Foreign Office, 28 Nov. 1914, in PRO FO115/1908, no. 3.
42. *Weekly Report*, 26 Sept. 1911. HDB: Oct. 1911, nos. 46–9 in IOLR IOR.POS.8972.
43. Telegram from Spring Rice to Foreign Office, dated 29 July 1915, in PRO FO371 2494 (103905).
44. *Weekly Report*, 21 Dec. 1915. HDB: Dec. 1915, nos. 709–11 in IOLR IOR.POS.9841.
45. *Weekly Report*, 2 Nov. 1915.
46. Thomson, *Queer People*, (op. cit.), pp. 98–9. *The Scene Changes*, op. cit., pp. 250–2.
47. *Queer People*, op. cit., p. 99.
48. Ibid., p. 98–9.
49. *Weekly Report*, 29 June 1915. HDB: July 1915, no. 520 in IOLR IOR.POS. 9840.
50. Ker, op. cit., p. 247. *Weekly Report*, 17 Aug. 1915. HDB: Aug. 1915, nos. 552–6 in IOLR IOR.POS.9840.
51. Letters from Nathan, MO5g/2, to Sperling, 29 Nov. and 4 Dec. 1915, in PRO FO371/ 2497 (181824).
52. Telegram from Sir Rennell Rodd, Rome, to Foreign Office, 1 Dec. 1915, in FO371/ 2497 (182672).
53. Letter from Nathan to Lyons, 31 Jan. 1916, in PRO FO371 2784 (17918).
54. He was still working in Rome at the end of the year. Letter from Rodd, Rome, to Foreign Office, in PRO FO371 2789 (191539). The Italian government only gave instructions for the careful examination of all Indians landing in Italy in January 1916. They excused their lack of action by referring to the state of Italian law, which did not allow police measures to be taken against whole categories of people, only against individuals. For this reason no round-up of Austrian and German citizens took place in Italy at the start of the war. '*Indians landing in Italy. Intimation that the Foreign Office have asked the Ambassador at Rome to deport to England all Indians landing in Italy, or failing that to intimate their names, keep them under observation, and prevent them crossing to Switzerland*'. HD(A): Feb. 1916, nos. 430–8 in IOLR IOR.POS.9841.
55. Ker, op. cit., p. 247. *Weekly Report*, 21 Dec. 1915. HDB: Dec. 1915, nos. 709–11 in IOLR IOR.POS.9841.
56. Intelligence in the Arab world was not a major concern of the Department of Criminal Intelligence. However, the Political and Secret Department noted that Private Cholmeley had sailed on 10 September to Jeddah where he was to serve as Criminal Investigation Department Officer, watching Indian pilgrims. There he served under Lieutenant Colonel C.E. Wilson, who reported to the Arab Bureau in Cairo. Telegram from the Viceroy, Foreign Department, to Cairo, 21 Sept. 1916, in PRO FO371 2789 (192896). In November 1916 Sub-Inspector Shaikh of the Bombay CID was working for Wilson in Mecca. Letter from C.E. Wilson, Jeddah, to the Director, Arab Bureau, 11 Nov. 1916, in PRO FO371 2790 (242004).
57. *Queer People*, op. cit., p. 100.
58. *The Scene Changes*, op. cit., pp. 250–1.

59. Ibid., pp. 250–2.
60. Ker, op. cit., p. 245.
61. Most notably Vincent Kraft, Germany's chief secret agent in the Far East, who was now working for the Singapore authorities.
62. Gifford is the model for the traitor Grantley Caypor in Somerset Maugham's *Ashenden Stories*.
63. *The Scene Changes*, op. cit. pp. 260–1. 'Memorandum of information obtained by an Indian during a recent visit to Switzerland', Jan. 1916, in Straits Settlements Correspondence, PRO CO273 450.
64. Letter from Wallinger to Cleveland, dated 29 June 1918. Wallinger wrote that 'the policy of allowing German schemes to develop in channels over which the British can exercise a surveillance in preference to forcing them by preventive action into unknown channels has been generally accepted here by experts with the most intimate knowledge of German workings. If we stop the Germans from spending thousands of pounds on wild-cat schemes for stirring up trouble in India which are so hare-brained as to be almost impossible of success, and can in any case be supervised by us, the time, energy and money which they undoubtedly do spend at present in this fashion will be diverted onto schemes and into channels of which we would be completely in ignorance, and which might ultimately prove a far greater danger to the Empire as a whole than all their present machinations can ever be'.
65. *Weekly Report*, 26 May 1914. HDB: June 1914, nos. 142–5 in IOLR IOR.POS. 9837.
66. *The Scene Changes*, op. cit., pp. 248–9, p. 305.
67. Scotland Yard gave him the codename 'Mr Jones' by Scotland Yard. Ibid., pp. 248–9, 304–5.
68. Ibid., p. 305. The first person whose attention he attracted was the British Military Attaché at Berne, who placed an informant with him. Telegram from Lieutenant Colonel W. Wyndham, Military Attaché, to Sir Horace Rumbold, Berne, 10 Oct. 1916, in PRO FO371 2789 (206530).
69. *The Scene Changes*, op. cit., pp.309–10.
70. *The Scene Changes*, op. cit., p. 310.
71. *The Scene Changes*, op. cit., pp. 257–8. Thomson did not reveal how Gullick proposed to entice Virendranath Chattopadhyaya onto French soil. In his short story *Giulia Lazzari* Somerset Maugham tells how Ashenden tried to get a fictitious Indian revolutionary leader named Chandra Lal into France, by using the latter's ex-mistress as the bait. There is no evidence that Gullick brought Hilda Howsin, the daughter of the Yorkshire doctor, with him to Switzerland, though it seems that she had been one of Chattopadhyaya's many lovers. *Giulia Lazzari* itself is a combination of the Mata Hari story with that of Gullick.
72. *The Scene Changes*, op. cit., pp. 257–8. *Weekly Report*, 23 Jan. 1916. Gullick's plan apparently did not lack inspiration for in May 1916 Thomson urged him to return to Switzerland, in another effort to capture Chattopadhyaya, even though the latter informed the *Daily Mail* that Thomson made him go to Germany against his will. *The Scene Changes*, op. cit., p. 288.
73. Andrew, op. cit., pp. 148–53.
74. Admittedly a similar overlapping of the jurisdictions of British intelligence networks existed in the Low Countries, where there was no Indian revolutionary activity. Interestingly of the four surviving *Ashenden Stories* which relate to events in Western Europe during the War, three deal either in their subject matter or in their source material, with Eastern nationalists. *Miss King* is about the Egyptians; the character Chandra Lal in *Giulia Lazzari* is clearly Virendranath Chattopadhyaya; and *The Traitor* is based on the life of Gifford, the Germans' Egyptian expert at Lausanne.
75. Copy of a note by Major J.A. Wallinger, 2 Jan.1917, in PRO FO371 3063 (263555/A/16).
76. This paragraph is based on references from the Kirke Diary given to me by Dr Nicholas

Hiley of New Hall College, Cambridge.
77. On 24 July 1919, Wallinger sent Cleveland a long memorandum entitled 'The Nearer East and the British Empire'. He was not sure who the author was, though he believed him to be 'an officer specially deputed by General Headquarters, Constantinople, to report on the situation in Switzerland.' *Defensive Measures Proposed for Dealing with Bolshevism*, HDA: Dec. 1919, nos. 1–7, IOR.POS.8622.
78. *Curriculum Vitae* of Sir John Wallinger, op. cit. Vickery left on an important mission to America in 1919 and was replaced by Major Pritchard, a Superintendent of the Indian Police. *Employment of Mr Newby vice Mr Vickery, pending Major P.A.R. Pritchard's assumption of the office.* HDB: July 1919, nos. 122–32 & K.W., IOLR IOR.POS.10516.

British Intelligence in North America, 1914–18

NAVAL INTELLIGENCE AND THE SECRET SERVICE,
AUGUST 1914–FEBRUARY 1917

With the outbreak of the First World War the plotting of Indian revolutionaries in the United States became one element in a complex of German intrigue based in America, whose objects were on the one hand the sabotage of Allied war supplies and on the other the disruption of the British Empire behind its front lines by causing unrest in Ireland and India. At another level, the centres of the Indian revolutionary movement in California and in New York were manifestations of the long-standing problem created by the United States government's protection of the nationalist enemies of the British Empire. In this light the Fenian incursions into Canada in 1866, 1870 and 1871 were early precursors of the Ghadr attempted insurrection of spring 1915 in the Punjab. The democratic traditions and neutrality of the United States allowed the insurgents to conduct their propaganda and to make their military preparations in safety.[1] This chapter will discuss the efforts of British intelligence both to counter German intrigue and to influence American official and public opinion against anti-British nationalists. The two themes are closely interrelated. The restrained activities of British intelligence in countering German plotting paid dividends when British agents sought American official favour for the prosecution of German and Indian conspirators. Robert Nathan was the first British officer ever to bring the nationalist enemies of the Empire to trial on American soil. The San Francisco conspiracy case which he organized was the longest case in American legal history, and resulted in the imprisonment of the leaders of the Ghadr Party in America.

236

Despite the old threat from Irish nationalists and the more recent activities of the Ghadr Party on the Pacific Coast, no department of the British government had made any contingency plans to set up an intelligence network in the United States upon the outbreak of war. The only extensive British intelligence system then operating in America was that built up by William Hopkinson, and that was restricted to the specialized surveillance of Indian revolutionaries. This system, as will be seen in the second part of this Chapter, survived the death of its creator, even though it received little encouragement from the Government of India. With the outbreak of war, New York and the German Embassy in Washington became the main centres of German intrigue.

The seriousness of the situation on the east coast had been ignored by the authorities in London, but impressed an officer on the spot. The British Naval Attaché in Washington, Guy Gaunt, volunteered to work 'in the intelligence-cum-propaganda line', and was granted permission to do so.[2] There is no evidence that he was following any plan of 'Blinker' Hall, the Director of the Intelligence Division of the Admiralty, to compensate for the slowness of the British Secret Service to establish 'any effective organization in the Americas'.[3] While Hall made full use of Gaunt's information, he was not in a position to aid him materially. Gaunt later complained that he had 'little money to spend, and no staff capable of tracking down the . . . conspiracies now being launched by the enemy'.[4] As late as spring 1917 his office staff in New York, where he did most of his work, consisted of just an office-boy and a typist.[5] Moreover, upon the outbreak of war it was precisely the absence of basic naval intelligence which most harmed the British, who were totally unprepared when the Germans converted some of their liners lying in US ports into commerce raiders and naval auxiliaries.[6]

From the start of the war Gaunt worked in close co-operation with the Consul-General at New York, Sir Courtenay Bennett, who had at his disposal the small Home Office Agency and a limited secret service fund with which he hired American detectives.[7] Gaunt first received additional assistance not from the Home Authorities but from Central European nationalists working under the Czech leader, Emanuel Voska. The latter offered Gaunt the assistance of his 80-strong network of agents who, being subjects of the Habsburg Empire, passed as supporters of Germany, though in reality they saw the war as an opportunity to further their national aspirations. Many

237

were employed by the Germans in sensitive positions as clerks and telephonists. On many occasions they proved of great assistance to the Naval Attaché.[8]

Whatever assistance Voska rendered Gaunt, the Germans were in a position to benefit far more from the support of anti-British nationalities living in the United States. Though they quickly squandered the potential of their Indian allies, the brief career of the saboteur Franz von Kleist Rintelen (of whom more below) showed the use which could be made of nationalist extremists.

Chapter 6 showed how many of the most able Indian revolutionaries left Canada and the USA shortly after the outbreak of war to participate in the disastrous Ghadr 'invasion' of the Punjab. It was only after this had taken place that the Indians and the Germans combined their efforts in America in a plan to send arms to Bengal.[9] The arms build-up started in the second half of October 1914. The plans were in the hands of Franz von Papen, the German Military Attaché, and Hans Tauscher, the US representative of the German armaments manufacturer, Krupps. The German Ambassador, Johann von Bernstorff, also participated in the scheme. Initially, things went very well for the conspirators, who had succeeded by the beginning of December 1914 in amassing nearly 11,000 rifles and 500 revolvers in a warehouse in New York. By the beginning of February 1915, the weapons were in California, ready for shipment to Bengal.

The Germans planned to land the weapons in Siam, and then transport them to India. They were easily able to concoct a cover story for their activities, which were a gross infringement of US neutrality laws. At this time, civil war was raging in Mexico. Tauscher claimed therefore that the shipment was intended for south of the border. The Germans acquired a Mexican middleman, Marcos Martínez, who in turn chartered a schooner, the *Annie Larsen*. The problem was that though the schooner could easily reach Mexico, it was not sufficiently seaworthy for the journey to Siam. Thus the Germans intended to transfer the weapons to another ship at an island off the Mexican coast.[10]

The Germans' first set-back was thanks to Gaunt and Bennett. By the middle of February they knew that the Germans had moved a large quantity of arms and that they intended to transport them to Mexico on board a ship named the *Annie Larsen*.[11] The British Ambassador, Sir Cecil Spring-Rice, protested to the State Department, but was informed that no breach of the US neutrality laws had taken place.[12] However, Gaunt's information was sufficient to get the FBI involved in the affair. The investigations which the Americans initiated into the *Annie Larsen* prompted her early departure from the United States on 8 March 1915. This was a disastrous upset for von Papen's plans. The Germans only managed to purchase a ship suitable for carrying the weapons as far as the Bay of Bengal on 6 March. This ship, the *Maverick*, set out after the *Annie Larsen* to a rendezvous on the Pacific island of Socorro. By the time the *Maverick* got there, the *Annie Larsen* had already left for the United States, where, on arrival, her cargo was seized. The British were possibly unfortunate that the two ships never met, since they might have seized the cargo. After Gaunt and Bennett's discoveries the Royal Navy was on the look-out. In the middle of May British and Canadian warships twice searched the *Maverick* whilst she was anchored off Socorro. Moreover, thanks to information received from a double-agent, the authorities at Singapore and the Indian police had full knowledge of the Germans' plans.[13]

The failure of the *Maverick* expedition did not discourage the Germans from attempting to send a second large arms shipment to India. In May 1915 Tauscher once again assembled a large quantity of arms in New York. However, by the first half of June the British Consulate-General was aware that these weapons were booked on board a ship of the Holland–America Line, the *Djember*, for passage to Surabaya in the Netherlands East Indies.[14] The Holland–America Line backed out of the contract when the British informed them of the origin of the cargo, though only after the Germans had taken the trouble of transporting the guns to the New York docks.[15]

Thus British intelligence in America had great success in scotching German attempts to ship arms to India, but this was due even more to the unsoundness of von Papen's plans than to the efficiency of Gaunt and Bennett's intelligence service. The scale of Tauscher's operations made their ultimate discovery likely. Von Papen devised a grandiose scheme to set India ablaze, thanks to which not a single cartridge got through to the beleaguered revolutionaries of Bengal who, ultimately, became demoralized as a result.

The limitations of British intelligence in North America were revealed soon after the fiasco of the *Maverick* expedition with the arrival from Mexico of the German secret service agent Franz von Kleist Rintelen, mentioned above. For a short time he achieved what Gaunt admitted was 'sensational success' as a saboteur.[16] A German-

American chemist, Dr Walter Scheele, provided Rintelen with a remarkably small and effective bomb. With the help of German and Irish stevedores and dock labourers, Rintelen set up a bomb factory in New York harbour. Also, thanks to their help, he had little difficulty in placing these bombs on board British ships and among British war supplies awaiting shipment. After a month the Allies found one of his bombs intact on board a crippled merchantman and Rintelen was forced to call off his campaign for fear of American action. However, he claimed to have destroyed 36 ships and to have damaged a very large quantity of stores on shore.[17] Rintelen's downfall was not, however, caused by the British. Von Papen and the German Naval Attaché, Boy-Ed (who was of German–Turkish parentage, hence his unusual name), were convinced that he had become a diplomatic liability because of plans which he had set afoot to cause trouble for the United States in Mexico, and because of his schemes to create labour unrest inside America. Their pressure led to his recall at the beginning of August 1915. On his way back he was captured by the British.[18]

The size of the German arms operations in America, if not their success, the audacity of German plans for sabotage, and the very continuance of the war which few had foreseen in 1914, made the development of British intelligence in the USA inevitable. However, despite Gaunt's success relative to the means at his disposal, the authorities in London decided not to expand the operations of naval intelligence there. The USA was instead given over to Mansfield Cumming and the Secret Service, or MI1c as it was more accurately known. In September 1915 he sent out to New York a two-man team, with the aliases of 'Smith' and 'Mansfield'. 'Smith', the head of the mission, was an officer who had experience only in India.[19] His true identity is not known.[20] Gaunt recalled of him that 'I could readily believe his story that he loathed the whole business'.[21] The mission failed, and within a few months both officers returned to London.

'Mansfield', the junior officer of the pair, however, had not found his intelligence duties so uncongenial and volunteered to return to New York to set up Section V, the American branch of MI1c. This man, whose real name was Sir William Wiseman, was ideally suited to work as a secret agent in the United States. His aristocratic background – he held a baronetcy dating back to 1628 – offered him entry into the highest social circles of America. Before the war he had worked in Mexico as representative of the London banking house of

Herndon's, which financed the Mexican government. In August 1915 he had enlisted into the Duke of Cornwall's Light Infantry where he attained the rank of Major. Early in 1915 he was gassed during the battle of Ypres and suffered impairment of his sight. Upon the recommendation of a friend of his father, and because of his familiarity with America, Cumming sent him for training at Scotland Yard and thence with 'Smith' to New York.[22]

Wiseman returned to New York in December 1915. Just before he left England he recruited a deputy, Norman Thwaites. Like Wiseman, Thwaites had been wounded on the Western Front; also like Wiseman, he had important pre-war experience in North America. Before the war he had worked for ten years as private secretary to Joseph Pulitzer, the owner of the New York newspaper, *The World*, and had subsequently been assistant foreign editor. He had easy entry into New York's high society. His cover as a journalist put him in an excellent position to obtain inside information from within US political circles where he had first-rate contacts.[23] Wiseman felt that Thwaites occupied an almost unique position. Frank Polk, the Counsellor to the State Department, was an old friend of his, while Frank Cobb, his former boss at the *The World*, had considerable influence on foreign affairs.[24] For the more technical side of his mission Thwaites was also very well qualified; educated in Hamburg as a boy, he had a native command of German and was familiar with German circles in America.[25]

Thwaites and Wiseman worked in close co-operation with Guy Gaunt but were not under his control.[26] They carried out enquiries at the request of 'Blinker' Hall, but were responsible only to Mansfield Cumming. At first they worked alone, but it was soon found necessary to expand MI1c operations in America. By the beginning of 1917 their personnel fell into two categories, MI1c's own staff and regularly employed agents.

The staff of MI1c came from varied backgrounds. The first to distinguish himself was John Gillan, an officer of the Special Branch of the Metropolitan Police whose services Basil Thomson had loaned to Section V.[27] Other officers came from backgrounds in the Services. Some of the most effective of the hired agents were German-Americans, whom MI1c, unlike the US intelligence organizations, did not regard as inherently untrustworthy.[28] But like the Home Office Agent before it, Section V was less successful in securing reliable Indian agents. In this respect they were in a weaker position than Carnegie Ross at San Francisco. Thwaites later recalled that in 1916:

I had been put in touch with certain not too reliable Hindu agents, who were alleged to be willing to furnish information concerning the seditious work of their co-religionists. One could never be quite sure of these gentry. If I was willing to pay five dollars for services rendered, I could not be quite certain that some other potential employer might not come along with an offer of ten dollars in consideration of supplying information about me or – uncomfortable thought – for value received in the direction of 'bumping me off'.[29]

These Indian agents had probably been serving already in the USA, possibly under Cunliffe Owen, the Home Office Agent, who still worked in New York. It is less likely that they had been sent out from India to support Section V's operations, since the Indian government at this time would not even provide agents for work on the Pacific Coast.[30]

MI1c's operations covered two basic areas: New York and the rest of the United States. It is not known how much the organization cost before the American entry into the war. However, in January 1918, before British Secret Service operations in America were cut back, the New York establishment was made up of ten regular officers, including Wiseman, plus an office staff. The total cost was $3,852 a month. The so-called Western Organization consisted of ten full-time agents, including some British officers, together with three agents who rendered occasional services, two of whom were Germans. This organization cost $3,354 a month. With the addition of other miscellaneous expenditures, the total monthly cost of MI1c in America in January 1918 was $8,816 or £1,852. These figures do not include a small contribution from the Government of India. However, throughout the war Indian operations were largely financed by MI1c itself, as part of its general duty of controlling nationalist extremists in the USA.[31]

MI1c at first attempted to conceal its existence from the United States authorities. Thwaites claimed that even the head of the New York police was not acquainted with any British intelligence officer except himself until after America entered the war.[32] Section V passed its information on to the Americans through Colonel Sherwood, the Chief Commissioner of the Canadian Police.[33]

The low profile of their operations in the United States did not prevent MI1c from obtaining important American assistance. Both

Gaunt and Thwaites, like Hopkinson before them, were very effective in securing the help of American officials of an intermediate rank. The most important of such officers was Inspector Thomas Tunney, the head of the New York bomb squad. This had been formed in 1913 to deal with the Mafia, but from 1914 onwards its time was devoted almost exclusively 'to the checkmating of German agents, enemy sabotage and Indian sedition'. This body was the most efficient undercover agency at the disposal of the American authorities during the First World War. Tunney, who was of Irish Protestant extraction, had a brother serving in the Royal Irish Constabulary. The assistance which he rendered Thwaites went well beyond the letter of the neutrality laws.[34] Nicholas Biddle, the Deputy Police Commissioner in New York before the US entry into the war, also gave important assistance to Section V.[35] Because of the help of these American officers the British were able to avoid the necessity of incurring the displeasure of Woodrow Wilson's regime either by employing a large secret service establishment of their own, or by pestering high officials anxious to maintain American neutrality for assistance against German plotters. The futility of the latter course had already been shown when Spring-Rice tried to use Gaunt's information to prevent the sailing of the *Annie Larsen*.

By its own account, the work of MI1c in American could be divided into five categories: counter-espionage; espionage; the surveillance of Irish nationalists; the surveillance of Indian nationalists; and 'time-consuming tasks less directly connected with the secret service'.[36] The surveillance of Indians will be discussed in the second part of this chapter. The surveillance of the Irish during the war, with which it was connected, was less important than might be thought, given the indignation in America at the vigorous suppression by the British of the Easter Rising in 1916.

Section V quickly established itself as an effective intelligence agency by two successes in countering German sabotage: early in 1916 an agent employed by MI1c discovered an important German plot to blow up the Welland Canal in Ontario;[37] and in March 1916 Thwaites conducted investigations leading to the discovery of Rintelen's bomb factory, which was still a major potential threat to Allied shipping.[38] It also performed important espionage functions. As early as April 1916 Wiseman was sending agents into Turkey and the Balkans.[39] In January 1917 J. A. Wallinger said that the introduction of agents into Germany from the USA had had considerable success.[40] Naturally, little work of this kind continued after America ended its neutrality.[41]

243

In the course of performing its other duties Section V did its best discreetly to influence American opinion. Before the American entry into the war there was no official British propaganda bureau in the United States. However, even before the arrival of Thwaites and Wiseman Gaunt had used contacts with American newspaper men.[42] Thwaites in particular lost no opportunity to create propaganda.[43] The battle for the mind of America which Section V waged in the press and by the forging of close personal ties with lower-ranking American officials was carried on at a higher level. Gaunt had formed close links with the Roosevelts and with Republican politicians, but failed to make any impression on Woodrow Wilson's Democrat administration. While certain important Democrat politicians regarded Thwaites with benevolence, Wiseman made the real breakthrough when he gained the friendship of Colonel House, Wilson's closest adviser. In January 1917 he spoke to House criticizing Gaunt's toying with the Republican Party and admitted that he was 'in direct communication with the Foreign Office'.[44] After the USA broke off relations with Germany he became the liaison officer for the British and American War Cabinets at House's suggestion.

By this time Section V had become a very special kind of intelligence service in America. Its public relations role with the US government and American people was if anything even more important than its very successful work against the Germans and their auxiliaries in the United States. None the less, up to the time America entered the war MI1c's operation in America had managed to retain a low profile. Not one complaint by Wilson's administration, which was hypersensitive to infringements of America's neutrality, is on record against it. In fact, the American government at its highest level remained unaware of the existence of MI1c on American soil, despite the amount of assistance which the British Secret Service had obtained from the US law-enforcement agencies. These achievements paved the way for the Government of India's successful campaign against its dissident subjects in the USA which culminated in the Chicago and San Francisco conspiracy cases.

BRITISH INTELLIGENCE AND THE GHADR CONSPIRACY IN AMERICA, 1914–18

By the end of 1915 the most enterprising Sikh revolutionaries had left America for India, while some of the most able Hindu leaders had

244

either gone to join the Indian National Committee in Germany, or to promote the schemes of the Ghadr Party in the Far East. In Canada the vigour of the revolutionary party was further sapped by the continuing feud between the disaffected Sikhs of Vancouver and the small party loyal to the Empire led by Hopkinson's old agent, Bela Singh. The Sikhs of California likewise became increasingly divided. Ram Chandra Peshawari, Har Dayal's successor as leader of the Ghadr Party, was a good speaker, but in other respects he was very unfitted for his command.

The *Khalsa Diwan* (Sikh Assembly) of Stockton, California, which was the most important Sikh organization in the western states, was the centre of opposition to Ram Chandra from within the Ghadr Party. By the early part of 1916 discontent had arisen over questions relating to the finance and control of the Ghadr movement. The Sikhs resented the way the Hindu leadership of Ghadr had sent their men to death and imprisonment during the 'invasion' of the Punjab, but would not give them the smallest say in decision-making. Sikh discontent was greatly accentuated by justified suspicions that Ram Chandra was embezzling funds. At the beginning of 1917 the divisions within the Indians' ranks were made formal when the *Khalsa Diwans* of Stockton and Vancouver combined in defence of Sikh orthodoxy and in opposition to the Ghadr Party. At the end of 1916 a well-known Sikh revolutionary leader, Bhagwan Singh, arrived in the USA and started a fierce leadership struggle with Ram Chandra, with the result that in February 1917 two separate *Ghadr* newspapers were being published in San Francisco.[45]

Not surprisingly the Germans soon became dissatisfied with the conduct of their Indian allies on the Pacific coast. At the end of 1915 von Bernstorff threatened to cut off their money supply.[46] But he did not do so. The Indians both on the west and the east coasts remained a serious potential threat to the British Empire. The very existence of centres of revolution in San Francisco and New York gave powerful moral support to revolutionaries in India, and remained the starting-point for Ghadr agents travelling to the Far East. Moreover, while the Indians were no longer a military force, the British still feared the effects of their propaganda in India and throughout the Far East. Certain publications issued by the Government of India after the war, which were written with the benefit of hindsight, stressed the inevitable failure of the Ghadr movement.[47] Yet the British authorities whom the Indian revolutionaries had set out to fight were few in

245

numbers – particularly in the Far East. The real anxiety which the existence of the Ghadr Party in America caused the Government of India is shown by the latter's readiness to deploy some of its best officers against it in 1917 and 1918.

Throughout 1915 the Indian authorities showed no inclination to improve their sources of information in America. While the officers of MI1c paid much attention to the affairs of Indians on the east coast after the beginning of 1916, there is no evidence that they were concerned with the doings of the Ghadr Party in California. The burden of controlling the Indians there fell upon the British consular authorities and upon the Canadian government.

It was not until March 1915 that the Foreign Office instructed the consular officers at San Francisco, Portland, New York, Chicago, Manila and Honolulu to report direct to the Government of India, to the Washington Embassy and to the Dominion Immigration Agent at Vancouver on the activities of Indian extremists. It thereby formalized a makeshift intelligence network which already existed. The most important elements in the scheme were Consul-General Ross at San Francisco and Consul-General Harrington at Manila. Ross had the assistance of the network of informers set up by Hopkinson. At the end of October 1915 this network received a very important addition in the person of a Parsi emigrant to the United States, Vishnu Das Bagai, who had been a friend of Ram Chandra in India. Before he left for the USA, the Inspector-General of Police of the North-West Frontier Province had given him Rs.700 in return for any information which came his way about the revolutionary party. For this reason he came to see Ross on his arrival in America. Ross trusted Bagai and set him to work among the Ghadr Party, where Ram Chandra entrusted him with the supervision of the party's finances.

In January 1916 Bagai informed Ross that he wanted to enter government service on a monthly salary of £20, in default of which he would emigrate to England.[48] Ross had no secret service funds at his disposal and referred Bagai's suggestion to the Government of India. In May 1916 the Home Department replied that they were unable to employ Bagai, but hoped that Ross would do so. They said that Bagai seemed 'somewhat addicted to talk too freely of his employment as a government agent . . .'. Ross did not accept this decision and wrote that it was 'unwise to lose connection altogether with a man . . . who has already established himself in the confidence of the agitators, as it would certainly take a long time for another man to get so far into the confidence of [Ram Chandra]' as Bagai then was.[49] Ross felt that he was receiving too little assistance in the surveillance of the Ghadr Party for which he was responsible. He wrote at the end of 1915 that he had 'no means of ascertaining, with any amount of accuracy, the real sympathies of British Indians . . .'[50] The Government of India was still extremely reluctant to risk being compromised in America. The need for good intelligence was subordinated to overriding diplomatic considerations. It was essential that pro-German propagandists should not be able to point to the 'oppressive arm' of the Empire on American soil. None the less Bagai continued to provide Ross with regular reports and, by 1917, was perhaps the most esteemed secret agent of the Indian empire.[51]

After the death of Hopkinson in October 1914 Ross had no personal contact with the Canadian authorities for some time. This was not because the Canadians were reluctant to take on again the liability of watching the Indians, but because they had no one qualified to do so. Hopkinson was replaced as Dominion Immigration Inspector by an officer named A.L. Jolliffe who, unlike Hopkinson, did not venture out of British Columbia.[52] The Canadians finally found the best replacement for Hopkinson in his old chief in the Vancouver Immigration Department, Malcolm Reid. When Hopkinson was alive Reid's knowledge of Indian affairs had been defective, but he soon remedied this. It seems that he began to concentrate on intelligence work. An MI1c report from early 1916 referred to the important work which he had done in this field.[53]

Another important factor explains the reluctance of the Government of India to set up intelligence operations in the USA in the first two years of the war. While agents could give warning of enemy schemes, there was nothing they could do to prevent plotting on American soil. Hopkinson himself had only been able to notify the Government of India of the movements of returning revolutionaries, and had not stopped them arming themselves. At the end of 1915 the American Department of the Foreign Office wrote that there was little chance of prosecuting Indian extremists in the USA for two reasons: the state of US law; and the attitude of the administration.[54] The Foreign Office believed that the evidence of crimes committed in India at the instigation of the San Francisco Ghadr Party rested solely on the word of the Government of India, which would not satisfy the American government, which would have to justify its action before 'a somewhat hostile public opinion'.[55] On the Pacific coast British influence over the media was weaker than anywhere else in America. The main newspapers published there were under the control of the Irish-American Hearst group, which acted 'in the closest understanding with German agents'.[56]

At the beginning of 1916, after going through the critical period of Ghadr plotting without an Indian expert in North America, the India Office decided to re-establish intelligence operations on the Pacific coast. They kept this operation so secret that even the DCI was not given details about it.[57] The officer whom the DCI was about to send out to establish an intelligence agency for the Far East was strictly prohibited from visiting the USA or Canada for fear that the India Office agent's 'work might be seriously prejudiced and even his life endangered'.[58]

If the India Office had undertaken a dangerous operation they selected a very special agent to carry it out. This was Robert Nathan, who by this time had been transformed from a senior civil servant into a top intelligence officer. He set up his headquarters in Vancouver at the beginning of May 1916. Nathan had certain characteristics in common with Thwaites and Wiseman. He seems, no less than they, to have been picked for his charisma and potential effect on the Americans with whom he came into contact.[59] Furthermore, he was well prepared to face legal problems involved in the prosecution of Indians since he had at one time trained as a barrister.

By the middle of June 1916 Nathan had established close contact with Ross, and taken over direct control of the latter's agents. Ross from this time on acted as Nathan's deputy.[60] However, Nathan's first important action was directed not against the Ghadr Party, but against the Indians on the east coast. In New York he had a room in Section V's office and the use of such of their staff as he required.[61] Nathan was subordinate to Wiseman, but his organization remained separate from that of MI1c throughout the war.

By the end of 1916 Dr Chandra Kanta Chakravarti had become 'the chief Indian agent of Germany in America'.[62] Nathan initially failed to get the American authorities to act against him for want of evidence, but then disclosed to them details of a bomb plot in which he was involved.[63] On 6 March the New York police raided Chakravarti's house. They at first found only a close German friend of Chakravarti, Ernst Sekunna, in the company of a little menial clad in a *dhoti*. Thwaites recalled that it was finally decided . . . to take everyone on the premises together with such papers and photographs as could be found. Alas for human vanity. Chakravarti had not only been photographed in various costumes and disguises, but he had been unwise enough to decorate his house with prints of himself in Persian costume, Turkish tarbouche, etc. Of course, he was immediately identified as the little half-naked cook.[64]

This capture was the start of the train of events which resulted in the two big conspiracy trials against the Indian revolutionaries in the United States. Much depended upon the willingness of Chakravarti to implicate his fellow Indians. At this time America was still not allied with Great Britain and Nathan's mission was concealed from the American government. Chakravarti was thus in a potentially strong position. However, Nathan benefited from Thwaites's friendship with Inspector Tunney and was allowed to participate in Chakravarti's interrogation. Thwaites recalled:

> We assembled in a large room . . . Behind a screen sat a wretched little Hindu, his knees imprisoned between the mighty legs of Tunney, who, with all the gentleness in the world was inviting his guest to come across with the details in the big plot.

Chakravarti would not do so, even though Nathan constantly passed notes over to Tunney on the other side of the screen. Then Sekunna was called in. Tunney informed him that Chakravarti had revealed all and given him pride of place among the German plotters. This broke Sekunna, whose testimony lasted for a full half hour during which he disclosed details of German plotting from the *Maverick* expedition onwards. Thwaites recalled that 'at 4am we mopped our foreheads once more, patted each other on the back and departed. Nathan, in high spirits, took me off to get nourishment'.[65]

The next day, 7 March 1917, the New York police allowed Nathan to go through the papers seized in Chakravarti's house and he found that they disclosed 'such an interesting connection with the German' that the case prepared against Chakravarti might even 'involve the whole question of plots against the Indian government in the United States'.[66] Wiseman sent Nathan and Thwaites to Washington to discuss the case with the State Department.[67]

In Washington Thwaites acted as cover for Nathan, who still could not see officials there without revealing his identity and 'imperilling his usefulness'.[68] The US authorities were reluctant to prosecute the Indian conspirators until they were given a guarantee against their own prosecution for past breach of the neutrality laws in harbouring German and India plotters. Nathan strongly supported the granting of this guarantee.[69] On Nathan's advice Thwaites prompted the State Department itself to start the expansion of the Indian secret service in America by asking for another officer to be sent out from England to help on the Chakravarti case.[70]

In response to the State Department's plea for help the British authorities despatched two assistants for Nathan. The men chosen represented a major contribution in human resources by the Indian Government to the war on the American front. Cleveland picked Godfrey Denham to represent the DCI.[71] The India Office selected Alexander Marr for service in America. He was a Scot who, like Nathan, had served in the ICS in Bengal. By 1915 he had attained the rank of Additional Secretary to the Political Department in that Province. In 1916 he had followed Nathan onto the staff of MI5, section G. In America his salary was paid entirely by the India Office.[72] He sailed from Liverpool on 7 April 1917.

By 21 June 1917 Nathan succeeded in his intention of developing the case against Chakravarti into as wide an action as possible, when the American authorities decided to make the case against the Ghadr Party at San Francisco into one of general conspiracy to aid the Germans by creating revolution in India. It was to begin with the very creation of the Ghadr Party and was to deal with all its military enterprises throughout the war. Finally it was decided to conduct two conspiracy cases. The first, which was tried at Chicago, was under the direction of Marr and Denham and ended with the conviction of three German agents on 29 October 1917.[73]

As early as March 1917, even before the American entry into the war, the extent of British Secret Service involvement in the preparation of the conspiracy trials was an open secret.[74] None the less, the US authorities did their best to conceal this assistance.[75] Significantly this knowledge excited little adverse comment. If the contacts between MI1c and the State Department procured both official sanction for the trials and official protection of the British agents conducting them, the very act of bringing the conspirators to justice neutralized the danger of a hostile reaction from American public opinion. The decision to stage the trials was a triumph not only of British diplomacy but also of British propaganda.

250

The great San Francisco trial started on 22 November 1917 and ended only in July 1918. The results were a foregone conclusion. The only issue was the quality of the publicity which the British could extract from the trial. The Indians played right into the hands of Nathan and Denham, who advised the counsel for the prosecution. The bitter divisions and suspicions which rent the Indian leadership were put on public show. The case reached a dramatic climax on 23 April 1918 when one of the accused, Ram Singh, shot Ram Chandra dead in the middle of the courtroom. As a British commentator remarked:

> In the Western States such incidents do not disturb the presence of mind of Assize Court officials: the deputy-sheriff whipped an automatic from his pocket, and from his elevated place at the back of the court, aiming above and between the intervening heads, shot the murderer dead.[76]

The sentences imposed by the American judge, on the other hand, were lenient; not one of the conspirators received a jail sentence in excess of three years. However, Nathan's team rightly considered that they had won a great victory over the Indian revolutionary movement. It would be unfair to criticize Denham's conclusions in the report he sent to Cleveland:

> I think the whole case is a great triumph and has done a lot to help us in this country. It has shown to the public the utter rottenness of the Ghadr Party and what lying, deceitful grafters men like Tarak Nath Das and C.K. Chakravarti were. More than this, it has been a very successful piece of propaganda work.[77]

Nathan wrote that the 'mere fact that a man is a Hindu now causes the ordinary American to suspect that there is something crooked about him'.[78]

Besides this propaganda victory, the Indian secret service had established close contacts with its American opposite numbers. This was important because the conspiracy cases weakened but did not destroy the Indian nationalist movement in the USA. The brief alliance between the British and American intelligence agencies against all radical activities in the USA will be discussed in the final chapter.

After the San Francisco case three aspects of Indian activity in America continued to worry the British. First, Indian nationalists continued to produce revolutionary literature in San Francisco, while the Ghadr Party itself tenaciously clung to life. Second, some Indian leaders had escaped to Mexico and were assisting German agents there. Finally, with the defeat of the extremist party, more moderate nationalists came to the fore in the USA, notably Lala Lajpat Rai who began to conduct a 'formidable agitation'.[79]

During the war various British intelligence agencies had co-operated to a remarkable degree against the 'Indian problem'. This had led to a great victory, but not as great as they had hoped. The United States continued to offer asylum to nationalist exiles and the need for intelligence there continued.

A NOTE ON GAUNT'S *THE YIELD OF YEARS*

In *The Yield of Years* Guy Gaunt claimed that he was responsible for the recall of Wiseman and the first station chief of MI1c in America at the end of 1915, describing them as 'gumshoe merchants'. Gaunt wrote further on, in partial contradiction of this, that Wiseman later returned to work under him. He professed to be offended that after the war people were mistakenly taking Wiseman for the former head of British intelligence in North America. This subterfuge is connected with the circumstances in which Gaunt's autobiography – in all other respects an accurate account – was written. Gaunt informed Wiseman in 1939 that the Admiralty had encouraged him to publish an account of his wartime experiences.[80] With the coming of the Second World War, the British were anxious to play down any implication that their intelligence services had been involved in bringing the USA into the First World War. In *The Yield of Years* Gaunt did not try to conceal the effort he had put into anti-German propaganda. However, he leads the reader to believe that secret service work was a dirty business which the British happily left to the Germans.[81]

At the same time that he denied the existence of the secret service in the USA, Gaunt also inaccurately refuted claims that Basil Thomson's Special Branch had operated in America during the war.[82]

NOTES

1. For the activities of the Fenians see J.A. Cole, *Prince of Spies* (London: Henri Le Caron, 1984), Chs. 1–8. For the involvement of Irish and German plotters in the USA with the Easter Rising see F.S.L. Lyons, *Ireland Since the Famine* (London: Fontana edn, 1982), pp. 339, 350–1, 363, 369, 395.

2. Guy Gaunt, *The Yield of Years* (London: Hutchinson & Co., 1940), pp. 136, 139.
3. Cf. Patrick Beesly, *Room 40* (Oxford: Oxford University Press, 1984), p. 227, who claims that 'Blinker Hall was not prepared to wait – if there was a vacuum he would fill it himself. He very quickly saw that there was a need to counter German activities in the States and in Central and South America . . . . .'
4. Gaunt, op. cit., p. 146.
5. Wiseman Papers, Yale University Library, MSS.666, Series I, Box 6, File 168: Undated letter from Gaunt to Hall; telegrams dated 9 and 12 May 1917; letter from Wiseman to Gaunt, 26 May 1917.
6. The liner *Kronprinz Wilhelm* alone sank 14 Allied ships totalling 58,000 tons after slipping out of New York harbour on 3 August 1914. Gaunt, op. cit., p. 146.
7. Bennett was Consul-General in New York from 1907 until the middle of 1915, when he retired, being replaced by Charles Bayley, who remained there until 1923.
8. E.V. Voska and W. Irwin, *Spy and Counterspy* (New York, 1940). Gaunt, op. cit., pp. 167–8.
9. More precisely the Germans and the Indians of New York. The Ghadr Party itself was not involved.
10. T.G. Fraser, 'The Intrigues of German Government and the Ghadr Party against British Rule in India, 1914–1918', University of London, unpublished PhD thesis (1974), Ch. 7, 'German attempts to arm the Indian revolutionaries'.
11. Spring Rice to Lansing, 16 Feb. 1915, PRO FO115 1895, no. 60. Memoranda on W.C. Hughes by the Consul-General, New York, dated 17 and 20 February 1915, PRO FO115 1895, no. 64.
12. Bryan to Spring Rice, 24 Feb. 1915, PRO FO115 1895, no. 73.
13. See Chapter 11.
14. Memo. by the Consul-General, New York, 1 July 1915, PRO FO115 1895, no. 171.
15. Testimony of Henry Muck, Ghadr Trial, IOLR MSS.EUR.C.138, Vol. 2, p. 920.
16. Gaunt, op. cit. p. 149.
17. A British Secret Service officer described Rintelen's bombs thus: 'a piece of cigar-shaped lead piping, harmless enough outwardly, but . . . it contained . . . both picric and sulphuric acid, with a protecting copper wall between. Given a certain amount of time, the two acids would eat through the copper and the result would be a fire that no ship's hose would put out.' Norman Thwaites, *Velvet and Vinegar*, (London: Grayson & Grayson, 1932), pp. 133–4, 152–3.
18. Gaunt, op. cit., p. 154.
19. YUL Wiseman Papers, obituary in the *New York Times* entitled 'Sir William George Eden Wiseman, 1885–1962', dated 18 June 1962. All the verifiable information in this obituary is wholly accurate. The past experience of this officer in India is no indication that the Indian government or the Department of Criminal Intelligence were taking the initiative in establishing Secret Service operations in the United States. During the war several officers of the Government of India and the Indian police were employed in Military Intelligence. See, for example, the list of names contained in PRO WO9944-A-3. Some, such as Robert Nathan, Alexander Marr and Stephenson were employed by MI5 to deal with Indian 'sedition' while still serving the Government of India. Others, however, worked solely for their new masters in Military Intelligence.
20. Anthony Read and David Fisher in *Colonel Z* (London: Hodder & Stoughton, 1984), p. 120, claim, without stating their source, that this officer 'had been recommended for the post by Lord Kitchener on the strength of his work as an intelligence officer on the North-West Frontier of India though he had never set foot in the United States.
21. Gaunt, op. cit., p. 172.
22. YUL Wiseman Papers, obituary entitled 'Sir William George Eden Wiseman, 1885–1962' from the *New York Times* 18 June 1962.
23. YUL Wiseman Papers, File 160, letter from Wiseman to Lieutenant Commander

Standing (Wiseman's opposite number on the staff of MI1c in London), 4 April 1916.

24. In 1917 Wiseman expected him to become the next head of the State Department. YUL Wiseman Papers, File 161, undated letter from Wiseman to Gaunt.

25. Thwaites never hid his liking for the Germans and admiration for their culture, particularly in its warlike manifestations.

26. For a discussion of Gaunt's claim in *The Yield of Years* that he was in charge of British intelligence in the United States until his return to active service in March 1918 see the Appendix at the end of this Chapter. In May 1917 after requests from Hall, Wiseman reported that he was 'extending all possible assistance to Gaunt', whose office staff was too small to cope with their work-load. YUL Wiseman Papers, File 168: undated letter from Gaunt to D.I.D.; two telegrams dated 9 May 1917; letter from Wiseman to Gaunt, 26 May 1917. At the beginning of 1917 Gaunt proposed a closer co-operation with MI1c by moving with his staff into its New York office. Wiseman did not approve this suggestion. YUL Wiseman Papers, File 162, two telegrams dated 8 Feb. 1917.

27. YUL Wiseman Papers, File 161, letter from Connop Guthrie to Wiseman, 21 Dec. 1916.

28. In March 1918 Wiseman wrote that 'None of the US Bureaux employ Germans whereas this office has several most dependable German agents who are trusted acquaintances in enemy circles . . .'. By this date MI1c had 'already discarded several of these German agents . . . but retained two . . .' YUL Wiseman Papers, File 173, memorandum entitled *Miscellaneous Functions of New York Office of British Military Attaché*, 28 March 1918.

29. He did not say at precisely what date in 1916 he started watching Indian affairs. *Velvet and Vinegar*, op. cit., p. 145.

30. In December 1915 the new Consul-General at New York, Clive Bayley, requested that Owen should participate in the exchange of information on Indian nationalists set up between the Government of India, the Canadian Immigration Department and British Consular Officers in the USA. At this time Spring Rice was wholly unaware of the Home Office Agent's existence (PRO FO115/1908, nos. 122 and 127). Cunliffe Owen seems to have worked with MI1c and, in 1918, was fully aware of Wiseman's very secret role as intermediary between the British and American War Cabinets.

31. Wiseman Papers, *Miscellaneous Functions of New York Office of British Military Attaché*, op. cit.

32. Thwaites, op. cit., p. 150. There are no references in the files of the US Military Intelligence Department (MID) in the National Archives, Washington, mentioning the existence of Section V, MI1c in the United States, until after the American entry into the war, when the British officially put their Secret Service in touch with the various departments of American intelligence.

33. Wiseman Papers, File 160, letter from Wiseman to Standing, 4 April 1916.

34. Gaunt, op. cit., p. 147. He wrote that 'The American secret service men went out of their way to treat me considerately; most of them were pro-English, and . . . accorded me every possible privilege'. Ibid., p. 166.

34. Thwaites, op. cit., Ch. 14, 'Inspector Tunney'. YUL Wiseman Papers, File 84, letter from Thwaites to Wiseman, dated 22 Nov. 1918: 'Suggestions as to Recognition of War Services Rendered by Persons in America.' Tunney wrote about his wartime experiences in his book *Throttled!* (New York, 1919), from which, at Thwaites's request, he omitted all references to the British Secret Service.

35. After the US entry he was put in full charge of US Military Intelligence in New York and worked in close co-operation with MI1c.

36. Both Gaunt and the officers of Section V found that much of their time was taken up by various miscellaneous tasks. Section V came to be seen as a general information bureau for various British departments – it carried out investigations for other Allied Embassies and Consulates. Indeed, relative to the operations of the French, Italians and

Russians even MI1c's operations in the USA were extensive. In 1917 Section V was not sure whether the Italians and Russians had intelligence services operating in the USA at all. Thwaites believed that French intelligence in the USA in 1917 consisted of only one officer. YUL Wiseman Papers, File 172, memorandum 'No. 3', entitled *Points to be taken up by W.W.*, 23 Oct. 1917.

37. YUL Wiseman Papers, File 160, letter from Wiseman to Standing, 4 April 1916.
38. Thwaites, op. cit., pp. 131–8. Ships in the New York docks were protected by private American detective agencies up till the US entry into the war. As the career of Rintelen had shown they were doing a bad job. Surprisingly, Gaunt knew little of the system in operation and the situation was only remedied in November 1916 when John Gillan tightened up these arrangements.
39. YUL Wiseman Papers, letter from Wiseman to Standing, 4 April 1916.
40. PRO FO371/3063 263555/A/16.
41. YUL Wiseman Papers, File 173, memorandum entitled *Notes on the Work of Section V in USA*, 11 Dec. 1917.
42. He was particularly close to his Australian compatriot, John Rathom, the editor of the *Providence Journal*.
43. In the middle of 1916 Thwaites returned to England and brought back a small exhibition of war trophies. YUL Wiseman Papers, File 175, Memorandum entitled On Relations of New York Office (Section V) and MI5, 3 Oct. 1918. A few months before this he had scored a notable triumph over the German Ambassador, von Bernstorff. While spending a weekend with a millionaire acquaintance on Long Island, Thwaites had been shown a picture of the German Ambassador with his arms around two women in bathing suits. He flicked the picture into a book, which he took to bed to read. The next morning the Russian Ambassador held a reception in his office to show neutral diplomats 'the enemy unmasked'. Gaunt, op. cit., pp. 192–3.
44. For Wiseman's diplomatic career see W.B. Fowler, *British-American Relations, 1917–1918: The Role of Sir William Wiseman* (Princeton: Princeton University Press, 1969).
45. For details of the Indian's squabbles see, generally, the *Weekly Reports* of the DCI.
46. *Weekly Reports* of the Director of Criminal Intelligence, Report for the week ending 21 Dec. 1915.
47. Especially the work of J.C. Ker of the Department of Criminal Intelligence, *Political Trouble in India, 1907–1917* (Simla, 1917; reprint, Calcutta: Editions Indian, 1973).
48. Letter from Carnegie Ross to the Viceroy, 24 Jan. 1916. PRO FO115/2067, no. 23.
49. Letter from H. Wheeler, Indian Home Secretary, to Ross, 31 March 1916 and letter from Ross to the Viceroy, 12 May 1916, in PRO FO115 2067, no. 123.
50. Letter from Ross to Sir Francis May, Governor of Hong Kong, 9 Nov. 1915, in PRO FO115/1908, no. 92.
51. Bagai's many reports are scattered through the PRO FO371 series 'Hindu Agitations' and series PRO FO115, the files of the Washington Embassy. In January 1917 the heads of British intelligence in the Far East, Ridout and Petrie, were considering sending Bagai on a very dangerous mission to infiltrate the German Embassy at Peking because he had 'done so well up to date'. PRO FO371 3065 (52534).
52. The first reference to Jolliffe is a letter addressed to him by Ross, 24 Feb. 1915, in PRO FO115 1907, no. 8.
53. Anonymous report dated New York, 12 Feb. 1916, in PRO FO371/2786.
54. Foreign Office Minute Papers in PRO FO371/2493 (21445).
55. The Foreign Office had in mind above all the Secretary of State, William Jennings Bryan, who had once written a pamphlet, *British Rule in India*, in which he expressed views severely critical of the imperial government. He resigned as Secretary of State in June 1915. Foreign Office Minute Paper entitled *Seditious Indian Literature*. 'Ghadr' in PRO FO371/2493 (91242).
56. Memorandum by Colville Barclay, 6 Sept. 1915. PRO FO115/1980 (60).

57. On 14 February 1916 Sir Charles Cleveland wrote that 'We have recently heard that the India Office are sending an officer to San Francisco. . . . .' HDA: Feb. 1916, nos. 496–514 in IOLR IOR.POS.7296.

58. Note by Secretary of the Judicial and Public Department on an Inter-Departmental Conference held at India Office on 10 March 1916 and telegram from Secretary of State to Viceroy, 17 April 1916. HDA: June 1916, nos. 285–95 in IOLR IOR.POS.7297.

59. Thwaites remarked in *Velvet and Vinegar*, p. 146, that Nathan was 'handsome and distinguished'. If anything, as various references in American documents show, he seems to have slightly overawed those with whom he came into contact.

60. Telegram from Ross to Spring Rice, 15 June 1916, in PRO FO115 2067 no. 140.

61. YUL Wiseman Papers, memorandum entitled *American Section MI1c*.

62. *Weekly Reports* of the Director of Criminal Intelligence, Report for the week ending 25 Nov. 1916. HDB: Nov. 1916, nos. 452–3 in IOLR IOR.POS.10511.

63. Telegram from Wiseman to the Foreign Office, New York, 7 March 1917. PRO FO115/2235 (35).

64. Thwaites, op. cit., p. 148. The Department of Criminal Intelligence's account published by Cleveland his Report for the week ending 21 April 1917 and adhered to by Ker in *Political Trouble in India* is the best example of the way in which the Department of Criminal Intelligence tended to mock Indian revolutionaries in its reporting. Indeed, if it strayed from dispassionate objectivity in its reports on political crime, this is accounted for by the well-developed sense of humour of some of its officers, foremost among whom was Sir Charles Cleveland. He wrote as follows:
   On entering the house the detectives found Dr Chakravarty in nothing more than a loincloth, practically in his native garb. He was said to have been doing a dance for Sekunna, who was reclining amid pillows on a long divan. The interior of the house was furnished in an Oriental style, while the garden in the rear had been arranged to give an impression of the Far East. HDB: April 1917, nos. 700–3 in IOLR IOR. POS.10513.

65. Thwaites, op. cit. pp. 146–9. Thwaites gave full credit to Tunney for the successful interrogation of Chakravarty. He wrote to Wiseman in his *Suggestions as to Recognition of War Services Rendered by Persons in America*, 22 Nov. 1918, that 'it was due to this gentleman's extremely clever cross-examination and untiring energy in the Chakravarty–Sekunna case that the San Francisco Hindu conspiracy was exposed, and the conviction of the accused made possible'.

66. YUL Wiseman Papers, File 164, letter from Wiseman to Spring Rice, 7 March 1917. Telegram from New York 8 March 1917, in PRO FO371 3065 (57135).

67. Letter from Wiseman to Spring Rice, 7 March 1917 in PRO FO115 2235, no. 35.

68. Telegram from Spring Rice to Foreign Office, dated 8 March 1917, in PRO FO371 3065 (50779).

69. Telegram from Embassy, Washington, 16 March 1917, in PRO FO115 2235, no. 50.

70. Telegram from Spring Rice to Foreign Office, 8 March 1917, in PRO FO371 3065 (50968).

71. Telegram from Viceroy, dated 17 March 1917, in PRO FO371 3065 (62023).

72. Telegram from Secretary of State to Viceroy, dated 21 March 1917; letter from T.W. Holderness, India Office, to Foreign Office, 24 March 1917, in PRO FO371 3065 (62909).

73. The agents Jacobsen, Wehde and Boehm were each sentenced to five years' imprisonment and a $13,000 fine. PRO FO115 2236. *Weekly Reports* of the Director of Criminal Intelligence, Report for the week ending 3 Nov. 1917.

74. On 21 March 1917 the *Columbia Spectator* wrote an article on the Chicago case in which it was stated that the US Attorney would 'with the assistance of the British secret service . . . attempt to prove that (Heramba Lal) Gupta was one of a number of Hindu residents in America who have been conspiring with Germans to stir up a revolt in India

256

. . . English secret servicemen claim to have followed Gupta's every movement in 1915. . . .' *Weekly Reports* of the Director of Criminal Intelligence, Report for the week ending 2 June 1917. HDB: June 1917, nos. 438–41 in IOLR IOR.POS.10513.
75. See for example, Ram Chandra's claim that British agents were behind the screen during his interrogation by Tunney in Report by Mr A. O'Gorman Munkhouse on the Hindu trial, 13 Dec. 1917, in PRO FO115 2236, no. 393.
76. Basil Thomson, *Queer People* (London: Hodder & Stoughton, 1922), p. 103.
77. *Weekly Reports* of the DCI, Report for the week ending 27 July 1918. HDB: July 1917, nos. 426–30 in IOLR IOR.POS.10513.
78. *Weekly Reports* of the DCI, Report for the week ending 12 Oct. 1918. HDB: Nov. 1917, nos. 43–5 in IORL IOR.POS.10514.
79. *Weekly Report* of the DCI for 23 June 1918. HDB: June 1918, nos. 491–4, in IOLR IOR.POS.10514.
80. YUL Wiseman Papers, Series III.
81. Gaunt, op. cit., pp. 172 and 190.
82. Ibid., p. 149.

11

British Intelligence in the Far East, 1914–18

BRITISH INTELLIGENCE AND GERMAN PLOTS, 1914–17

The seriousness of the threat to the security of the Indian empire which Indian nationalists living in the Far East posed only became clear some months after the outbreak of the First World War. By means of its newspaper, the *Ghadr*, the revolutionary party had spread the message of revolt to Indian expatriate communities throughout the Far East.[1] The insurrection in the Punjab was a miserable failure but the complete success of the Indian government in suppressing it was in no way due to the efficiency of imperial intelligence in the Far East. Apart from a small agency for watching Chinese nationalists at Hong Kong and naval intelligence stations there and at Singapore, 'British intelligence' did not exist at all in the area. Once they had left America, India depended for information about the progress of the returning Ghadr revolutionaries upon reports provided by the Foreign and Colonial Offices.

The failure of the campaign in the Punjab by no means marked the end of the Ghadr Party. There were still several hundred Sikh watchmen spread through towns on the Chinese coast, whose potential to cause trouble greatly exceeded their numbers since almost all were ex-soldiers and in the conditions of post-revolutionary China had easy access to arms.[2] In Siam likewise, the majority of a Sikh community numbering several thousands was violently anti-British and dangerously close to the Burma military police. The latter was composed entirely of Indians and was the key to the control of Burma.[3] The Philippines were an important gathering-point for Indians leaving the United States for the Far East. On the other hand, the islands of the

Netherlands East Indies – Java, Borneo, the Celebes and New Guinea – had few British Indian inhabitants, but were the home of a sizeable and patriotic German community. The geographical extent of the islands and the difficulty of their terrain made it difficult for the British to keep an effective watch over them.[4] In the first half of 1915 the diplomatic and consular authorities in these areas were uniformly alarmed by Indian and German plotting, and they turned naturally to the Government of India for assistance. It was not forthcoming.

Despite the Russo-Japanese war of 1904–5, which resulted in the emergence of Japan as a major regional power, and China's Revolution of 1911, which further increased the instability of that country, the Far East in 1914 had remained the forgotten backyard of the Indian empire. Though India was the obvious base for any system of British intelligence in the Far East, its strategic outlook in 1914 was still governed by nineteenth century conditions. In the nineteenth century the foreign policy of the Government of India had centred on the protection of the Raj from overt military threats, and for this reason was directed almost exclusively against the danger from Russia which it perceived on the North-West Frontier. The evaporation of the threat from Russia after the signing of the Triple Entente by Britain, France and Russia in 1907, encouraged India to live in a splendid isolation of its own. Despite the growth of a revolutionary movement within India after 1907, the British were slow to credit their native subjects, other than the *bhadralok* of Bengal, with the capability of doing them real harm. The Germans had greater foresight. Unable to strike at the Indian empire by conventional means, they turned to novel means of colonial subversion. The numbers of the German and Indian plotters, and of the British intelligence officers deployed to thwart them, were minute in comparison with the vast armies fighting on the Western Front and against the Turks. Yet the stakes at issue were considerable. British intelligence in the Far East grew to play a vital role in protecting the British Empire behind its front lines.

The DCI would have faced serious problems in meeting all the requests for assistance which it received from British local authorities in the Far East. However, it flatly refused to act as a truly imperial intelligence agency when thus encouraged to become one. Cleveland took a remarkably calm view of the situation. Already before the war, in June 1914, he had formulated the policy to which his Department adhered until late 1915. He felt that secret service activity in the Far East was bound to be a waste of the Raj's limited resources because it could only defend against rather than prevent plots against India. In particular he thought that the governments of Japan, China and the Netherlands East Indies would not welcome the presence of British agents on their territory. He believed that the efforts of the DCI and of the Indian police as a whole should be confined to India, which was the ultimate end of all German and Indian intrigue in the Far East.[5] The DCI had already played a vital role in co-ordinating the control of returning Ghadr revolutionaries by the Indian CIDs in Spring 1915.[6] Cleveland's 'Fortress' India proved impregnable to the overseas plots of Germans and Indian revolutionaries throughout the war.

The Germans took over control of Indian revolutionary activities in the Far East and North America only after the failure of the insurrection in the Punjab. At the beginning of 1915 they attempted to strike at India from two directions. Their first plan was to supply arms from the United States to the revolutionaries of Bengal. By March 1915 this scheme had fallen through. The SS *Maverick*, which had the task of delivering the weapons, was hounded by British warships throughout her journey and was observed by British consular officers at every port of call.[7] An important role of the British Navy throughout the war was to isolate the Dutch East Indies as a centre of Indian–German intrigue.[8] While Britain had command of the seas – which it had completely after the Battle of the Falkland Islands in December 1914 – the possibility of Germany sending arms in bulk shipments to the coasts of India was slight. Cleveland had understood this, unlike the Germans.

The Germans' attempt to infiltrate India by land was no more successful. In the first half of 1915 they tried through the agency of a few Indian and German agents to mobilize the Sikh population of Siam and to cause mutiny in Burma. The odds were heavily against their success. The Siamese government went out of its way to help the British, who had close control over police operations undertaken to suppress the German plot. Since before the war two officers of the Burma police, E.W. Trotter and R.C. Whiting, had been respectively Acting Commissioner and Deputy-Acting Commissioner in Bangkok. Moreover, Danish police officers employed by the Siamese government in its police force gave unofficial assistance to the British.[9] By the beginning of September all the leading conspirators in Siam had either been executed or were on their way in chains to Singapore.[10]

An important factor in the swift success of the British operation in Siam was the ability of two successive ambassadors, Crosby and

260

Dering, to act as intelligence officers. They made sure that they had full knowledge of the movements of the Indian community throughout Siam. Indeed, everywhere in the Far East from the beginning of 1915 British Embassies and Consulates started to acquire intelligence functions. All were initially hampered by their inability to acquire reliable Indian agents and by a lack of secret service funds, neither of which were provided by the Government of India in the first part of 1915, when German-Indian plotting appeared at its most dangerous. Nevertheless in April 1915 Davidson, the Vice-Consul at Yokohama was controlling his own Indian agent, while in February 1916 Rentiers, the Consul-General at Manila, formally set up a two-man intelligence agency paid for by a £35-a-year secret service grant from London.[11]

Beckett, the British Consul at Batavia (Jakarta) in the Netherlands East Indies, had a particular, if fortuitous success in acquiring his agent. At the end of June 1915 a man of mixed German and Swedish parentage contacted him, promising him information about German plots in return for financial remuneration. Beckett agreed to the suggestion, and the man, whose true name remains unknown, was given the code-name 'Oren'. The information which he gave helped fill in the jigsaw puzzle of German plotting in the Pacific, whose first pieces Gaunt and Bennett had laid with their discovery of the American end of the plot. 'Oren' gave the British firm evidence that the *Maverick* had never received any arms cargo whatsoever, as well as details about the Helfferich brothers, through whom the German Foreign Office intended to implement its plans in the Netherlands East Indies.[12]

British intelligence in the Far East in 1915 was very makeshift in character, but it amounted to more than just a concerted effort by the Foreign Office to make up for the absence of an imperial intelligence system in the Far East. From early in 1915 intelligence activity there was closely watched by Whitehall. The formation of the interdepartmental committee to deal with the problem of 'Hindu agitations' was described in Chapter 9.

As far as British intelligence in the Far East had a local centre, this was Singapore. It was a natural focus for intelligence operations, being not only an important military base, but also the naval headquarters of the Far East. In 1915 the commanding officer there, Colonel (later Major General) Dudley Ridout, assumed a prominence in all matters relating to British intelligence in the Far East which he was to retain throughout the war. Ridout (pronounced 'Rid-out') was a 49-year-old veteran of the Boer War, in which he had served as a Staff Officer in the Intelligence Department. The seriousness of the Indian problem and the weakness of British power in the East was brought home to him almost as soon as he assumed his command on 5 February 1915. On 15 February a mutiny broke out among the 5th Light Infantry, an Indian Muslim regiment stationed at Singapore. The insurrection owed little to Indo-German plotters, though rather more to Pan-Islamist agitators working independently, and was soon suppressed, though only after French, Russian and Japanese assistance was called in, as well as that of a group of head-hunters from Borneo, and only after 40 Europeans had been killed.[13] Immediately after the mutiny Ridout set about improving the sources of information at his disposal. As a result Singapore became the sorting-house for intelligence in all the region. He and the interdepartmental committee in London worked together in close co-operation from an early date.[14]

Ridout's predecessor as commanding officer at Singapore had recently brought back from India a native agent. The latter, astonishingly, had never been allowed to work among the troops.[15] Ridout changed this. At the same time he took it upon himself to perform intelligence activities on a far wider geographical scale than those conducted by the Foreign Office. He secured a second agent from the Indian police, who was the first assistant sent from outside to help the British authorities in Bangkok at the height of the Indo-German plotting in June 1915.[16] Ridout acquired agents wherever he could. In August 1915 he sent an Austrian-British and an American agent to the Philippines. Neither proved successful. The Austrian-British agent was unable to discover what was going on in Indian circles in Manila, since he could not understand Indian languages. The American agent was later disgraced when Ridout discovered that the reports which he had submitted had actually been written by Consul-General Rentiers.[17]

Ridout's efforts to improve his sources of intelligence at Batavia also met with little success. In October 1915, at the recommendation of Consul-General Beckett, he took into employment a drunken Dutchman, Nederveen Meerkerk. After initially satisfactory service, he proved to be a braggart and was sent back to Holland in December 1916.[18] Ridout's difficulties in finding agents are wholly understandable. It was very difficult for the British consular authorities, whether in Singapore, North America or Europe, to secure native agents. If some of Ridout's agents were flamboyant, the system really depended upon the reports provided by more sober, though correspondingly more anonymous, residents of these areas. The services of the captains of coastal traders were particularly important. Whatever the quality of some of the men he employed, Ridout gave valuable, if sometimes only moral, support to the consular authorities in controlling Indian and German activities.

Ridout's main work was done within Singapore itself. He was greatly assisted throughout the war by a Parsi officer of the Bombay police, Deputy Superintendent Hector Kothavala. Kothavala came to Singapore in April 1915 as interpreter in the trial of an Indian revolutionary. Ridout felt that he was needed in Singapore and had him seconded to the War Office.[19] The success of counter-espionage at Singapore against the Germans and Indian revolutionaries was to a considerable extent due to Kothavala's work. He proved, according to Ridout, practically the only man able to control the two Indian agents already in Singapore. Kothavala's services were most important in interrogating a series of German agents who passed through Singapore in 1915, and from whom he secured full details of the failed German arms plots.[20]

The most important capture of all was a German agent named Vincent Kraft. Even before leaving on his mission, Kraft had intended to work for the British. He presented himself to the British authorities in Holland early in 1915. They would not help, but this did not deter him from visiting Beckett at Batavia at the end of July 1915. Beckett also dismissed him, but notified Ridout of Kraft's departure for Singapore. He was arrested there on arrival on 3 August 1915.[21] It took little on the part of Ridout and Kothavala to persuade him to become their double agent, codenamed 'X', on a pay of £2 per day.[22] Those who met him found Kraft an intriguing character. An Indian secret service officer who later interviewed him recorded that:

> To describe him personally is difficult, for his face changes its expression seldom, perhaps once in several hours – we might, however, liken him to a well-inflated bullfrog, placidly digesting his heavy meal.[23]

For the Germans, Kraft was a surprising choice as a secret agent, though he did have local knowledge of the Netherlands East Indies, since he had been born there. If his own account is to be believed, he had been a soldier in Flanders in 1914 where he had been wounded. Wesendonck, the Indian specialist on the German Foreign Office's Intelligence Bureau for the East, recruited him in hospital at Lille in

April 1915. According to another variant of his adventures, which Kraft also gave to the British, he had committed some offence in the army and was given a choice between the firing-squad and a secret service mission to Great Britain.[24]

Whatever the truth about his recruitment, it is clear that Kraft intended to betray the Germans from the beginning. He devised an elaborate plan involving the Netherlands East Indies. He proposed that the German inhabitants there should be armed and sent on a raid to the Andaman Islands, where the Government of India kept its political prisoners. The latter were then to be sent as an invasion force to India accompanied by the Germans. This plan, which Kraft had devised only for future sale to the British, and possibly to save his own skin, received the full support of the German Foreign Office.[25] In Singapore Kothavala proved the only man capable of handling Kraft, who was of a very temperamental disposition, and in August the two proceeded to Shanghai and Peking, where Kraft and the German authorities drew up plans for gathering arms for the assault on the Andamans. At the last minute the Germans called off the raid, which had been scheduled for Christmas Day 1915.[26] However, Kraft's main use to the British lay in the clear indications which he provided of the miscarriage of German plans, which reduced the need for extensive intelligence in the Far East.[27] Kraft also had the duties of spreading German propaganda in India and of co-ordinating the activities of Indian revolutionaries. British intelligence reports from Europe proved that the Germans still had absolute confidence in him and that the substance of his information was accurate.[28]

A second important capture at Singapore occurred at the end of 1915 and, according to Ridout, was the result of Kothavala's sharp detective work. The captive was a Chinese named Sing Kwie whom the Germans had sent through Singapore bearing bank drafts amounting to a huge Rs.100,000 or £6,600, with which they hoped to 'buy' a native regiment in Calcutta.[29]

By the end of 1915 there existed three distinct groups in the Far East providing information about Indo-German plotting: India itself; Ridout at Singapore; and the various consulates and embassies. The only real link between them all was the interdepartmental intelligence committee thousands of miles away in London. Because of Cleveland's 'Fortress India' policy, India did not take the lead in establishing an intelligence network in the Far East in 1914 and 1915. However, Ridout's secret service activities outside Singapore met with variable success and the pressure towards greater Indian involvement in Far Eastern intelligence continued.

At the beginning of 1915 the Department of Criminal Intelligence still believed that the local diplomatic and consular authorities should find their own native agents. This the embassy at Bangkok and the Burmese officers in the Siamese Police had consistently failed to do. They pleaded a complete ignorance of Indian affairs and an inability to place their work in the general context of the Indian revolutionary movement.[30] Finally, in August 1915, when effective moves had already been taken to suppress the Indo-German plot, Cleveland sent David Petrie to assist Dering in Bangkok.[31] The gradual establishment of the Indian intelligence system in the Far East dates from this action. In 1915 Petrie was a natural choice to send to Siam since, while convalescing from the wounds received in the Budge Budge affray, he had spent the first half of that year in compiling a 'Who's Who' of the Indian revolutionary movement in the Far East and North America entitled the *Ghadr Directory*.[32]

Petrie's mission did not mark a complete breach of the rules which Cleveland had established in 1914 against extensive Indian involvement in the Far East. In Autumn 1915 both Cleveland and Petrie decided that even though the Ghadr plot in India had been completely defeated, the DCI still could not find high-ranking police officers for all the places in the Far East which had requested them. However, they agreed, after Petrie's reconnaissance in Siam, that India would have to provide expert guidance for the consular authorities in some form. They seem, moreover, to have become worried that India was being left out of intelligence arrangements in the Far East. Petrie wrote that

> if India had been more closely associated in the handling of [Kraft's] information at Singapore in the early stages of the enquiry, the Government of India would have been saved some lakhs of rupees spent on an elaborate system of precautions'.[33]

The Department of Criminal Intelligence decided that while it could not set up an expensive system of intelligence in the Far East, Petrie should be sent there for the duration of the war as a special officer with a brief to set up a network of agents in all the important trouble spots.[34]

In February 1916, upon his return from Siam, Petrie submitted a plan for the establishment of his Far Eastern agency to the Government of India. The system which he proposed was to comprise only seven agents, one of whom was already working at Hankow in China. By the DCI's estimate it would involve a net increase in their annual expenditure of only Rs.36,400 or about £1,933; by the higher estimate of Cleveland it would still cost only Rs.50,000 or £2,400. Petrie realized that the problems of distance in the Far East prevented his exercising direct control over all these agents. For example, with Singapore as his headquarters it would take him three days to get to Bangkok, 10–12 to Hong Kong and over 14 to Japan. Therefore, of necessity, the network of Indian agents depended on close co-operation with the diplomatic and consular authorities. They were to control the agents. Petrie described his own role within the system thus:

> It will be my special function to see that the information obtained from the different sources is co-ordinated and to see that the general situation is so understood that local officers can intelligently deal with the particular aspects of it with which they find themselves confronted.[35]

In March 1916 Petrie's project was discussed in London at a meeting of the interdepartmental committee. The discussions were based on a misunderstanding of Petrie's intentions. The Whitehall departments believed that the DCI wanted to set up an intelligence network independent of the Foreign Office and of Ridout. None the less the discussions reveal much about the status of India as an intelligence centre within the Empire. By the end of 1915 there had been a vast increase in the numbers of personnel employed by the home intelligence agencies. The staff of all the departments of Military Intelligence, for example, amounted to about 6,000 men.[36] This was far more than the small number of officers employed by the Indian Department of Criminal Intelligence. The interdepartmental committee felt that only the offices in London were capable of collating information received about German plots on a worldwide level. Thus in effect it held London to be a much more important centre of Far Eastern intelligence than Delhi. The interdepartmental committee saw Ridout as the most important intelligence officer in the Far East because they knew and trusted him. Petrie was unknown in London.

The operation of the intelligence system formed around the diplomatic and consular officers had already pointed up a potential danger that the activities of local officers might lead to serious diplomatic complications if they were not closely watched by London. Because the Dutch government took no action to deport German plotters in the Netherlands East Indies, Consul-General Beckett became obsessed that its secret service in the islands was working hand-in-hand with the Germans.[37] He even proposed to establish an 'elaborate scheme' for the protection of the Dutch government in the Netherlands East Indies.[38] The Foreign Office became alarmed, for they realized that the Dutch administration was 'antiquated and easy-going', and that even if it had tried to restrain the Germans they would have 'put on the screw at The Hague'.[39]

Some important men within military intelligence, if not all the government departments represented on the Committee, blamed the DCI for having till then served India's interests before those of the Empire as a whole. The Committee was anxious that the existence of an intelligence system in the Far East should not multiply the conflicts of interest between London and Delhi. Thus the committee ruled that Petrie should only work in the Far East as an adviser to the diplomatic and consular authorities.[40] Furthermore, he was not allowed to visit the Pacific coast of North America, which was the base of the Ghadr Party, since this might endanger the work of Robert Nathan, the senior Indian officer working there under the control of the secret service. Nor was he allowed to place agents anywhere within the Far East unless local diplomatic and consular authorities requested him to do so. Above all, the committee stressed that Petrie should do nothing that might impair the authority of General Ridout.

The determination of the interdepartmental committee to keep all intelligence activity in the Far East firmly under its control was also reflected in its relations with the government of Australia. In June 1916 the Governor-General asked that Australian intelligence agents should be allowed to work at the Consulates of Manila and Batavia. The interdepartmental committee was unanimously hostile to this moderate request.[41] They informed the Australians that a multiplication of intelligence networks in the Far East would have harmful effects. But the committee frankly acknowledged the real reason for blocking Australian entry into the imperial intelligence system – the impossibility of keeping secrets in Australia.[42]

Except that Petrie was barred from working in North America these rulings meant little in practice.[43] The only important diplomatic and consular officers in the Far East who had not so far asked for the assistance of the Indian government were those in Japan.[44] At the beginning of May 1916 the Tokyo Embassy urgently requested Indian agents.[45] Petrie wrote in reply to the authorities in London:

The modifications which I suggest are all made in the light of my experience in the Far East. I found no difficulty then in establishing a practical and mutually satisfactory system of relations. All that I ask is to be given free hand to do this again, and I am confident that I shall find no difficulty in meeting half way any wishes on the part of the local officers.[46]

From May to August 1916 Petrie went on a preliminary tour during which he visited Singapore, Hong Kong, China, Japan, the Philippines and the Netherlands East Indies.[47]

An important outcome of the tour was the establishment of good personal relations with Ridout, who wrote:

From a full discussion with Mr Petrie it is evident that he wishes to work in the closest co-operation and co-ordination with existing organizations and that he has no desire to displace anything which is working well.[48]

Petrie likewise established cordial relations with the diplomatic and consular officers whom he met.[49] The Ambassador at Peking immediately recommended that the Indian network should be made permanent.[50]

BRITISH INTELLIGENCE IN CHINA, 1914–18

In the first two years of the war British intelligence in China amounted to no more than small, makeshift agencies in Hong Kong and Shanghai. A 'Joint Naval and Military Intelligence Bureau' was formed at Hong Kong upon the outbreak of the Chinese revolution in 1911 'when the need for close co-operation between the two services became evident'. Its duties were very limited and it was not intended to gather political intelligence. After the outbreak of war the Bureau became the 'Military Intelligence Department of China Command', with headquarters at Hong Kong. This change in title did not, however, entail a notable increase in the scope of its activities. Though it employed Chinese agents, the intelligence diary which it issued was composed of military reports and summaries of Chinese political events, which appear to have been drawn largely from press and consular reports. It was not concerned with German and Indian subversion.[51]

From the Government of India's point of view Hong Kong was of the greatest strategic importance late in 1914 when Indian revolutionaries stopped there on their way back from America and the Far East. The Captain Superintendent of the Hong Kong Police, McI. Messer, took vigorous action, assisted by officers of the Punjab CID, who had been sent over on special duty. There was no permanent staff of Indian intelligence officers at Hong Kong.

During the first three years of the war British intelligence in northern China did not exist in any form, while agents from southern China were unable to operate there because of their ignorance of the local dialects and conditions.[52] In November 1916 the Embassy in Peking complained that 'we are quite powerless here in the matter of watching the Indian suspects who visit Peking at no infrequent intervals'. However, the commander of the Embassy Guard, Captain Ross Thomson, had previously worked in the Burma police, and at the Embassy's request attempted to get in touch with 'one or two local Indians'.[53] But at the end of the war there was still no regular and effective secret service organization in Northern China.

After his tour in the Far East, Petrie concluded that the most important centres of the Indian revolutionary movement abroad now lay in China and Japan.[54] His headquarters were therefore placed at Shanghai, which he regarded as the part of China most troubled by Indo-German intrigues. He wrote:

> The port is . . . an International Settlement in which theoretically, if not actually, British and enemy interests are looked upon with an equal eye. Consequently there has been no check on the coming or going of revolutionary Indians, and the presence of the German Consul-General, who is the reputed head of German underground intrigue in the East, has served to make Shanghai a hot-bed of German-Indian plotting.[55]

In the early part of the war British intelligence operations against the Germans in Shanghai were carried out by a naval staff officer, Captain J.M. Seigne, and by an ex-merchant, Mr Canning, who represented China Command.[56] It seems that Canning played a passive role which involved no more than transferring to Hong Kong information collected by other agencies at Shanghai.[57] Captain Seigne, on the other hand, kept a watch on Indo-German arms plots in Shanghai while performing the general duties of naval intelligence.[58] But he was not suited for this work. In January 1916 the Ambassador at Peking, Sir John Jordan, wrote that 'it is virtually impossible to deal with general statements made with the air of assurance and authority which characterize nearly all Captain Seigne's reports'.[59] Colonel French, the head of MI1(a), dismissed these reports as 'fairy stories', and the Foreign Office regarded his work generally as 'a waste of money'.[60]

Seigne showed poor judgement in his selection of agents. His most unfortunate choice was a naturalized British subject of Romanian origin named Rothman, who had already left the employment of the Hong Kong Military Intelligence Department in bad favour. The Governor of Hong Kong remonstrated against Seigne's use of him at the end of 1915.[61] These complaints were vindicated in July 1917 when Rothman publicly denounced Seigne as a British agent at the trial of a German agent in Shanghai.

Even after this incident Seigne continued to represent British naval intelligence in Shanghai. By the end of 1916 his main role was to act as a front for other more capable intelligence officers, including David Petrie, who worked in Shanghai.[62] In a similar manner Guy Gaunt, the station chief of naval intelligence in the USA, principally worked as a cover for the main intelligence operation there, which was conducted by Mansfield Cumming's MI1(c), the Secret Service.[63]

Despite Seigne's incompetence, the British were potentially in a very strong position in Shanghai because they had the majority of the officers of the Shanghai municipal police in their pay. This force included an Indian contingent of 500 Sikhs and 50 Muslim policemen together with 175 watchmen. Their loyalty to the British remained firm.[64] Captain E.M.I. Barrett, Assistant Superintendent of Police, who had been an officer in a Sikh regiment of the Indian Army, commanded the contingent.[65] He was assisted by Buddha Singh, a Sikh officer who had served in the Shanghai municipal police since 1902. The Captain Superintendent in charge of the municipal police claimed that 'the knowledge which has been gained regarding the movements and doings of Ghadr agents in Shanghai and its environs is chiefly due to the loyalty and zeal of [Buddha Singh]'.[66]

Despite the vigilance of Barrett and his men, considerable difficulties lay in the way of the surveillance of Indian and German suspects in Shanghai. Like the diplomatic and consular authorities in 1915, the Shanghai municipal police found that work against Indian nationalists necessitated the assistance of officers of the Government of India who were familiar with the history of Indian political crime. As late as January 1917, Barrett remarked on 'the lack of capable detectives to watch the movements of the highly educated and clever [Indian] revolutionist . . . The international police is not properly equipped for this work . . .'[67] He also complained about the state of the law in China, feeling that 'the facilities for dealing with sedition among natives of India in Shanghai and for the punishment of serious crimes, uncovered by the Orders-in-Council, are, to say the least, most unsatisfactory'.[68]

But the main difficulty impeding the effective working of British intelligence in Shanghai was the attitude of the officer in command of the municipal police, Captain Superintendent Kenneth McEuen. Accord to the Consul-General at Shanghai, Sir Everard Fraser, McEuen clung to 'extreme views of the international character of the municipal police force', which hampered the efforts of Barrett and other officers to exploit it to full effect on behalf of the Empire. McEuen commanded a special intelligence staff which had been formed to watch Chinese 'sedition'. Thanks to his neutral stance in the war these 'detectives [showed] little zeal for [British] interests and [were] not allowed to be stimulated by rewards from the British authorities'.[69]

At the same time that Petrie was setting up an Indian intelligence network in China, Captain Hilton Johnson, an officer of the Shanghai municipal police, successfully established that force as a regular British intelligence agency. To overcome McEuen's obstruction of the full use of the Shanghai municipal police in the service of British interests, Hilton Johnson secretly encouraged the Foreign Office to order the establishment of an intelligence bureau in Shanghai and recommended himself as officer in charge of McEuen's special intelligence staff.[70] He had a strong claim to this position since he was the only British police officer in Shanghai who spoke fluent Mandarin Chinese.[71] He made an arrangement with the Foreign Office to report on Indian unrest there without informing the Captain Superintendent.[72] In October 1916 McEuen yielded to pressure from the Consul-General,[73] and turned over his intelligence staff to Hilton Johnson.[74] At the same time the War Office appointed Hilton Johnson as its representative in Shanghai, though he remained an officer of the Shanghai municipal police. At the end of October 1916 Fraser reported that 'just recently . . . Hilton Johnson has begun to get information'.[75]

In Autumn 1916 the various intelligence agencies operating in Shanghai were grouped together into the 'Shanghai Intelligence Bureau'. This was an informal committee which met under the chairmanship of Sir Everard Fraser, the Consul-General. Captains Barrett and Hilton Johnson of the Shanghai municipal police, Petrie, Seigne

271

and Canning regularly attended its weekly meetings.[76] The committee's activities were restricted to the co-ordination of political intelligence and 'to facilitating such local action as [might] be desired' by the individual officers sitting upon it. The duties of these officers were unchanged, the only difference being that they now had to keep the Bureau constantly informed.[77] The different members of the Bureau continued to obtain funds from various sources. Petrie received money from the DCI, whereas the Admiralty and the War Office supplied Seigne and Hilton Johnson respectively.[78] Fraser, on the other hand, received secret service funds from the Embassy at Peking. Likewise the members all employed agents individually.[79] In January 1917 Fraser reported that the Bureau was working satisfactorily.[80]

Petrie's Indian network was therefore successfully grafted onto the existing intelligence system in the Far East which had grown up in 1915 when India shunned involvement there. Petrie now intended to spend most of his time in Shanghai and was given the rank of Vice-Consul by the Foreign Office and an office in the Shanghai Consulate.[81] In October 1916 he started placing his agents, who were either native Indian police officers of the rank of Sub-Inspector or Inspector, or were civilian agents whom he had recruited on his own initiative.[82] A Muslim was sent to Batavia in the Netherlands East Indies, while a very important agent, whose work will be discussed later, was sent to Japan.[83]

In China, Petrie's network was confined to the coastline. His plans there received an immediate set-back. On 10 February 1917 the first agent whom he had employed, 27-year-old Sub-Inspector Harnam Singh, was assassinated at Nanking. The circumstances of his death caused Petrie considerable distress and embarrassment. According to Petrie, Harnam Singh had impeccable credentials for a secret mission to China. He had firsthand knowledge of the country, having served as an interpreter in the Shanghai municipal police between 1906 and 1910, before joining the Indian police in 1913. Late in 1915 he accompanied Petrie to Siam where he did 'admirable work'. Harnam Singh then volunteered to work under Petrie in China, arriving in Nanking late in October 1916.[84] The Indians in China knew that he had been thrown out of the Shanghai municipal police, for 'having mixed himself up in . . . factional quarrels and bickerings'. Petrie thought that this blot on his record might provide a suitable cover. In fact the revolutionaries distrusted Harnam Singh from the start and he did nothing to allay their suspicions. He arrived in China with an Indian

272

servant which, Petrie noted, was 'an appanage not usually found with a dismissed Sub-Inspector of Police who is reduced to coming out to China to seek his living', and delivered a lecture on loyalty at the Sikh temple at Shanghai, which was 'hardly a fit topic for a dismissed police officer who was to worm himself into the good graces of revolutionary plotters'.

Harnam Singh's indiscretions grew worse when he got to Nanking. Petrie had not realized that he was a hardened drinker – a habit which he now indulged heavily. To his cost he chose a dedicated revolutionary as his companion, and poured out to him tales of his deeds in the imperial service in Siam. This proved the last straw to a Sikh named Atma Ram, who was then living in Nanking in constant fear, after escaping arrest in Siam. By the time Harnam Singh became aware that his life was in danger he was doomed. He pleaded desperately with the British Consul to arrange his transfer, but the latter did not have the authority to do so. Petrie wrote sorrowfully that 'it will be a lasting regret to me that during the closing days of Harnam Singh's life I was still en route from India to China'. A few days after Harnam Singh made his request, Atma Ram shot him down in the street.[85] As Petrie sadly noted: '*Quem Deus perdere vult, prius dementat*'.[86] On the practical side, Petrie felt that the tragic episode demonstrated the necessary dependence of the Indian intelligence system in the Far East upon the local consular officers.[87]

Harnam Singh's conduct was not typical of Petrie's agents. In March 1917 another of Petrie's men, Jagjit Singh, went to Hankow in search of the revolutionary leader Bhagwan Singh. The British Consulate General there were aware of his true identity and, in order to remove any suspicions the revolutionaries might have about him, they had him arrested and put on trial, but then released him for want of sufficient evidence. Jagjit Singh next saw the German Consul who gave him money and sent him to Shanghai to seek Bhagwan Singh.[88]

By the beginning of 1917 the Government of India 'did not think that there was much risk of [German-Indian plots] being put into practice'.[89] but they remained conscious of their vulnerability and kept up vigilance even when the alarms were difficult to take seriously.[90] In Bengal the Indian police had only recently started to make real headway in suppressing terrorism. British intelligence in the Far East continued to perform a crucial role in keeping Bengal isolated from German aid and from the Indian revolutionary movement abroad.

Neither General Ridout nor Petrie believed that the Germans

had really given up their efforts to bring down the Indian empire. While acting in close collaboration with Petrie, Ridout thought that the Indian organization was unlikely to discover much about German activities in the Far East. He noted in November 1916 that little had been heard of German secret service activity in the Far East for some time and that it was wholly un-German in character to quit. He concluded that the Germans must be using a better class of agent, whom British intelligence had failed to detect. He proposed, therefore, to send Kothavala to Peking disguised as an Indian revolutionary to infiltrate the German secret service in China.[91] Petrie agreed to the plan, though he thought that Ridout's suspicions were ill-founded. He wrote at the end of 1916:

> Better class Germans were wearied of these intrigues and plottings; the riff-raff who were employed as agents had failed, disclosures had taken place and the good name of Germany had been dragged in the dirt; money had been lavishly spent and nothing had been achieved; was it worth while, they had begun to ask, to persevere with schemes which so far had ended only in discredit, expense and failure.[92]

His assessment proved correct.[93] The War Office, on the other hand, was enthusiastic about Ridout's plans. Even in January 1917 Colonel French of MI1(a) was suspicious of Indian intelligence, doubting whether the Department of Criminal Intelligence should even be informed if Kothavala was sent to China.[94] The entry of China into the war on the Allied side in February 1917 rendered the whole scheme redundant, though it did not put a stop to the smouldering Indian unrest in that country.[95]

By the beginning of 1917 British intelligence in the Far East had developed into two distinct spheres of activity. The first sphere was centred on Singapore and had come into being as a result of the efforts of General Ridout. It basically amounted to a heterogeneous collection of agents working in the Straits Settlements and in the Netherlands East Indies. During the war this area of British intelligence activity became more systematized. From the end of 1917 the General Staff at Singapore, which now had an intelligence department made up of three British staff officers, started to produce monthly intelligence summaries.[96] But despite this, Singapore intelligence remained very dependent upon the personal initiatives of General Ridout.

The second sphere of British intelligence activity in the Far East, which consisted of the diplomatic and consular officers and of the Indian intelligence network, had no local centre. While the Foreign Office had ultimate control of diplomatic and consular officers, the aim of their intelligence duties in the Far East was the defence of India and they depended increasingly for support and advice upon the agents of the Indian police. There was a remarkable absence of conflict between the 'Singapore network' and the 'Indian network' on the one hand, and between Indian agents and the diplomatic and consular officers on the other. This co-operation was in marked contrast to the bitter conflicts which broke out between different British intelligence services operating in Europe and in North America. This is the clearest reflection of the acute sense of imperial vulnerability which was created first by the Indian and German plots of 1914 to 1916, and which was nurtured thereafter by widespread suspicions of Japan.

The second reason for the cohesiveness of British intelligence operations in the Far East was the supremacy of control maintained by the interdepartmental committee in Whitehall, which retained the last word in all matters of intelligence strategy in the region, despite the great distances separating London from the Far East. On the other hand, the main danger of conflict within the system lay not between the 'Singapore network' and the 'Indian network' but between Indian interests and Whitehall. This conflict came briefly to a head at the end of 1917.

At the end of September 1917 the Department of Criminal Intelligence informed Petrie that Lieutenant Oelsner of the German General Staff was intending to proceed through China to Japan, and there to take charge of Indian–German plots. Petrie was only informed in April 1918 that Oelsner was under Kraft's command. Petrie wrote to Cleveland:

> you will realize that I am hardly doing justice to my feelings in merely saying that I was surprised to learn the truth as to his relationship with 'X' . . . The authorities in London seem to have displayed a curiously ill-advised want of confidence in their officials out here in failing to enlighten them as to the true position of men like . . . Oelsner.

Petrie complained that his men and the Shanghai municipal police had been seeking high and low for Oelsner for several months. He particularly resented that 'the confidence so carefully withheld from us was bestowed in full measure upon the Japanese Ambassador in

London' with the result that the full details of Oelsner's mission were published a few days later in a Japanese newspaper. Petrie concluded 'this is reducing intelligence work to the level of the comic opera'.[97]

This judgement was unfair. By this date the pooling of resources of different British organizations in the Far East – the War Office, the Foreign Office and the Indian Police – was seen as natural and desirable. The system was still not truly imperial in that it was run entirely by the British. London continued to block Australian participation in imperial intelligence. None the less, the degree of co-operation achieved in the Far East by the end of the war could not have been foreseen in 1915.[98] The struggle of the British Empire with Indian revolutionaries and their German allies is probably the only area of the intelligence history of the First World War in which human intelligence played a decisive role.

BRITISH INTELLIGENCE AND JAPAN

In January 1915 the Japanese government shocked the Allies by its attempt to impose a virtual protectorate on China with the presentation of the 'Twenty-One Demands'. Over the year the Allied cause sank to a low ebb and the British government became concerned that Japan's commitment to the Anglo-Japanese alliance might waver.[99] These fears reached their height in the middle of the year when the Japanese government did not prevent certain newspapers printing attacks on Great Britain's prosecution of the war and on its imperial policies.[100] Japan remained faithful to the alliance. None the less, British suspicions of its policy grew and were encouraged partly by the failure of the Japanese government to take effective action against Indian revolutionaries who had taken refuge in Japan, and partly by numerous cases of Japanese espionage throughout the Far East.[101]

On 1 December 1915 the Japanese government failed to fulfil a promise to deport a prominent Indian revolutionary named Heramba Lal Gupta and a mysterious character whom the British correctly suspected of being Rash Behari Bose, who had assisted at the attempt on the Viceroy in 1912, and had played a major role in organizing the failed Ghadr insurrection in the Punjab in 1915. The two Indians escaped to the house of the Japanese ultra-nationalist leader, Toyama Mitsuru. The Japanese never recaptured them.[102] The shielding of these and other Indian revolutionaries was part of what the British

Foreign Office and the Government of India increasingly regarded as Japanese encouragement of the Indian revolutionary movement.[103]

The British could not dismiss Indian revolutionaries in the Far East as a potential threat to the Empire. If the numbers of Indian plotters remained small, so too did imperial resources. On a practical level the shielding by the Japanese of Rash Behari Bose and other revolutionaries was a serious matter, but in the eyes of British officers in the East and of policy-makers in London and Delhi it assumed an even greater symbolic importance. During the war British statesmen in both London and Delhi as well as officials on the spot in the Far East had difficulty in understanding the behaviour of a nation which equalled many European countries in economic and military strength but which, to their surprise, sometimes deviated from European standards of conduct. The shielding of the revolutionaries was a uniquely clear-cut issue over which the British could gauge the readiness of the Japanese to behave according to their own British codes of honour. The case polarized the suspicions which the British Embassy at Tokyo, the Foreign Office and the Government of India had of Japanese conduct on other matters.

British suspicions were based to a large extent upon the reports which they received from their secret service, whose development in Japan the Foreign Office had initially opposed. The Foreign Office believed that 'owing to the scarcely friendly attitude of the Japanese government over Indian sedition' the presence of an Indian agent would soon become known.[104] But it yielded to pressure from the Tokyo Embassy which was uneasy at its lack of information about Indian affairs. The British secret service in Japan came into existence at the end of April 1915 when the Ambassador at Tokyo, Conyngham Greene, instructed his Vice-Consul at Yokohama, Charles Davidson, to send him information on Indian nationalist propaganda printed in Japan. Davidson himself was the most important component of the network of agents which grew up around him. There was nothing in his background disposing him to distrust Japan. He was both a scholar of the Japanese language and an admirer of Japanese culture. His work was held in high esteem by Greene, who himself had been very pro-Japanese before 1915 but became increasingly disillusioned thereafter. In August 1915 Davidson found a valuable assistant in Rahim Baksh, a Punjabi Muslim merchant, whom the revolutionaries trusted as an intermediary.[105]

The intelligence arrangements based on Yokohama did not

develop further until Petrie visited Japan in July 1916. He unreservedly distrusted the policies of the Japanese government and disliked the country and its inhabitants from the moment he set foot there. He came to the conclusion that

> It is clear that we must for the present regard Japan as a country in which purely Indian intrigue will be allowed to flourish unrebuked, and in which it may even receive a certain amount of official, or, at any rate, unofficial, encouragement. I do not see that we can do very much to arrest this, but it is clear that it will be to our advantage to know as much as we can of the doings of Indian revolutionaries while they are on Japanese soil, and to watch the course of this dalliance between them and the Japanese people.[106]

In October 1916 he despatched two agents to Japan, whom Davidson was to control. They were unknown to one another, and went under the codenames 'P' and 'Q'.[107] 'P' was a remarkable man. His name was Professor Pandit Hari Prasad Shastri and he came ostensibly to teach Indian philosophy at Tokyo. In India he had been acquainted with Rash Behari Bose.[108] Both he and 'Q' were astounded by the reception which they received in Japan when it became known that they were Indian nationalists.[109] Shastri's reports soon led Davidson and Greene to conclude that the Indian revolutionary movement in Japan was far more important than they had realized. Furthermore they felt that each successive report from 'P' proved the support which Indian revolutionaries enjoyed among prominent Japanese.[110] In the course of 1917, assisted by his social status, Professor Shastri mixed with important Japanese nationalists.[111] However, at no time did he act as an *agent provocateur*.

The Indian secret service occupied a peculiar position in Japan. The consular authorities were not able to secure agents operating within Japanese ultra-nationalist groups and could approach them only by employing Indian agents. Furthermore, the Indian secret service was the only political intelligence service operating inside Japan during the war. It is not surprising that the information which it revealed of Japanese connivance with Indian nationalists carried great weight.

At the end of 1916 'P' and 'Q' discovered that the mysterious Indian who had escaped deportation was indeed Rash Behari Bose. The Government of India held it essential that he should be brought to justice. But the Japanese government claimed to be unable to locate him. In January 1917 Davidson employed a former Japanese policeman named Samejima to do this for them and in May 1917 he succeeded.[112] However, by this time it was clear that the Japanese had no intention of deporting Bose.

Davidson continued to trace Bose's movements, employing a second Japanese agent in August 1917.[113] Over the course of that year he came to control a variety of informants. He had a Japanese hotelier in his pay,[114] and took charge of a Chinese agent who paid a brief visit to Japan.[115] It appears that at one stage Davidson was paying an official inside the Japanese Ministry of Foreign Affairs for information.[116] It is not possible to say precisely how many agents he controlled.[117] However, the most important agents were 'P' – 'Q' was redeployed in China in January 1917 – Rahim Baksh, and the two Japanese agents. By 1918 the Tokyo Embassy was in receipt of an annual secret service allowance of £500, paid by the Foreign Office, which was a relatively large sum.[118] At the beginning of 1918 the cost of the whole secret service organization in North America was £1,500.[119]

The agents' reports were invariably detached in tone. Moreover, the number of agents employed ensured that the British were not dependent on any one of them. But these reports did not reach London and Delhi unprocessed. The covering letters which Davidson attached were shot through with his feelings of outrage at the treachery of the Japanese in protecting Rash Behari Bose, which had become the touchstone of Japanese official probity by early 1917. Petrie added further interpretations hostile to the Japanese. I shall argue below that these opinions were fundamentally sound, based as they were on an appreciation of Japanese tendencies to expansion seen throughout Asia.

Davidson and his agents, particularly Professor Shastri, distinguished the activities of the Japanese government from those of ultra-nationalist pressure groups working on the government. They stressed the weakness of the Japanese ministers over the Indian question as much as their lack of honesty. They believed that the representatives of first Count Okuma's (1914–16) and then General Terauchi's (1916–18) Cabinets went in fear of their lives before the secret societies who were protecting the Indians.[120] The British were uncertain of the extent to which the Japanese government used the secret societies for its own ends. They were convinced, however, that certain members of the government, especially Terauchi's Foreign Minister, Baron Goto, were more ready to dally with the ultra-nationalists than other members of the Cabinet.[121] Moreover, the agents reported that some of the ultra-nationalist groups were in receipt of Japanese government funds. The general impression created by British intelligence in Japan was that successive governments took an opportunist line towards the secret societies.[122] This was a moderate assessment. There is strong evidence that the Japanese government had greater control over the secret societies than the British suspected. Since the assassination attempt upon Count Okuma in 1889 the Japanese police had kept the secret societies under close surveillance, and they did not have the independent power with which Davidson credited them.[123] It is significant that the Japanese agents searching for Rash Behari Bose were warned off by the police.

By far the most important secret group in Japan were the Shina (China) Ronin. They were divided into several branches, the most famous of which was the Black Dragon Society. This grew up in the 1890s with the object of encouraging the Japanese government to annex the Amur region of China. Its great leader was Toyama Mitsuru, the protector of Rash Behari Bose. The Shina Ronin became violently hostile to Great Britain after it blocked the Twenty-One Demands on China in 1915. Intelligence reports from Japan showed how the ultra-nationalist groups provided a strong and continuous pressure on successive governments in favour of Japanese expansion in Asia. Information about the potential long-term threat from the ultra-nationalists obtained from within Japan was supported by various cases of the secret societies' espionage abroad, which came from different sources.

Even before 1914 the Government of India had considered setting up a special counter-espionage agency to watch Japanese visitors, whose suspicious movements encouraged 'a great feeling of doubt as to Japan's probable attitude towards India and trouble in India, in the event of Great Britain being involved in a Continental war'.[124] No such agency was established even when the increase of Japanese trade caused by the war brought a large influx of Japanese to India.[125] The Government of India admitted that in 'attempting to gauge the activities of Japanese in India [it had] been greatly handicapped by the absence of any system whereby a close scrutiny could be kept over them'. Native officers of the Indian police were unable to perform the surveillance of foreigners effectively. Often they were ignorant even of the English language. Thus the Indian police were 'seldom quite certain that the names of the Japanese [were] correctly given, and seldom [were] able to trace the real identity of a suspicious Japanese visitor'. Consequently the information which the Government of India possessed by the end of the war about Japanese espionage was frequently 'inconclusive'.[126]

But the Government of India believed that the quantity of cases of suspected espionage involving Japanese more than counterbalanced the uncertainty created by the inadequancies of police surveillance. By the end of the war the DCI had collected 'voluminous' papers on the subject. Often the Japanese gave misleading or false statements when questioned. In many cases they flagrantly contravened movement restrictions. The Government of India were particularly concerned about Japanese activity in Tibet and Yunnan which were areas of strategic importance.[127]

Probably the majority of the suspect Japanese were engaged in commercial espionage. The Indian police were particularly concerned about the activities of the leading Japanese firm in India, the Mitsui Busan Kaisha. In this case there was a definite overlap between the firm's unfair trading practices and its indulgence in political mischief.[128] The Government of India believed that its representatives and others in Japan spoke in support of Indian nationalism in order to gain the goodwill of Indian consumers. However, some Japanese suspects were entirely concerned with political work. The first case to cause real offence was that of Okakura Kakuzo, a distinguished Japanese visitor who, in 1913, was caught giving advice to Bengali revolutionaries.[129]

The important connections of some Japanese suspects disturbed the Government of India. One such case is indicative both of the very suspicious, not to say eccentric, character of Japanese movements in India and of the difficulties facing the police in understanding what was really going on. Count Otani was a descendent of the Imperial House and had been a Buddhist Abbot until forced to resign after speculating his Temple's funds on the Tokyo Stock Exchange. In 1914 and 1916 he went to India professedly to study Buddhist remains. The DCI suspected that 'his interest in Buddhist research is more political than religious and that he regards a Buddhist revival as an important step towards the political headship of Japan in Asia'. When the Government of India contacted Count Otani in order to render him honour, he left hurriedly for Japan, saying that he needed treatment for a heart disease.[130] Later in 1916 the Shanghai Intelligence Bureau reported that he had made an astonishing recovery and was about to begin a tour of China.[131]

The most important case of Japanese espionage in India concerned a scholar of Tokyo's Keio University. In May 1918 Professor Kazunobu Kanokogi went to India on a three-year visit, ostensibly to study Sanskrit philosophy. He was one of the few Japanese that the Indian police were able to keep fully under observation.[132] British intelligence in Japan reported that he was 'an enthusiastic promoter of the Pan-Asiatic Movement' and the DCI made arrangements to keep a watch on him. On arrival in India he fell in with a police agent.[133] In November 1918 the Calcutta police arrested him and found documents which proved his connection with the Indian revolutionary movement.[134] Worse, members of the Mitsui Busan Kaisha had agreed to take to Japan correspondence written on behalf of Bengali terrorists. The DCI concluded that 'the case of Kanokogi shows . . . that certain Japanese in India have behaved in a most improper and outrageous manner and that a great deal of suspicion was more than justified'.[135] This opinion was restrained. To the Government of India the Kanokogi case was the last straw. The Viceroy, Lord Chelmsford, informed the Secretary of State that

> The case of Kanokogi . . . has strikingly confirmed our apprehensions of the danger of a powerful section of the Japanese people, with or without their government's sanction, engaging in a campaign of spying and incitement to sedition in India itself.[136]

The evidence of widespread Japanese espionage in Asia which the Indian police provided was supported by the monthly intelligence summaries of the Intelligence Department of the General Staff at Singapore. Singapore intelligence, like the Government of India, found that it was not easy to substantiate this information, though the number of suspected cases of espionage was large.

The Straits Settlements (Singapore) Command also believed that the Japanese had done much spying in the Netherlands East Indies. According to Singapore intelligence, after the Russo-Japanese War Japanese military and naval officers made detailed studies of the islands with little attempt at concealment. The Japanese naval intelligence officer at Singapore later boasted of the efficiency of his espionage operations in Dutch territories.[137] Since then, 'Japanese spy stories, often absurdly exaggerated, but often founded on truth, [were] current in the East Indies'. By 1913 the Dutch regarded Japan with little short of terror. Moreover, as in India, the period saw a growth of unrest, in which Japanese 'adventurers' were implicated.[138]

In another important way the British intelligence agencies which had sprung up throughout the world after 1914 encouraged British suspicions of Japanese support for Asian nationalism. Throughout the war British intelligence in America and in the Far East provided information that many Indian revolutionary agents received their mail in Japan both in their own names and under the cover of Japanese addressees.[139] The Japanese government persistently failed to perform an adequate censorship over the Indians' mail and over certain anti-British publications.[140]

David Petrie was convinced that Japan was bent on expansion in China under the banner of Pan-Asianism. It was perhaps natural for an Indian officer to seize upon those utterances in the Japanese press which cast Japan in the role of protector of the Asiatic races living under colonial regimes. Yet Petrie's views were soundly based. His suspicions of Japanese policy were no more intense than those of Greene and Davidson.[141] In May 1918 he drew up a memorandum on Japan's encouragement of nationalism in Asia, which he admitted was 'only the expression of my own views on a new and comparatively unknown subject.' He wrote:

> I am conscious that a good deal of what I have written is of a highly controversial character and that even the Pan-Asiatic movement itself may be regarded in some quarters as a mere mare's nest. I am all the more anxious then, that my early and essentially tentative contribution to the subject should not be accepted as in any sense a final and authoritative pronouncement.[142]

Neither Petrie, nor Ridout who shared his views, were concerned as much with any immediate danger from Japan, as with the threat which its growing commercial and political involvement throughout the Far East posed in the long term. The Empire's experience of German plots during the war, which had been sustained by the German residents of the Netherlands East Indies, encouraged these views. Petrie wrote:

> We have seen the dangers of German 'peaceful penetration' in the past, and the Japanese are now pursuing a similar policy in the Straits Settlements and the Dutch East Indies.[143]

Petrie frankly referred to Japanese agents in the area as 'invaders' and maintained that the first task of the secret service in Japan was to obtain information about their 'inner activities'.

283

Petrie's fears of Japan coincided with and reinforced those of the Foreign Office. The Far Eastern Department wrote:

> Mr Petrie . . . conclusively shows that Pan-Asia . . . amounts to pure Pan-Japanism . . . She is out for her own hand: her own aggrandizement comes first, and, so far as this can be enhanced by the expulsion of the white man from Asia, just so far and no further is she Pan-Asiatic at heart. That is to say, so far as the more jingoistic Japanese are concerned, and there are very many jingoists in Japan these days.[144]

Sir John Jordan, the Ambassador at Peking, made the main criticism of Petrie's views. He distrusted the Japanese no less than Petrie, and recognized that 'China is in the melting pot and . . . is practically being put up to auction, with only one bidder at the sale . . .' None the less he did not agree with 'Petrie and others' who foresaw 'a great pan-Asiatic movement . . . under the direction of Japan'. In Jordan's opinion the war marked no more than 'a temporary eclipse of western influence'. But Jordan's opinions were based on two misconceptions. First, he believed that economic prosperity was making the Japanese soft, and that consequently they had started to decline as a military power. Second, he foresaw that Anglo-American co-operation in the Far East would deny the Japanese all possibility of expansion in China and thus encourage their decline as a major power. He concluded that after the war

> Great Britain and America . . . [would] represent the moral and material strength of the New World. Anglo-Saxon influence [would] dominate the East and China [would] turn to the people who will give her justice and fair play.[145]

Although Petrie's views found favour with the Foreign Office, the Department of Criminal Intelligence did not broadcast them as the official opinion of Indian intelligence. In the *Weekly Reports* of the Department of Criminal Intelligence which were drawn up under the supervision of Sir Charles Cleveland there were no references to Pan-Asianism. As late as May 1918 the DCI expressed a remarkably moderate opinion on the Japanese press. They reported that Japanese newspapers naturally took an anti-British point of view on certain issues but that on occasion they had printed articles which were very friendly to the British Empire. Thus the DCI held that it was 'dangerous to gauge the real attitude of a paper from any single article which it may publish'.[146]

Similarly, as late as 1918 the DCI communicated a report in which the writer stated that 'there is little or no anti-British feeling or sentiment anywhere in Japan and the people on the whole are very keen on maintaining intact the Anglo-Japanese Alliance'.[147] The DCI felt that the 'Pan-Asiatic party in Japan . . . and its disreputable left wing' were the main difficulty in the way of good relations with Japan. This was the most moderate interpretation possible at this date.[148] Indian intelligence as a whole, therefore, cannot be accused of promoting anti-Japanese feeling among the authorities in London and Delhi, who were by no means dependent upon a monolithic picture created by British intelligence in the Far East.

It is impossible to say to what precise extent imperial policies were influenced by the views of Petrie and Ridout. With regard to the suspicion of Japan which they encouraged, there is no doubt that they were preaching to the converted. The anxiety of those who interpreted British intelligence in the Far East, particularly of Petrie, Ridout, Davidson and Greene, corresponded closely with that of the makers of British policy in London and Delhi. In a *Memorandum on Anglo-Japanese Relations* for presentation to the Imperial Conference in March 1917, the British Foreign Office drew up a balance sheet in which Japan's services to the Allies in the war were weighed against its disservices. Japan's encouragement of 'the use of its territory as a focus of intrigue on the part of the most active and dangerous Indian seditionists' headed the list of points on which 'Japan has failed the Allies'. The Foreign Office held that the disservices outweighed the services. They concluded that at best Japanese policy in the war was opportunist and that at worst Japan was 'bent on pursuing a *realpolitik* as evil as Prussia's'. In support of this conclusion the Foreign Office wrote that the acts of successive Japanese governments, the speeches of many prominent public figures combined with intelligence reports received from many sources 'prove that national aspirations [were] being followed up by methods almost identical with those employed by the Germans'.[149] These opinions were no less hostile to Japan than those of the other Departments of State in Whitehall.

On the other hand, even at the end of 1917 not all the departments represented on the interdepartmental intelligence committee dealing with the Far East were convinced of Japanese official dishonesty.

Yet this moderation was not warranted. To see why this was so it is necessary to return to the adventures of Vincent Kraft.

In the second half of 1917 Kraft went on an important secret service mission in Mexico. Even after the exposure of the Zimmermann telegram in which the Germans had proposed an offensive alliance with Mexico in the event of the United States entering the war on the Allied side, the German Foreign Office continued its plot to stir President Carranza to attack the United States. More importantly, as Kraft revealed, the Germans wanted to implicate Japan in support of German plots.[150] In March 1918 Kraft and Lieutenant Oelsner were despatched to Japan on the secret mission referred to in the previous section of this Chapter. Ambassador Greene hoped to use Kraft's services to penetrate the Japanese dealings with Indian revolutionaries.[151] However, the Director of Naval Intelligence, Admiral 'Blinker' Hall, and the Director of Military Intelligence, General Macdonogh, disregarded Greene's opinions because they felt it to be unethical not to inform their Japanese ally of enemy activities on his doorstep.[152] On 22 March a Japanese newspaper revealed discoveries made about German activities in Japan and warned of Kraft's imminent arrival there under a codename.[153] Greene wrote that 'I was hardly prepared for so drastic a breach of confidence' by the Japanese Foreign Office.[154]

The Kraft episode is typical of a disquieting disregard for British susceptibilities displayed by Japanese high officials which continued after the war. A Japanese national named Hideo Nakao had worked for the German secret service in Mexico at the same time as Kraft. His activities were exposed in the San Francisco conspiracy trial which led to the conviction of most of the members of the Ghadr Party in the United States. Hideo Nakao escaped to Japan where his movements were watched by Davidson's agents. The British informed the Japanese government of Nakao's presence with a view to obtaining his deportation, which was clearly in accordance with the law. Instead Nakao disappeared, only to be found by British intelligence working for the Japanese government at Vladivostok. The Government of India concluded that this discovery confirmed that 'he was all along in the employment of the Japanese government'.[155]

The most obvious influence of intelligence on imperial foreign policy is revealed in the Indian 'Brief about Japan' at the Conference of Versailles. This consisted of nine articles of complaint. Eight of them were concerned with the Japanese encouragement of the Indian revolutionary movement and espionage against India.[156] The Government of India concluded;

> It is hard to resist the conclusion that the Japanese Government's inaction and assistance given by individual Japanese to individual revolutionaries [amount to] a deliberate policy favouring Indian revolutionary attempts to embarrass us during the war.[157]

Perhaps it is not legitimate to ask what would have been the consequences to the British Empire had no intelligence service developed in the Far East during the war. British political intelligence agencies grew up there in response to the immediate military threat posed by German and Indian plotters between 1914 and 1916. In this field British intelligence was very successful in defending the Empire, though the completeness of its success was due to the lack of co-ordination and over-ambition of its adversaries. But Germany's campaign of subversion in the Far East left the Empire with both an awareness of its vulnerability and with intelligence agencies dedicated to seeking out any potential threat.

It is important to consider what would have happened if British intelligence worldwide had not been so vigilant in seeking out evidence of Japanese 'misdeeds'. Undoubtedly the trust of the imperial authorities in London and Delhi in their Japanese ally would have been less easily undermined. The deep sense of outrage felt throughout British governing circles at Japan's conduct during the war was nurtured by a complex of indications of Japanese 'treachery' provided by intelligence in Japan, China, the Straits Settlements, North America and India, of which the suspected shielding of Rash Behari Bose by the Japanese government was just the most obvious and emotive example. This evidence as a whole seemed at the time to prove conclusively that Japan could not be trusted as an ally. Much has been said of the shock and anger of the Japanese at Britain's abrupt termination of the Anglo-Japanese Alliance at the Washington Conference of 1921. But on the British side the feeling was widespread and deep that Japan was not fit to be an ally.

Whatever the moral factors guiding Britain's decision to end the Alliance, that decision was primarily based on rational calculations. Here too the influence of British intelligence is clear. The most important impression created by British intelligence in the Far East in its complexity was not any set view of Japan's exploitation of 'Pan-

Asianism', or of the untrustworthiness of all Oriental governments, but an overwhelming sense of imperial weakness.

Since concern about imperial vulnerability led to the development of British intelligence in the Far East it is natural to suspect that this encouraged exaggerated British perceptions of the real threats to their interests in the area. But, in fact, there was a fundamental difference between Britain's attitudes to Indian and German plots, which by the end of 1916 it knew to be futile, and its justified anxiety about Japanese intentions following the presentation of the Twenty-One Demands. Intelligence did not create a strong distrust of the aims of Japanese foreign policy on the part of the imperial government. This distrust had existed before the war and had been greatly increased in 1915.[158] In warning of Japanese espionage, British intelligence only underlined what was written on the wall by the end of the First World War. Japanese power had grown greatly in Asia and rivalled that of the British Empire. Further Japanese expansion in China was a likelihood in the long term, which the Empire alone could not stop. In paying heed to their intelligence services in the Far East, the British governments in London and Delhi refused to bury their heads in the sand.

However, British intelligence in Japan might be accused of paying too much attention to issues which were ultimately trivial. Above all, it is arguable that the case of Rash Behari Bose should never have been allowed to assume real importance in the deterioration of Anglo-Japanese relations during and after the war. However, this case was hardly an isolated example. British suspicions of Japan which centred on this case were supported by a large number of reports from British intelligence around the world about Japanese espionage. However, during the First World War the at best ambivalent attitude of the Japanese government towards Indian revolutionaries, of which the Indian secret service gave ample details, was seen by the British as one of the most clear-cut cases of Japanese malevolence. Thus the development of the Indian intelligence system in the Far East had consequences which went far beyond the surveillance of Indian revolutionaries.

If British intelligence in the Far East encouraged fears of imperial weakness, these fears were justified and the overall picture created by British intelligence was objective. The great variety of human intelligence agencies supplying reports on Japan, and the universality of their hostility to Japan, probably strengthened the influence of intelligence on policy. By 1917 British intelligence in the Far East, which had been virtually non-existent on the outbreak of war, had, as the case of Japan shows, become an essential factor in the formulation of British foreign policy at an imperial level. Equally, by this date the imperial government recognized that the various intelligence agencies in the Far East played a vital role in imperial defence.

NOTES

1. There are a vast number of intelligence reports relating to the Indian problem throughout the world, but particularly in the Far East, from 1915 to 1919 in the Foreign Office Series entitled 'Hindu Agitations', which is contained in volumes PRO FO371 2493–97, 2784–91, 3063–9, 3422–7 and 4243–4.
2. *Sedition among the Sikhs at Hankow*, in HDA: Aug. 1914, nos. 2–6, IOLR IOR.POS. 7147. *Spread of the Ghadr Movement in the Far East. Scheme for placing an Officer from India in charge generally of sedition in Siam, Dutch East Indies, Philippine Islands, China and Japan.* HDB: Oct. 1915, nos. 369–74, IOLR IOR.POS.9840.
3. *Proposal that a Secret Agent be sent to Siam to investigate and report on Indian sedition there. Despatch of Mr Petrie to Siam in connection with the appointment of an Indian Secret Agent there*, in HDB: Aug. 1915, nos. 414–39, IOLR IOR.POS.9840.
4. PRO FO371 2493 (101405), Minute Paper. Even as late as 1918 the British were concerned that the Germans might find support among the Arab population of the islands. Series PRO FO228, Embassy and Consular Archives: Peking Legation and Embassy, Vol. 3210, Secret Intelligence: Naval Intelligence Slips, no. 279. Slip signed F.C.T. Tudor, Commander-in-Chief, China Station, dated 9 Oct. 1918.
5. Memorandum by Cleveland of 28 July 1914 in *Plot connected with the seditious movement to poison British officials at Shanghai*, in HDA: Aug. 1914, nos. 7–14, IORL IOR.POS.7147. *Question of establishing Intelligence Agencies at Hankow and other places*, in HDA: Sept. 1914, no. 210, IOLR IOR.POS.7148.
6. For example, *Discussion as to the best means of exercising effective control over Indians returning from America and the Far East via Colombo*, in HDA: April 1915, nos. 96–300, IOLR IOR.POS.7151.
7. For details of German and Indian plots see T.G. Fraser, 'Germany and Indian Revolution, 1914–1918', in *Journal of Contemporary History*, Vol. 12, No. 2 (1977). For the contribution of the British Navy in preventing German arms shipments in 1915 see telegram from the Naval C in C, Singapore to Admiralty, 5 August 1915, in PRO FO371 2494 (109583), and telegram from the Viceroy of 11 Aug. 1915, in PRO FO371 2494 (109157).
8. Foreign Office, Confidential Print, no. 11697, *Memorandum Respecting Japan and the East Indies.*
9. From Dering, Bangkok, to Ridout, Singapore, dated 12 April 1916, in Foreign Office Series PRO FO628, Thailand: General Correspondence, Vol. 33, file 352.
10. There are many documents on Siam in FO Series FO371, 'Hindu Agitations'. See particularly Letter from Crosby to Grey, 29 April 1915, in PRO FO371 2493 (79215); letter and enclosures from Dering to Foreign Office, 6 and 7 Aug. 1915, in FO371 2495; (128631/128633); letter from Dering to FO, dated 8 Sept. 1915, in FO371 2496 (149891); letter from Dering to FO, 25 Oct. 1915, in FO371 2497 (182522); 'Weekly note for the information of the Viceroy in letter from A. Hirtzel, India Office, to FO, in FO371 2784 (3761); letter from Dering to FO, 12 June 1916, in FO371 2788 (145020); letter from Dering to FO, 28 Aug. 1916, in FO371 2789 (201170); letter from Dering to FO, 27 July 1917, in FO371 3068 (176681). The work of Trotter and Whiting was praised by the Government of India after the war. Chelmsford Papers, telegrams

to and from the Secretary of State, 1917, IOLR MSS.EUR.E.264/8, part I, page 341; ibid., part II, pp. 466–7; India Office Library and Records.

11. Undated memorandum by the Manila Consulate on its Secret Service activities, PRO FO371 2785 (39674).

12. In October 1915, Beckett wrote:

> It has been, I believe, entirely due to his [Oren's] information as to a German plot against our Indian Empire that the resultant extensive precautionary measures have been taken, and the Government of India are now, aided by other supplementary information, well on their guard against any surprise attack. I have received letters from the Government of India expressing their warm appreciation of and their gratitude for the assistance thus rendered.

Though 'Oren' was certainly useful to the British, this claim is exaggerated. The British were now aware of the extent of German plots because of the information which they had gathered in America, Burma, and Europe, as well as India itself. Letter from Beckett to Grey, 28 Oct. 1915, FO 371/2497 (183235).

13. For details of the mutiny see R.W.E. Harper and Harry Miller, *Singapore Mutiny* (Singapore: Oxford University Press, 1984).

14. Letter from War Office to India Office, 7 March 1916, in *Deputation of Mr D. Petrie as Intelligence Officer for the Far East in connection with Indian Sedition*, in HDA: June 1916, nos. 285–95, IOLR IOR.POS.7297.

15. Letter from Ridout to War Office, 18 Aug. 1915, in PRO CO273, Singapore Correspondence, Vol. 435.

16. See reports by the Singapore agent drawn up in June 1915, in HDB: Aug. 1915, nos. 414–39, op. cit., and letter from Dering to Foreign Office, in PRO FO371 2494 (105135).

17. Memorandum from the Consulate-General, Manila, to the Foreign Office, 2 Dec. 1915, in Foreign Office Series PRO FO115/1908. *General Report on the German and Indian revolutionary movements in the Philippine Islands*, in PRO FO371 2787 (120162).

18. Letters from Consul-General Beckett, Batavia, to the Foreign Office, 28 Oct. 1916 and from Ridout to War Office, 11 Jan. 1917 in PRO FO371 2790 (247617).

19. *Correspondence on the subject of the deputation of Hector R. Kothavala, Deputy Superintendent, Bombay Presidency, to the Straits Settlements Government*, in HDB: Nov. 1916, nos. 389–406, IOLR IOR.POS.10511.

20. Ibid. Letter from Ridout to War Office, 5 Oct. 1915. Letter from Ridout to Chief of General Staff, Simla, India, 7 Oct. 1919 in *Grant of leave to Mr Kothavala*, in HDA: Jan. 1920, nos. 129–50A, IOLR IOR.POS.8622.

21. Telegram from Beckett, Batavia, 30 July 1915 in PRO FO371 2495 (124371).

22. Letter from Col. French, MI1(a), to Foreign Office, 16 Feb. 1918 in PRO FO371 3423 (51442).

23. Memorandum by Rayment, Newby and Wallinger, 13 Nov. 1917, in PRO FO371 3069 (223219).

24. Continuation of memorandum by Rayment, Newby and Wallinger in PRO FO371 3069 (23290).

25. As soon as he arrived in the Netherlands East Indies he wrote to Consul-General Beckett offering to work as a British informer. Beckett, however, did not trust him. Letter from Beckett to Grey, 30 July 1915, in PRO FO371 2495 (124971); telegram from Ridout to War Office, 23 Sept. 1915, in PRO FO371 2495 (135663).

26. See Fraser, 'Germany and Indian Revolution', op. cit.

27. However, David Petrie, the head of Indian Intelligence in the Far East from 1915 to 1918 'distrusted and disliked' Kraft. '"X" is an impostor and a humbug. At no stage has he ever been actuated by anything except the most sordid of pecuniary motives.' Letter from Petrie to Cleveland, 9 April 1918, in PRO FO228 2944.

28. See various references to 'X' in the *Weekly Reports* of the Director of Criminal

Intelligence.

29. Letter from Ridout to the Governor, Straits Settlements, 6 Jan. 1916, in PRO FO371/2784, (32430).
30. On the other hand, the Consul at the town of Chiengmai on the Burmese border showed more initiative. By October 1915 he had two Indian 'informants' at his disposal. Memorandum on Laddha Singh, PRO FO628 31, file 345.
31. Memorandum by Cleveland, 27 Sept. 1915, in HDB: Aug. 1915, nos. 414–39, op. cit.
32. A later copy of the Ghadr Directory is contained in IOLR V/27/262/6 (New Delhi, 1934).
33. Memorandum by Petrie 9 Feb. 1916 in *Sedition in the Far East. Proposed deputation of Mr D. Petrie, Superintendent of Police, Punjab and Criminal Investigation Department, as Indian Intelligence Officer in the Far East*, H.D.(A): Feb. 1916, nos. 496–514, IOLR IOR.POS.7296.
34. An outline of this scheme received the authorization of the Secretary of State for India on 16 Sept. 1915. Telegram from Secretary of State, 16 Sept. 1915, in *Spread of the Ghadr Movement in the Far East. Scheme for placing an officer from India in charge generally of sedition in Siam, Dutch East Indies, Philippine Islands, China and Japan*, HDB: Oct. 1915, nos. 369–74, IOR.POS.9840.
35. Memorandum by Petrie, Feb. 1916, in HDA: Feb. 1916, nos. 496–514, op. cit.
36. *Historical Sketch of the Directorate of Military Intelligence During the Great War, 1914–1919*, in PRO WO32 10776 XCA 8181.
37. Beckett had, however, been vigorous and capable in his surveillance of German plotters. He controlled the double agent 'Oren'. Early in 1915 the Government of India refused to provide him with the £100 secret service allowance which he had requested. Letter from W.A.D. Beckett to Foreign Office, 30 July 1915, in PRO FO371 2495 (124371).
38. Undated Foreign Office Minute Paper of early 1916 in PRO FO371 2786 (82056).
39. Foreign Office Minute Paper of October 1916, in PRO FO371 2790 (247617).
40. Letter from War Office, 7 March 1916; note by the Secretary, Judicial and Public Department on Inter-Departmental Conference held at the India Office on 10 March 1915; minute by Admiral Hall, 7 March 1916 in *Deputation of Mr D. Petrie as Intelligence Officer for the Far East in connection with Indian sedition*, in HDA: June 1916, nos. 285–95, IOLR IOR.POS.7297.
41. Telegram from Munro Ferguson, Governor-General of Australia, to the Secretary of State for the Colonies, 25 June 1916; Minute Paper by Admiral Hall, Director of Intelligence Division, Admiralty, 4 July 1916. PRO FO371/2787 (124426).
42. Memorandum by 'Blinker' Hall, DID, 4 July 1916, in FO371 2787 (124426). Not surprisingly the Australians were resentful of their exclusion from the imperial intelligence system. The Governor-General wrote that 'It is difficult to imagine how absolutely in the dark this government was at the commencement of this war as to all that was going on to the north of Australia. This lasted till we were sent Germans for internment from Ceylon and Singapore . . . The only current news obtainable is on the return of Australian destroyers from patrolling northern waters . . .' Letter from R.N. Ferguson, to Colonial Secretary, 2 Aug. 1916, in PRO FO371 2789 (1911235).
43. However, Petrie was placed in close communication with Robert Nathan, the Indian officer in North America.
44. Letter from Ridout to War Office, 3 May 1916 in PRO FO371 23786 (85175).
45. Greene had suggested that the Indian government should send a secret agent to Japan as early as June 1914. Telegram from Greene, Tokyo, to Jordan, Peking, 20 June 1914, in FO228/2299.
46. Memorandum by Petrie, 28 March 1916, in *Proposed deputation of Mr Petrie as Intelligence Officer for the Far East in connection with sedition*, in H.D.(A): April 1916, nos. 89–91, IOR.POS.7296.

47. *Note on a recent tour in the Far East*, by Petrie, 4 Dec. 1916, in FO371 3065 (63504).
48. Letter from Ridout to War Office, 26 May 1916, in *Further correspondence regarding the deputation of Mr Petrie as Intelligence Officer in the Far East in connection with Indian sedition*, H.D.(A): April 1917, nos. 370–82, IOR.POS.8611.
49. Hankow and Nanking: Petrie to Jordan, 28 Aug. 1916, PRO FO228/2702 (no. 80).
50. Telegram from Jordan to Foreign Office, 11 Aug. 1916, PRO FO228/2702 (69).
51. Letter from War Office to Colonial Office, 30 Aug. 1923, in PRO CO537, Supplementary Correspondence, Vol. 757.
52. Note signed 'W.W.G.', 16 Jan. 1918, in PRO FO228 2944.
53. Letter from Alston, Peking, to Foreign Office, PRO FO228 2703 (no. 16).
54. *Note on a recent tour in the Far East*, op. cit.
55. Ibid., pp. 4–5.
56. Telegram from Consul-General Fraser, 8 Oct. 1916, and memorandum by MI1(a), in PRO FO371 2789 (200623).
57. He played an insignificant role in the meetings of the Shanghai Intelligence Bureau which was formed at the end of 1916.
58. The first documentary reference about him is for 22 Nov. 1915.
59. Jordan continued: 'Captain Seigne finds no difficulty in disposing of the recent trouble with the Shanghai Arsenal and of apportioning to Japanese and Germans their respective shares in this adventure. He asserts that the late Admiral Tseng was the only official at Shanghai who was not in German pay and that Germans and Chinese rebels conjointly arranged for his assassination.' From Jordan, Peking, to Foreign Office, 19 Jan. 1916, PRO FO228 2672. As early as November 1915 the Governor of Hong Kong was complaining about the way in which Seigne was discharging his duties as Naval Staff Officer at Shanghai. From Alston, Peking, to Singapore, 29 July 1917, PRO FO228 2674 (no. 49).
60. Minute by Col. French of MI1(a) in PRO FO371 2790 (217693). Note on telegram from Shanghai to Peking, PRO FO228 2703 (no. 55).
61. From Alston, Peking, to Singapore, 29 July 1917, PRO FO228 2674.
62. Admiral Hall, the Director of Naval Intelligence, did not lose faith in Seigne. On 21 June 1917 Captain Seigne informed the Intelligence Bureau that 'in view of the importance attached by the Admiralty to the activities of Sun Yat Sen, a private arrangement [had] been made by his office, irrespective of steps previously taken by the Bureau, to have Sun's house watched'.
63. Telegram from Shanghai to Peking, 22 June 1917, PRO FO228 2674 (no. 42).
64. There were no other European officers in the section, which even in 1910 was considered to be under strength. Letter from Barrett to the Captain Superintendent of Police, 11 March 1915. PRO FO228 2299, no. 40.
65. Note by Wilkinson, Consul, Hankow, entitled 'Sedition Amongst Sikhs at Hankow', 21 May 1914, in PRO FO228 2299.
66. Undated letter from K. McEuen to Fraser, PRO FO228 2703 (no. 70).
67. Report entitled 'Indian sedition in Shanghai during 1916' by E.M. Barrett, 13 Jan. 1917, PRO FO228 2703 (no. 70).
68. Letter from E.I.M. Barrett, to the Captain Superintendent of Police, 11 March 1915. PRO FO228 2299, no. 40.
69. From Fraser to Jordan, 27 Oct. 1916, PRO FO228 2703 (no. 16).
70. Ibid.
71. Foreign Office Minute Paper, Oct. 1916, in PRO FO371 2790 (217693).
72. Within Shanghai he complained about McEuen's attitude before the Consul-General and other British officers.
73. Telegram from Ambassador Jordan, Peking, 14 Oct. 1916 in PRO FO371 2789 (205875). Telegram from Jordan, 30 Oct. 1916, in PRO FO371 2790 (217693).
74. From Fraser to Jordan, 27 Oct. 1916, PRO FO228 2703 (no. 16).

75. Ibid.
76. A large number of reports of the weekly meetings of the Shanghai Bureau and of the suspects' history sheets which it drew up are contained in Series FO228, Embassy and Consular Archives: Peking Legation and Embassy.
77. Telegram from Foreign Office to Jordan, Peking, 9 Nov. 1917 in PRO FO371 2790 (23808).
78. Letter from Naval Intelligence Division to Foreign Office, 14 Nov. 1916, in PRO FO371 2790 (223808).
79. Notes on Intelligence Bureau meeting of 8 March 1917, in PRO FO228 2706.
80. Telegram from Alston, Peking, 6 Jan. 1917 in PRO FO371 3063 (5205).
81. Owing to the lack of experienced Indian intelligence officers, there was no possibility of his having a deputy. From Consulate-General, Shanghai, to Alston, Peking, PRO FO228 2704 (no. 36). Home Department, Government of India, to Jordan, Peking, 10 Feb. 1917, PRO FO228 2703 (no. 125).
82. Memorandum by Petrie, dated February 1916, in H.D.(A): Feb. 1916, nos. 496–514, op. cit.
83. Letter from Beckett, Batavia, 28 Oct. 1916, in PRO FO371 2790 (217363).
84. Letter from the Director of Criminal Intelligence to the Secretary to the Government of India, Home Department, 21 Nov. 1917, in *Grant of pensions to the family of late Sub-Inspector Harnam Singh, who was assassinated at Nankin*, in H.D.(A): April 1918, nos. 140–5 and K.W., IOR.POS.8616.
85. Petrie noted that 'it seems almost to have been a case of *Quem deus perdere vult, prius dementat*'. He maintained that while irresponsible, Harnam Singh had been an intelligent and potentially capable man. Letter from Petrie to Alston, 23 April 1917, in PRO FO228 2704.
86. 'God first makes mad him whom he wishes to lose'.
87. Letter from Giles, Consul, Nanking, to Alston, Peking, 3 Feb. 1917, PRO FO228 2703 (no. 113).
88. Letter from W.F. Handley-Derry to Hoare, dated 5 March 1917; and letter from Wilkinson, Hankow, to Fraser, Shanghai, 27 Feb. 1917, FO228 , no. 11.
89. Letter from J.W. Nelson, Department of Criminal Intelligence, to D.S.B., Karachi, 20 March 1917, in *Alleged smuggling of arms into India by German-Indian plotters*, HDB: June 1917, nos. 521–32. IOLR IOR.POS.10513.
90. In February 1917, for example, the Consul-General at San Francisco reported that the Ghadr Party were trying to send 50,000 rifles from islands in the Pacific to India enclosed in teak logs. None the less the Government of India ordered precautions to be taken.
91. Telegram from General Ridout to the Secretary, War Office, 22 Nov. 1916, in PRO FO371 2791 (263555).
92. *Note on a recent tour in the Far East*, op. cit., p. 4.
93. The Naval General Staff at Singapore reported that with two exceptions 'The Far East was not visited by any itinerant conspirator of the first rank in 1917'. Memorandum by Admiral F.C.T. Tudor, 20 May 1918, FO228 3210 (no. 251).
94. Note by Colonel French of MI1(a), 17 Jan. 1917, in PRO FO371 2791 (263555). In the end, however, the interdepartmental committee decided that double agents should be fed into the hypothetical German secret service network in China by the Shanghai Bureau.
95. Letter from the Director of Military Intelligence to Ridout, 13 Jan. 1917, in PRO FO371 3063 (7078).
96. For details of the Intelligence Staff at Singapore see *Confidential War Diary of the General Staff, Straits Settlements Command*, for February 1919, in FO371 4244 (66005).
97. Letter from Petrie to Cleveland, 9 April 1918, PRO FO228 2944.
98. The representatives of the interdepartmental committee in London were more

sanguine about the danger from German plots than either Petrie or Ridout. In answer to Petrie's complaints, Major John Wallinger, the representative of the DCI in London, wrote to Cleveland on 29 June 1918: 'If we stop the Germans from spending thousands of pounds on wild-cat schemes for stirring up trouble in India which are so hair-brained as to be almost impossible of success, and can in any case be supervised by us, the time, energy and money which they undoubtedly do spend at present in this fashion will be diverted onto schemes and into channels of which we would be completely in ignorance, and which might ultimately prove a far greater danger to the Empire as whole than all their present machinations can ever be'. Letter from Wallinger to Cleveland, 29 June 1918, PRO FO228 2944.

99. Report by F. Ashton-Gwatkin entitled *The Japanese in the South Seas: A Historical Sketch*, in Yokohama Consulate Correspondence: From India and Singapore. PRO FO262 1419.

100. In their *Brief Against Japan* for presentation at the Versailles Peace Conference, the Government of India claimed: 'We know that Germany attempted to subsidize certain Japanese papers to publish attacks on Great Britain. The fact that such attacks were allowed at all in the press of an Allied country is significant enough.' *The Indian Brief Against Japan* [at the Conference of Versailles] in Yokohama Consulate Correspondence: From India and Singapore, PRO FO262 1419.

101. The consequences of Japanese protection of Indian revolutionaries in Japan are discussed in T.G. Fraser, 'India in Anglo-Japanese Relations during the First World War', in *History*, Vol. 63, No. 209 (October 1978). Fraser criticizes the British government in London – he does not mention what the Government of India thought about Japan – for what he sees as their absurd narrow-mindedness in letting the Bose case harm Anglo-Japanese relations. Fraser's argument, however, fails on a number of grounds. Most importantly he does not discuss the numerous shocks to the Anglo-apanese Alliance which occurred during 1915, or the various subsequent actions of Japanese foreign policy which Britain saw as a danger to the Empire. The British never attached importance to the shielding of Indian revolutionaries in Japan alone. It had significance only when set against the background of the Japanese threat to China and of Japanese espionage throughout the Pacific and in India, which he does not mention. Moreover Japanese protection of Indian revolutionaries was a serious matter in itself. The Empire's defences were very weak during the war and Rash Behari Bose had already shown how much damage a single terrorist could do. The shielding of German agents was hardly to be expected of Britain's ally. Finally, Fraser describes the British secret service in Japan as incompetent on the basis of one insignificant piece of evidence: the reporting on one another of agents 'P' and 'Q'. That amusing situation continued for only a very short time.

102. For details of British efforts to have the Indians arrested and their escape see: letter from T.W. Holderness, India Office, to Foreign Office, dated 17 Sept. 1915, and Foreign Office Minute Paper, in PRO FO371 2495 (133802); undated Foreign Office Minute Paper of Autumn 1915, in FO371 2496 (1475350); Foreign Office Minute Paper by R. Sperling, 26 Nov. 1915, in FO371 2496 (178747); telegram from Greene to Foreign Office, 2 Dec. 1915 and Foreign Office Minute Paper, in FO371 2497; telegram from Greene to Foreign Office, 5 Jan. 1916 and Foreign Office Minute Paper, 19 Feb. 1916, in which Beilby Alston concluded: 'The Japanese government have certainly not acted as allies in any sense over this case – and their attitude in regard to it is in keeping with the trend of public opinion in that country'; FO371 2784 (31444).

103. The defeat of a European power by Japan in the Russo-Japanese war was widely held to have stimulated Indian nationalism. But fear of Indian revolutionaries drawing inspiration from Japan and of Japan courting the favour of the Indian nationalist movement did not greatly concern the British before the First World War. The Government of India heard many accounts of the strong racial prejudice shown by the Japanese

to Indians living in Japan. Moderate Indian nationalists were disillusioned by Japan's expansionist policy in Korea. The subject of Japanese influence on Indian opinion is discussed, for example, in the *Weekly Report* for 10 Aug. 1907, in HDB: Aug. 1907, nos. 135–45. IOLR IOR.POS.8959.

104. Undated Minute Paper in PRO FO371 2786 (85175).
105. Memorandum from Davidson to Secretary, Home Department, Government of India, 26 April 1915, in PRO FO371 2493 (77951). Letter from Davidson to Viceroy, 16 Aug. 1915, in FO371 2496 (150249).
106. *Report on a recent tour*, op. cit., p. 7.
107. On only one occasion, however, did they inform upon one another. Letter from Greene to Foreign Office, 15 Jan. 1917, in PRO FO371 3065 (40716).
108. Letter from Greene to Foreign Office, 10 Oct. 1916, and report by agent P., 4 Nov. 1917, in PRO FO371 2790 (234310). Letter from Davidson to Greene, 24 Jan. 1917, in FO371 3066 (644778).
109. Note by Davidson, 28 Nov. 1916, in PRO FO371 3063 (8834).
110. Ibid. Letter from Greene, to Foreign Office, 7 Dec. 1917, in PRO FO371 3064 (31152).
111. On one occasion 'P' gave dinner to Mr Shonobu of the Japanese Foreign Office along with the nationalist writers Oshikawa and Okawa. Report by Agent P., 30 Sept. 1917, in PRO FO371 3069 (216196).
112. Samejima's first report was submitted to Davidson on 12 Jan. 1917. PRO FO371 3065 (40716).
113. The second agent, 'Sa', was engaged in August 1917. Letter from Davidson, dated 27 Sept. 1917, in PRO FO371 3069 (216183).
114. Letter from Davidson, dated December 1918, in PRO FO371 4244.
115. Letter from Davidson, 18 June 1917, in PRO FO115 2235 (236).
116. Letter from Davidson, 18 June 1917, in PRO FO115 2236.
117. At the end of 1917 the highest numbered codename on record at Yokohama was 'A15'.
118. Telegram from the Viceroy, 19 Sept, 1919, in Yokohama Consulate Correspondence: From India and Singapore, PRO 262 1419.
119. YUL Papers, Series I, Box 6, Folder 177, 'List of salaries and other monthly expenditure' of MI1(c) in the USA, 27 Jan. 1918.
120. For example, letter from Greene, to Foreign Office, dated March 1917, in PRO FO371 3066.
121. Letters from Davidson, dated August 1917, in PRO FO371 3069 (162957) and FO371 3068 (182541).
122. Davidson's views are summarized in a memorandum entitled *Japan's policy towards India, 1915–1917*, drawn up by the India Office in June 1918. PRO FO371 3424 (102176).
123. There are many Japanese police surveillance reports on the secret societies in Library of Congress, Washington.
124. *The Indian Brief Against Japan*, op. cit.
125. Report by Ashton-Gwatkin entitled *The Japanese in the South Seas, A Historical Sketch*, March 1919, in Yokohama Consulate Correspondence: From India and Singapore, FO262 1419.
126. Letter from the Government of India to the Secretary of State, 4 May 1917, in British Foreign Office Confidential Print, no. 123198.
127. In *The Indian Brief Against Japan*, op. cit., the Government of India stated that the movements of Japanese agents in Tibet and on the frontier in particular caused them to view with distrust all Japanese visitors whose business and occupation were not fully established.
128. *Weekly Report* of the Director of Criminal Intelligence, 16 June 1919, in HDB 1919, nos. 701–4. IOLR IOR.POS.10516.

129. See the *Weekly Reports* of the Director of Criminal Intelligence.
130. *Weekly Report* for 9 Sept. 1916, in HDB: Sept. 1916, nos. 652–6, IOLR IOR.POS. 10511.
131. *Weekly Report* for 21 Oct. 1916.
132. *The Indian Brief Against Japan*, op. cit.
133. Telegram from the Viceroy, Foreign Department, to the Foreign Office, 26 Feb. 1919, in PRO FO371 4244.
134. *Weekly Report* 3 March 1919, in HDB: April 1919, nos. 148–52. IOLR IOR.POS. 10515.
135. *Weekly Report* dated 16 June 1919, in HDB: June 1919, nos. 701–4. IOLR IOR.POS. 10516.
136. Telegram from Viceroy to Secretary of State, dated 2 December 1918, in Chelmsford Papers, IOLR MSS.EUR.E.264/9.
137. *Memorandum respecting Japan and the East Indies*, 8 Sept. 1921, in Confidential Print no. 11697.
138. Ashton-Gwatkin, in a report dated 24 March 1919, pointed to the connection of the Japanese with the nationalist Sarikat Islam organization. Yokohama Consulate Correspondence: From India and Singapore, PRO FO262 1419.
139. The Shanghai Intelligence Bureau also provided miscellaneous pieces of information about Japanese assistance to Indian revolutionaries. In the *Indian Brief Against Japan*, op. cit., the Government of India wrote that 'it is noticeable that Indian conspirators were helped by the Japanese in other parts of the Far East . . .'
140. *The Indian Brief Against Japan*, op. cit.
141. Davidson was convinced that if serious trouble broke out in India, the Japanese would exploit the situation by selling their aid at an exorbitant price to the British, or else they would break the Alliance and intervene on behalf of the rebels. FO371 2787.
142. Letter from Petrie to Cleveland, 16 May 1918, in PRO FO228 2947.
143. Ibid., p. 18.
144. Minute Paper, signed 'W.W.L.', 27 May 1918, in PRO FO228 2947.
145. Letter from Jordan to Langley, 29 May 1918, PRO FO350 16.
146. This opinion about the Japanese press was presented as that of 'a very high authority on all matters concerning modern Japan'. *Weekly Report*, 11 May 1918, in HDB: May 1918, nos. 581–4. IOLR IOR.POS.10514.
147. This report was entitled 'An Indian gentleman's views on Japan'. *Weekly Report*, 1 June 1918, in HDB: June 1918, nos. 491–4, IOLR IOR.POS.10514.
148. *Weekly Report*, 16 June 1919, in HDB: June 1919, nos. 701–4. IOLR IOR.POS.10516.
149. *Memorandum on Anglo-Japanese Relations*, dated March 1917, in Confidential Print, no. 10845.
150. Memorandum by Rayment, Newby and Wallinger, op. cit.
151. Telegram from Greene, Tokyo, 30 Nov. 1917, in PRO FO371 3369 (229390).
152. *Notes drafted by D.M.I. and D.I.D. for Lord R. Cecil to communicate if thought fit to Japanese Embassy*, in PRO FO371 3069 (234133).
153. PRO FO371 3424 (88360).
154. Ibid.
155. *The Indian Brief Against Japan*, op. cit.
156. These articles related to: the behaviour of Japanese in India; the harbouring of Indian revolutionaries in Japan during war; Hideo Nakao; the attacks on the Government of India in the Japanese press during war; the Kanokogi case. The last article in the list concerned Japan's unfair trading practices in India during the war.
157. Chelmsford Papers, telegram from Viceroy to Secretary of State, 29 Jan. 1919, IOLR MSS.EUR.E.264/10.
158. See, for example, *Memorandum on the Japanese occupation of Pacific Islands*, 22 Dec. 1915, in Confidential Print, no. 10777.

12

India, 1919–24

The world is in a state of extreme unrest and it is of utmost importance for government to have full information regarding that unrest. We surely ought to have learned the lessons the war has taught us, and be awake and on our guard.

Godfrey Denham, Shanghai, April 1920.[1]

Victory in the First World War did not bring peace for the Raj. By the end of 1919, the Government of India had to face a complexity of new threats which had emerged very rapidly. Most serious was the concerted opposition to British rule centred on the person of Gandhi and stretching thoughout British India. This was a far stronger movement than the short-lived unrest of 1907–8 and was the most serious challenge to the Raj since the Indian Mutiny of 1857.

At the same as internal security in India deteriorated, new foreign threats emerged, which might potentially have exploited the many grievances that had accumulated during the last years of the war. The most immediate danger came from Afghanistan, which invaded India in 1919. Japan represented another, though ill-defined, menace. The activities of Japanese agents in India and throughout South-East Asia were by no means a mortal threat to British power at this time, but they contributed to the Government of India's general state of unease. So, to a greater extent did the plotting of the Bolshevik regime which took power in Russia after the October Revolution of 1917. Immediately Lenin made clear his intention to undermine the British Empire by fostering revolution in India.

These were just the direct threats to the Raj. At the same time, the British Empire was faced with outbreaks of unrest elsewhere. In 1919, Egypt, which had been peaceful under British occupation since 1882, saw a series of nationalist demonstrations, though the British succeeded in suppressing them by the end of the year. In Ireland, however, outright rebellion had broken out in 1919. The fighting lasted until December 1921, when Ireland, with the exception of the six counties of the north, received dominion status. British rule in the south was effectively over.

Thus in 1919, the Raj found itself as vulnerable as it had been during the war. The question to be addressed in this chapter is to what extent did British intelligence heighten the government's sense of vulnerability, and to what extent did the complex of imperial intelligence agencies which emerged during the First World War continue to protect the Empire against internal and overseas threats, particularly by keeping India largely free from subversion by foreign powers? But, first, more needs to be said about the causes of Indian unrest.

An immediate cause of the unrest which shook India was the disruption which resulted from the war. By 1918, India was hit by serious economic dislocations which led to rampant inflation and a marked deterioration in living standards. Worse, summer that year brought the outbreak of a devastating influenza epidemic, which killed six million people according to official statistics, though the real number is likely to have been much higher. Another source of concern to the Government of India was the increasing demands put forward by the Indian National Congress, which by 1917 was calling for home rule within the British Empire. This was all the more serious because the Congress's strength was to grow exponentially under the leadership of Gandhi. In 1914, it had still been essentially a gentlemen's political club; in 1919 it was able to accomplish what had seemed impossible – the mobilization of a popular movement stretching throughout India.

The power of Indian nationalism was the product not only of Gandhi's leadership and tactics, but also of grave mistakes by the British. The first of these was the decision to shelve all debate about political change in India for the duration of the war. This only led to frustration on the part of moderate nationalists, and to the increase of their demands. More serious were a series of errors in the course of 1919, when the Raj reeled from disaster to disaster. In February the government introduced the so-called 'Rowlatt Act' into the Indian legislatures. This provided for the continuance of wartime powers of arrest into peacetime. It provided for the restriction of political suspects' movements, and even their imprisonment without trial.[2] The effect was disastrous. Indian moderates were outraged because they felt they were now being subjected to a potential police state regime which would be unthinkable in Britain. The Rowlatt Act put an important card in Gandhi's hand, since it enabled him to organize opposition at an all-India level; this was something which had not been seen before, even during the troubles of 1907. Gandhi set 6 April 1919 as his 'national day of humiliation'. The response was a series of strikes and political rallies in many towns throughout India.

What was the role of Indian intelligence in the formulation of the Rowlatt Act? The simple answer is, a very considerable one. The political police in India had gained influence during the war, although this was very temporary. The strategies which Sir Charles Cleveland had carried out had been very successful. He had been right to concentrate the scanty resources of the Indian police on the revolutionary movement at home before setting up an intelligence system in the Far East. Despite the claims of his critics in the United Province and in Bengal, he had behaved with restraint in conducting arrests. By 1915 he was an influential adviser to the government rather than the outcast which he had been before the war. Cleveland had a very close ally in Sir Reginald Craddock, the most able of the Viceroy's Council, who was Home Member from 1912 to 1917. Above all, the DCI had influence because it was the repository of information reaching India from different intelligence agencies abroad. The influence of the DCI was thus very marked in the drawing up of the Rowlatt Act.

Two important intelligence officers assisted Lord Chief Justice Rowlatt and his associates on the Sedition Committee, which enquired into the causes of the Indian revolutionary movement and drew up recommendations for dealing with it. The first was James Campbell Ker of the DCI. Ker was better aware than any man in India, apart from Cleveland, of the extent of the Indian revolutionary movement at home and abroad. From October 1914 to February 1917 he served on special duty at Army HQ, Simla, with the task of making a detailed study of the documents connected with the Indian revolutionary movement in India, Asia, Europe and America.[3] In December 1916, Cleveland suggested that he should be employed for six months on summarizing the information on record in the DCI on the 'political and revolutionary agitation in India since the year 1907'. This work was distributed to the government as *Political Trouble in India*.[4] From February to November 1917, Ker worked on special duty under the DCI, acting as assistant to the Sedition Committee.[5] After reading his documents, Rowlatt and his colleagues concluded that even before the war it was recognized that the forces of law and order working through the ordinary channels were beaten. We are convinced that that was the state of affairs even at that date.

The Bengal police also had a say in the drawing up of the anti-terrorist laws when, in November 1917, Charles Tegart was suddenly recalled to assist the Committee from the Western Front in Flanders, where he had volunteered for service.[6]

There is no doubt that the 'Rowlatt Act' was the product of the outlook of the police who, for the first time, were able to influence a political decision of wide importance. But the passing of the Act can only be explained if the attitude of the DCI and Home Department is understood. Their outlook is inexplicable if viewed in purely Indian terms. The seeming willingness of the police blindly to cause trouble for themselves by encouraging such unpopular legislation can only be explained by the worldwide threat posed by the Indian revolutionary movement and by the seriousness of the situation in Bengal in the years 1907–16. For indeed, the undermanned Bengal police had been losing the war against the terrorists until the Defence of India Act was passed. The Government of India, the India Office, and the police agreed that this should not happen again. The main reason for the passing of the Rowlatt Act was the Government of India's desire to keep existing suspects locked up, in order to avoid a recurrence of the Bengali terrorist problem at a time when conditions in India were so unsettled. The Liberal Secretary of State, Edwin Montagu, agreed to the Act reluctantly, but even he recognized that the danger of revolution could not be risked.[7]

A major problem with the Rowlatt Act was its timing. In a sense the police and the Government of India were the victims of their own success. By 1918, neither the terrorists of Bengal, nor the Indian revolutionaries abroad appeared a threat to the Raj. Furthermore, the Government of India had always tried to conceal from the public the extent of its wartime distress at the actions of the terrorists. The result was that few educated Indians understood the government's motives in introducing such obnoxious legislation. The cardinal mistake was to apply the Rowlatt Act not only to Bengal, but throughout India. It cannot be stressed too strongly that this momentous decision is inexplicable without reference to the virulence of German and Indian plotting against the Raj on worldwide level throughout the war. The Rowlatt Act was not so much an arrogant act by a victorious imperial power, as a recognition by the Indian police of their own weakness.

The second disaster of 1919 came in April. At this time the Punjab was in a state of great unrest. Riots were taking place and there was great agitation for Indian self-government. The situation was made worse by developments across the border in Afghanistan, which now had an anti-British Amir, Amanalluh. War with the Afghans seemed likely at any time. This was the background to the violence which took place in the city of Amritsar, the administrative capital of the Punjab.

On 13 April a vast crowd gathered for a political rally in the city's enclosed Jallianwalla Bagh gardens, even though the Local Government had banned all public meetings. The crowd was greeted by the local commanding officer, Brigadier-General Reginald Dyer, and his troops. Without warning, Dyer's men opened fire, killing 379 and wounding 1,200. Indian opinion was traumatized. Before the massacre, Gandhi and his many followers had hoped to co-operate with the British government which, under the Secretary of State, Edwin Montagu, and the Viceroy, Lord Chelmsford, promised a package of constitutional reforms. In response to the Amritsar massacre, Gandhi launched his Non-Co-operation Movement in 1920 with the backing of the Indian National Congress. Gandhi now eschewed all co-operation with what he described as an evil regime, and announced his intention of giving India self-government within a year. He called on Indians to boycott all association with the government, to refuse to pay taxes and to buy only native goods. His success was such that by the beginning of 1921 it seemed as if British rule in India was coming to an end.

There is no obvious connection between the operations of the DCI and CIDs, and the disastrous situation in the Punjab. Though the DCI provided the Government of India with daily reports on the situation in the province, there was little they could do to bring quiet to the province. The severe measures of martial law which the government imposed owed something to fears of a revival of the Ghadr movement, but the local CID reported that the old revolutionaries were not stirring.[8]

A third mistake of British imperial policy strengthened Gandhi's position. Over the course of 1919, it became clear that Britain intended to impose very harsh terms on the defeated Ottoman Empire. This led to great disquiet among Indian Muslims. For, while the overwhelming majority of Muslims had backed the Allied cause in the war, they viewed the demise of the last significant Muslim power in the world with horror. As Sultan-Caliph, the Ottoman ruler continued to have for them both a religious and a political significance. Few Indian Muslims viewed his possible elimination with calm. In 1919–20 a small group of Indian Muslims developed a fierce campaign for the rescue of the Ottoman Empire. The key leaders were the Pan-Islamist Ali brothers, whom the British had released from prison in 1919. The so-called Khilafat (Caliphate) Movement attracted a far wider base of support than the British had anticipated, given the loyalty of the Indian Muslim community during the war. Worse, in June 1920, Gandhi and the Khilafat leaders joined forces in the Non-Co-operation movement, which meant that not only was Gandhi leading an all-India movement, but also one which embraced both the major religious communities of the sub-continent.

Up to a point, the Khilafat Movement can be classified as an intelligence failure. As with the introduction of the Rowlatt Act, the Government of India and the DCI failed accurately to assess the strength of popular opinion, in this case Muslim attachment to the institution of the Caliphate. The absence of Pan-Islamic agitation after 1914 encouraged this error. Again, the police were the victims of their own success. An important reason for the weakness of Pan-Islamism during the war was the effectiveness of the security measures taken against the small group of Pan-Islamist leaders. None the less, the connection between Indian intelligence and the Khilafat Movement should not be pressed too far. The Government of India was concerned about the possible effects on Indian Muslims of the harsh measures which London was preparing to impose on the Ottoman Empire. Delhi had urged a restraint which Lloyd George's government at home ignored.

Already by the beginning of 1919, British rule in India was faced by serious unrest. The first foreign power to attempt to exploit the internal weaknesses of the Raj was Afghanistan. Throughout the war, the Amir, Habibullah, had sought to keep Afghanistan out of the conflict. But in 1918 his position was weakening, and pressure from the anti-British faction centred on his son, Amanullah. Habibullah had not made things easy for himself. First, he had squandered the money which the British had provided in order to keep his subjects sweet. Second, he had created enemies for himself through his over-developed taste for his subjects' wives and daughters. He was killed by an assassin in February 1919 and Amanullah seized the throne.

Amanullah's hatred of the British was even stronger than it had been during the war. He seriously believed that the Christian powers of Britain and France intended to destroy Islam. Furthermore, he greatly overestimated the weakness of British rule in India. He was encouraged in this view by a group of Indian revolutionaries under the Wahati leader, Obeidullah, who still resided in Kabul. Amanullah launched a propaganda campaign which played on Indian hostility to the Rowlatt Act and upon the outrage at the Amritsar Massacre. On 4 May 1919, Amanullah launched an invasion of India, which he hoped would lead to a great uprising in the Punjab.

The British were caught unawares by the invasion, which shows that their intelligence operations in Kabul were as ineffective as they had been during the war. Within the North-West Frontier Province bordering Afghanistan, however, the local CIDs operated quickly to arrest all the main Afghan and Indian agitators who might be working on Amanullah's behalf, and send them off to Burma. No risings took place in support of the Afghans, and by 13 May the India Army had vigorously repulsed Amanullah's invasion.

Despite the wishes of Amanullah, Gandhi and the Pan-Islamists, British rule in India was to last for another quarter century. Partly this was because many of the causes of the unrest were temporary. The economic distress did not last. Gandhi proved unable to keep his opposition to the Raj on a non-violent footing, calling off his first Non-Co-operation Movement in February 1922. The Khilafat Movement collapsed when Turkey's new leader, Musafa Kemal, abolished the Caliphate without any prompting from the British in 1924. But a key role in the survival of the Raj lay in the policies of the British rulers. Despite the Rowlatt Act, and despite the Amritsar Massacre, they essentially remained committed to the fundamental tenet which had guided their policies since the end of the nineteenth century: the need to conciliate moderate Indian opinion. A key component of this policy was to restrict the role of the political police in India.

The continuance of the threat from foreign-backed subversion which the British perceived did not lead to any change in official ideology. Neither the Government of India nor the India Office had any intention of ruling India through the police. In January 1918, the Secretary of State for India, Edwin Montagu, warned the Viceroy, Lord Chelmsford, that:

I have an uneasy feeling that the CID is being used not merely as a great detective agency, but as an instrument of government; that its activities are too widespread; that it is growing too rapidly; that it is convenient, but very dangerous, to govern by means of your police.[9]

Montagu stressed that the DCI and the CIDs must remain entirely criminal investigation departments and not meddle in politics. But his remarks about the size of the police were mistaken.

It is true that on 21 March 1918, the Government of India renamed the Department of Criminal Intelligence the Department of Central Intelligence.[10] Yet it continued to watch political criminals, not politicians in general. Besides the government's continuing need to conciliate Indian moderate opinion – particularly during the intro-duction of the Montagu–Chelmsford Reforms of 1919 – the activities of the DCI and the CIDs were limited by their small size.

The permanent officer staff of the DCI was practically the same in 1918 as it had been in 1907. The only additional officer now serving with the department, was the 'Assistant Examiner of Questioned Documents'. The Director was still paid the Rs.3,000 starting salary which he received in 1904.[11] Furthermore, little had changed in the DCI's lower ranks. At the beginning of the war the DCI set up a counter-espionage section. This was a clerical establishment co-ordinating the work of the provincial police. It did not initially involve an increase in staff. In August 1918 a specialized clerical department was set up, which had consisted of four clerks and a typist. At this time the Government of India was 'not satisfied that sufficient grounds exist[ed] at present for placing this establishment on a permanent footing'.[12] In May 1920 the Secretary of State sanctioned the continued employment of an officer on special duty for counter-espionage work for two years from the date of the official termination of the war.[13] He expected this post to 'be continued for a very considerable time to come' since, because of the emergence of the Bolshevik threat and continued suspicions about Japan, the Government of India intended to exercise 'a stricter control than in pre-war days over the movements within India of foreigners generally'.[14] In no sense did the existence of the counter-espionage section of the DCI justify Montagu's accusation that the Government of India was governing through its police.

At the end of the war, there was a turn-over in the DCI's leader-ship. In March 1918 Denham was appointed to 'the temporary post of Deputy Inspector-General on the establishment of the Director,

Criminal Intelligence' for six months.[15] P.M. Stewart, an Assistant Superintendent of the Bombay Police, replaced Sempkins on deputation to the DCI. He had come to Cleveland's notice in several important CID cases.[16] H.V.B. Hare-Scott became Deputy Director of Central Intelligence in 1919.[17] At the end of that year an Indian Muslim, Abd al-Majid, became Assistant Director.[18] In April 1919, H.E. Horsfield was appointed Personal Assistant to the Director of Central Intelligence; the duties of this post were now wholly political.[19]

The most significant change in the DCI's leadership came with the end of Sir Charles Cleveland's reign in November 1919. Despite his successes during the war, Cleveland left India an embittered man. He had long had the ambition to replace Sir Reginald Craddock in the important office of Home Member of the Government of India. In June 1916 he complained to Sir Malcolm Seton, the head of the Judicial and Public Department of the India Office, that his connection with intelligence, which was still widely regarded as a dirty business, was prejudicing his career. He wrote:

> I understand that in some quarters it is supposed that the DCI is by nature the *bête noire* of the Indians and must therefore be degraded rather than promoted. If a man junior to me gets the post my career in India ends . . . I want a fair field and no favour. But I don't want to finish up prematurely merely because my name never occurs.[20]

When Cleveland did not get the job, he resigned from the ICS three years before his retirement was due. He had served as Director of Criminal Intelligence for nine years. Even on the financial level, Cleveland was a disappointed man. His services had not made him wealthy. At the beginning of 1919 he complained that he was not receiving the same salary as many of his juniors.[21] He begged the Government of India to allow him the chance of 'earning a little money by directorships and companies'.[22] A final irritation to Cleveland was his official letter of thanks. This was written by Sir William Marris, the Government of India's newly appointed Home Secretary. For a long time, Marris had been one of Cleveland's main detractors within the administration.[23] Cleveland's fortunes clearly show that Montagu was wrong in his description of British India as an embryonic police state. Intelligence officers remained a necessary evil to the Raj. Cleveland's influence was thanks only to the war and declined when it was over. To many members of the government, Cleveland was someone best forgotten.

The Viceroy offered the post of officiating Director of Central Intelligence to David Petrie, but he was too exhausted to accept it.[24] Instead, the post fell to Cecil (later Sir Cecil) Kaye. Kaye's background was in the Indian Army. When the First World War broke out he was made Deputy Chief Censor, serving under Cleveland's direction. In this capacity he acquired a reputation because of his skill at breaking codes.[25] Kaye was confirmed in his appointment as 'Director, Central Intelligence' on 7 May 1920, and held the office until his retirement in 1925.[26]

COMMUNISM IN INDIA

The emergence of Gandhi as a leader capable of uniting nationalist opposition on an all-India level was the main threat to the Raj which emerged after the First World War. In the past, Indian intelligence had been very effective in crippling all efforts at armed resistance to British rule in India. However, Gandhi's techniques of non-violent protest were difficult for the British to counter. Another challenge arising at this time came from the Bolshevik regime in Moscow. Soviet Russia replaced the Germans as the main supporter of Indian revolutionaries. Despite some initial uncertainty about the power of Communism to win support in India, the British very soon found out that the threat of Communist subversion there was not nearly as serious as the German intrigues during the war which had caused serious difficulties in Persia, led to great uncertainty about the intentions of the Afghan regime and threatened to stoke up the terrorist campaign in Bengal. When they faced the Bolshevik threat, the British benefited from the experience they had gained in the earlier struggle against the Germans. Nor were they materially unprepared. The intelligence apparatus in India, the Far East, Europe and North America was now brought to bear on the remnants of the Indian revolutionary movement which the Bolsheviks were rallying to their cause.

On coming to power in the October Revolution of 1917, Lenin immediately expressed his hostility to the British Empire. He repudiated the Anglo-Russian Convention of 1907 which had ended the rivalry between the British and Russian empires in Asia. In

December 1917, he pledged Bolshevik support for revolution in the colonial regimes, calling on the peoples of Asia to overthrow their European masters. After the end of the First World War, the Bolsheviks perceived Britain as their main enemy, and were to continue to do so until the German invasion of the Soviet Union in 1941. Lenin came to the conclusion that the weakest part of the British Empire was India. He stated in 1920:

> England is our greatest enemy. It is in India that we must strike them hardest.[27]

If a strong Communist movement could be established in India, ultimately leading to revolution there, then Britain's economic and military power would be gravely weakened on a global level. The agency for achieving this end was the Third Communist International, or Comintern as it is commonly known, which was established in Moscow in March 1919 in order to spread the Bolshevik revolution throughout the world.

When they came to power, Lenin and the Bolsheviks had two major problems with their ambition to foster revolution throughout Asia. First, they were faced by civil war at home, and their power within Russia was not consolidated until the end of 1920. By the time that they were in a position to launch their campaign against the Raj, conditions in India had changed. The Afghans, whom the Bolsheviks hoped to stir up, had been heavily defeated in 1919 and unrest within India had died down by 1922. Secondly, Lenin and the Bolsheviks knew very little about conditions in either British India or elsewhere in Asia. For example, Lenin held the belief in 1917 that the majority of India's population were Muslims.[28]

The Bolsheviks initially believed that they would be able to pose a military threat to British India. They intended to do this by instigating another Afghan invasion, which would be supported by risings within India. The main Bolshevik representative in Kabul was Obeidullah Sindhi, a Sikh convert to Islam who had played a prominent role in the earlier German plots centred on Afghanistan.[29] In 1919 he was the Wazir, or Prime Minister of the 'Provisional Government of India', which the small group of Indian revolutionaries still lingering in Kabul had formed.[30] At some time around after the end of 1916, Obeidullah drew up a scheme for the creation of 'The Army of God', which was to liberate India. Its main aim was to bring about an alliance between the rulers of the Ottoman Empire and Afghanistan. At Tashkent, the

Bolsheviks provided military training for a group of a hundred or so Muslims who had fled India during as a result of the Khilafat Movement. But it is difficult to take Bolshevik invasion plans seriously. Obeidullah's 'Army of God', was pure farce. It had no fewer than 12 field-marshals and 48 generals of various grades, but could muster only two captains and one lieutenant; it had no other ranks.[31] It is true that the Afghan government was bitter at its recent defeat at the hands of the British, and toyed with the Bolsheviks; but Amanullah, like previous Amirs, had no more intention of selling his independence to the Russians than to the British. In October 1922 he expelled all the Indian revolutionaries from Afghanistan.[32] Amanullah's hostility to Communist subversion made the infiltration of agents into India much harder in the future.[33]

After the failure of their activities in Afghanistan, the Bolsheviks concentrated on an attempt to build up a strong Communist organization in India. Their aim was to set up Communist cells and to penetrate the existing nationalist movement. Their main agent in this scheme was M.N. Roy. Roy, whose real name was Narendra Nath Bhattacharji, had already achieved some note as a revolutionary. He had been the right-hand man of the important Bengali terrorist leader, Jotindra Nath Mukherji, and had taken part in several terrorist acts before escaping from India in 1915. He had played a prominent part in the *Maverick* affair, serving as the link between the Germans and the Bengali revolutionaries. Roy spent the next few years in the United States, and then Mexico, where he was recruited by the famous Comintern agent, Mikhail Borodin. In April 1920 he arrived in Moscow, where he made a strong impression on Lenin. Roy played an important role in the initial Bolshevik plan to stir up Afghanistan. Thereafter he was the main Indian organizer of Comintern subversion in India.

The Comintern trained its Indian agents in two centres: Tashkent and Moscow. In 1921 the Bolshevik government set up the 'Communist University of Toilers of the East'. This was a school for revolutionaries who were sent to work throughout Asia, though mainly in India. By April 1922, Roy had trained 22 'students', the first of whom he had sent into India in the summer of 1921.[34]

By this time, Moscow was keener than ever on its campaign against India. The Bolsheviks' key aim when they came to power was to cause revolution throughout Europe. These attempts failed completely. In 1923, the Comintern made its last bid to cause revolution in the West, when it called on the German workers to rise. This action was a miserable failure, and it seemed clear to the Communists that their only chance of spreading the revolution in the short term was to strike at the colonial empires in Asia. The Comintern saw its Indian operations as a key part of its work, proposing that the funds allotted to subversion in India should be more than quadrupled in 1924.[35] The Comintern was, however, unaware of exactly how poor the performance of its Indian agents had been. Furthermore, British intelligence played a vital role in the Comintern's failure in India.

Initially, the Government of India showed much concern at the emergence of the Bolshevik threat at a time when India was rent by internal unrest. Intelligence measures were quickly taken to combat Bolshevism. In June 1919 the Viceroy, Lord Chelmsford, informed the Secretary of State, Lord Montagu, that the Government of India 'was not yet armed to combat' Bolshevik subversion satisfactorily, but that urgent measures were being taken to remedy this situation.[36]

> All authorities concerned are alive to the importance of intercepting Bolshevik agents and literature . . . But with our vast frontier we must rely in the main on the evil being tapped at its source by means of intelligence systems at all chief centres of Bolshevik activities . . .[37]

The British intelligence operations against the Bolshevik threat can be divided according to specific geographical areas. First, there were the forward bases to which the Viceroy referred. These were situated at Meshed in north-eastern Persia, on the western flank of Afghanistan and at Kashgar in Chinese Turkestan, on Afghanistan's eastern flank. Second, there were the operations of the Indian police inside India. Third, there were the operations of various British intelligence organizations which now emerged to combat Bolshevism in the Far East, as will be discussed in the next chapter. Finally, in North America and Europe, existing Indian intelligence operations continued against the Indian revolutionary movement.

Intelligence operations against the Bolsheviks at Meshed were under the control of General Sir Wilfrid Malleson, the commander of the British forces which had occupied northern Persia at the end of the war. Malleson ran agent networks in Central Asia and watched the movements of Bolshevik agents into Persia.[38] One of his chief aims was to observe and prevent any contacts between the Bolsheviks and the Afghans. Malleson complimented himself on the effectiveness of this aspect of his work in a speech which he made to the Royal Central Asian Society in London in 1922:

> Having, through numerous agents in both camps, a fairly accurate notion of what was going on, and of how these two interesting parties were seeking how best to take each other in, we made it our business to keep each side unofficially informed of the perfidy of the other. The Afghans about this time, hearing that there was a serious and promising anti-Bolshevik rebellion throughout Ferghana, were gauche enough to send special emissaries there with letters and presents for the leaders of the insurgents. This information we felt it our duty to bring to the notice of the Bolsheviks.[39]

The forward base at Kashgar was run from the British Consulate-General. There, Colonel Percy Etherton, who was Consul-General in the period 1918–22, carried out duties similar to those of Malleson. He ran agents inside Afghanistan and Soviet Central Asia, and checked the attempts of the Communists to send agents into India. This was not a difficult task because the only route to India through Chinese Turkestan was via the Karakoram pass, which was narrow, difficult and long. It took about two weeks to cross. Another important duty of British intelligence at Meshed and Kashgar was to monitor Communist radio traffic.[40]

The Indian police had very few resources to devote to the Bolshevik threat in 1919. On 25 November, Sir William Marris, the Indian Home Secretary, wrote that 'though actual proof of Bolshevik activity in India is small, a serious situation might develop unless systematic protective measures are taken'. As a result, the Government of India appointed two officers to advise it on the Bolshevik question. The first served under the DCI and dealt with information on Bolshevik activities in India. The second served under the Foreign and Political Department to deal with Bolsheviks outside India. Furthermore, most of the Local Governments were ordered to attach a Bolshevik expert to their staff.[41]

British intelligence operations against the infiltration of Comintern agents thus amounted to the small-scale intelligence operations at Meshed and Kashgar, and the equally discreet preparations of the Indian police. None the less, by the beginning of 1920 the Government of India felt confident that it was capable of meeting the challenge. On 28 January 1920, Chelmsford sent the following telegram to Montagu:

Work has now been co-ordinated by officers specially appointed for counter-propaganda, co-ordination of intelligence, both internal and external, and organizational measures to keep Bolshevist emissaries and propaganda out of India . . .[42]

Two years later, the Government of India still felt no need to expand its intelligence operations against the threat from the Comintern which, it was now becoming clear, was a hollow one. In December 1922, the new Viceroy, Lord Reading, informed London:

We are of opinion that our existing organization for dealing with all these activities is not inadequate, although it may require supplementing.[43]

Why, then, did the Government of India feel so confident against the threat of Comintern subversion? There are three general answers. First, Indian intelligence found it very easy to take effective measures against Comintern agents. Second, the political climate in India was not receptive to Communist ideas. Finally, the quality of the Comintern's Indian agents, from Roy downwards, was very poor.

It was relatively easy for the Indian police to catch Comintern agents. There were only three routes by which they could enter India, all of which were difficult. First, there was the western Khyber Pass through Afghanistan. Agents arriving by this route were awaited by the local CID at Peshawar. Second, there was the western route through the Pamir mountains over the Karakoram pass. Agents taking this route were even more exposed than those going through Afghanistan. The police arrested ten of Roy's agents who went by this route at the beginning of 1922. Finally, there was the sea route through the Persian Gulf. This too was by no means easy, since the Indian CIDs were keeping a sharp look out for Comintern agents at the ports. Some of Roy's agents did get through, but even then they found the police were after them. Cecil Kaye, the Director of Central Intelligence, noted in February 1923:

We definitely know a considerable number of Roy's agents arrived in India, and are on the tracks of the few of whose existence in India we are aware, but whose identity is still untraced . . .[44]

The Home Department supported this conclusion in a report of June 1923:

A considerable number of these Bolshevik agents succeeded in reaching India, the first arriving towards the end of 1921. In the majority of cases they were either arrested at once or they found the police so hot on their trail that they fled the country without having carried out their mission. Two of them, however, Nalini Gupta and Shaukat Usmani, achieved a certain amount of success, and it was through their efforts that Communist centres came into being in Calcutta and in the United Provinces (Benares and Cawnpore). From the beginning of 1922, Roy followed up the despatch of these agents by sending a flood of printed propaganda pamphlets to India through the post.[45]

Arrest and surveillance was the first weapon in the police armoury. Another was censorship of mail. Already in 1922, the police had learned much from Roy's correspondence with his agents, which they were regularly reading.[46] In their confidential handbook, *Communism in India 1924–27*, the DCI regularly quoted Roy's correspondence. Petrie who, as Director of Central Intelligence, was responsible for this book, commented that Roy's letters had 'been an unfailing source of information of proved accuracy as to the movements of men, money and literature'.[47] In their task of reading revolutionary mail, the DCI were assisted by the Indian climate, which often caused messages written in 'invisible' ink to become legible.[48]

Intercepting letters was not the only means by which the British were able to read secret Communist correspondence. From 1920 to 1927 they were able regularly and extensively to read Soviet codes, including those of the Comintern.[49] From 1920 British signals intelligence intercepts proved that the Comintern was deeply involved in attempts to subvert India,[50] and also provided detailed insights into Soviet policy at the highest levels. In 1923, for example, the British were fully aware of the amount of money, two million gold roubles, which the Comintern had allotted for propaganda in the East, as well as the fact that the economic plight of the Soviet Union resulted in the reduction of this sum by a half.[51]

Finally, the police had considerable success in infiltrating such Communist organizations as there were in India at this time. The Home Department commented in a memorandum of 1924:

Obviously the best means of obtaining information regarding an organization is from members of the organization itself, and most provinces in which Roy has followers have attained some results by this means. The most successful province in this respect is possibly Bengal, from where fairly detailed information of the activities of Roy's party in Calcutta and elsewhere has been forthcoming for the last 18 months. The Punjab CID has also furnished very useful information, and a certain amount has emanated from Madras . . . Bombay, however, has been distinctly unsuccessful in the aquisition of information, and apart from interception of correspondence practically nothing of interest has been ascertained there.[52]

A major reason for the success of the police in combating the Comintern's plans to subvert India lies in the incompetence of Roy and his Indian agents. The DCI were quite frank about this in their reports to the Government of India. Petrie concluded in 1927 that practically all the Communist agents under Roy, including Roy himself, had 'proved to be greedy opportunists, lacking in scruples and principles and even in common honesty'.[53] Worse, they lacked discipline and organization. As Petrie put it, another 'radical defect in Roy's team was that while every one was prepared to lead, few or none were prepared to follow . . .' All of them, in his view, were men of 'ordinary calibre'.[54] The contrast here with the Bengali terrorists of the First World War is marked. One of the agents detected had simply used the money which the Comintern provided in order to build himself a house. Another, named Ghulam Hussain, was supposed to be Roy's 'centre' in the key Punjabi city of Lahore. Hussain also pocketed his revolutionary funds. When arrested he brazenly claimed that he had been doing the British a favour in 'preventing this money from being devoted to the purposes for which it was sent'.[55] Even some European Communist visitors to India were dismayed by the poor performance of Roy's team. At the beginning of 1925, an Englishman, Percy Glading, went on a secret mission to India for the Communist Party of Great Britain. On reading his correspondence, the DCI were gratified to hear that he had not met a single 'convinced' Communist during his tour.[56]

The DCI was easily able to handle the new threat from familiar revolutionaries flying the red flag. By 1923, Roy's main agents were in police custody. They were put on trial and convicted the next year in the Cawnpore conspiracy trial, where the judge referred to their aims as 'absurd and unbelievable'. Even the DCI showed a condescending sympathy to the prisoners, which it described as 'deserving as much of contempt as of prosecution and punishment'.[57] Petrie concluded, in an assessement of the Cawnpore trial for the Government of India, that it proved what had long been obvious, namely that

> not only did Roy not succeed in establishing a live, working Communist Party in India, but that even those persons who grouped themselves together under that title were a poor enough semblance of any kind of a 'party'.[58]

More important than Petrie's assessment of the trial, though, is that of Indian moderate nationalist opinion. Annie Besant, who was no friend of the Raj, claimed that the trial 'conclusively proved the existence of a Bolshevik plot in India'.[59] Clearly the counter-subversive measures which the Government of India had taken had not alienated Indian public opinion. This was the crucial test of their success. Indian intelligence remained both discreet and effective.

Indian intelligence during the First World War had been equally effective in countering German-backed subversion in India. Despite this, the police had been a major contributer to the disastrous internal security policies which the Government of India followed after the war when it introduced the Rowlatt Act. In the case of the Communist threat, the case was very different, and the DCI served as a calming influence on the government. From the very moment that the threat of Communist subversion against India emerged in 1919–20, police reports showed a high degree of calm. This contrasted with the occasional uneasiness about the Communist menace displayed by the Viceroy. In December 1920, the Home Department, after consultation with the DCI, felt it necessary to comment on Lord Chelmsford's worries. The Secretary of the Home Department wrote as follows:

> The Secretary of State is evidently very impressed by the fact that Roy has secured £10,000 but our experience is that [this amount] will not go very far in the country, and unless Roy produces very tangible and large results, which I regard as very improbable, the Russians are not likely to go on financing him on a large scale; whilst therefore a close watch is necessary, I see no ground for supposing that the danger is acute or very formidable; and this is also Col. Kaye's view.[60]

The Home Department realized that Bolshevik agents were trying to enter India but even at this date, when all India was in ferment, they

314

did not make much of this new, and still undeveloped, danger. The Home Secretary continued:

> It is possible that men have entered the country who have been supplied with money from Russian sources, on the understanding that they would carry on Bolshevik propaganda; but once in India their connection with Bolshevism has gone no further than taking Soviet money. Probably most of these so-called agents had no intention of carrying out their contracts; they desired to return to India and had no objection to return with money obtained at the cost of promises which they knew it would be impossible to enforce.[61]

The Home Department and the DCI were aware that the Bolsheviks might possibly exploit the existing unrest which centred on Gandhi and his first Non-Co-operation Movement. But this concern was not great in the first place, and did not last long. By 1922, when conditions in India were much more settled, the Home Department and the DCI were reporting that India was simply not a fertile ground for Communism. This is quite the opposite conclusion to that of the Comintern at this time. The Home Department recognized that Gandhi had got through to the Indian masses, rallying them to the nationalist cause, but they felt that he and his political message amounted to quite a different phenomenon from the message of Communism, which was bound to be far weaker than a political platform drawn up on nationalist lines. Furthermore, by 1922, even Gandhi had apparently failed and as the Home Department noted at the end of the year:

> The masses themselves have been disillusioned and failed promises of a new heaven on earth, in which no taxes or rents will be paid, will not now make anything like the appeal they did 18 months ago.[62]

It is particularly revealing to compare the attitude of Indian intelligence towards Communist subversion with that of the British domestic security services, MI5 and the Special Branch. In the early 1920s, the latter were gripped by a deep anxiety about Communist infiltration of the British labour movement, and regarded this as a very significant factor contributing to the serious industrial unrest which affected Britain in the early 1920s.[63] In India a wave of labour

315

unrest accompanied Gandhi's first Non-Co-operation Movement, and the situation was potentially far more serious; it seemed, after all, far more likely that the Raj might be overthrown than the British government at home. None the less, the DCI's reports dismissed the connection between Bolshevik subversion and strikes as insignificant. The Home Department reported at the end of 1920:

> The labour unrest in large industrial centres is an obvious instance where Bolshevik influence might be suspected . . . It is therefore not difficult to show a certain connection with Russian ideas, but up to the present no proof has been obtained of any Russian money behind the labour agitation. The rise in prices and economic causes generally are sufficient in themselves to explain the present epidemic of strikes.[64]

Thus, from early on the Home Department and the DCI were aware of the weaknesses of Communism and India and of why this was so. Without doubt, their appreciation of local conditions was vastly superior to that of their Comintern adversaries. But there was one other, perhaps crucial, reason why Roy and his agents were so ineffective at this time, and it was this which gave the Government of India great cause for concern. Roy's main adversary was not just the Indian police, but also Gandhi. Gandhi from 1919 onwards had gained such a commanding position over the Indian nationalist movement that it proved almost impossible for the Communists to gain a foothold within it. In assessing the work of the Comintern in 1927, Petrie wrote:

> The first, and possibly the chief, cause of Roy's lack of success in founding a live Communist Party in India arose out of the special circumstances of the years during which he was most active. Roy, as John the Baptist of Communism, endeavoured to introduce into India the idea and practice of mass action for the enforcement of political demands; but he could scarcely have got to work before he must have realized that 'a greater than John the Baptist' had already forestalled him. This was no other than 'Mahatma Gandhi', whose Non-co-operation campaign produced a mass movement which, while owing nothing in spirit and conception to Communism, was far more widespread and formidable than anything that Roy could possibly have created, even if he had had a completely clear field.

With a demi-god like Mr Gandhi leading the Non-co-operation

movement, there was no one to harken to the purely secular preachings of a puny earthling like Roy.[65]

Indian intelligence had little difficulty in countering the threat from Indian revolutionaries in Bolshevik clothing. Communist subversion in India continued but was never to pose any threat to the Raj. During the First World War and subsequently against the Bolsheviks, élite sections of the Indian police had countered relatively small numbers of Indian revolutionaries, though, as the case of Bengal showed, the stakes had sometimes been high. This kind of 'war' was, it turned out, relatively convenient for the police to wage. If, during the war, they had been mainly concerned with a particular kind of violent opposition to the Raj, so too political violence was what they were equipped to destroy. The investment of the government in the upper cadres of the police brought good results.

But there was little that the DCI and the CIDs could do to halt the non-violent protests against the Rowlatt Act which Gandhi organized in 1919. Anti-terrorist laws, indeed, could not be used against him, since by no stretch of the imagination was he a terrorist or an anarchist. Gandhi understood the British government and refused to confront it on its own ground. The mass non-violent protests he organized, which soon got out of hand, had to be dealt with by the ordinary underpaid district constables. The weaknesses of the Indian police, and of the Indian government which they protected, had never been clearer. In the Punjab in 1919, the results were disastrous.

The events in the Punjab in 1919 revealed the limits of what intelligence could achieve. The Amritsar massacre was an aberration the government had never intended. General Dyer's act in firing on the crowd in the Jallianwalla Bagh represented a return to the political conditions of the late eighteenth century when, in default of the restraints of mass public opinion and of government ideology, large-scale use of armed force was acceptable on the part of the security forces. In 1919, the government could have recourse to violence only at the cost of weakening the basis of its own rule. This happened at Amritsar. During the war and afterwards, Indian intelligence had performed the vital role of keeping the government from this dilemma. It had prevented Indian terrorists and revolutionary 'agitators' of various creeds from stirring up popular unrest. But it could do nothing to stop Gandhi's first Non-Co-operation Movement, launched in response to the Amritsar Massacre.

317

NOTES

1. Letter from G.C. Denham, Shanghai, to Grant Jones, 12 April 1920, PRO FO228/3214.
2. The provisions of the Rowlatt Act have been summarized as follows: 'First, the committee recommended permanent changes in the criminal law, to enable accused persons to be promised protection against criminal acts as an inducement to implicate accomplices, to make the possession of prohibited documents an offence, to give powers to order released prisoners to give security and notify their residence, and to allow evidence of previous convictions in cases of sedition.

   'Secondly, they recommended legislation on the lines of the Defence of India Act to be held in reserve and applied as necessary by notification to specified areas in stages. In the first stage, there should be provision for the trial of seditious crime by three high court judges without juries, committal proceedings, or appeal . . . In the second stage, there should be power to require suspects to give security and report their movements, to restrict their residence, and to order them to abstain from particular activities such as journalism or attendance at meetings. In the last stage, there should be power to imprison suspects, and to search premises without warrant. Independent men should examine informally the evidence in cases in which these powers were used before final orders on them were made. In addition, there should be power to supply any of these provisions without notification to persons already restricted under the Defence of India Act when it expired.' A. Rumbold, *Watershed in India* (London: the Athlone Press, 1979), pp. 135–6.
3. Note by H. Wheeler, 12 Aug. 1914, in *Retention for a Further Period of the Service of Mr F.S.A. Slocock, (Inspector-General of Police in the Central Provinces) for Employment under the Director, Criminal Intelligence, in Connection with Enquiries Arising out of the Outbreak of War*, in HDD: Sept. 1914, no. 79, IOLR IOR.POS.10612.
4. Letter from the Director of Criminal Intelligence to the Secretary to the Government of India, Home Department, 15 Dec. 1916, in *Deputation of Mr J.C. Ker, ICS, for a Period of 6 Months to Summarize the Information on Record in Director, Criminal Intelligence's Office* in HD/Pol: March 1917, no. 126, IOLR P/10176.
5. *Anarchy in India. Appointment of a Committee to Investigate the Whole Question of Indian Anarchism* in HDA: April–June 1917, IOLR IOR.POS.8612.
6. *Representation by Mr C. Tegart Regarding his Acceptance of a Commission in England and his Conduct in the Matter of Relieving Mr D. Petrie in the Far East*, in HDB: July 1919, nos. 122–32 & KW, IOLR IOR.POS.10516.
7. Montagu to Chelmsford, 10 Oct. 1918, in IOLR MSS.EUR.E.264/4.
8. O'Dwyer, *India as I Knew It* (London: Constable and Co., 1925), Ch. XVII, 'The Punjab Rebellion of 1919'.
9. Letter from Montagu to Chelmsford, 1 Jan. 1918 in Chelmsford Papers; Letters, Secretary of State, IOLR MSS.EUR.E.264/4.
10. *Raising the position of the Director, Criminal Intelligence, in the Warrant of Precedents and changing the Director's designation from 'the Director of Criminal Intelligence' to 'the Director of Central Intelligence'*, HD/Pol: March 1918, nos. 151–3 in IOLR P10176.
11. *Revision of the Rates of Pay of the Deputy Director, and Assistant Director, Central Intelligence, Consequent on the Introduction with Effect from 1 January 1919, of Time Scale of Pay for the Officers of the Indian Imperial Police*, in HD/Pol: Nov. 1919, nos. 166–9, IOLR P/10597.
12. Letter from the Under-Secretary to the Government of India, Home Department, to the Director, Central Intelligence, 30 July 1918, in *Addition of 5 Men to the Clerical Establishment of the Office of the Director, Central Intelligence, for the Duration of the War and for 6 Months Thereafter*. HD/Pol: Aug. 1918, nos. 190–2 in IOLR P/10373.
13. Telegram from the Secretary of State to the Viceroy, 6 May 1920, in *Sanction to the Extension, for Two Years, of the Appointment of an Officer under the Director of*

Central Intelligence, to Deal with Contre-Espionage against Suspicious Foreigners.
HD/Pol: June 1920, nos. 126–7 in IOLR P/10839.

14. Telegram from the Viceroy to the Secretary of State, 20 Feb. 1920 in *Proposed Extension for a Period of Two Years, of the Deputation of an Officer under the Director, Central Intelligence, to Deal with the Subject of Contre-Espionage against Suspicious Foreigners.* HD/Pol: Feb. 1920, nos. 222–4 in IOLR P/10839.

15. Letter from J.H. DuBoulay, Secretary to the Government of India, Home Department, 14 March 1918, in *Proposed Creation of a New Temporary Post on Rs.1,500 under the Director, Criminal Intelligence, Carrying the Rank of a Deputy Inspector-General of Police, and to Appoint Mr Denham to it.* HD/Pol: March 1918, nos. 89–90 in IOLR P/10372.

16. Letter from the Director, Central Intelligence, to the Secretary to the Government of India, Home Department to the Secretary to the Government of India, Home Department, in *Grant of 3 Months' Privilege Leave to Mr F.R. Sempkins, Officer on Special Duty under the Director, Central Intelligence, with Effect from 21 November 1918.* HD/Pol: Dec. 1918, nos. 159–74 in IOLR P/10373.

17. In May 1919 he was seconded to the Delhi administration to serve as Superintendent. *Emoluments of Mr H.V.B. Hare-Scott, Deputy Director, Central Intelligence Department, During the Period he Held Charge of the Appointment of Senior Superintendent of Police of Delhi.* HD/Pol: June 1919, nos. 38–41 in IOLR 10596.

18. Letter from A. MacLeod, Under-Secretary to the Government of India, Home Department, to the Director, Central Intelligence, 28 February 1920, in *Sanction to the Secretary of State to Revised Rates of Pay for the Deputy Director and Assistant Director, Central Intelligence.* HD/Pol: April 1920, nos. 59–63 in IOLR P/10839.

19. *A Proposal that the Restriction Regarding a Maximum Placed upon the Pay to be Drawn by the Personal Assistant to the Director, Central Intelligence, Should be Removed.* HD/Pol: May 1920, nos. 164–75 in IOLR P/10839.

20. Letter from Cleveland to Seton, 23 June 1916. Seton Papers; Letters to Seton, IOLR MSS.EUR.E.276/6.

21. Letter from Cleveland to the Secretary to the Government of India, Home Department, 14 January 1919 in *Representation by Sir Charles Cleveland, Director, Central Intelligence, for the Grant to him of the Maximum of the Personal Allowance of Rs.500-1000-1,000 sanctioned for him with Effect from 1 January 1919.* HD/Pol: March 1919, nos.21–2 in IOLR P/10596.

22. Letter from Cleveland to the Secretary to the Government of India, Home Department, 29 August 1919, in *Request of Sir Charles Cleveland, KCI, KBE, Director, Central Intelligence, for Permission to Undertake, While on Leave in India, Directorships of Companies, and to Receive Honorarium for Such Works.* HD/Pol: Nov. 1919, no. 180 in IOLR P/10597.

23. Letter from Sir William Marris, Secretary to the Government of India, Home Department, to Sir Charles Cleveland, 18 November 1919, in *Appreciation of the Services of Sir Charles Cleveland, KCIE, KBE, During his Tenure of the Office of Director, Central Intelligence.* HD/Pol: Dec. 1919, nos. 1–2 in IOLR P/10597.

24. Telegram from the Viceroy to the Secretary of State, 9 August 1919. Telegram from the Secretary of State to the Viceroy, 27 August 1919, in *Grant of Combined Leave for Six Months to Sir Charles Cleveland, KCIE, KBE, Director of Central Intelligence, and his Subsequent Retirement from the Indian Civil Service.* HD/Pol: Nov. 1919, nos. 63–83 in IOLR P/10597.

25. He was formally confirmed in this office on 7 May 1920.

26. Notification no. 846, dated 7 May 1920 in *Confirmation of Colonel C. Kaye, as Director, Central Intelligence.* HD/Pol: May 1920 in IOLR P/10839.

27. Quoted in Peter Hopkirk, *Setting the East Ablaze. Lenin's Dream of an Empire in Asia* (Oxford: Oxford University Press, 1986), p. 1.

28. J. Gallagher, *The Decline, Revival and Fall of the British Empire* (Cambridge: Cambridge University Press, 1982), p. 92.
29. James Campbell Ker, *Political Trouble India 1907–1917* (Reprint, Calcutta: Editions Indian, 1973), p. 279.
30. *Weekly Reports of the DCI*, June 1919, nos. 494–7, in Cecil Kaye, *Communism in India 1919–1924* (Reprint, Calcutta: Editions Indian, 1971), p. 128.
31. David Petrie, *Communism in India 1924–1927* (Reprint, Calcutta: Editions Indian, 1972), p. 68.
32. Kaye, *Communism in India* (Reprint, Calcutta: Editions Indian, 1973), p. 55.
33. Ibid., p. 205.
34. Ibid., p. 22.
35. Petrie, op. cit., pp. 71–2.
36. Hopkirk, op. cit., p. 120.
37. Ibid., p. 119.
38. Ibid., pp. 2, 81.
39. Ibid., p. 81.
40. Ibid., pp. 81, 96.
41. Letter from Sir William Marris, Secretary to the Government of India, Home Department, to all Local Governments and Administrations except Buram, Assam, Coorg and Delhi, 25 November 1919, in *Defensive Measures Proposed for Dealing with Bolshevism* in HDA: Dec. 1919, nos. 1–7, IOLR IOR.POS.8622.
42. Telegram from Viceroy to Secretary of State, 28 Jan. 1920, in Kaye, op. cit., p. 131.
43. Telegram from Viceroy to Secretary of State, 21 December 1922, in Kaye, op. cit., p. 214.
44. 'Notes in the Intelligence Bureau of the Home Department', signed C. Kaye, 7.2.23, in Kaye, op. cit., p. 204.
45. Quoted in Kaye, op. cit., p. 239.
46. Kaye, op. cit., pp. 21, 245.
47. Petrie, op. cit.
48. Hopkirk, op. cit., p. 176.
49. C.M. Andrew, *Secret Service* (London: Heinemann, 1985), p. 259.
50. Ibid., p. 269.
51. Kaye, op. cit., p. 52.
52. Ibid., pp. 324–5.
53. Petrie, op. cit., p. 67.
54. Ibid., p. 68.
55. bid., p. 67.
56. Ibid., p. 96.
57. Ibid., p. 64.
58. Ibid., p. 172.
59. Quoted in Petrie, op. cit., p. 1.
60. Kaye, op. cit., pp. 199–200.
61. Ibid.
62. Telegram from S.P. O'Donwell to the Secretary of State, 18 Dec., 1922, in Kaye, op. cit., pp. 199–200.
63. Andrew, op. cit., Ch. 9.
64. Kaye, op. cit., pp. 151–2.
65. Petrie, op. cit., pp. 65–6.

13

British Intelligence in North America and the Far East, 1918–24

During the First World War, British intelligence played a significant role in imperial defence by keeping foreign subversion out of India. The intelligence organizations based on Delhi attempted, with great success, to discover hostile plans towards the Raj, and to stem them at source. It was to a considerable degree thanks to British intelligence in North America that Ghadr plans to raise the Punjab in 1915 failed as completely as they did. Even more important was the British success in preventing the Germans from supplying the terrorist movement in Bengal with arms. After 1917, there was not much that the British could do to prevent the preparation of plots within Bolshevik Russia, which was an overtly hostile power, but the intelligence services continued to play an important role in imperial defence by countering the activities of the Bolsheviks and their Indian accomplices in North America and the Far East. In the latter region, however, various British intelligence organizations were even more concerned about Japanese subversion against the colonial powers than they were about the Communist threat.

NORTH AMERICA

The entry of the United States into the First World War on the Allied side gave the British an unprecedented opportunity to take the offensive against what had once been the most important centre of Indian 'sedition' abroad. They were in a powerful position to carry this out. By 1918 MI1c and its Indian section had attained a great deal of influence over various American intelligence agencies, to the extent that in April 1918, Thwaites, the deputy head of the British Secret Service in the United States, expressed his hope that 'gradually we shall be able to wean the United States authorities from dependence upon us'.[1] But the entry of the United States into the war was the occasion for a reorganization of British intelligence operations in America, which was ultimately to have wholly negative results. In March 1918 MI5 was put in charge of British intelligence in America.[2] This immediately led to confusion and conflict within British ranks. Wiseman, the head of MI1c's operations in the United States, commented on the bitterness which his chief, Mansfield Cumming, or 'C' as he was known, felt at MI5's intrusion. In March he wrote in a letter to a friend:

> Poor C. is very much hurt about the transfer of the N.Y. office to the MI5 man . . . It does seem rather tough that, after his organization has built up the business and carried it on satisfactorily for over two years, it should now be taken away from him bodily and I think he feels it very much.[3]

Worse was to come, because the authorities in London considered scrapping British espionage in the United States altogether.[4] On 6 April 1918, London ordered Thwaites to dismiss all his staff not engaged in purely MI5 work.[5] At this point, the Government of India intervened. They insisted on continuing the work of Robert Nathan, their chief intelligence officer in North America, and the subsidy which they paid toward MI1c's operation in America. Thus at least Nathan's section continued as before. At the end of 1918, Indian intelligence played the leading role in North America, as it had done before the war.[6] In July 1918, Wiseman introduced Nathan to Colonel House as the man 'who knows more about the Bolshevist organizations in this country than any other man'.[7]

MI1c hoped to capitalize on their success in the San Francisco conspiracy trial, and to utilize their influence over the Americans by cementing a close alliance between the American and British intelligence services against radicals of all kinds. This was made possible by the Russian Revolution at the end of 1917 and the ensuing 'Red scare' in the United States. The British greatly played upon the Americans' fears of subversion. The US Military Intelligence Department recalled that there were

several classes of investigations which the British were . . .

particularly interested in. These included Sinn Fein activities, Hindu activities, Negro activities (especially as they . . . became part of the activities of all darker peoples), international radical organizations and individuals, and radical affairs of all kinds in the United States.

Nathan tried to convince the Americans, and not without initial success, that there was a serious armed threat from radicals within the United States, whose total military strength he represented at 600,000 men.[8]

The apparent success of Nathan's plans was shown at the end of the year, when the British were able to secure US support against the powerful Irish nationalist cause in America at a time when trouble in Ireland was escalating to the point of revolution. In September 1918 the leading Irish-American nationalist paper, *The Gaelic American* published a notice calling upon Irish-Americans to register themselves with the Republican Provisional Government in Ireland. This was a breach of the US Espionage Act. The US Department of Justice was eager to prosecute and requested Nathan's assistance.[9] He began to work very closely with the Americans.[10] Now a close alliance of the British and American intelligence services had a real chance of coming into being.[11]

In January 1919, Nathan became head of the British Secret Service in North America.[12] He was officially on the staff of MI1c, but remained in close contact with the Government of India, which was the main beneficiary of his work. But that same month the American Military Intelligence Department decided that no further exchange of information on radicals with Nathan was permissible.[13] Exactly a year later, the British were asked to wind up their counter-intelligence operations in the United States.[14] Possibly the failure of the intelligence alliance was inevitable after the United States' return to neutral power status. None the less, it is significant that no US intelligence agency pressed for the British to stay.

What had caused this dramatic reversal in Nathan's fortunes? It is clear that the position of MI1c and Indian intelligence in the USA had deteriorated because of the lack of support which they received from London. What India held as vital, MI5 did not see as so important. Wiseman complained:

If Kell [the head of MI5] is not interested in contre-espionage in the States – particularly Irish and Hindoo affairs – I should like to know who is?

Even more seriously, MI5 officers did not have the diplomatic skills of MI1c and the officers of Indian intelligence, who had been very popular with their American colleagues. Relations between the British and American intelligence agencies in New York deteriorated after the MI5 take-over. The decline had already started after the end of 1917, when Kell sent out his officer, Harran, to be Military Control Officer in New York. Wiseman reported that 'evidently, on instructions from Home, he takes highhanded action and refuses to accept advice from Embassy and Consulate'.[15] By the end of 1918, relations between MI5 and the Americans had got much worse. The US Military Intelligence Department suspected MI5 officers stationed at American ports of using their privileges to interrogate American merchants in pursuit of commercial intelligence.[16] This was the real reason for the Americans' sudden turning on their former allies.

The failure of the grand alliance between British and American intelligence was a blow to the British, but it did not mean that the United States would become a stronghold for revolutionaries intent on destroying the Empire, as it had been before the war. The Ghadr organization still existed in North America. It was, however, much weaker than it had been before 1915. Moreover, while as hostile as ever to the British, it found no great attraction in the Bolsheviks, with whom its leaders toyed, to no effect whatsoever, over the course of the 1920s.[17]

None the less, after the official expulsion of British intelligence from the United States, the Government of India took secret steps to set up its own small covert agency on the Pacific coast independently of MI1c and MI5. It started to do so even before Nathan's own operations were curtailed. This basically amounted to the resurrection of the old system under Hopkinson. The India Office selected another Indian policeman to fill his place at Vancouver. He was Wallinger's deputy, Vickery, who, conveniently, had relatives in San Francisco.[18] This amounted to a careful and limited response to what was now a very small threat. Cleveland commented that 'the success of the work depends on personal ability and character far more than experience and seniority'.[19] This was just as it had been when Hopkinson had, to all intents and purposes, been British intelligence in North America before 1914.

THE FAR EAST

For British intelligence in the Far East, the end of the First World War did not mark a complete break with the past. Reactions to the Bolsheviks were less dramatic than in Europe, where they preoccupied all intelligence services from 1918.[20] In British eyes, the new Russian threat at this time by no means outweighed the potential danger from Japan, and so the anti-Japanese orientation of imperial intelligence in the Far East continued after the war. The Indian revolutionary problem was the main stimulus in this direction.

In 1919, the Foreign Office discontinued the allowance of £500 for secret service work which it had paid to the Tokyo Embassy. This work was of the greatest importance to the Government of India,[21] which began to pay a yearly allowance of £200 for Japanese intelligence, a very sizeable sum by Indian standards.[22] Thus in Japan, as in the United States, the Government of India provided the main stimulus for the continuance of British intelligence operations after the war. In May 1919, Davidson was appointed full Consul at Tokyo. This post was specially created for him so that he could more effectively control his agents. The Foreign Office wrote in connection with Davidson's promotion:

> Davidson's services have been invaluable and there appears to be no one else capable of taking up his special work. All the information we have here indicates that Japan is likely to be a centre of sedition for some time to come and it is therefore very desirable that Mr Davidson's services should be retained, for the present at any rate.[23]

At Singapore, the main focus of British counter-intelligence after the War was also Japanese subversion. In July 1917, General Ridout, who directed *ad hoc* intelligence operations from the Straits Settlements, recommended the appointment of an officer to watch the activities of the Japanese in the Malay States, the Netherlands East Indies and neighbouring regions. This officer was to watch 'the large numbers of Japanese of various classes . . . who reside or travel about in . . . the South Seas and who are suspected of adding spying or anti-European agitation to their ostensible occupations'.[24] In London, Colonel French, the head of MI1a, the intelligence liaison office, agreed that the appointment of a 'Japanese expert' at Singapore was essential.[25] Kothavala, whose services had not involved Japanese counter-espionage, returned to India at the end of 1918.[26] The officer selected for the appointment early in 1919 was Davidson's former assistant at the Yokohama Consulate and fellow Japanese scholar, Frederick Ashton Gwatkin. He was seconded to the War Office.

In China, the Shanghai Intelligence Bureau continued to operate, as did the Indian secret service. Denham replaced Petrie as Vice-Consul and the DCI's representative at Shanghai in February 1919.[27] The British Legation at Peking found the Indian secret service to be the most effective part of the Bureau. Its other elements were pre-occupied by the Bolsheviks from the end of the war. However, the Legation thought that the quality of their work, though not that of Denham, had declined and that they attached 'an exaggerated importance' to what they heard.[28]

A new element in the complex of British intelligence organizations in the Far East was provided by the involvement of MI1c, the secret service. At the beginning of 1918, Mansfield Cumming was trying to recruit an employee for general service in the Far East, with the exception of Singapore. His main duty was to be the 'observation of Japanese designs'.[29] He was due to start work in June 1918. By 1923, the secret service had a second representative working in Canton in southern China. They set great store on working independently of other organizations in the region. Lee Warner, the head of the Far Eastern section of the secret service, noted at this time that

> the success of the SIS Intelligence depended to a large extent on their keeping a free hand in the matter of personal contact with a new and untried branch of government work, which in the case of the Hong Kong Bureau must of necessity be less secret as an organization than their own.[30]

The next important development affecting British intelligence in the Far East was the establishment of the Malayan Bureau of Political Intelligence in 1922. The discussions leading to its creation began in November 1920. They are interesting because they show the reasons which the British believed necessitated good intelligence in the Far East. The Colonial Office divided the threats to the security of Singapore into two headings: 'external' and 'internal'. The topic 'India' headed the list of external threats because of the existence there of 'active sedition and non-co-operation'. It was followed by, in order: Netherlands East Indies, in which 'sedition' was rife; Siam, where there were possible movements against the throne; China, which 'hardly had a government'; and Japan where 'dangerous [Indian] sedition' continued. Two of the four 'internal' dangers directly concerned India: these were religious trouble amongst Hindus, Muslims and Sikhs; and 'active agents . . . employed by the Japanese, the Pan-Islamists and the seditionists'. The Malayan Bureau's duties were fundamentally political. Basically it was established to collect information that was not purely naval, military or criminal. It did not replace the Intelligence Section of the General Staff of the Straits Settlements Command which Ridout had formed, or the Naval Intelligence Department at Singapore. It was intended to take over 'matters of purely political interest' which were at that time being handled by the GOC Singapore, and the CIDs of Singapore and Kuala Lumpur. This basically meant reporting to the government on 'all political agitation and movements in Malaysia' and all foreign political movements which might affect Malaysia. It was to ensure a flow of intelligence to the government and to the local authorities by issuing *Abstracts of Intelligence* at regular intervals. It had the task of co-ordinating the flow of information from Singapore and to the Department of Central Intelligence in India. It was also to carry out propaganda work in the Malay Peninsula.[31]

The Malayan Bureau was not set up until 1922 because the financial situation in Malaya prohibited large-scale expenditure on intelligence. It started life with a minimum staff and only one officer, A.S. Jelf. Jelf was an officer of the Malayan Civil Service who had served in the Peninsula for 22 years. In 1917 Ridout detailed him for 'contra espionage and political work generally'. During the early part of 1918 he was engaged on similar work at MI5. Despite its small size, the Malayan Bureau quickly established a reputation for efficiency. On 30 August 1923 the War Office reported:

The [Army] Council feel that the establishment at Singapore of the Malayan Bureau of Political Intelligence in 1922, in which the fighting services are represented, has resulted in a remarkable improvement in the general intelligence organization of the Empire. This Bureau presents, and gives a wide distribution to, the considered views of experts on all political developments throughout Malaya. Its monthly bulletin supplies a useful and necessary corollary to the intelligence notes isssued by the local general staff, who, from the guidance given them as to the political situation by the director of the Bureau, are able to concentrate on the consideration of those purely military problems which are most likely to arise.

By this time, the monthly reports of the Malayan Bureau were carrying 'a good deal of weight in military and naval intelligence circles'.[32]

Hong Kong remained the weak link in British intelligence in the Far East. According to a War Office report of 1923, the information received from there had been inadequate 'for some time'. This was not, however, of direct concern to India. The main concern expressed in London was that 'with the increasing importance of the Far East from an imperial point of view and the constant state of disruption in China . . . nothing short of a first-class intelligence organization is adequate for Hong Kong'. As a result, the War Office decided to set up an organization on the lines of the Malayan Bureau.[33]

By the end of 1923, a large number of British intelligence agencies were operating in the Far East. These were the Indian Department of Central Intelligence based at Shanghai; the Shanghai Municipal Police; the General Staff at Singapore; the Japanese organization run from the Yokohama Consulate – as well as the post-war additions, namely, the two SIS officers, the Malayan Bureau, and the reorganized apparatus at Hong Kong. Only one organization was specifically concerned with the threat from Bolshevism. This was the Indian Special Bureau of Information, which the Government of India had set up at Delhi in June 1920. Its first Director was Colonel W.F. O'Connor. The Special Bureau's field of interest was the Far East, and it was intended to draw together all the material concerning the Bolsheviks which the various intelligence agencies operating in that region provided. The information which it processed was distributed in the form of a *Weekly Diary*. It did not employ its own agents.[34]

A truly co-ordinated imperial response to the worldwide problem of nationalist subversion against the Empire did not come into being during the war, nor did it develop after the war. There is no evidence, however, that this affected the performance of counter-espionage in the region. During the war, the co-operation of various British intelligence agencies had impressive results against the Indian nationalists in the Far East, and a considerable degree of co-operation had been achieved between the DCI, the Foreign Office and Military Intelligence based at Singapore. There is no sign that this situation deteriorated in the 1920s. This was a a marked contrast to the post-war performance of British intelligence in the United States, where the conflict between

328

the secret service and MI5 in 1918 had harmed the collective interests of the intelligence community.

NOTES

1. Letter from Major N.G. Thwaites to Colonel H.A. Packenham, 9 April 1918, in YUL Wiseman Papers, Series I, Box 6, Folder 174.
2. *Memorandum on Scope and Activities of MIIc New York*, dated 27 April 1918 in YUL Wiseman Papers, MSS.666, Series I, Box 6, File 174.
3. Letter from Wiseman to 'Billy', 3 March 1918, in YUL Wiseman Papers, MSS.666, Series I, Box 1, File 4.
4. Memorandum entitled *Miscellaneous Functions of New York Office of British Military Attaché*, dated 28 March 1919 in YUL Wiseman Papers, MSS.666, Series I, Box 6, File 173.
5. Letter from Thwaites to Wiseman, 9 April 1918 in YUL Wiseman Papers, MSS.666, Series I, Box 6, File 174.
6. Telegram from Secretary of State to Viceroy, 11 Feb. 1919. Chelmsford Papers; Telegrams, Secretary of State, Vol. 4 in IOLR MSS.EUR.E.264/10.
7. Letter from Wiseman to House, 22 July 1919 in YUL House Papers: MSS.4665, Series I, Box 123, File 123 4332.
8. Memorandum entitled *British Espionage in the United States*, dated 15 Feb. 1921, in NAW MID 9944-A-178.
9. Telegram from Wiseman to Foreign Office, 19 Sept. 1918 in YUL Wiseman Papers, MSS.666, Series I, Box 5, File 142.
10. He served as translator of Indian letters which the US Military Intelligence Department intercepted. Leter from Office of MID, 302 Broadway, New York City, to Director of [US] Military Intelligence, 14 Oct. 1918 in NAW, MID 9771-56. Various reports submitted by Nathan to the US authorities are contained in the files of the Military Intelligence Department, in the National Archives, Washington, DC. For example, a memorandum entitled *Some Notes on the Constitution and Activities of the Irish Revolutionary Party in America*, filed in October 1918. NAW MID 9771-56.
11. This is shown by a memorandum entitled *Proposals for System of Direct Cooperation Between US, Canadian and British Negative Intelligence Organizations*, which was drawn up by the US Military Intelligence Department in September 1918. NAW MID 10566-274.
12. Letter from Wiseman to Thwaites, 20 Jan. 1919 in YUL Wiseman Papers, Series I, Box 3, File 84.
13. Telegram from K.C. Masteller, Colonel, General Staff, to Captain J.B. Trevor, 20 Jan. 1919. Telegram from Captain J.B. Trevor, New York, to US Director of Military Intelligence, 29 Jan. 1919. NAW MID 10153-330-1/2.
14. Memorandum entitled *British Espionage in the United States*, dated 15 Feb. 1921. NAW MID 9944-A-178.
15. Telegram from Wiseman to Reading, 17 Sept. 1918 in YUL Wiseman Papers, MSS.666, Series I, Box 3, File 78.
16. *Memorandum of British Secret Service Activities in this Country*, dated 2 Nov. 1920 in NAW MID 9771-45.
17. See various passing references tgo the Ghadr Party in C. Kaye, *Communism in Indian 1919–1924* (Calcutta: Editions Indian, reprinted 1971) and in D. Petrie, *Communism in India 1924–27* (Calcutta: Editions Indian, reprinted 1972).
18. Telegram from Secretary of State to Viceroy, 3 Feb. 1919; Telegram from Secretary of State to Viceroy, 11 Feb. 1919 in Chelmsford Papers: Telegrams, Secretary of State,

Vol. 4 in IOLR MSS.EUR.E.264/10.
19. Note by C.R. Cleveland, dated 10 July 1919, in *Employment of Mr Newby vice Mr Vickery, Pending Major P.A.R. Pritchard's Assumption of the Office. Calculation of Mr Vickery's Deputation Allowance*, HDB: July 1919, nos. 122–32 and KW in IOLR IOR.POS.10516.
20. See, for example, C.M. Andrew, *Secret Service* (London: Heinemann, 1985).
21. Undated telegram from the Viceroy, in Yokohama Consulate Correspondence: From India and Singapore, FO262/1419.
22. From Tokyo Embassy to Viceroy, 3 Oct. 1919. In Yokohama Consulate Correspondence: From India and Singapore, FO262/1419.
23. PRO FO371/4244 (68049).
24. Ridout added: 'If an effective watch is to be kept on these people it will be necessary to employ a number of minor agents, either of their own nationality or drawn from the natives of the country in which they happen to be, since no Europeans would be likely to succeed in living amongst them and in being trusted by them'. Letter from Greene, Tokyo, to Ridout, 5 Oct. 1917 in PRO FO371/3069 (217756).
25. French to Campbell, 4 Jan. 1918 in PRO FO371/3069 (244302).
26. *Grant of Leave to Mr Kothavala*, in HDA: Jan. 1920, nos. 129–50A in IOLR.POS. 8622.
27. *Grant to Mr Petrie, CIE, CBE, Intelligence Officer in the Far East, of Combined Leave for One Year and Ten Months from 9 May 1919 With a Lien on his Appointment Throughout the Period of Leave. Appointment of Mr G.C. Denham, CIE, as Intelligence Officer in the Far East*, in HDA: June 1919, nos. 671–94, IOLR IOR.POS.8621.
28. Letter from British Legation to Fraser, Shanghai, 7 April 1920 in PRO FO228/3214.
29. *Grant of Leave to Mr Kothavala*, in HDA: Jan. 1920, nos. 129–50A in IOLR.POS. 8622.
30. Unsigned, undated Colonial Office memorandum in CO537 757.
31. Colonial Office Minute Paper, signed 'C.W.G.', 25 Nov. 1921; Letter from Sir L.M. Guillemard to Churchill, 18 Oct. 1921 in PRO CO537/904.
32. Letter from War Office to Colonial Office, 30 Aug. 1923, 083/5445 (M.I.2), in PRO CO547/757.
33. Colonial Office note signed 'S.N.G.' dated 2 Aug. 1923, in CO537 757.
34. 'Indian Special Bureau of Information 1920–1921' in PRO FO228/3216.

Conclusion

By 1917, the British had defeated the Indian revolutionary movement both within the sub-continent and abroad. After the war the Bolsheviks failed to stoke up the embers of the cause, which had all but burned out. To some extent, the Raj's success lay in the rashness and incompetence of its adversaries. But this is only a partial explanation. During the war, Indian revolutionaries, though never united, had put up a significant challenge to British rule. This is quite clear from the events in Bengal between 1914 and 1916, even without consideration of the wide geographical spread of the revolutionaries. Ultimately the revolutionaries achieved little concrete, except to engender fear in the minds of their rulers. These fears were not unjustified.

British intelligence on a global scale played the key role in defeating the Indian revolutionaries and first their German, then their Bolshevik, supporters. During the war, Indian intelligence and the imperial intelligence agencies which assisted it had proved able to knock on the head any armed threat to the Raj from abroad. Indeed, by fighting their battles on foreign soil, even in such unlikely environments as the United States, they had reduced the need for coercion at home and assisted the government in pursuing the policies of conciliation which it needed to rally India to the war effort. The Rowlatt Act was an aberration from the normal line of government policy, which was taken up again with respect to the Bolsheviks. The struggle of the British Empire with Indian revolutionaries and their German allies is possibly the only area of the intelligence history of the First World War in which human intelligence played a decisive and exclusive role.

The problem of Indian revolutionaries abroad was important not only in its own right, but also because of the developments in British imperial intelligence to which it led. It was the primary cause for the

331

development of British intelligence in the Far East and a very important stimulus to the development of the British secret service in America. By the end of the war intelligence had become necessary not just to the protection of the Raj, but to imperial defence in general.

The continuing existence of a worldwide Indian revolutionary problem had the strongest influence upon the attitude of the Indian government towards intelligence abroad. This is not a statement of the obvious, since until the end of 1915 the Government of India was very reluctant to allow the DCI to operate overseas. Before then, its attitudes were little different from those of its nineteenth century predecessors; namely, intelligence operations ought to be temporary and, if possible, not conducted at all, so as to avoid the danger of diplomatic complications. But the activities of Indian revolutionaries during the war, and the ability of Indian nationalists to secure the support of foreign powers, led the Government of India to see its overseas intelligence operations as permanent. In 1918 there was no longer any question that the Indian counter-intelligence network in China should be scrapped. In America, the Government of India took steps to set up its own small covert agency on the Pacific coast independently of MI1c and MI5, even before their operations were curtailed.

Developments in intelligence during the war do not point to the resurgence of official confidence in the Empire. Rather the growth of intelligence reflected official belief in the fragility of the Empire. The Victorians did not establish intelligence on a formal footing because they felt confident of their position in India. The growth of British intelligence agencies dedicated primarily or in part to combating the Indian revolutionary movement throughout the world is a clear sign that the British perceived the position of the Empire to be weakening during and after the First World War. The intelligence networks whose fundamental concern was the defence of the Indian empire may have been disconnected, but they all combined to produce a picture of imperial vulnerability. Clear indications of the impact of intelligence reporting on domestic and foreign policy were provided by the introduction of the Rowlatt Act in 1919, and by the attitude of the British and Indian governments towards Japan from the end of the war.

However, the fears which Indian intelligence created were not misplaced. By 1919, the Indian empire was faced with a far more threatening domestic scene, after Gandhi unleashed his first Non-Cooperation Campaign, as well as an array of potential dangers which had not existed during the Raj's days of splendid isolation from 1907 to 1914. The outlook facing British rule in India in the years just after the war was bleak. Yet, far from encouraging panic and loss of confidence, the intelligence networks defending the Indian empire, tended to instil confidence in the regime. This was clear from their reporting on the threat from Bolshevism, which almost from the outset they played down. The British governments in London and Delhi were outraged at Bolshevik plotting. None the less, the Government of India did not see the emergence of the threat of Communist subversion as a radical new development. Rather it appeared, in the early 1920s, to be a partial rekindling of the old revolutionary fires. In many ways the early activities of the Bolsheviks repeated, with more use of the pen than the bullet, old German schemes for colonial subversion.

The effectiveness of British intelligence in combating the Indian revolutionary movement does not imply a greater willingness on the part of the Raj to use repression against its Indian subjects. It is true that by the end of the First World War intelligence had become an indispensable tool of government. It is equally true that the intelligence agencies at the disposal of the Raj, both at home and overseas, remained very small in scale. There are several reasons why this was so, and they all reveal a notable continuity with British practices of the nineteenth century. It is perhaps misleading to talk about Victorian attitudes to intelligence. When faced by foreign or internal threats, the nineteenth century rulers of India had had ready recourse to intelligence. It was only because these threats were intermittent that they had never really systematized their intelligence. When threats to the Raj became permanent, after the First World War, so too Indian intelligence became a permanent component of the government.

The British rulers of India in the 1920s had no greater respect for secret police forces than their Victorian predecessors. Opposition to the development of a political police force from within the Government of India continued throughout the war. The war did not bring about a reliance upon intelligence. Defence to a significant extent was subordinated to the dictates of an unwritten imperial ideology. This outlook was shared by the DCI, which consistently refused to generate its own growth by feeding the Government of India with scare stories about the revolutionary movement.

Sentiment, though strong, was not the only explanation for this British aversion to spying on their own subjects. The ideological stance of the British was sincere, but it was also convenient. For one thing,

India's poverty left it too poor to pay for a specialized police force, secret or otherwise. India could not have supported an extensive intelligence service, any more than it could support a modern army.

An equally potent reason for restricting the work of intelligence within India and abroad was a lasting belief that too extensive an intelligence organization could only be counter-productive. In North America and in Europe, the British benefited from the co-operation of the local authorities precisely because their intelligence operations were so small in scale. Even more important, within India the British realized that their rule depended on maintaining the support of moderate public opinion. This they could only achieve by restricting their intelligence apparatus. In Bengal, during the First World War, this commitment to the conciliation of Indian moderate opinion came within a hair's breadth of destabilizing the Raj. It is significant that the size of the Indian CIDs only increased greatly in the 1940s when British rule in India was visibly coming to an end. During the First World War, and in the subsequent campaign against Bolshevik subversion, the real British victory lay not in the numbers of revolutionaries they succeeded in killing or convicting, but in how few British it took to fulfil this task.

Bibliography

A. PRIMARY SOURCES

1. *Official Records*

India Office Library and Records
Home Department, Political Proceedings, A Series
Home Department, Political Proceedings, B Series
Home Department, Political Proceedings, Deposits
Home Department, Police Proceedings
Judicial and Public Department Proceedings
Political and Secret Department Proceedings
V/27 Official Publications Monographs

National Archives, Washington
Military Intelligence Department Files

Public Record Office, Kew, London
CO42 – Canada, Despatches
CO273 – Straits Settlements Correspondence
CO537 – Supplementary Correspondence
FO115 – USA General Correspondence
FO228 – Embassy and Consular Archives: Peking Legation and
            Embassy
FO262 – Yokohama Consulate Correspondence
FO350 – Jordan Papers
FO371 – USA Files, 'Hindu Agitations' (1915–18)
FO628 – Thailand Correspondence
FO882 – War of 1914–18: Arab Bureau Papers

2. *Private Papers*

Bertie Papers, Public Record Office (FO800)
Chelmsford Papers, India Office Library and Records
Cross Papers, India Office Library and Records
Hirtzel Papers, India Office Library and Records
House Papers, Yale University Library
Lytton Papers, India Office Library and Records
Morley Papers, India Office Library and Records
Northbrook Papers, India Office Library and Records
Seton Papers, India Office Library and Records
Tegart Papers, India Office Library and Records
Wiseman Papers, Yale University Library

3. *Published Primary Sources*

James Campbell Ker, *Political Trouble in India, 1907–1917* (First published 1917, ed. Mahadevaprasad Saha, Calcutta, 1973)
Sir Cecil Kaye, *Communism in India, 1919–1924* (First published 1924, ed. Subodh Roy, Calcutta, 1971)
Sir David Petrie, *Communism in India, 1924–1927* (First published 1927, ed. Mahadevaprasad Saha, Calcutta, 1972)
Sedition Committee 1918 Report (First published, 1927, reprint, New Delhi, 1973)
Sir Horace Williamson, *India and Communism* (First published 1933, ed. Mahadevaprasad Saha, Calcutta, 1976)

B. SECONDARY SOURCES

Andrew, Christopher M., *Secret Service, The Making of the British Intelligence Community* (London: Heinemann, 1985)
Ansari, K.H., 'Pan-Islam and the Making of the Early Indian Muslim Socialists', *Modern Asian Studies*, Vol. XX, No. 3 (1986)
Arnold, David, *The Madras Police* (Oxford, 1987)
Arnold, David, 'The Armed Police and Colonial Rule in South India, 1914–1947', *Modern Asian Studies*, Vol. II, No. 1 (1977)
Ashton, S.R., *British Policy Towards the Indian States, 1905–1939* (London: Curzon Press, 1982)
Bailey, F.M., *Mission to Tashkent* (Oxford: Oxford University Press, 1992)

Barrier, N.G., *Banned: Controversial Literature and Political Control in British India, 1907–1917* (Columbia: University of Missouri Press, 1974).

Beesly, Patrick, *Room 40. British Naval Intelligence, 1914–1918* (Oxford: Oxford University Press, 1984)

Blake, S.P., 'The Patrimonial-Bureaucratic Empire of the Mughals', *Journal of Asian Studies*, Vol. XXXIX, No. 1 (November 1979)

Bose, Arun Coomer, *Indian Revolutionaries Abroad, 1905–1922: In the Background of International Developments* (Allahabad: Indian Press Private, 1971)

Bray, N.N.E., *Shifting Sands* (London: Unicorn Press, 1934)

Brown, E.C., *Har Dayal: Hindu Revolutionary and Rationalist* (Tucson: University of Arizona Press, 1975)

Brown, Judith M., *Gandhi's Rise to Power. Indian Politics 1915–1922* (Cambridge: Cambridge University Press, 1972)

Brown, Judith M., *Modern India. The Origins of an Asian Democracy* (Oxford: Oxford University Press, 1985)

Brust, Harold, *I Guarded Kings. The Memoirs of a Political Police Officer* (London: Stanley Paul, 1935)

Cashman, R.I., *The Myth of the 'Lokamanya': Tilak and Mass Politics in the Maharashtra* (Berkeley: University of California Press, 1975)

Chandra, Bipan, with Mukherjee, Aditya, Panikkar, K.N., and Mahajan, Sucheta, *India's Struggle for Independence* (New Delhi: Penguin, 1989)

Chirol, Sir Valentine, *Indian Unrest* (London: Macmillan, 1910)

Cole, J.A., *Prince of Spies: Henri Le Caron* (London: Faber & Faber, 1984)

Darwent, Charles, 'Mystery of the Medina', *Observer Colour Supplement*, 12 July 1987.

Das, M.N., *India Under Morley and Minto. Politics Behind Revolution, Repression and Reforms* (London: George Allen & Unwin, 1964)

Datta, V.N., *Madan Lal Dhingra and the Revolutionary Movement* (New Delhi: Vikas, 1978)

Dignan, Don, *The Indian Revolutionary Movement in British Diplomacy, 1914–1919* (New Delhi: Allied, 1983)

Dilkes, David, *Curzon in India* (2 vols.) (London: Rupert Hart Davis, 1969–70)

Dodwell, H.H. (ed.), *The Cambridge History of India* Vol. VI, 'The Indian Empire'. (Cambridge: Cambridge University Press, 1932)

Faruqi, Zia-ul-Hasan, *The Deoband School and the Demand for Pakistan* (Bombay: Asia Publishing House, 1963)

Fowler, W.B., *British-American Relations, 1917–1918. The Role of Sir William Wiseman* (Princeton: Princeton University Press, 1969)

Fraser, Thomas Grant, 'The Intrigues of German Government and the Ghadr Party Against British Rule in India, 1914–1918' (University of London, unpublished PhD thesis, 1974)

Fraser, T.G., 'Canada and the Sikh problem, 1907 to 1922', *Journal of Imperial and Commonwealth History*, Vol.7, No. 1 (Oct. 1978)

Fraser, T.G., 'Germany and Indian Revolution, 1914–18', *Journal of Contemporary History*, Vol. 12, No. 2 (1977).

Fraser, T.G., 'India in Anglo-Japanese Relations during the First World War', *History*, Vol. LXIII, No. 209 (October 1978)

French, David, 'Spy Fever in Britain', *Historical Journal*, Vol. XXI (1978)

Gallagher, John, *The Decline, Revival and Fall of the British Empire* (Cambridge: Cambridge University Press, 1982)

Garnett, David, *The Golden Echo* (Vol. 1) (London: Chatto & Windus, 1953)

Gaunt, Sir Guy, *The Yield of Years: A Story of Adventure Afloat and Ashore* (London: Hutchinson, 1940)

Griffiths, Sir Percival, *'To Guard My People': The History of the Indian Police* (London: John Murray, 1971)

Gupta, Anandswarup, *The Police in British India 1861–1947* (New Delhi: Concept Publishing Company, 1979)

Gupta, Hiralal, *Journal of Indian History*, Vol. 37 (August 1959)

Harper, R.W.E. and Miller, H., *Singapore Mutiny* (Singapore: Oxford University Press, 1984)

Hartley, Stephen, *The Irish Question as a Problem in British Foreign Policy, 1914–1918* (London: Macmillan, 1987)

Hopkirk, Peter, *Setting the East Ablaze. Lenin's Dream of an Empire in Asia* (Oxford: Oxford University Press, 1986)

Hopkirk, Peter, *The Great Game. On Secret Service in High Asia* (London: John Murray, 1990)

Hunter, W.W., *Life of the Earl of Mayo* (2 vols.) (London: Smith, Elder & Co., 1876)

Johnson, Gordon, 'Partition, Agitation and Congress: Bengal 1904 to 1908', *Modern Asian Studies*, Vol. VII, No. 3 (1973)

Johnston, Hugh, *The Voyage of the 'Komagata Maru'. The Sikh*

Challenge to Canada's Colour Bar (Oxford: Oxford University Press, 1979)

Kautilya, *The Arthashastra*, translated by Rangarajan, L.N. (New Delhi: Penguin Books India, 1992)

Kipling, Rudyard, *Kim* (first published October 1901)

Kruger, Horst, 'Har Dayal in Deutschland', *Mitteilungen des Instituts für Orientforschung*, Vol. X, No. 1 (1964), p. 145

Leggett, George, *The Cheka. Lenin's Political Police* (Oxford: Oxford University Press, 1986)

Lowe, Peter, 'The British Empire and the Anglo-Japanese Alliance 1911–1915', *History*, Vol. LIX, No. 181 (June 1969)

Majumdar, R.C. *et al.* (eds), *The History and Culture of the Indian People* (Bombay: Bharatiya Vidya Bhavah, 1951–77)

Maugham, W. Somerset, *Collected Short Stories*, Vol. III (London: Heinemann, 1951)

Moberly, Sir Francis, *The Official History of the War. The Campaign in Mesopotamia 1914–1918*, Vols. I-II (London: His Majesty's Stationery Office, 1925)

Morgan, Gerald, 'Myth and Reality in the Great Game', *Asian Affairs*, Vol. LX [new series, Vol. IV, part I (February, 1973)]

Morris, L.P., 'British Secret Service Activity in Khorassan, 1887–1908', *Historical Journal*, Vol. 27, No. 3 (1984)

Nish, Ian, 'Japanese Intelligence and the Approach of the Russo-Japanese War' in Andrew, Christopher and Noakes, Jeremy (eds), *Intelligence and International Relations 1900–1945* (Exeter: Exeter University Press, 1987)

O'Dwyer, Sir Michael, *India as I Knew It* (London: Constable & Co., 1925)

Persits, M.A., *Revoliutsioneri Indii v Strane Sovetov* (Moscow: Izdate L'stvo 'Nayka', 1973)

Popplewell, Richard, 'The Surveillance of Indian "Seditionists" in North America, 1905–1915' in Andrew, Christopher and Noakes, Jeremy (eds), *Intelligence and International Relations 1900–1945* (Exeter: Exeter University Press, 1987)

Popplewell, Richard, 'The Surveillance of Indian Revolutionaries in Great Britain and on the Continent, 1903–1914', *Intelligence and National Security*, Vol. 3, No. 1 (January 1988)

Popplewell, Richard, 'British Intelligence in Mesopotamia, 1914–1916' in Handel, Michael I. (ed.), *Intelligence and Military Operations* (London: Frank Cass, 1990)

Porter, Bernard, *The Origins of the Vigilant State. The London Metropolitan Police Special Branch before the First World War* (London: Weidenfeld & Nicolson, 1987)

Porter, Bernard, *Plots and Paranoia. A History of Political Espionage in Britain 1790–1988* (London: Unwin Hyman, 1989)

Powe, Marc B., 'The Emergence of the War Department Intelligence Agency: 1885–1918' (University of Kansas, unpublished MA thesis, 1974)

Pratap, Mahendra, *My Life Story of Fifty-Five Years* (Dehra Dun, 1947)

Read, Anthony and Fisher, David, *Colonel Z. The Secret Life of a Master of Spies* (London: Hodder & Stoughton, 1984)

Reisner, I.M. and Goldberg, N.M. (eds), *Tilak and the Struggle for Indian Freedom* (New Delhi: People's Publishing House, 1966)

Richards, J.F., *Mughal Administration in Golconda* (Oxford: Oxford University Press, 1975)

Robbins, Keith, *The First World War* (Oxford: Oxford University Press, 1985)

Rumbold, Sir Algernon, *Watershed in India, 1914–1922* (London: The Athlone Press, 1979)

Sareen, Tilak Raj, *Russian Revolution and India, 1917–1921* (New Delhi: Sterling Publishers, 1977)

Sareen, Tilak Raj, *Indian Revolutionary Movement Abroad, 1905–1921* (New Delhi: Sterling Publishers, 1979)

Sarkar, Sumit, *The Swadeshi Movement in Bengal 1903–1908* (New Delhi: People's Publishing House, 1973)

Seal, Anil, *The Emergence of Indian Nationalism. Competition and Collaboration in the Later Nineteenth Century* (Cambridge: Cambridge University Press, 1971)

Singh, Khushwant, *A History of the Sikhs* Vol. 2, 1839–1974 (New Delhi: Oxford University Press, 1977)

Sharmasastry, R., *Kautilya's Arthasastra* (Mysore: 1951)

Short, K.R.M., *The Dynamite War* (Dublin: Gill and Macmillan, 1979)

Spratt, Philip, 'Blowing Up India' (unpublished copy held by India Office Library and Records)

Taylor, Philip Meadows, *Confessions of a Thug* (Oxford: Oxford University Press, 1986)

Teague-Jones, Reginald, *The Spy Who Disappeared. Diary of a Secret Mission to Russian Central Asia in 1918* (London: Victor Gollancz, 1990)

Tegart, C.A., 'Terrorism in India', speech delivered before the Royal Empire Society (London, 1932)

Thapar, Romila, *A History of India*, Vol. 1 (London: Penguin, 1966)

Thomson, Basil, *Queer People* (London: Hodder & Stoughton, 1922)

Thomson, Basil, *The Scene Changes* (London: Doubleday, Doran & Co., 1939)

Thwaites, Norman, *Velvet and Vinegar* (London: Grayson & Grayson, 1932)

Trivedi, S.D., *Secret Services in Ancient India. Techniques and Operation* (New Delhi: Allied Publishers Private, 2nd edn, 1988)

Tuchman, Barbara, *The Zimmermann Telegram* (London: Constable, 1959)

Tunney, Thomas, *Throttled!* (New York, 1919)

Visram, Rozina, *Ayars, Lascars and Princes. Indians in Britain 1700–1947* (London: Pluto Press, 1986)

Winstone, H.V.F., *The Illicit Adventure: The Story of Political and Military Intelligence in the Middle East from 1898 to 1926* (London: Jonathan Cape, 1982)

Index

DCI, *see* Department of Criminal Intelligence

Deccan, 11

Decentralization Commission, 71–2, 76–7

Defence of India Act (1915), 171, 174–5, 180, 188, 190, 205, 207, 210–12, 300

Defence of the Realm Act, 174, 205

Dehra Dun, 87, 113

Delhi, 62, 78, 80–2, 84, 87, 173

Delhi Bomb Plot, 64, 80–91, 114, 154, 156, 167–8, 191, 276

Delhi Durbar, 78–80, 113

Democrat Party, US, 244

Denham, Godfrey Charles, 81, 86–7, 105–6, 111, 191, 210, 250–1, 297, 304–5, 326

Denmark, 230

Deoband, 185–6

Deodhar, Gopal Krishna, 77

Department of Central Intelligence (DCI): anti-Bolshevik measures, 309–15, 317, 325; attitude to Japan, 235; establishment of, 304–6; Malayan Bureau and, 327, 328; post-war operations in United States, 324–5

Department of Criminal Intelligence (DCI): assessment of revolutionary strength in Punjab, 171; Assistant Deputy Director of, 67; Assistant Director of, 67, 191; Assistant Examiner of Questioned Documents, 304; attitude to Japan, 284–5, 304; clerks and servants of, 67, 192–3, 304; cost of, 48–9, 78; counter-espionage, 304; creation of, 42–5; Deputy Director, 79, 191; detective staff of, 68–9, 93n, 191; Director of, 49–50, 54n, 191; efficiency of, 54n, 65–6, 78, 82–5, 88–9; espionage, *see* use of secret agents; establishment of Far Eastern Agency, 264–7, 273; Financial Department of, 68; fingerprint bureau of, 67; First World War and, 166; Gandhi and, 301–2, 317; geographical information of, 169; graphologist of (Government expert in handwriting), 67, 191; Home Office Agency, New York and, 148–9, 157, 237; ideological outlook of, 90–1, 149–50; intelligence on Afghanistan, 185; linguistic capabilities of, 179; location of, 50; Montagu's suspicions of, 303–4; objectivity of reporting, 66; Pan-Islamism and, 179, 302; Personal Assistant to Director of, 67–8, 72, 191; photographic section of, 67, 92n; proportion of political to criminal cases of, 191–2; relations with Canadians, 152, 156–7, 160; relations with CIDs, 66, 73–8, 88–9, 169–70, 222, 260; relations with India Office, 248; relations with Scotland Yard, 127, 130, 132–6, 139–40; relations with J.A. Wallinger, 1914–18, 230–1; renamed Department of Central Intelligence, 304; Rowlatt Act and, 300; Secret Service funds of, 48, 54n, 72, 82; setting up of operations in Europe, 136–41; staff during First World War, 191–3, 304; strategy for dealing with revolutionary movement, 90, 160–1, 169–70, 234n, 247–8, 259–60, 264–5, 274, 299; surveillance of foreigners, 74–5, 280–1; use of secret agents, 47–8, 69–73, 90–1, 136–7, 156–7, 222; *Weekly Reports* of, 65–6, 68, 221, 284

Department of the Interior, Canadian, 151–3

Dering, Herbert, 260, 265

Dhanushkodi, 170

Dhingra, Madan Lal, 125, 130–1

Director of Criminal Intelligence, *see* Stuart, Stevenson-Moore, Cleveland, Kaye, Petrie

Djakarta, *see* Batavia

Djember, 239

Dominion Immigration Inspector, *see* Jolliffe, A.L.

Dost Mohammed, 20

Dubé, Vishna, 225, 229

Dublin, 70, 88

Dufferin, Lord, 24–5, 26, 28–9, 36, 50, 52, 61

Duke, Sir William, 168

Durand, Sir Mortimer, 23

Dyer, Brigadier-General Reginald, 301

'Dynamite War', 46, 88, 125–6

Easter Rising, 243

Eastern Bengal and Assam (EBA), 102–3, 104, 110; CID of, 52, 57–8, 70, 75, 103–4, 106–8, 111–13; Muslims of, 78–9, 91; police of, 107–9, 111–12; Special Branch of, 106

Edinburgh, 139

Edwards, William, 27

Egypt, 179, 182, 226–7, 297

Egyptian Intelligence, 226, 233n

UNIVERSITY OF PLYMOUTH
LIBRARY SERVICES (EXMOUTH)
DOUGLAS AVENUE
EXMOUTH
DEVON EX8 2AT